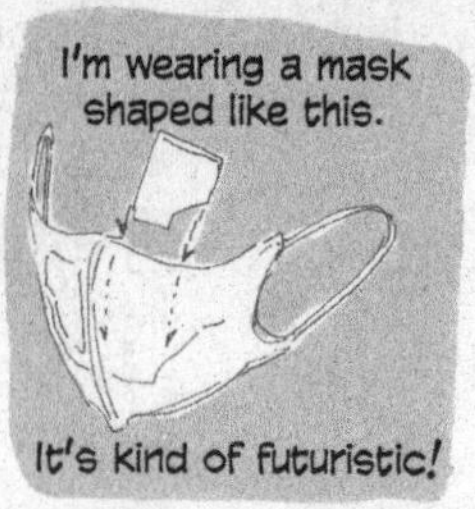
I'm wearing a mask shaped like this.
It's kind of futuristic!

I was sick a lot last year, especially during the second half. Actually, I have a cold as I'm writing this. This is what happens when all you do is create manga. And so my resolution for this year is to not catch a cold.

-Tite Kubo

Bleach is author Tite Kubo's second title. Kubo made his debut with *ZOMBIEPOWDER.*, a four-volume series for *Weekly Shonen Jump*. To date, *Bleach* has been translated into numerous languages and has also inspired an animated TV series that began airing in the U.S. in 2006. Beginning its serialization in 2001, *Bleach* is still a mainstay in the pages of *Weekly Shonen Jump*. In 2005, *Bleach* was awarded the prestigious Shogakukan Manga Award in the *shonen* (boys) category.

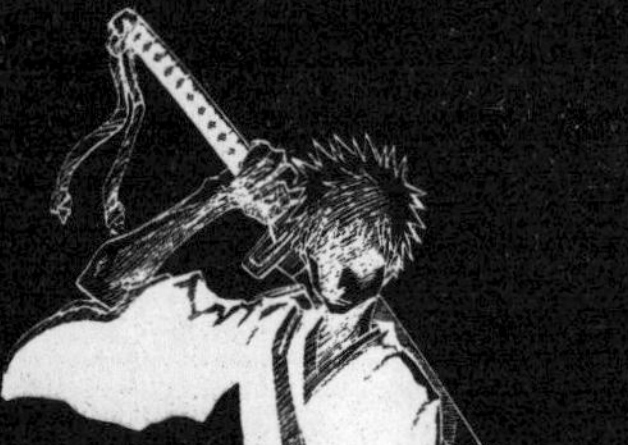

BLEACH
Vol. 43: KINGDOM OF HOLLOWS
SHONEN JUMP Manga Edition

STORY AND ART BY
TITE KUBO

English Adaptation/Lance Caselman
Translation/Joe Yamazaki
Touch-up Art & Lettering/Mark McMurray
Design/Yukiko Whitley, Kam Li
Editor/Alexis Kirsch

BLEACH © 2001 by Tite Kubo. All rights reserved. First published
in Japan in 2001 by SHUEISHA Inc., Tokyo. English translation rights
arranged by SHUEISHA Inc.

The rights of the author(s) of the work(s) in this publication to be so
identified have been asserted in accordance with Copyright, Designs and
Patents Act 1988. A CIP catalogue record for this book is available from
the British Library.

The stories, characters and incidents mentioned in this publication are
entirely fictional.

No portion of this book may be reproduced or transmitted in any form
or by any means without written permission from the copyright holders.

Printed in the U.S.A.

Published by VIZ Media, LLC
P.O. Box 77010
San Francisco, CA 94107

10 9 8 7 6 5 4 3 2 1
First printing, July 2012

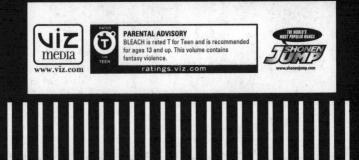

VIZ
MEDIA
www.viz.com

RATED
T
FOR
TEEN

PARENTAL ADVISORY
BLEACH is rated T for Teen and is recommended
for ages 13 and up. This volume contains
fantasy violence.

ratings.viz.com

THE WORLD'S
MOST POPULAR MANGA
SHONEN JUMP
www.shonenjump.com

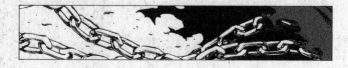

Decay is my friend
Night is my servant
I wait for you in a palace of elm
While I let the crows peck at my body

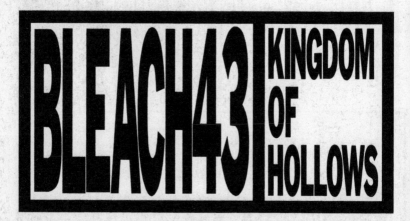

BLEACH43 KINGDOM OF HOLLOWS

STARS AND

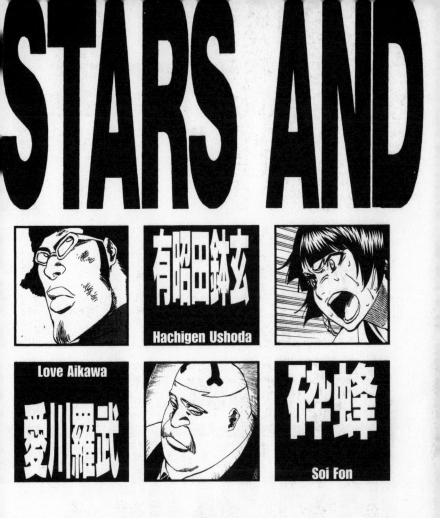

有昭田鉢玄
Hachigen Ushoda

Love Aikawa
愛川羅武

砕蜂
Soi Fon

plot

When high school student Ichigo Kurosaki meets Soul Reaper Rukia Kuchiki his life is changed forever. Soon Ichigo is a soul-cleansing Soul Reaper too, and he finds himself having adventures, as well as problems, that he never would have imagined. Now Ichigo and his friends must stop renegade Soul Reaper Aizen and his army of Arrancars from destroying the Soul Society and wiping out Karakura as well.

While Ichigo defeats Ulquiorra in Hueco Mundo to save Orihime, the Thirteen Court Guard Companies battle it out with the Espadas in Karakura. But when Aizen himself appears on the battlefield, things look grim indeed for the Soul Reapers. Then a dangerous new element is introduced into this already explosive mix with the arrival of the Visoreds. And there's one question on everyone's mind--whose side are they on?

BLEACH ALL STORIES

リリネット
Lilinette

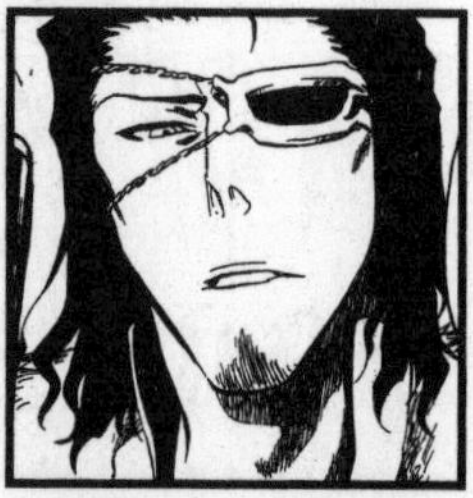

バラガン
Barragan

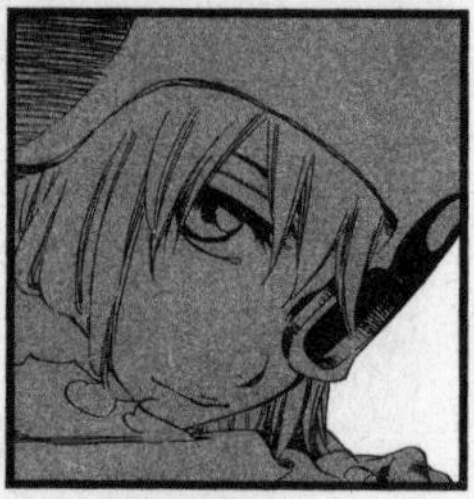

Stark
スターク

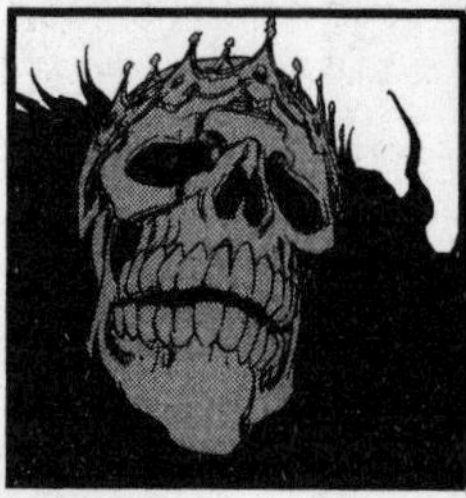

BLEACH43

KINGDOM OF HOLLOWS

Contents

368. The Fearless Child

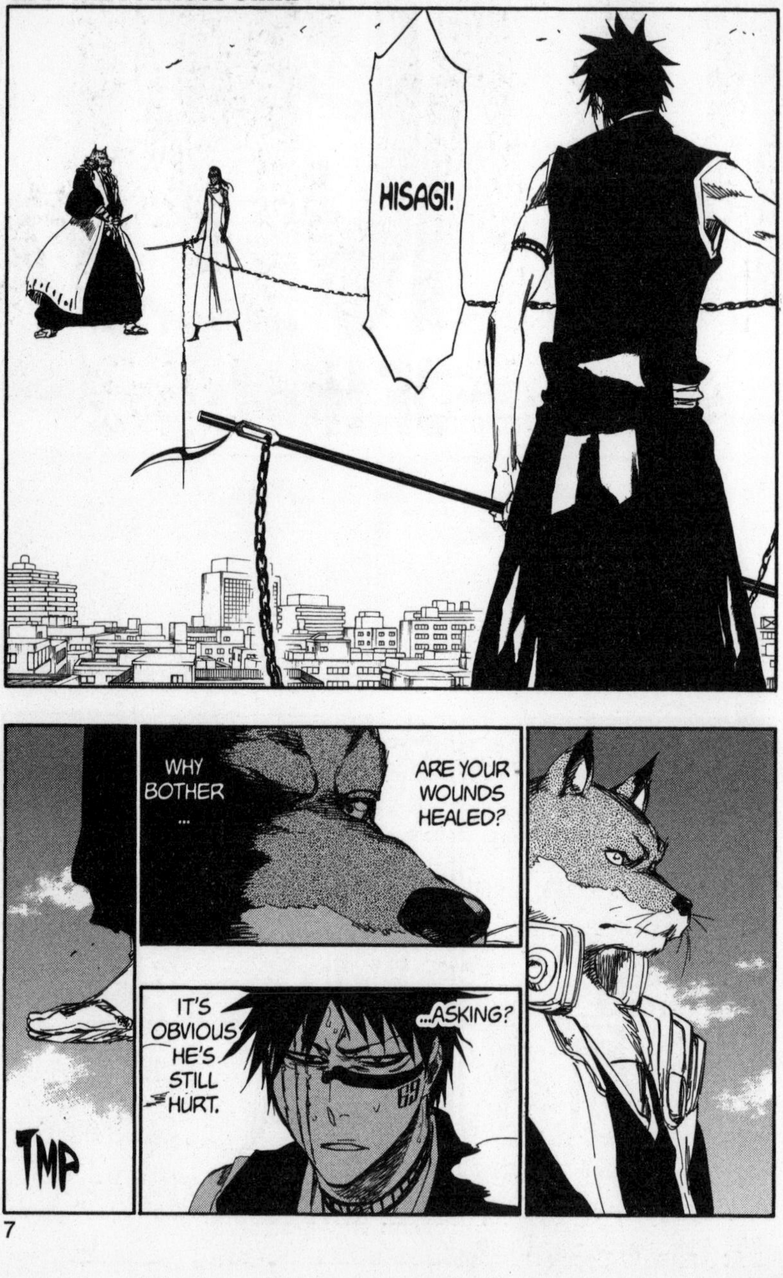
HISAGI!
ARE YOUR WOUNDS HEALED?
WHY BOTHER ...
...ASKING?
IT'S OBVIOUS HE'S STILL HURT.
TMP

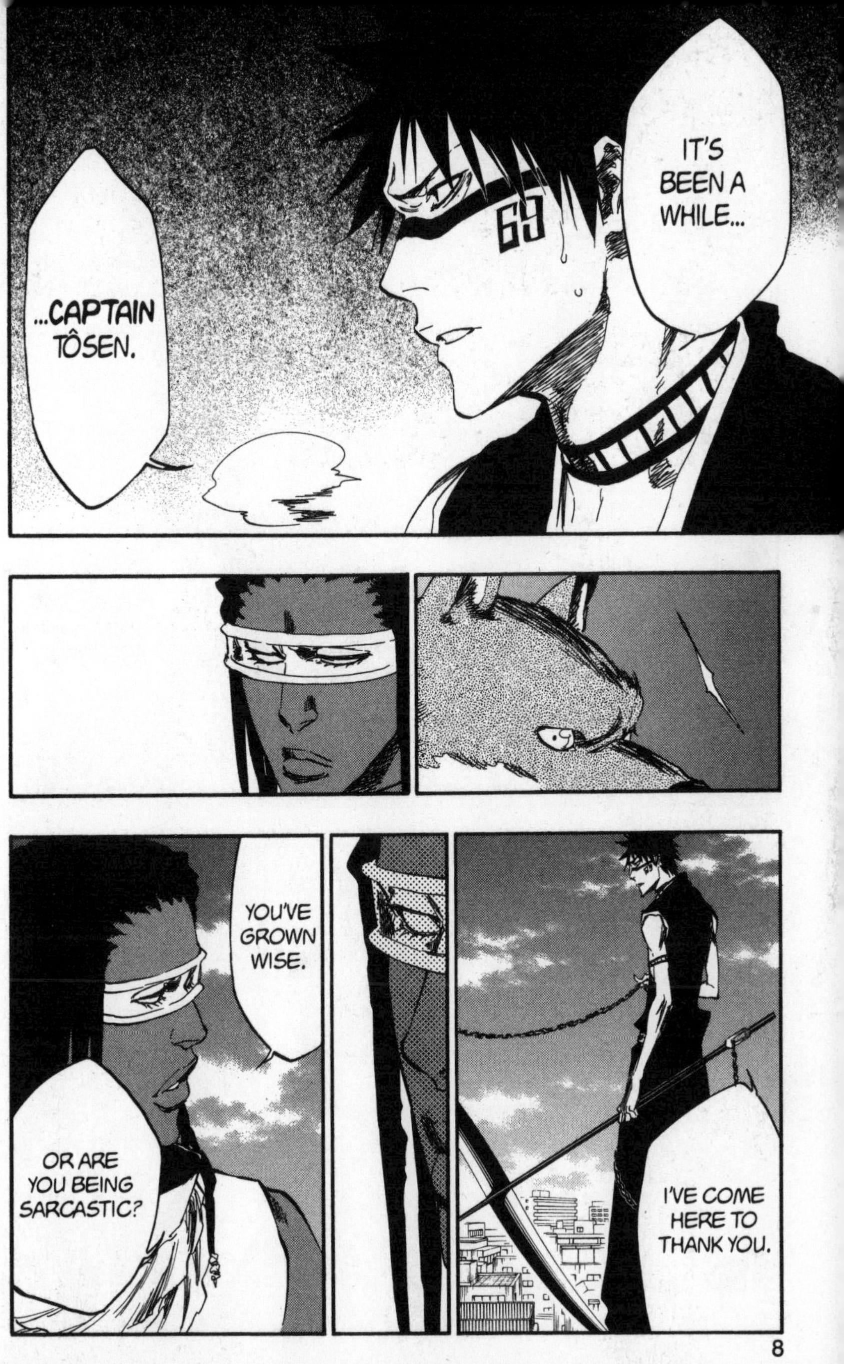
IT'S BEEN A WHILE...
...CAPTAIN TÔSEN.
I'VE COME HERE TO THANK YOU.
YOU'VE GROWN WISE.
OR ARE YOU BEING SARCASTIC?

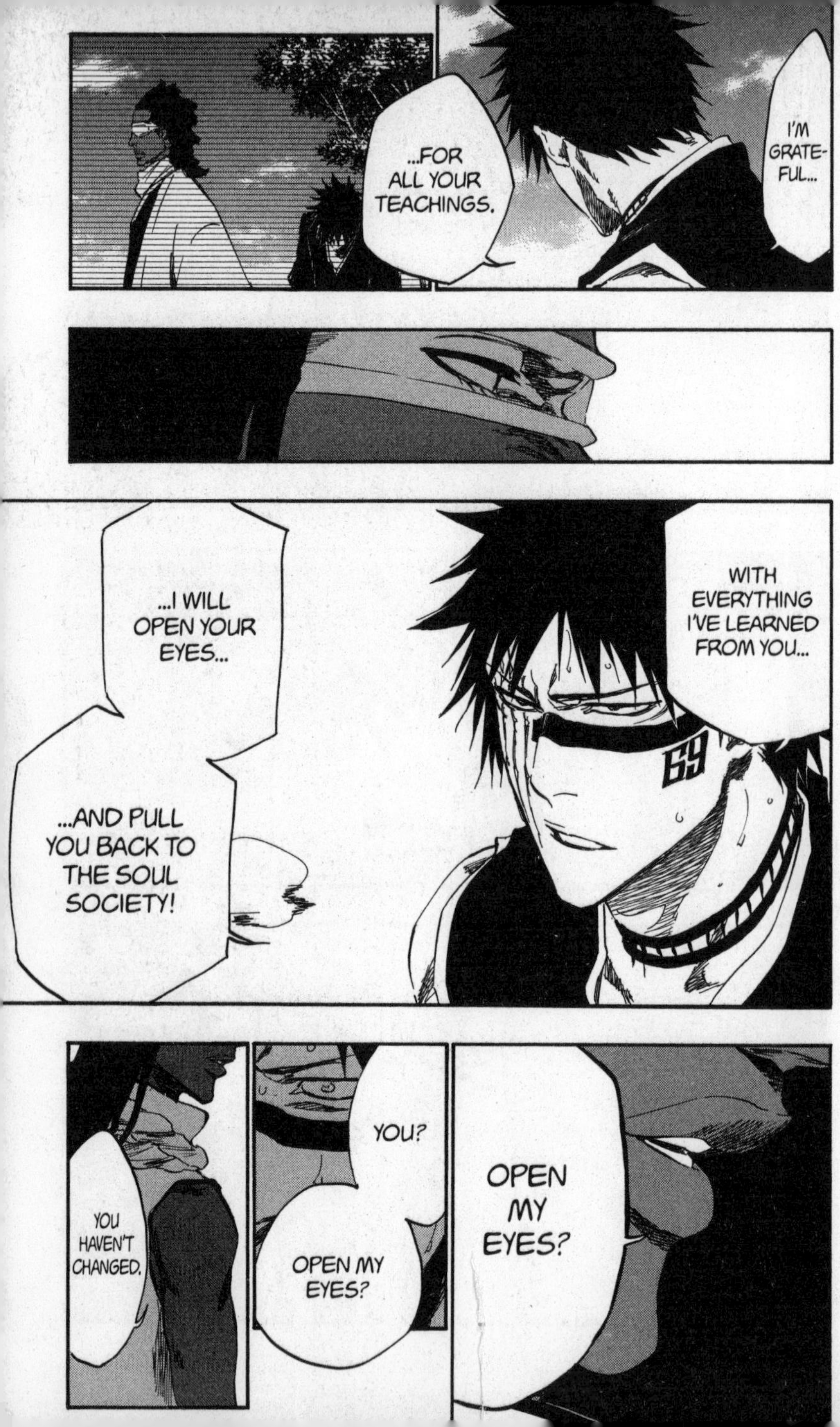
I'M GRATEFUL...
...FOR ALL YOUR TEACHINGS.
WITH EVERYTHING I'VE LEARNED FROM YOU...
...I WILL OPEN YOUR EYES...
...AND PULL YOU BACK TO THE SOUL SOCIETY!
OPEN MY EYES?
YOU?
OPEN MY EYES?
YOU HAVEN'T CHANGED.

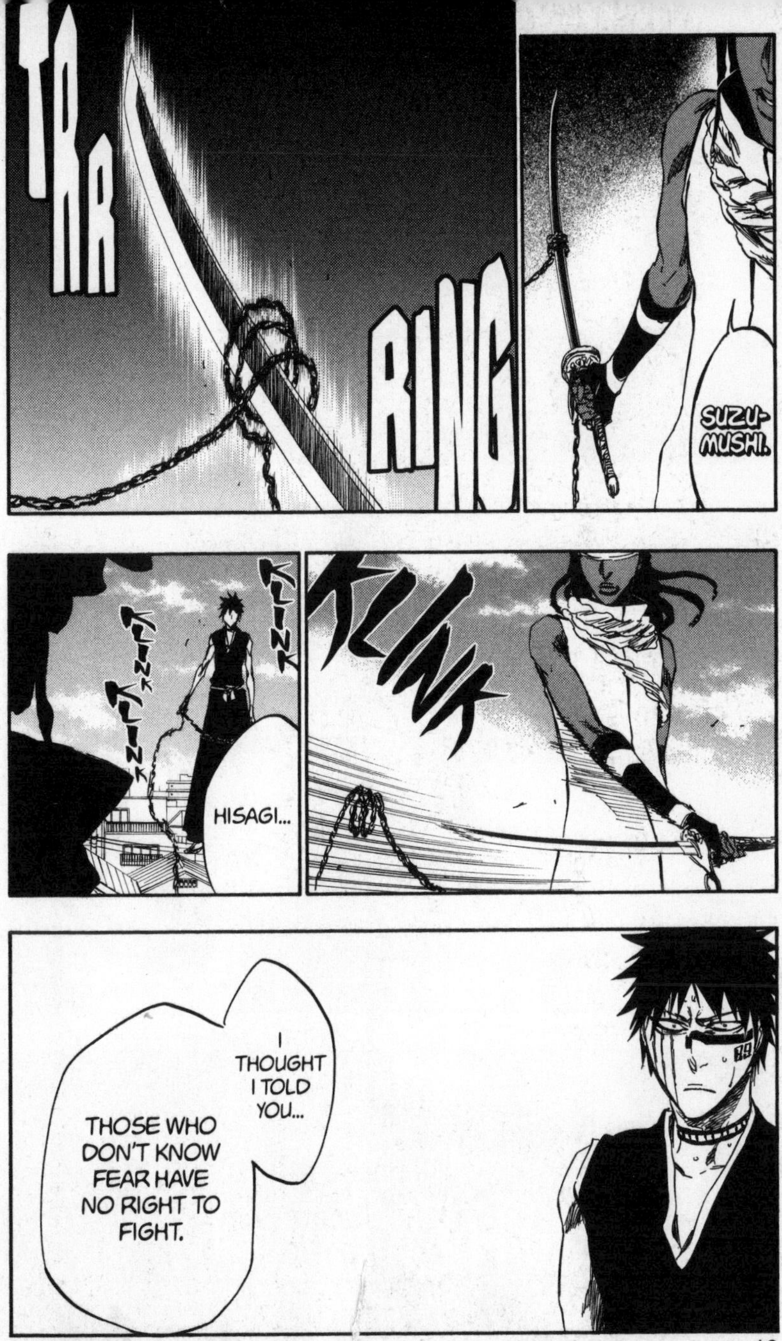
SUZU-MUSHI.
RING
TARR
KLINK
KLINK
KLINK
KLINK
HISAGI...
I THOUGHT I TOLD YOU...
THOSE WHO DON'T KNOW FEAR HAVE NO RIGHT TO FIGHT.

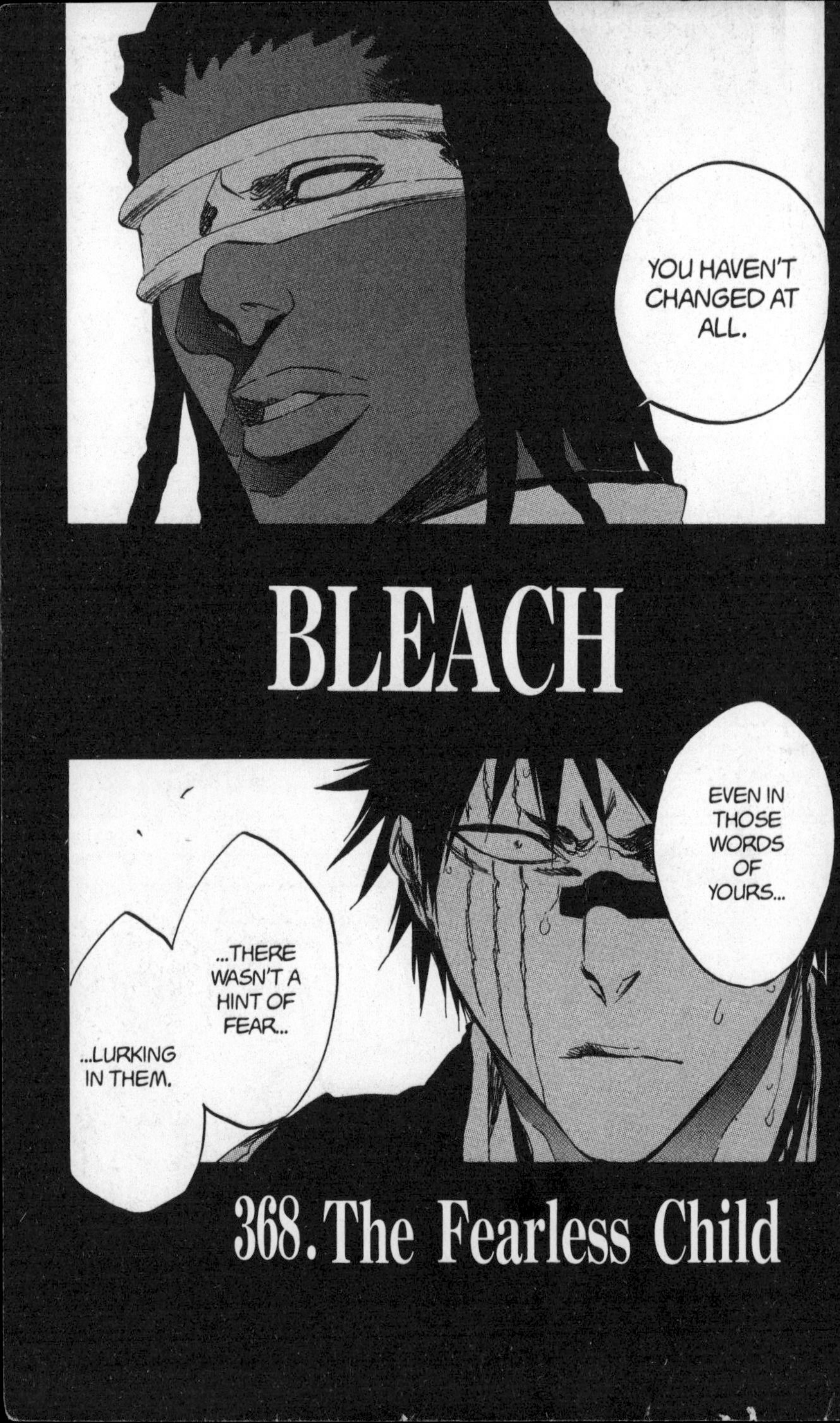
YOU HAVEN'T CHANGED AT ALL.
BLEACH
EVEN IN THOSE WORDS OF YOURS...
...THERE WASN'T A HINT OF FEAR...
...LURKING IN THEM.
368. The Fearless Child

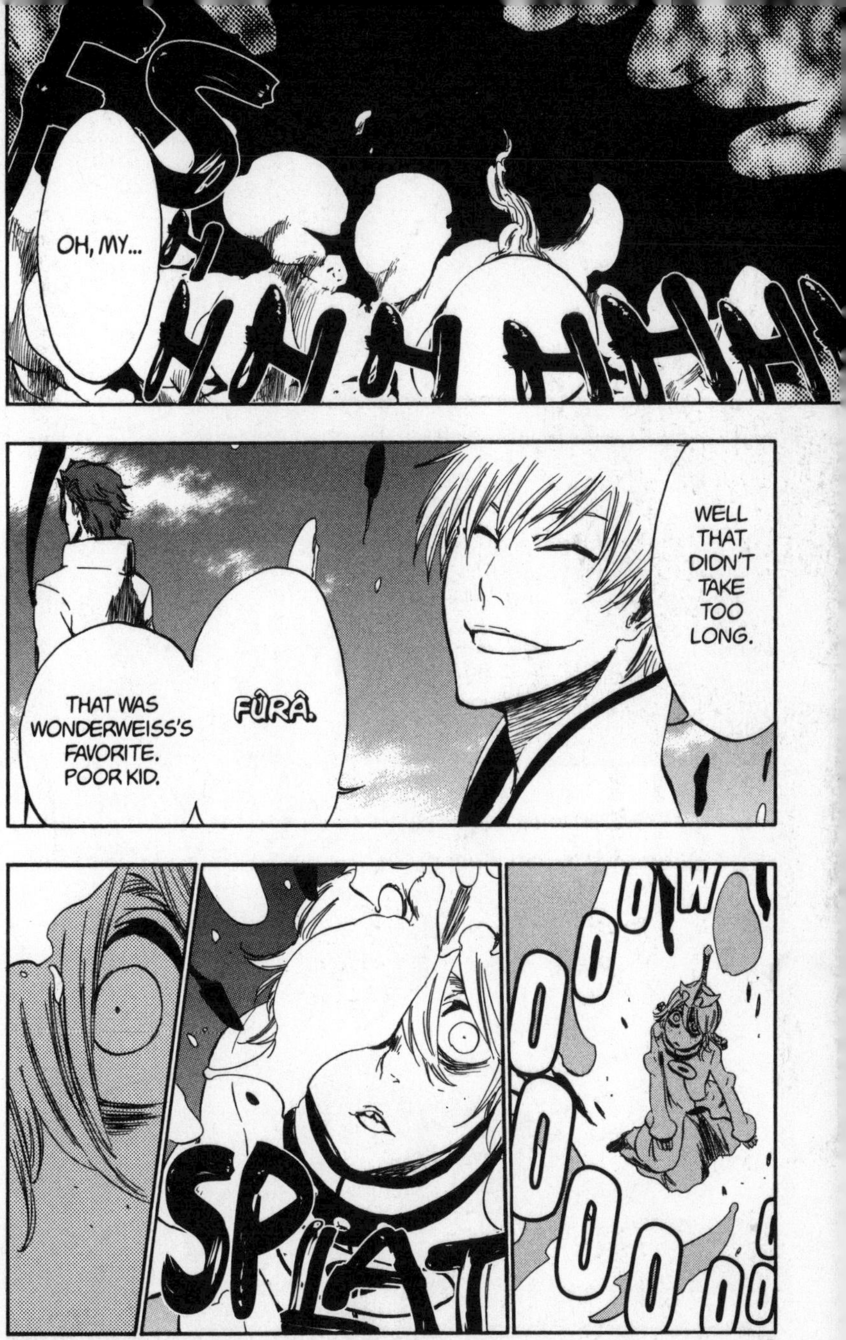
OH, MY...
WELL THAT DIDN'T TAKE TOO LONG.
FÛRÂ.
THAT WAS WONDERWEISS'S FAVORITE. POOR KID.
SPLAT

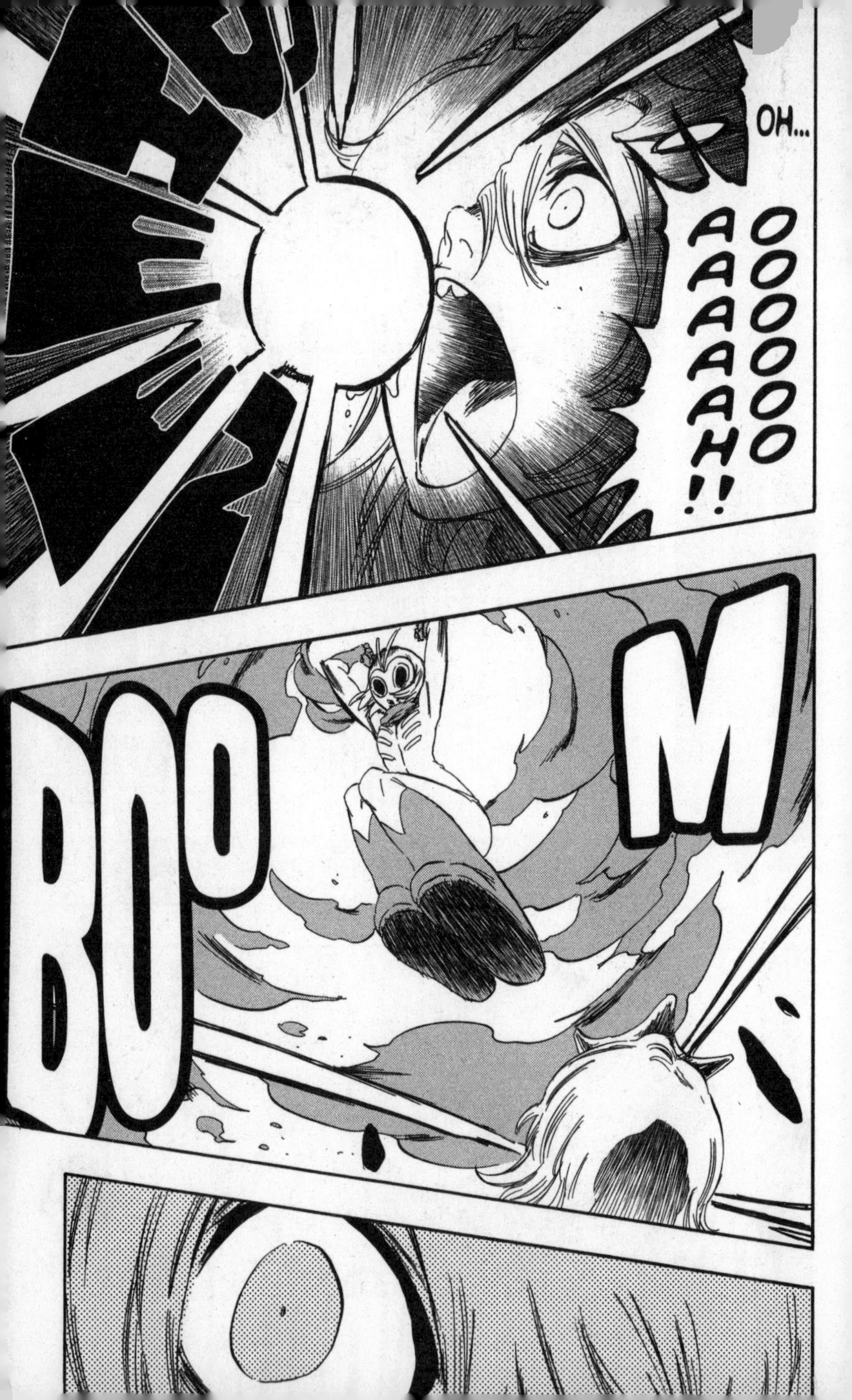
OH...
OOOOOO
AAAAAH!!
BOOM

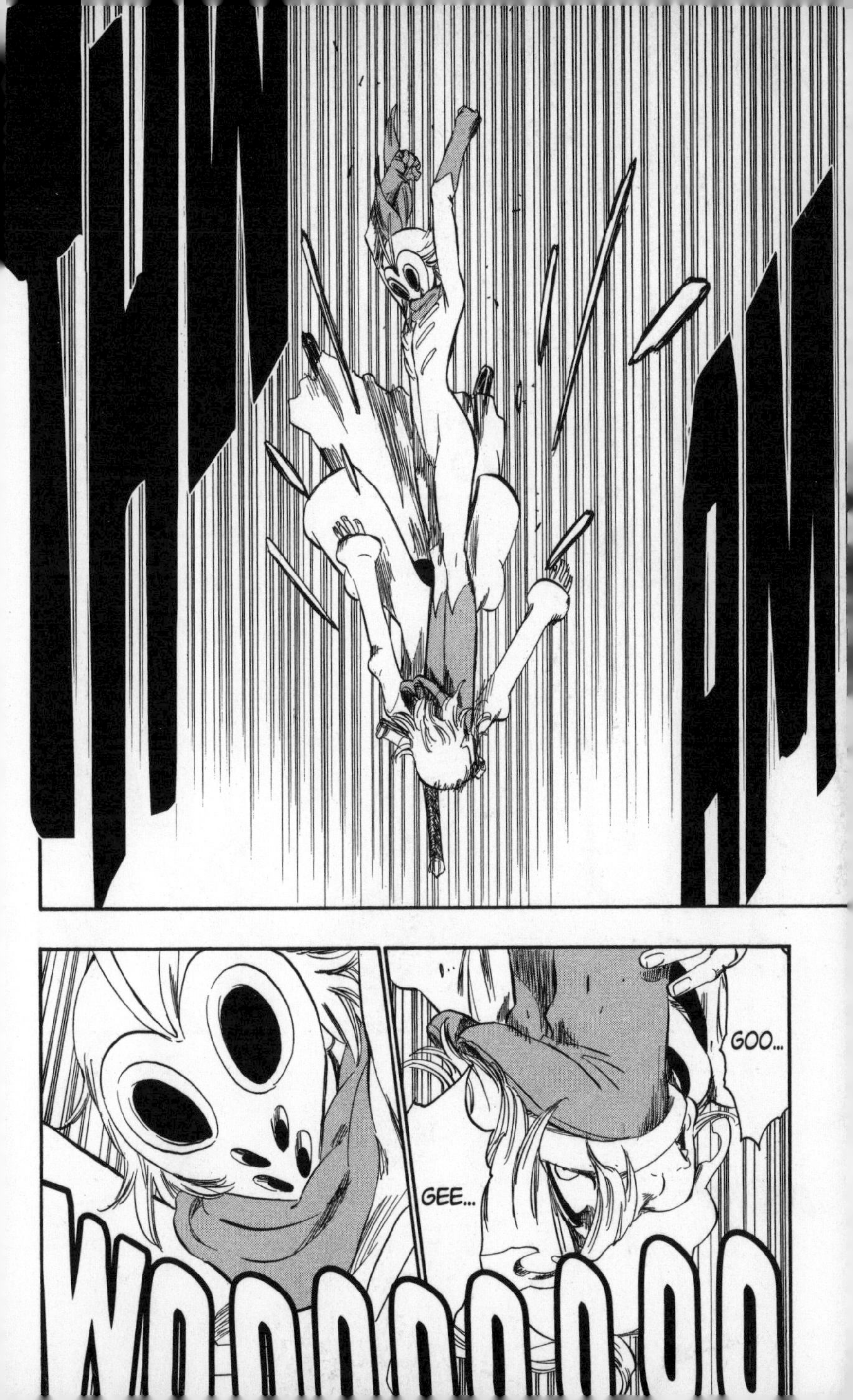
THW
AM
...
GOO...
GEE...
WOOOOOOOOO

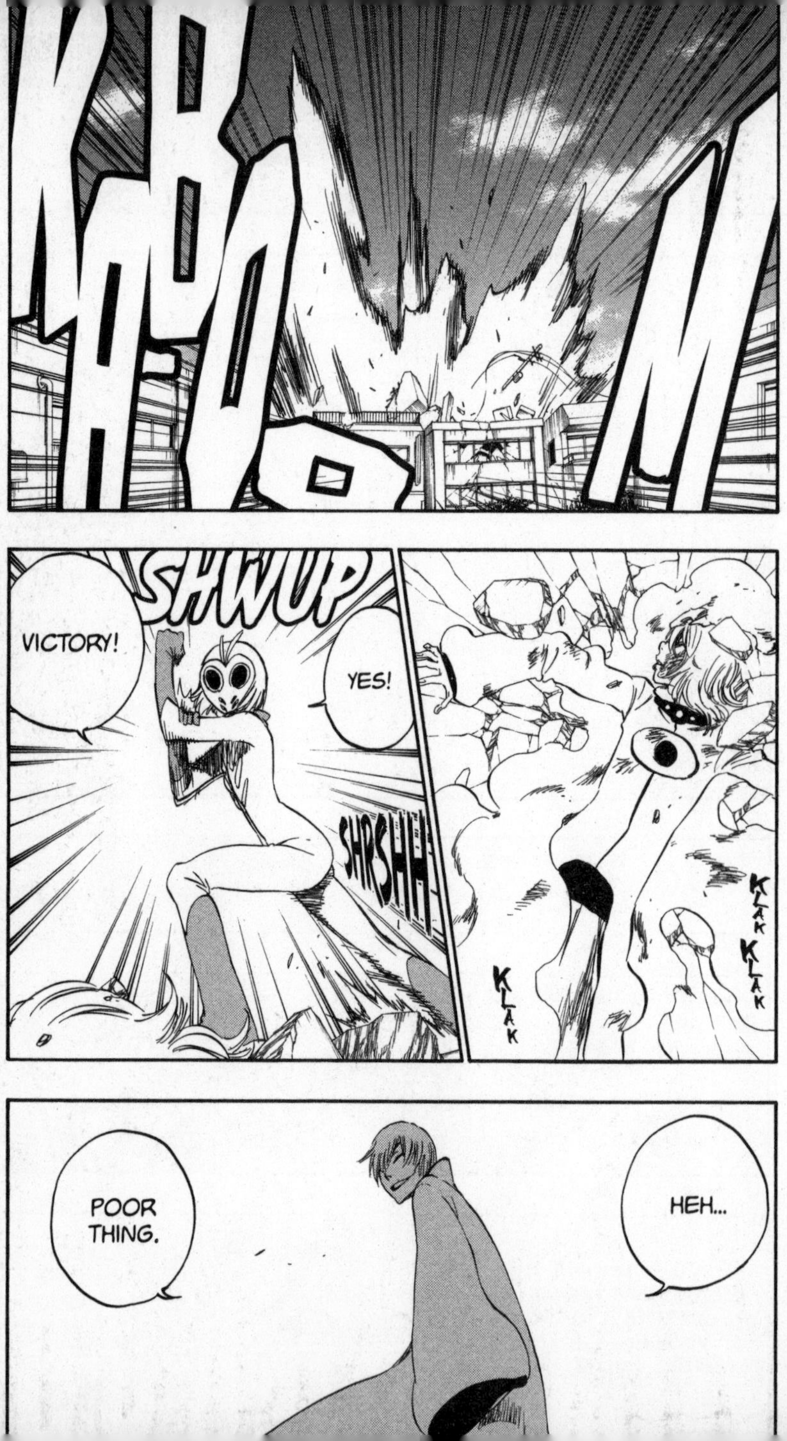
KABOOM
KLAK KLAK
KLAK
SHWUP
YES!
VICTORY!
SHRSHH
HEH...
POOR THING.

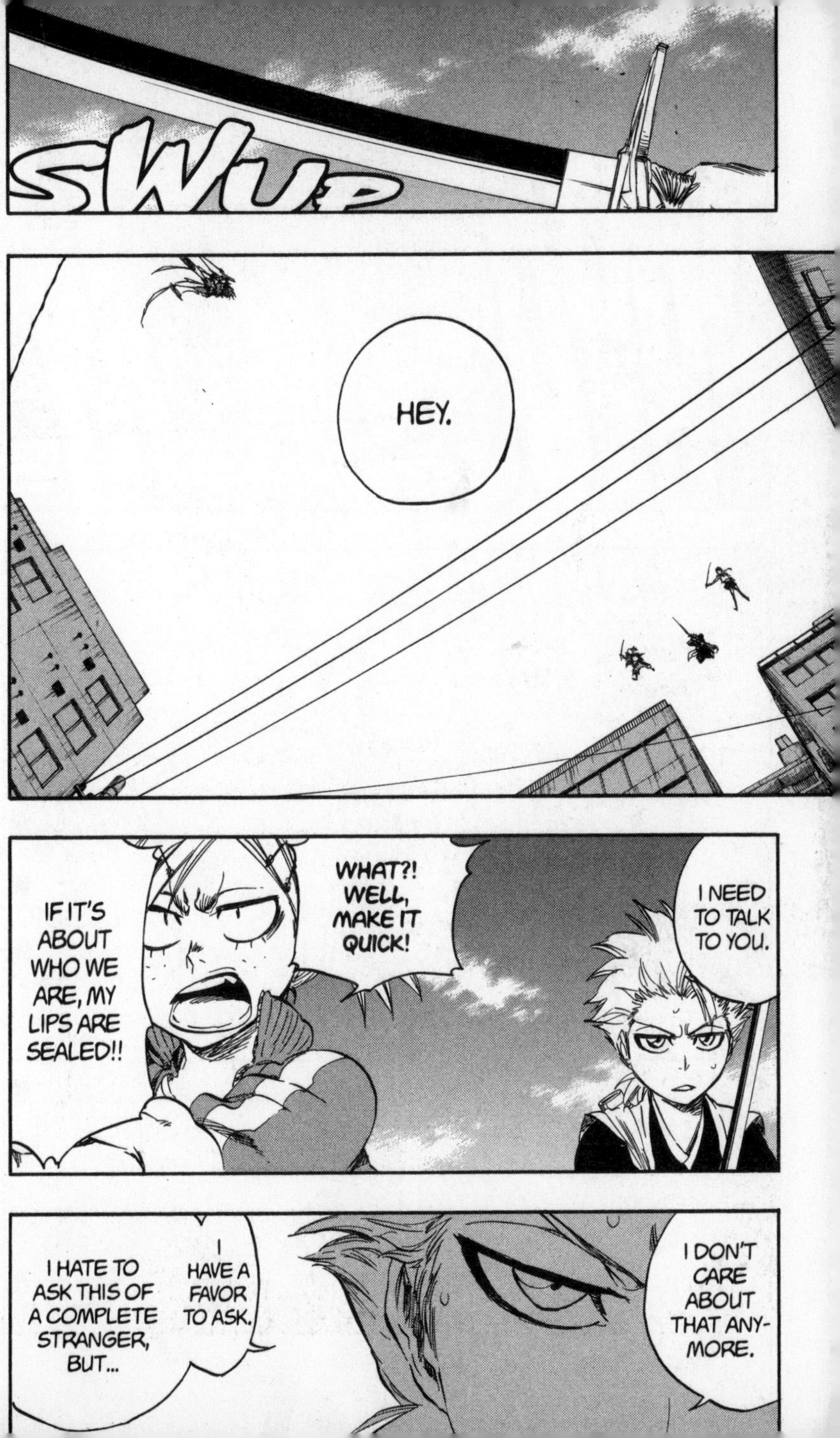
SWUP
HEY.
I NEED TO TALK TO YOU.
WHAT?! WELL, MAKE IT QUICK!
IF IT'S ABOUT WHO WE ARE, MY LIPS ARE SEALED!!
I DON'T CARE ABOUT THAT ANY-MORE.
I HAVE A FAVOR TO ASK.
I HATE TO ASK THIS OF A COMPLETE STRANGER, BUT...

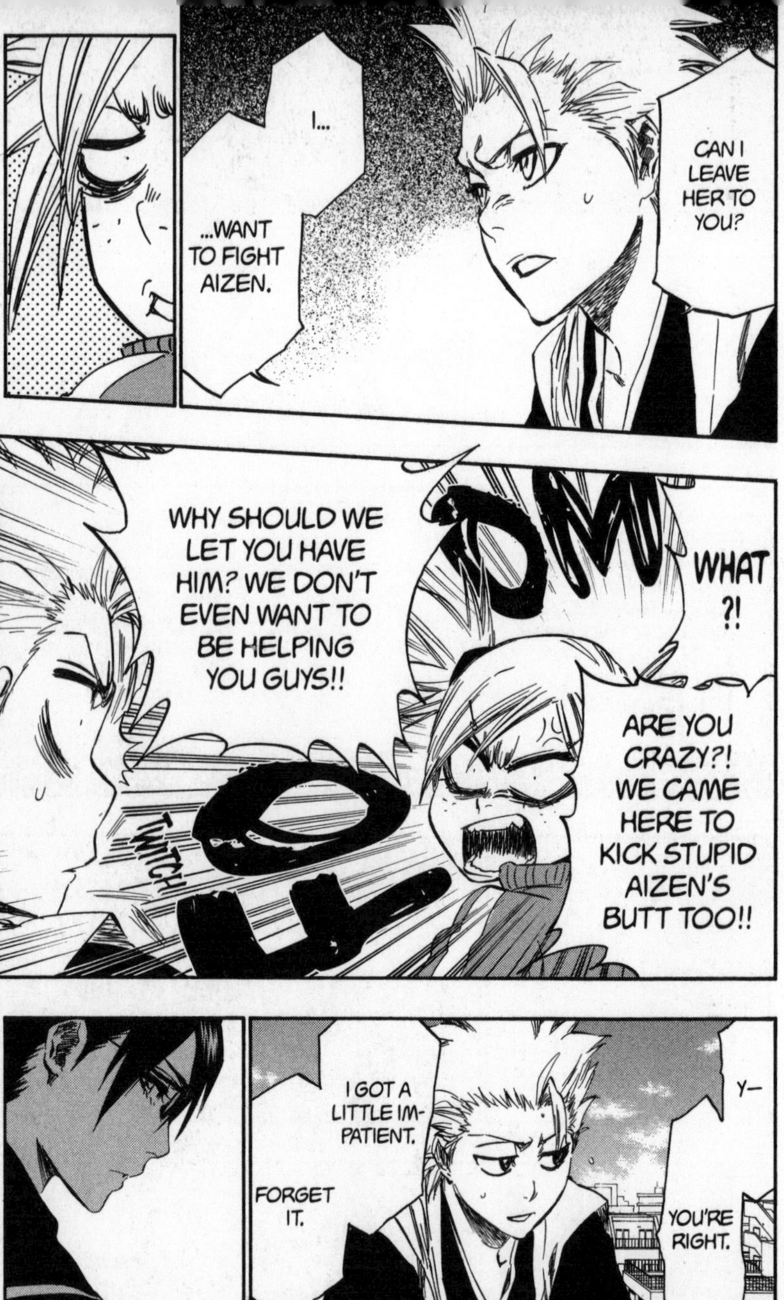
CAN I LEAVE HER TO YOU?
I...
...WANT TO FIGHT AIZEN.
WHAT ?!
ARE YOU CRAZY?! WE CAME HERE TO KICK STUPID AIZEN'S BUTT TOO!!
WHY SHOULD WE LET YOU HAVE HIM? WE DON'T EVEN WANT TO BE HELPING YOU GUYS!!
TWITCH
Y—
YOU'RE RIGHT.
I GOT A LITTLE IM-PATIENT.
FORGET IT.

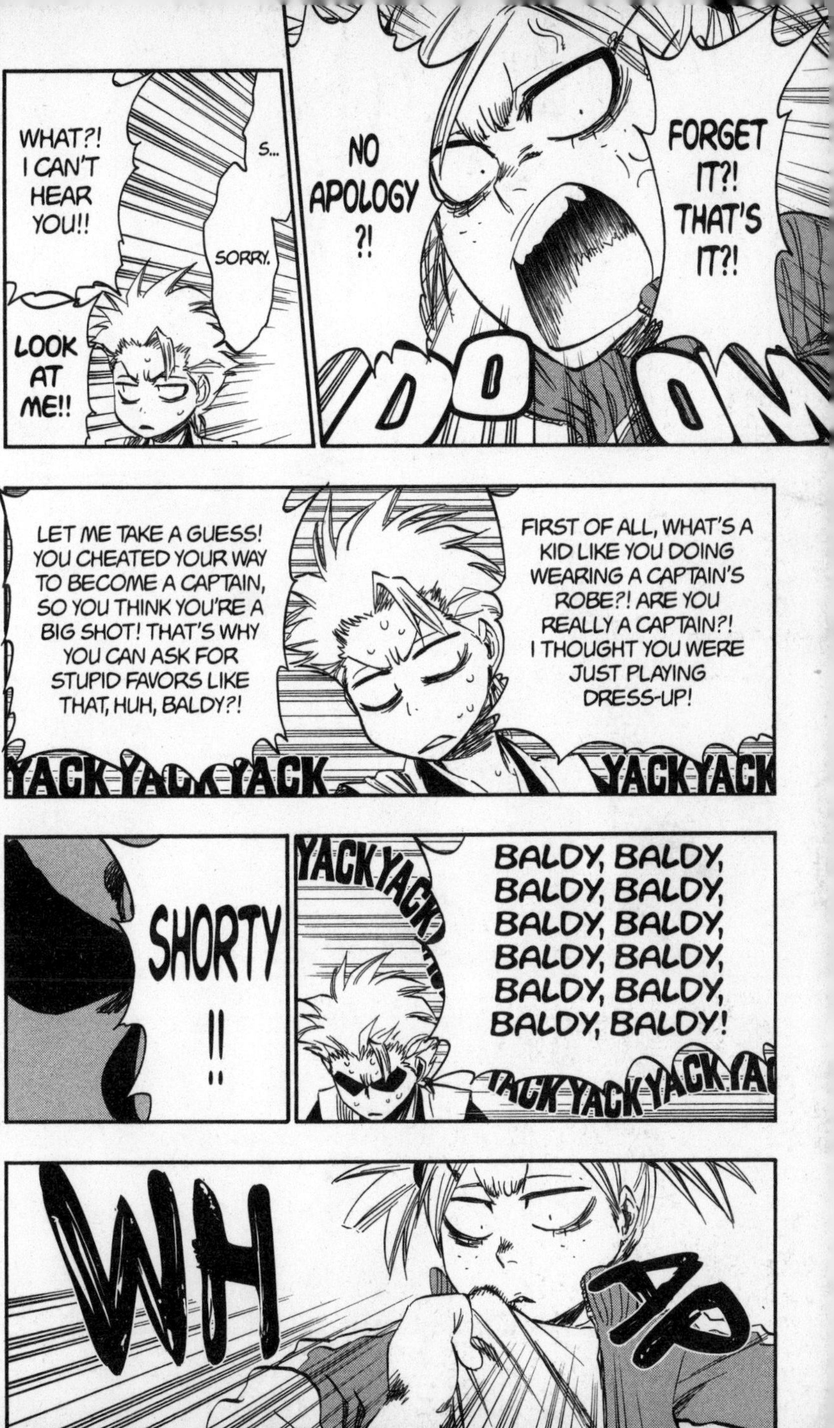
FORGET IT?! THAT'S IT?!
NO APOLOGY ?!
DOOM
S...
SORRY.
WHAT?! I CAN'T HEAR YOU!!
LOOK AT ME!!
FIRST OF ALL, WHAT'S A KID LIKE YOU DOING WEARING A CAPTAIN'S ROBE?! ARE YOU REALLY A CAPTAIN?! I THOUGHT YOU WERE JUST PLAYING DRESS-UP!
YACK YACK
LET ME TAKE A GUESS! YOU CHEATED YOUR WAY TO BECOME A CAPTAIN, SO YOU THINK YOU'RE A BIG SHOT! THAT'S WHY YOU CAN ASK FOR STUPID FAVORS LIKE THAT, HUH, BALDY?!
YACK YACK YACK
BALDY, BALDY, BALDY, BALDY, BALDY, BALDY, BALDY, BALDY, BALDY, BALDY, BALDY, BALDY!
YACK YACK
YACK YACK YACK
SHORTY !!
WHAP

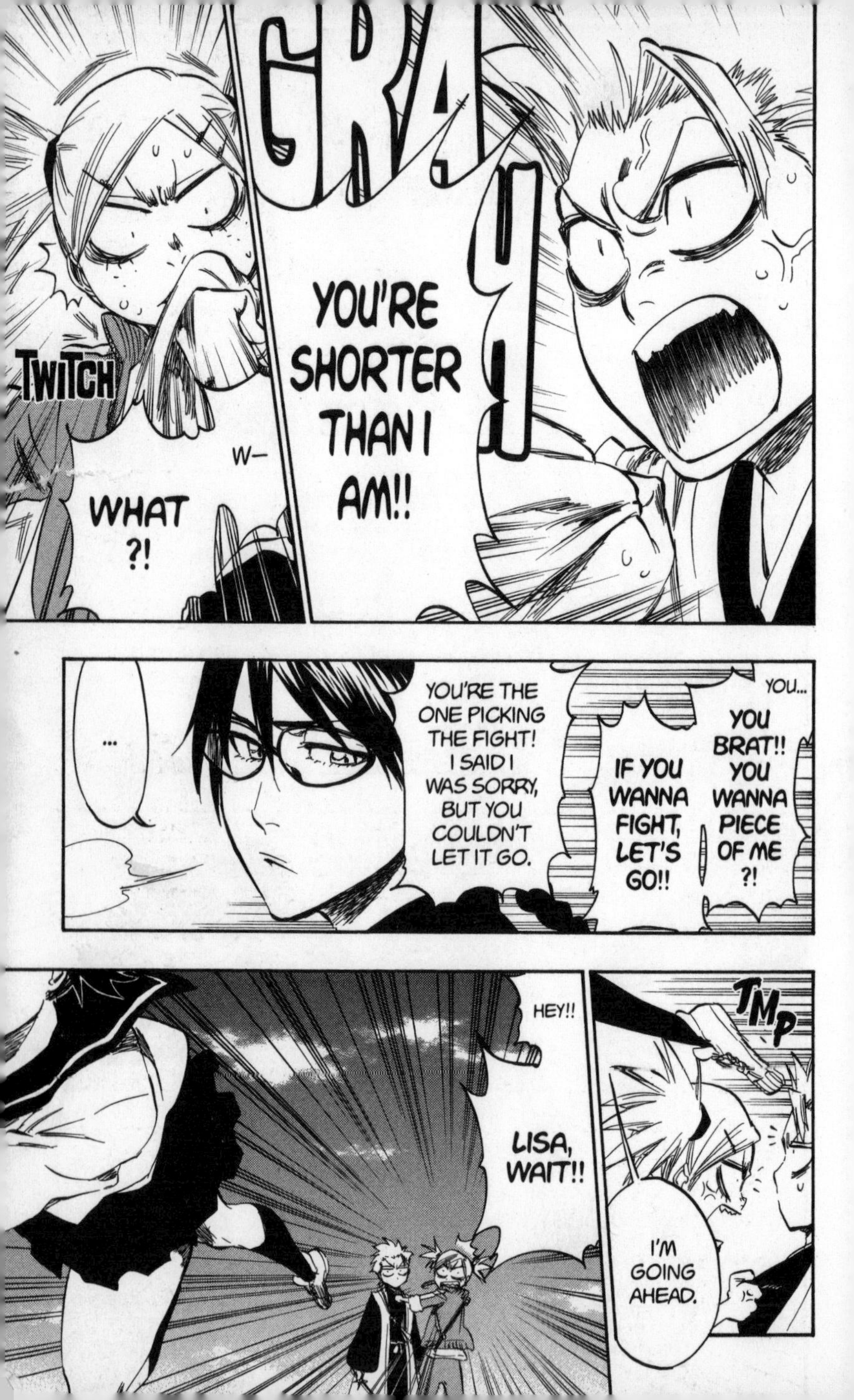
YOU'RE SHORTER THAN I AM!!
W—
WHAT ?!
TWITCH
YOU...
YOU BRAT!! YOU WANNA PIECE OF ME ?!
IF YOU WANNA FIGHT, LET'S GO!!
YOU'RE THE ONE PICKING THE FIGHT! I SAID I WAS SORRY, BUT YOU COULDN'T LET IT GO.
...
TMP
I'M GOING AHEAD.
HEY!!
LISA, WAIT!!

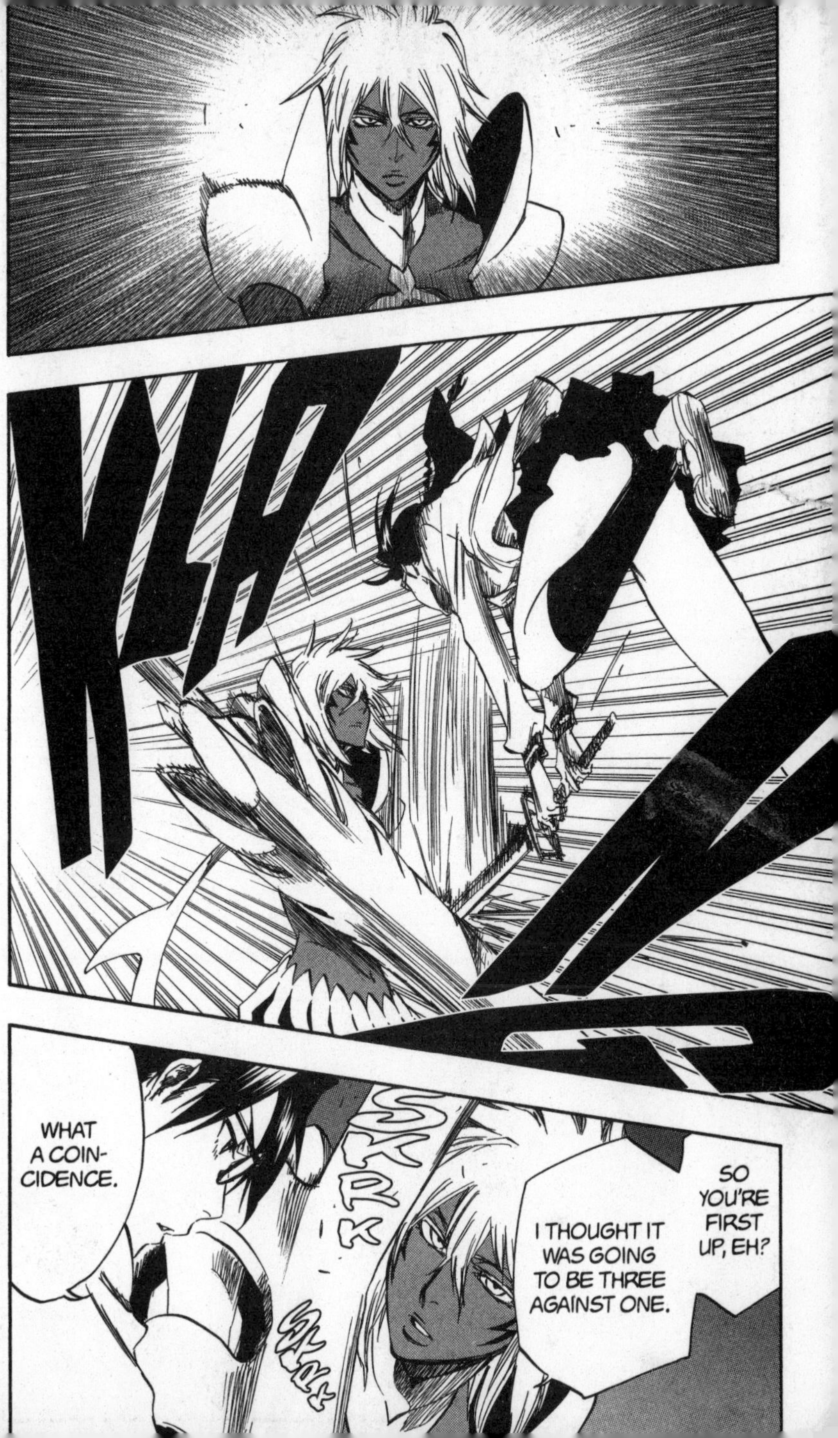
SO YOU'RE FIRST UP, EH?
I THOUGHT IT WAS GOING TO BE THREE AGAINST ONE.
SKRK
WHAT A COIN-CIDENCE.

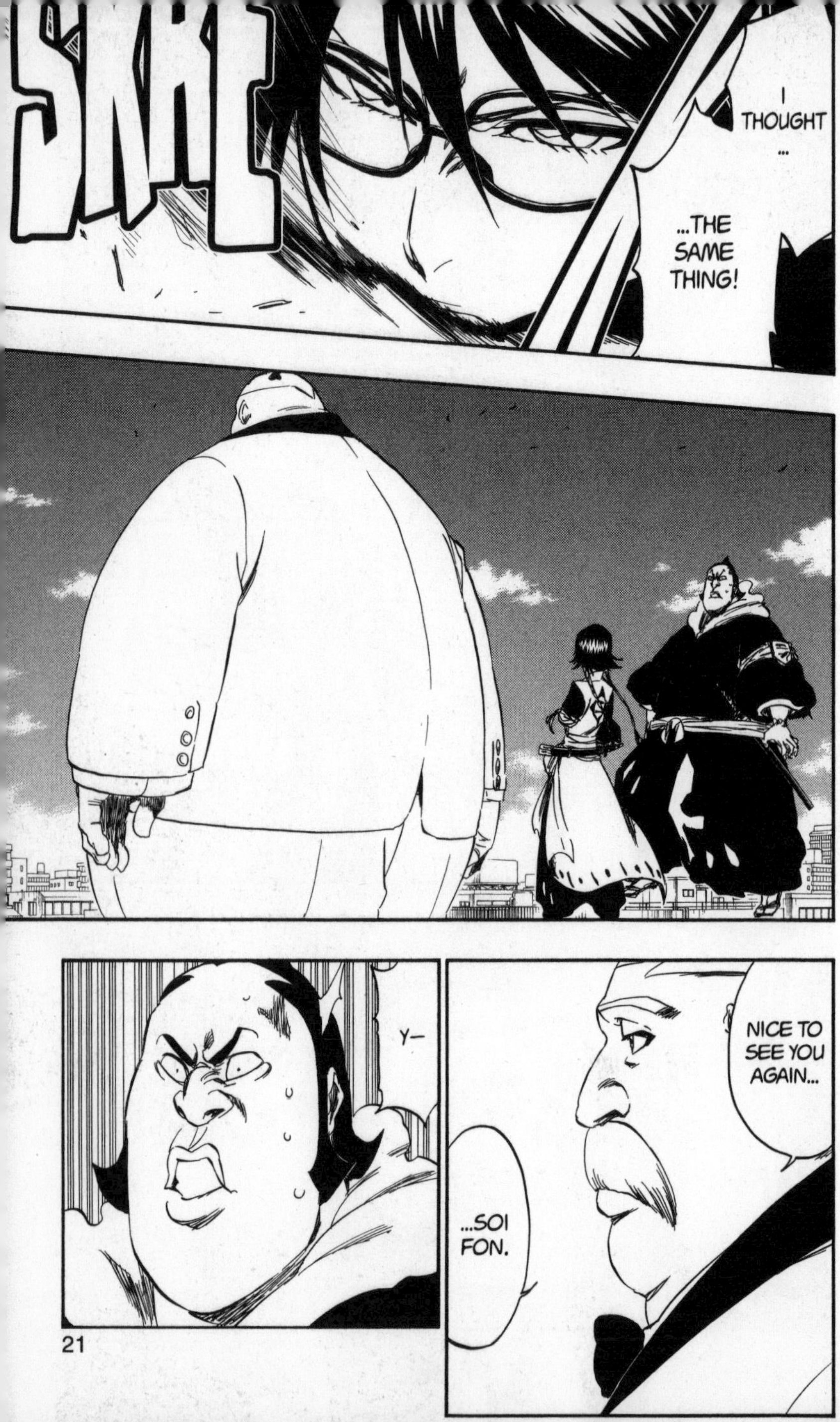
I THOUGHT ...
...THE SAME THING!
SNAP
NICE TO SEE YOU AGAIN...
...SOI FON.
Y—

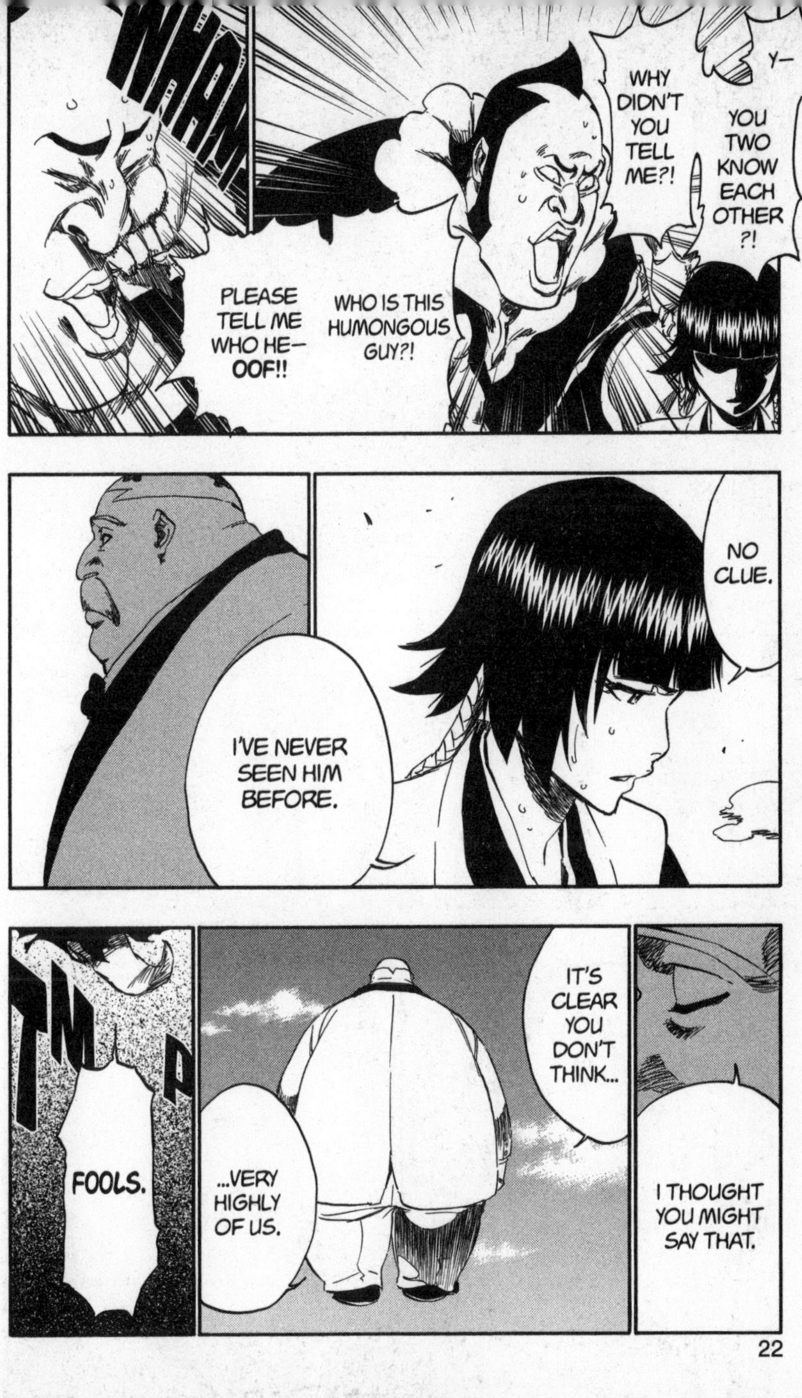
Y—
YOU TWO KNOW EACH OTHER?!
WHY DIDN'T YOU TELL ME?!
WHO IS THIS HUMONGOUS GUY?!
PLEASE TELL ME WHO HE— OOF!!
NO CLUE.
I'VE NEVER SEEN HIM BEFORE.
I THOUGHT YOU MIGHT SAY THAT.
IT'S CLEAR YOU DON'T THINK...
...VERY HIGHLY OF US.
TMP
FOOLS.

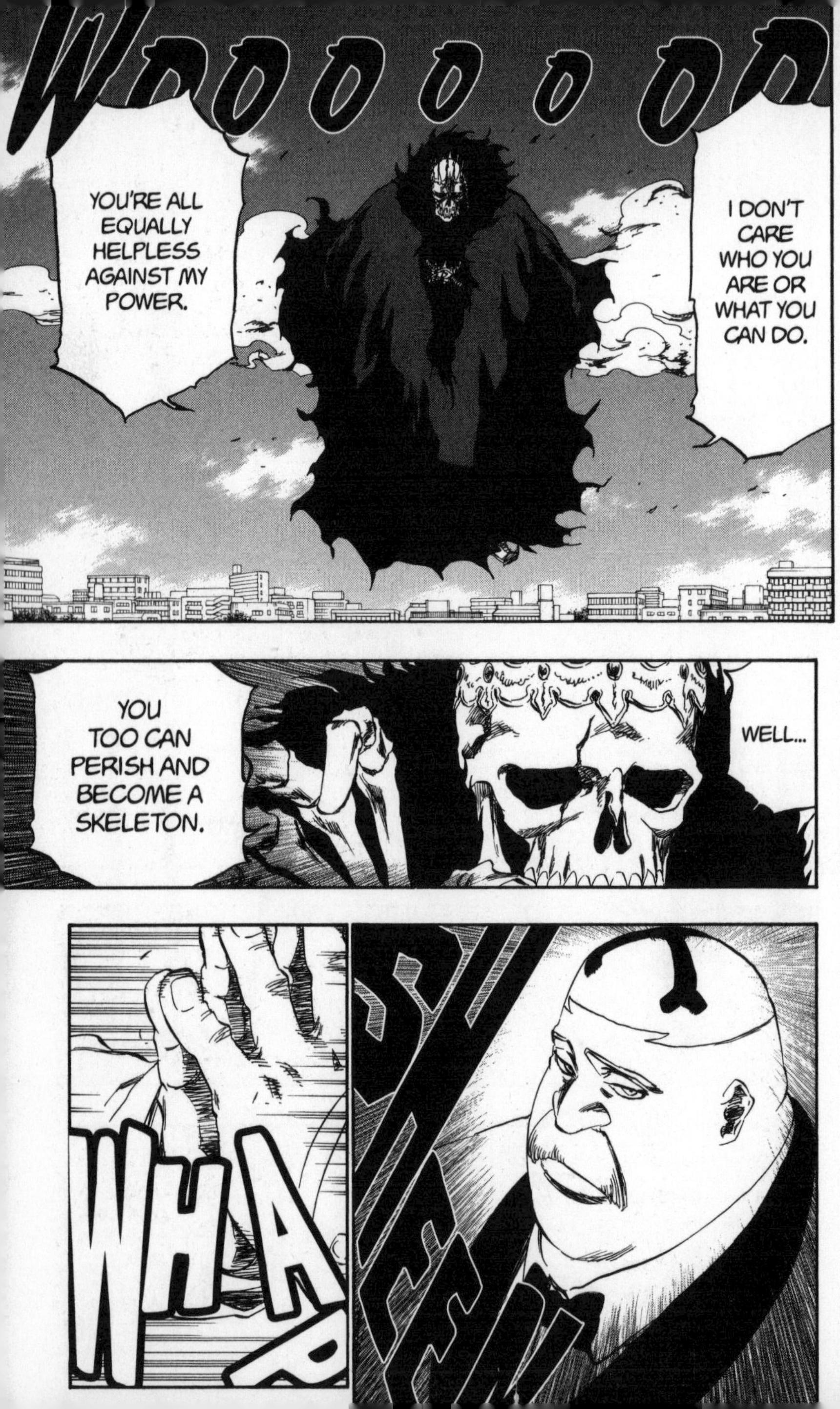
I DON'T CARE WHO YOU ARE OR WHAT YOU CAN DO.
YOU'RE ALL EQUALLY HELPLESS AGAINST MY POWER.
WELL...
YOU TOO CAN PERISH AND BECOME A SKELETON.

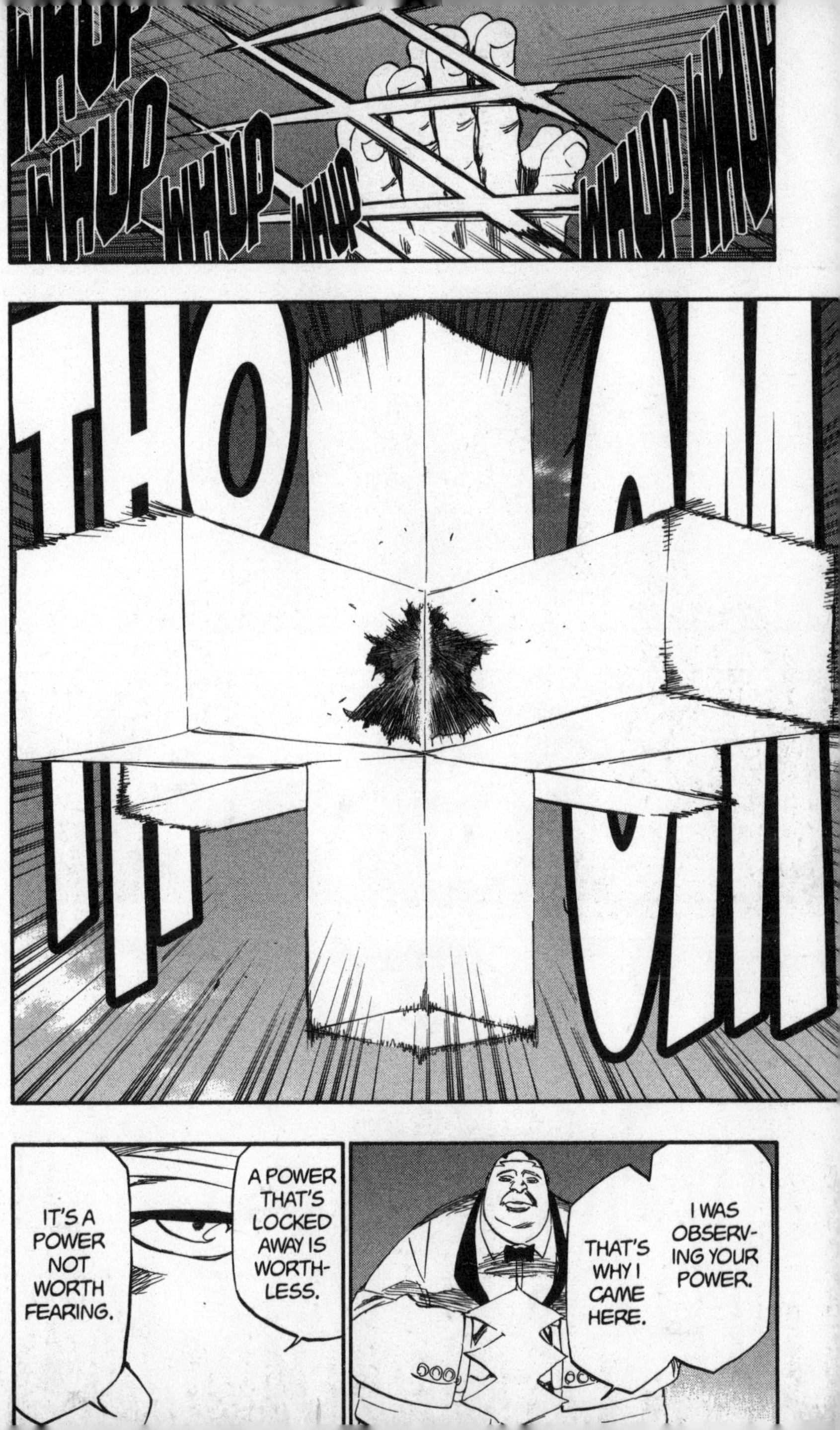
WHUP WHUP
WHUP WHUP WHUP WHUP
THOOM
I WAS OBSERV-ING YOUR POWER.
THAT'S WHY I CAME HERE.
A POWER THAT'S LOCKED AWAY IS WORTH-LESS.
IT'S A POWER NOT WORTH FEARING.

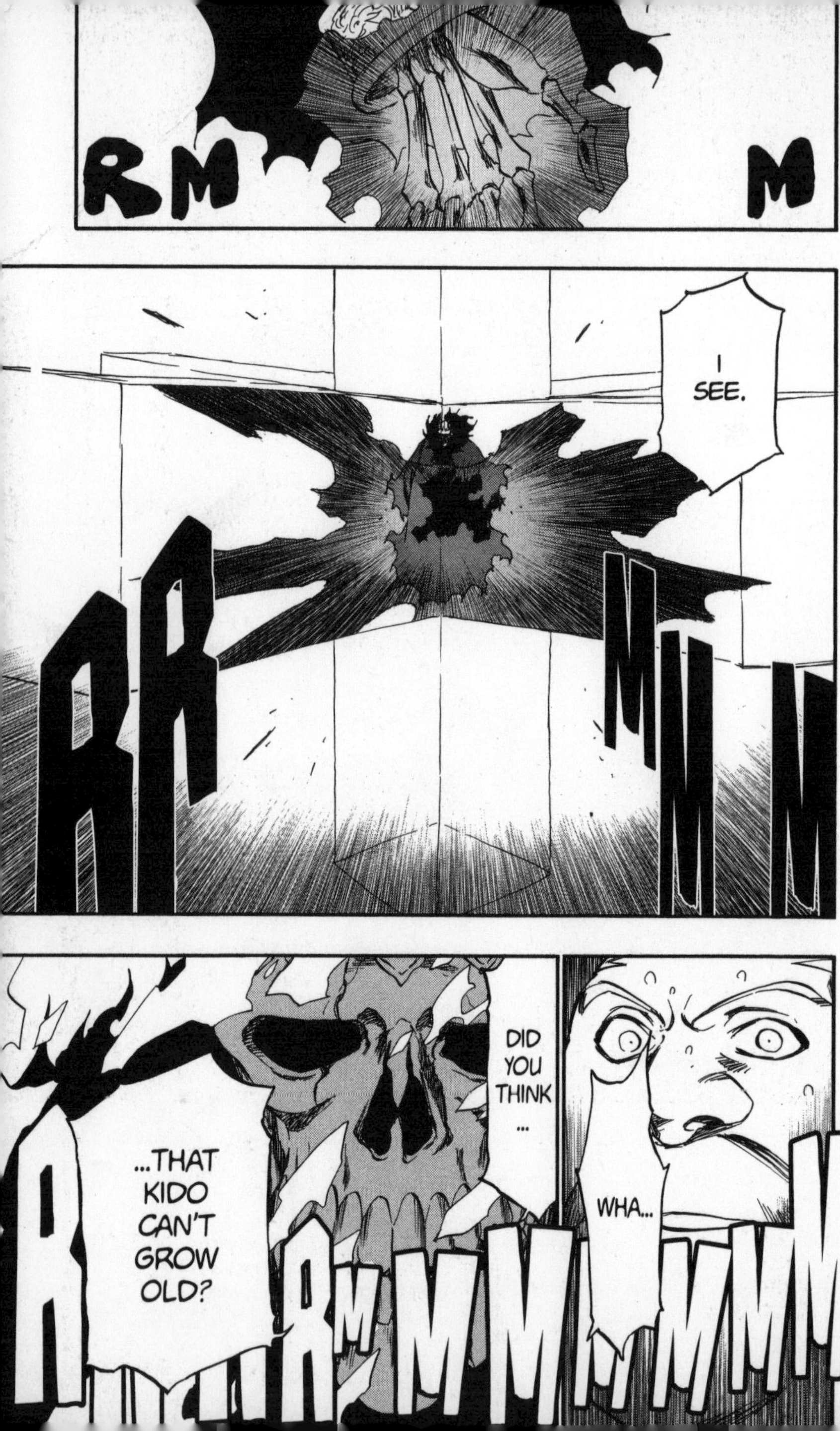
RM
M
I SEE.
RR
MMM
WHA...
DID YOU THINK ...
...THAT KIDO CAN'T GROW OLD?

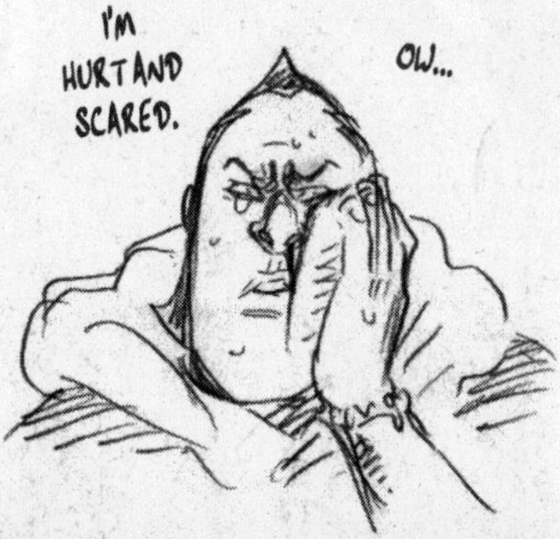
OW...
I'M HURT AND SCARED.

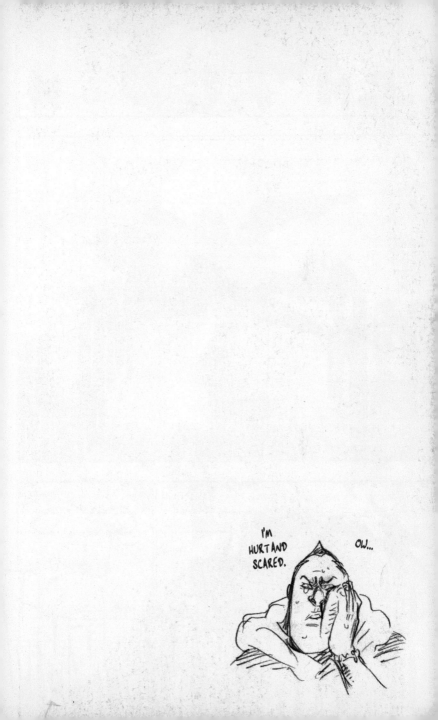

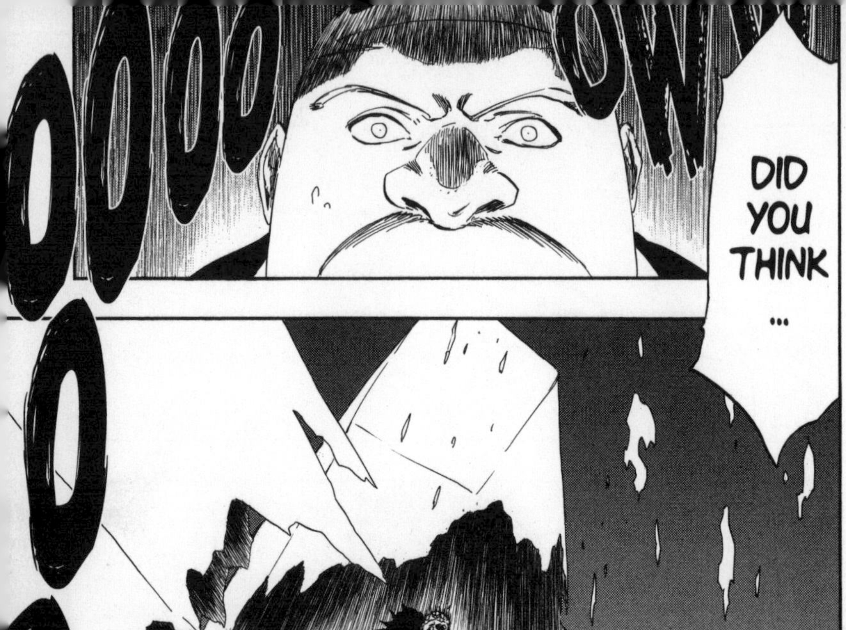
DID YOU THINK ...
...THAT KIDO CAN'T GROW OLD?

369. Spit on Your Own God

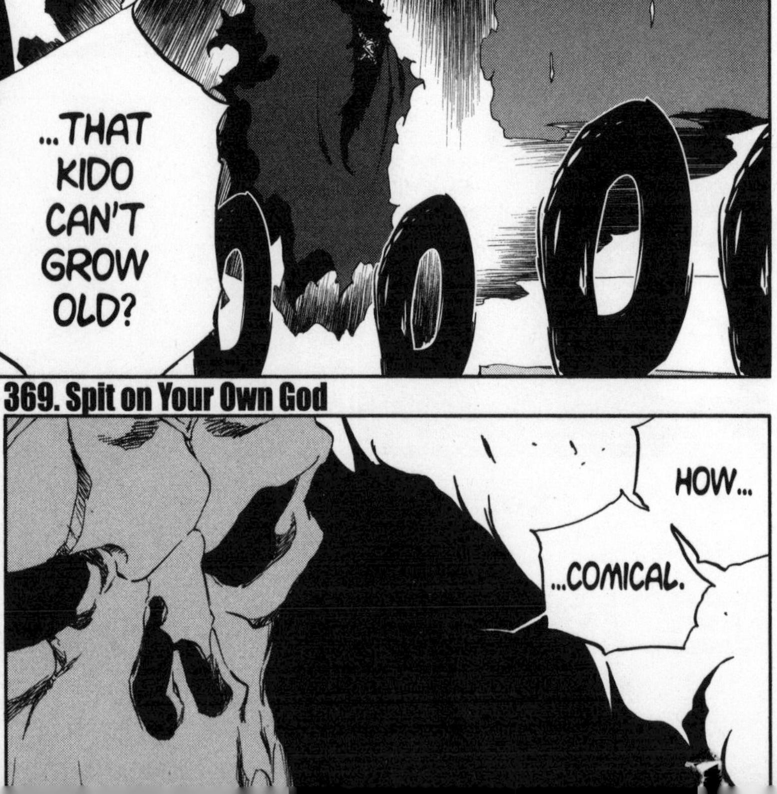
HOW...
...COMICAL.

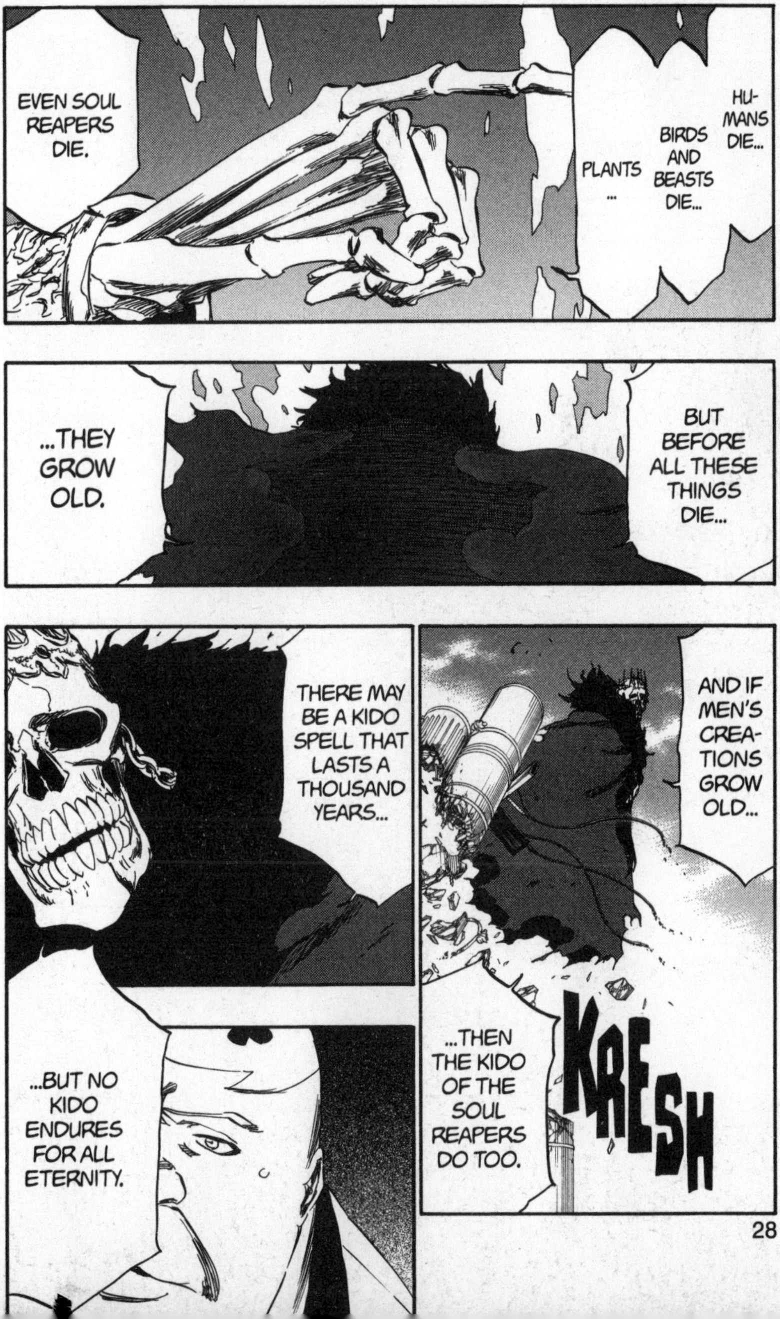
HU-MANS DIE...
BIRDS AND BEASTS DIE...
PLANTS...
EVEN SOUL REAPERS DIE.
BUT BEFORE ALL THESE THINGS DIE...
...THEY GROW OLD.
AND IF MEN'S CREA-TIONS GROW OLD...
KRESH
...THEN THE KIDO OF THE SOUL REAPERS DO TOO.
THERE MAY BE A KIDO SPELL THAT LASTS A THOUSAND YEARS...
...BUT NO KIDO ENDURES FOR ALL ETERNITY.

READ THIS WAY

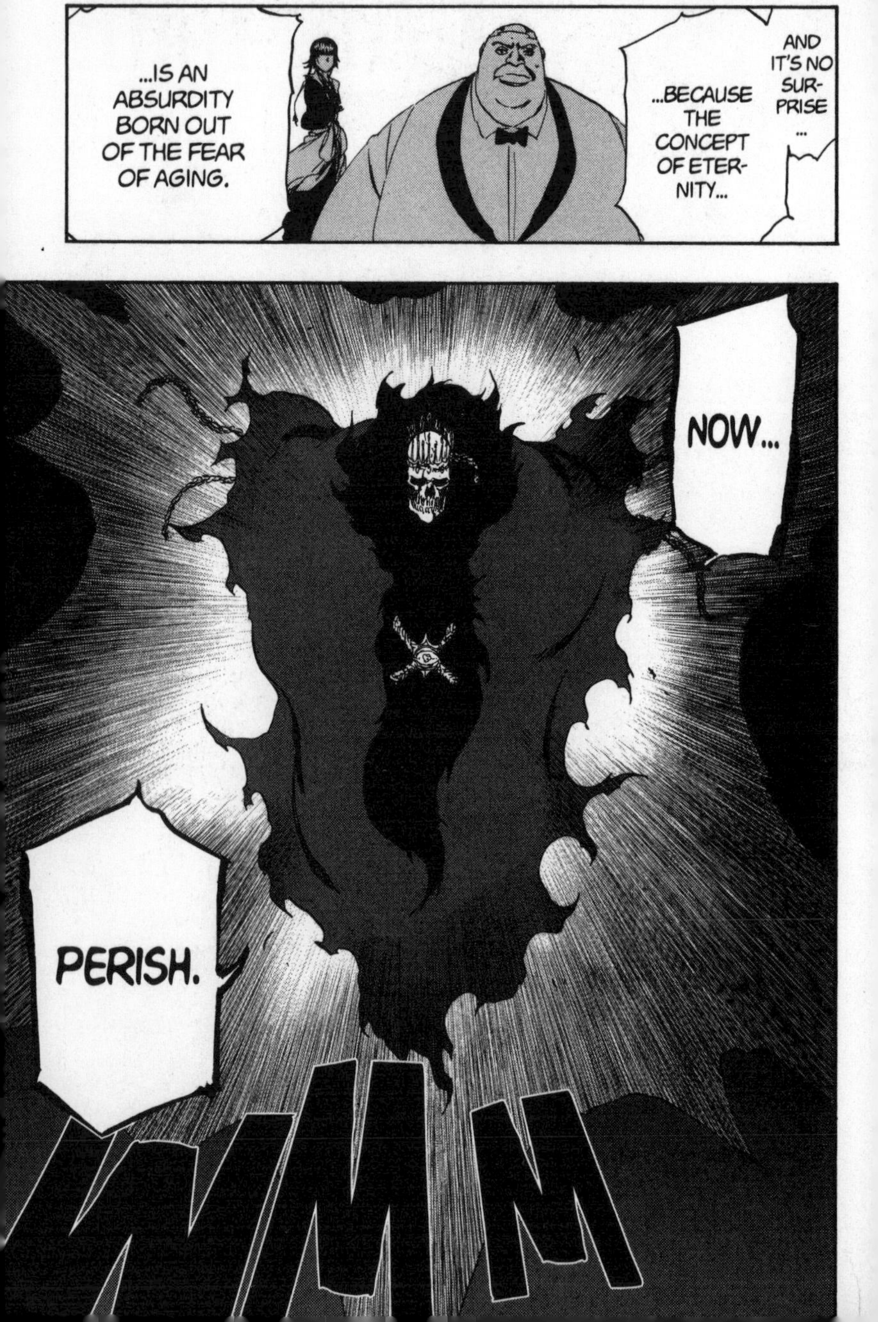
AND IT'S NO SURPRISE...
...BECAUSE THE CONCEPT OF ETERNITY...
...IS AN ABSURDITY BORN OUT OF THE FEAR OF AGING.
NOW...
PERISH.

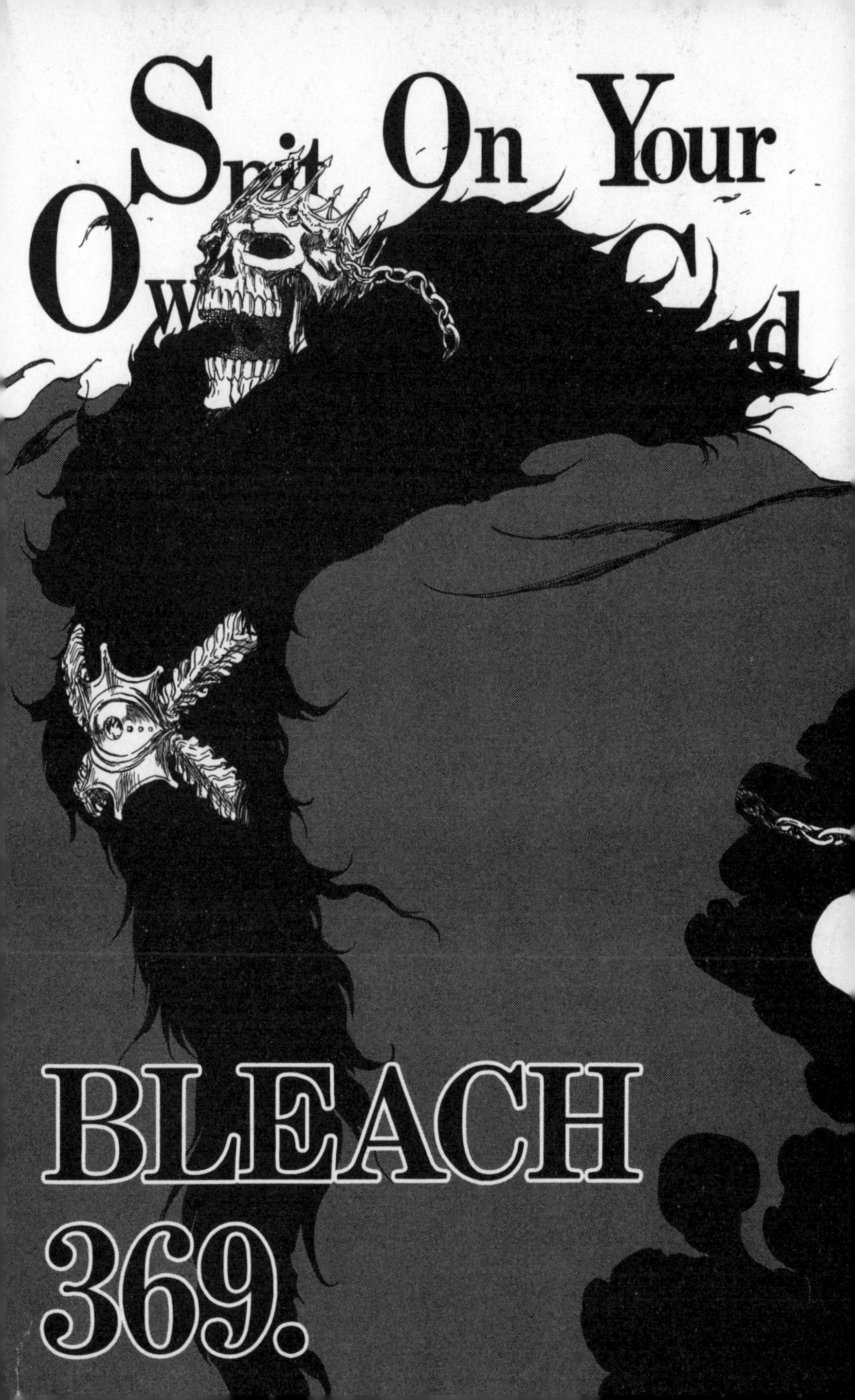
Spit On Your
BLEACH
369.

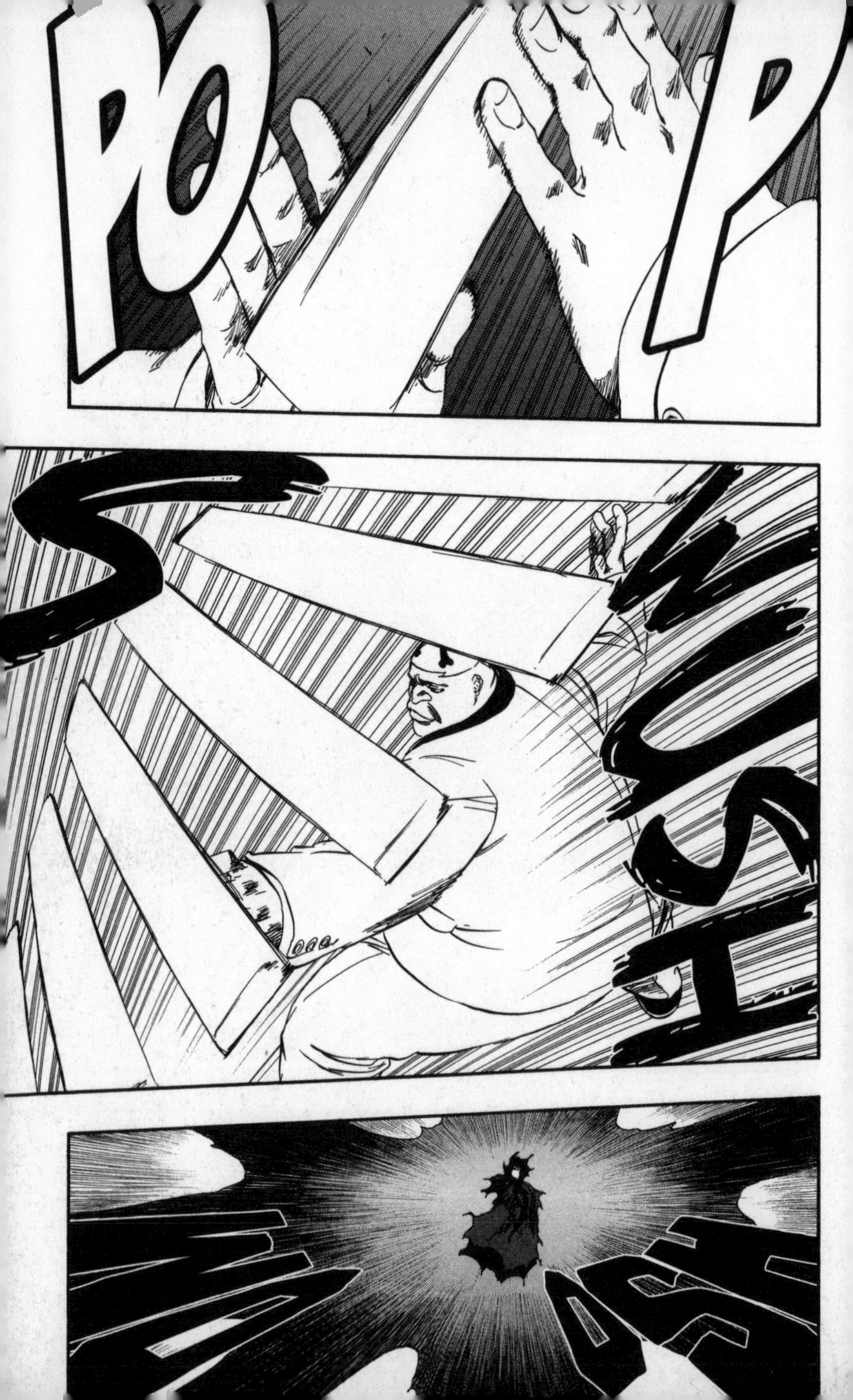
POP
SWUSH

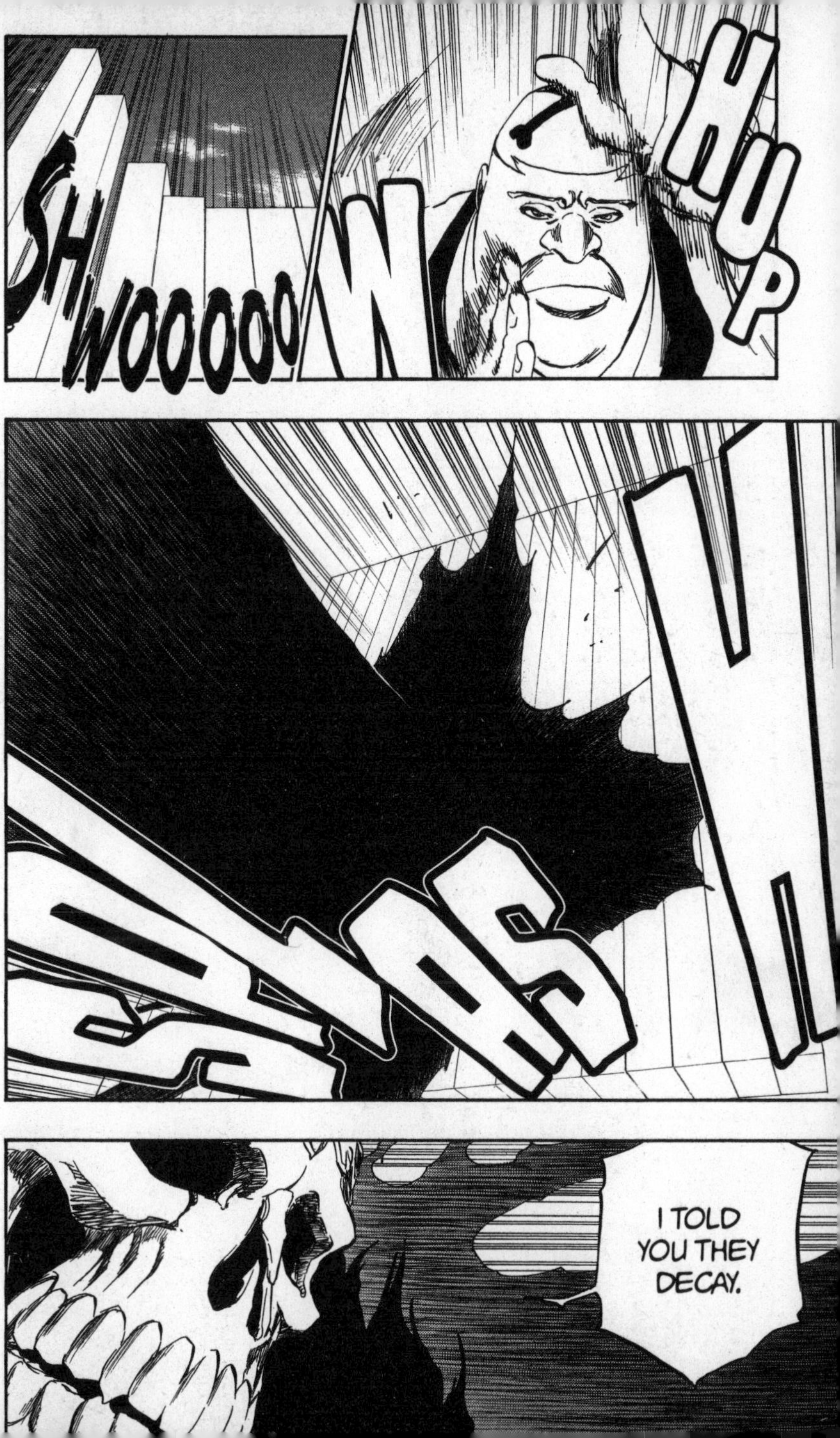
HUP
SHWOOOOOWN
I TOLD YOU THEY DECAY.

READ THIS WAY

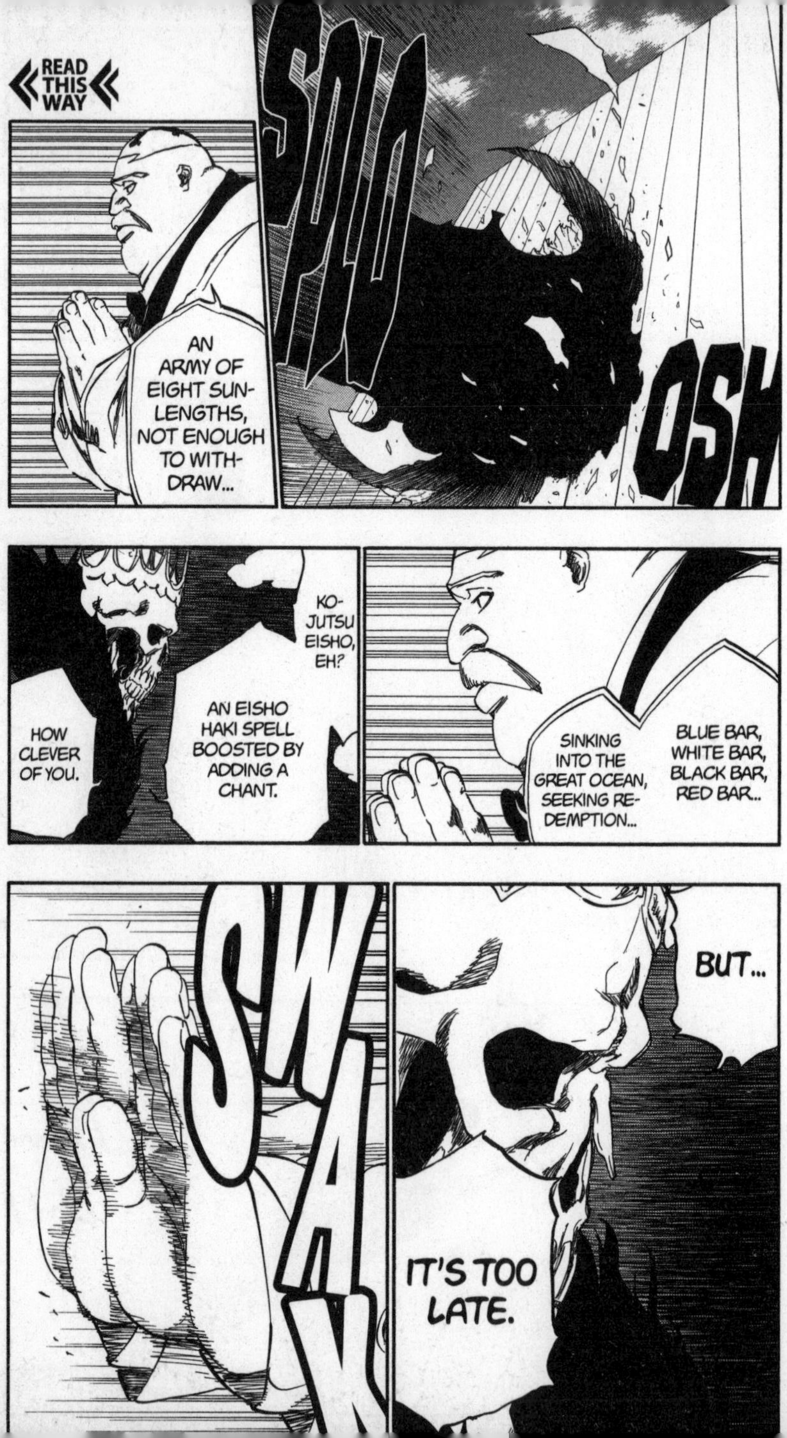
AN ARMY OF EIGHT SUN-LENGTHS, NOT ENOUGH TO WITH-DRAW...
BLUE BAR, WHITE BAR, BLACK BAR, RED BAR...
SINKING INTO THE GREAT OCEAN, SEEKING RE-DEMPTION...
KO-JUTSU EISHO, EH?
AN EISHO HAKI SPELL BOOSTED BY ADDING A CHANT.
HOW CLEVER OF YOU.
BUT...
IT'S TOO LATE.

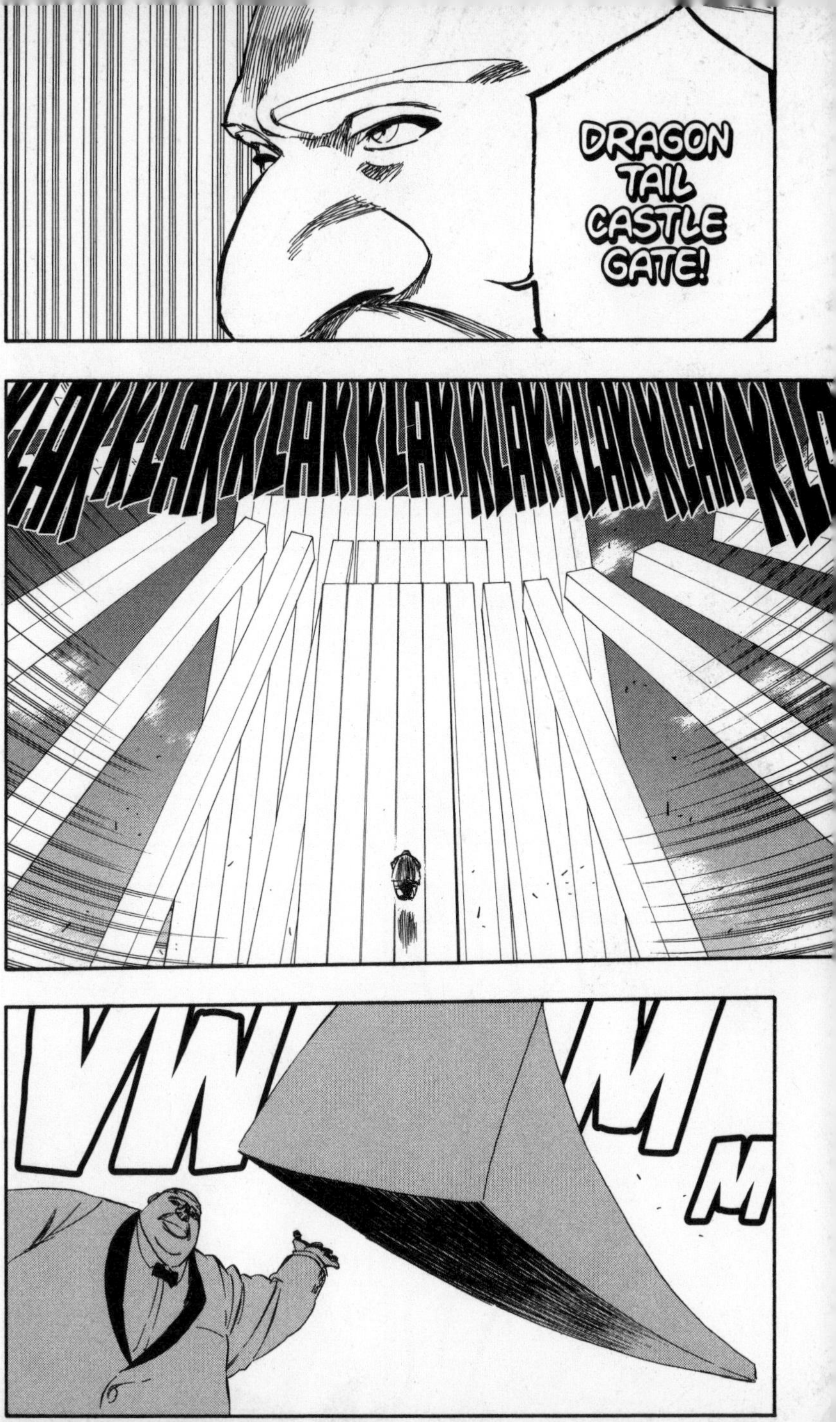
DRAGON TAIL CASTLE GATE!
KLAK KLAK KLAK KLAK KLAK KLAK
VW M M

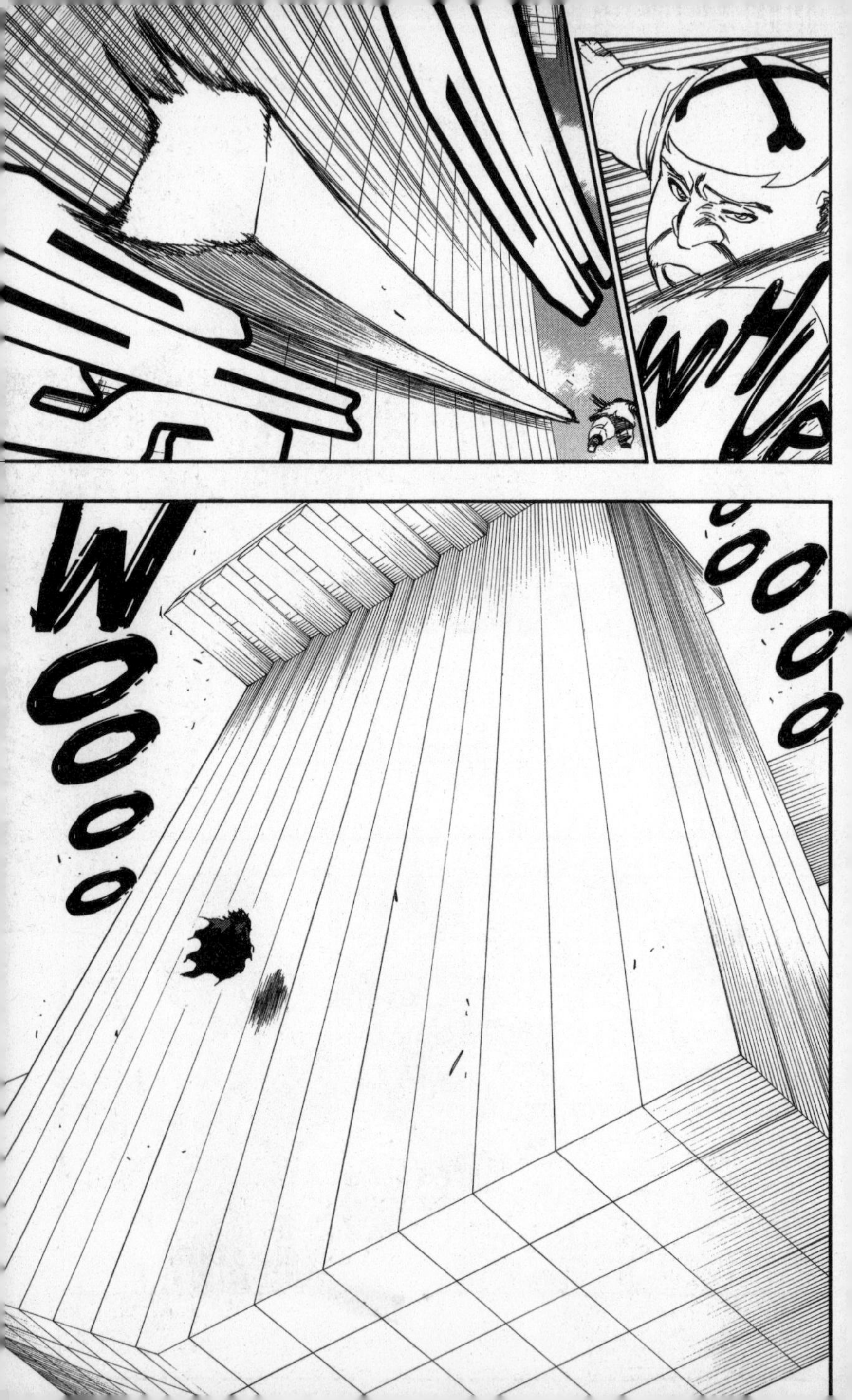
WHOOOOOO
WOOOOO

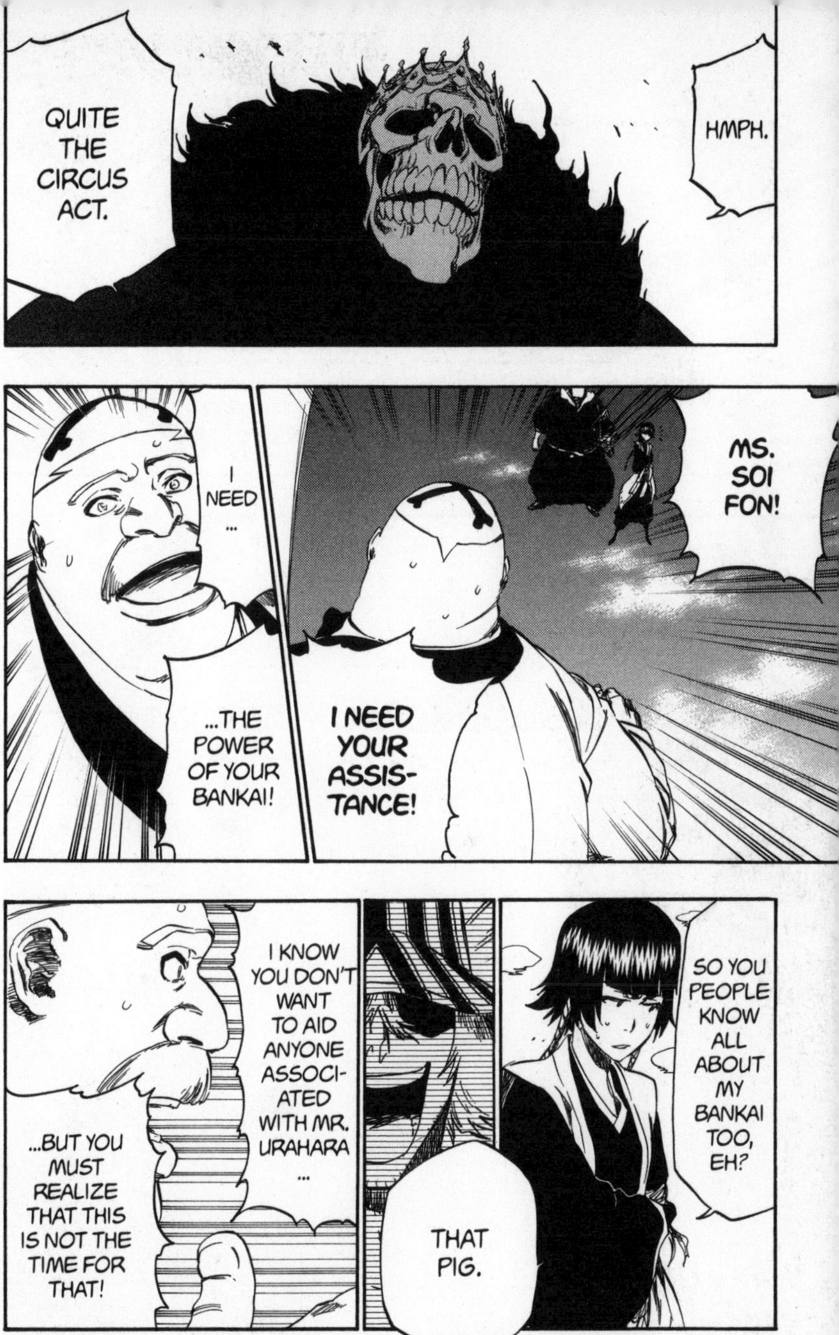
HMPH.
QUITE THE CIRCUS ACT.
MS. SOI FON!
I NEED YOUR ASSISTANCE!
I NEED...
...THE POWER OF YOUR BANKAI!
SO YOU PEOPLE KNOW ALL ABOUT MY BANKAI TOO, EH?
THAT PIG.
I KNOW YOU DON'T WANT TO AID ANYONE ASSOCIATED WITH MR. URAHARA...
...BUT YOU MUST REALIZE THAT THIS IS NOT THE TIME FOR THAT!

READ THIS WAY

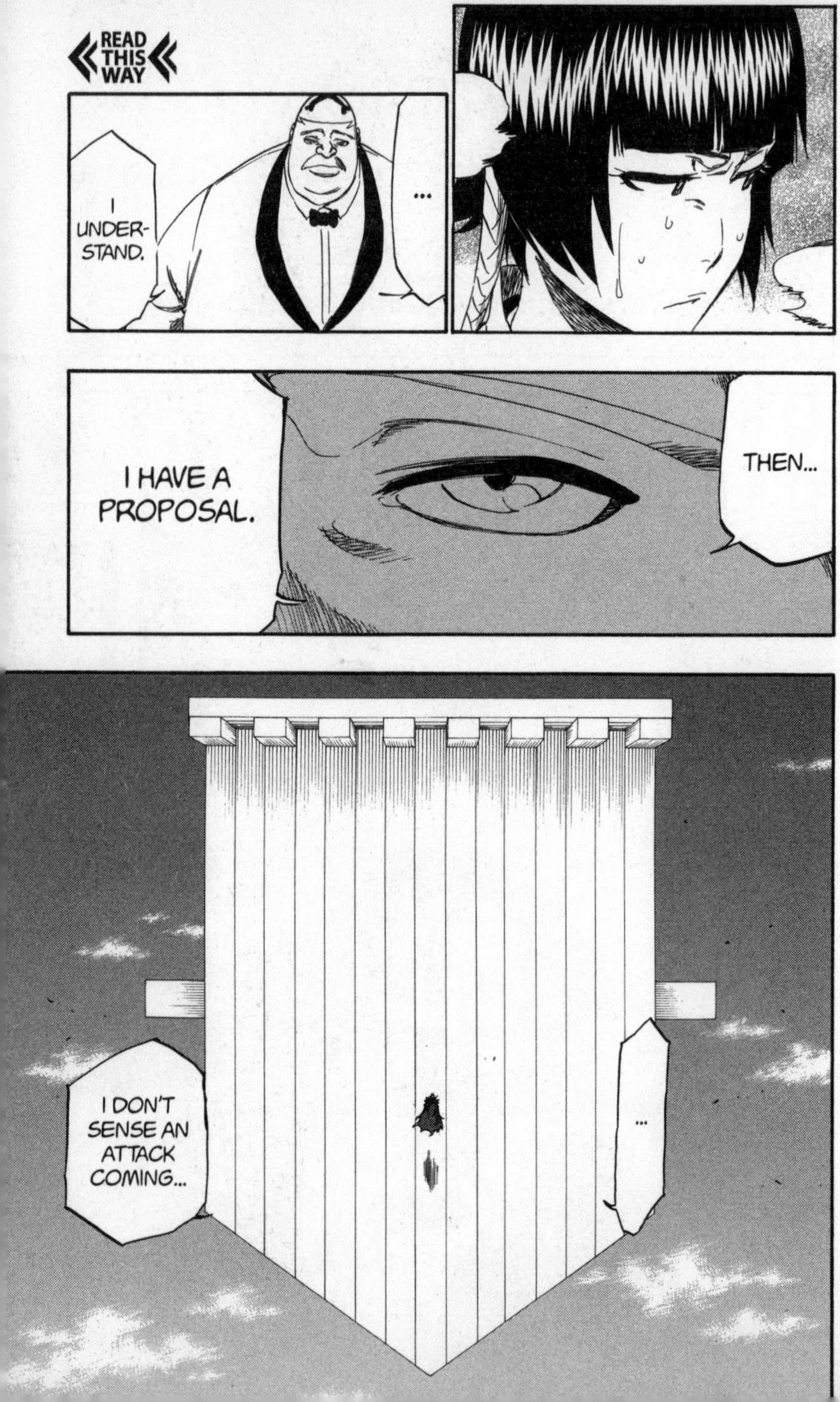
...
I UNDER-STAND.
THEN...
I HAVE A PROPOSAL.
...
I DON'T SENSE AN ATTACK COMING...

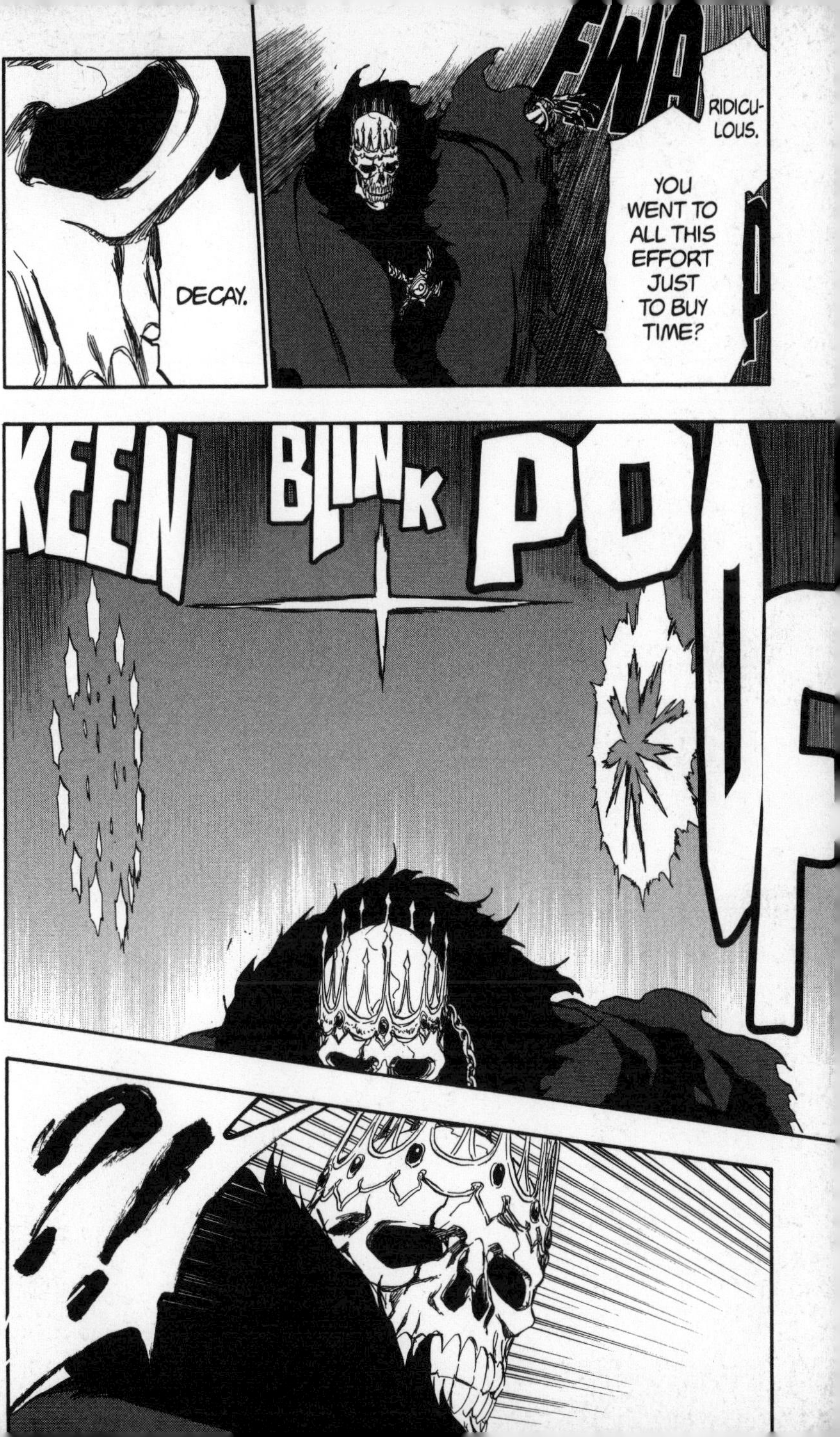
RIDICU-LOUS.
YOU WENT TO ALL THIS EFFORT JUST TO BUY TIME?
DECAY.
PO
BLINK
KEEN
?!

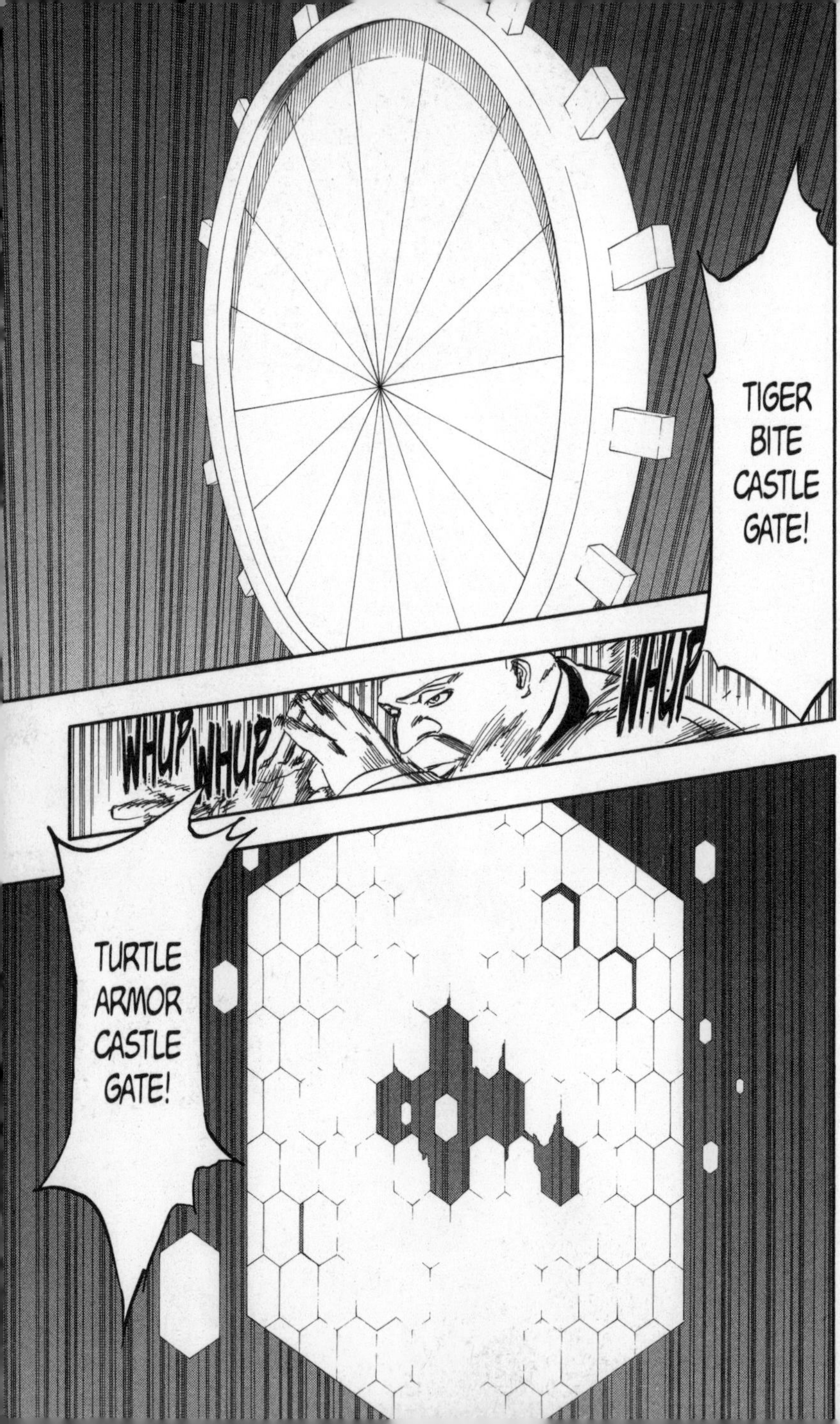
TIGER BITE CASTLE GATE!
WHUP
WHUP
WHUP
TURTLE ARMOR CASTLE GATE!

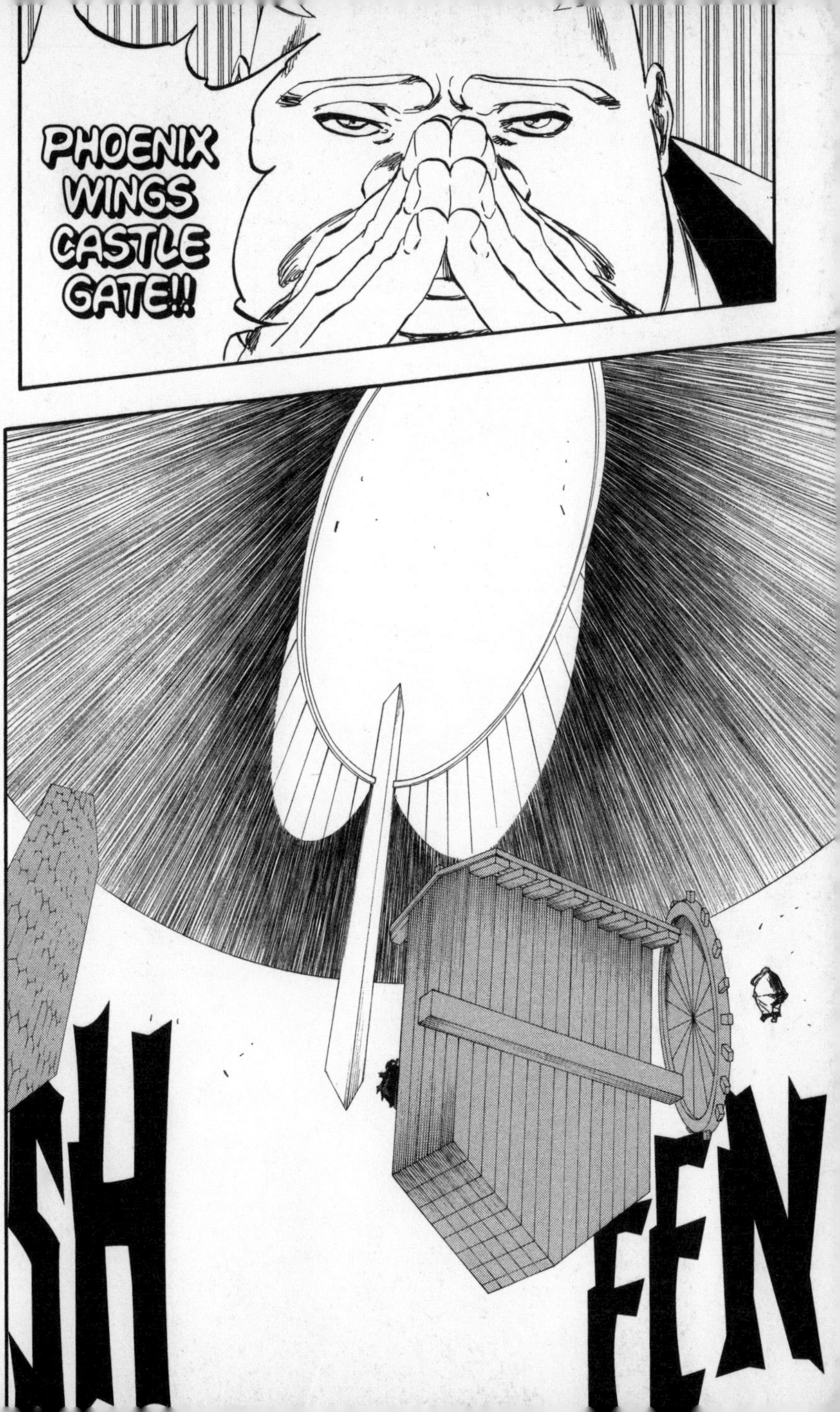
PHOENIX WINGS CASTLE GATE!!
SH FEN

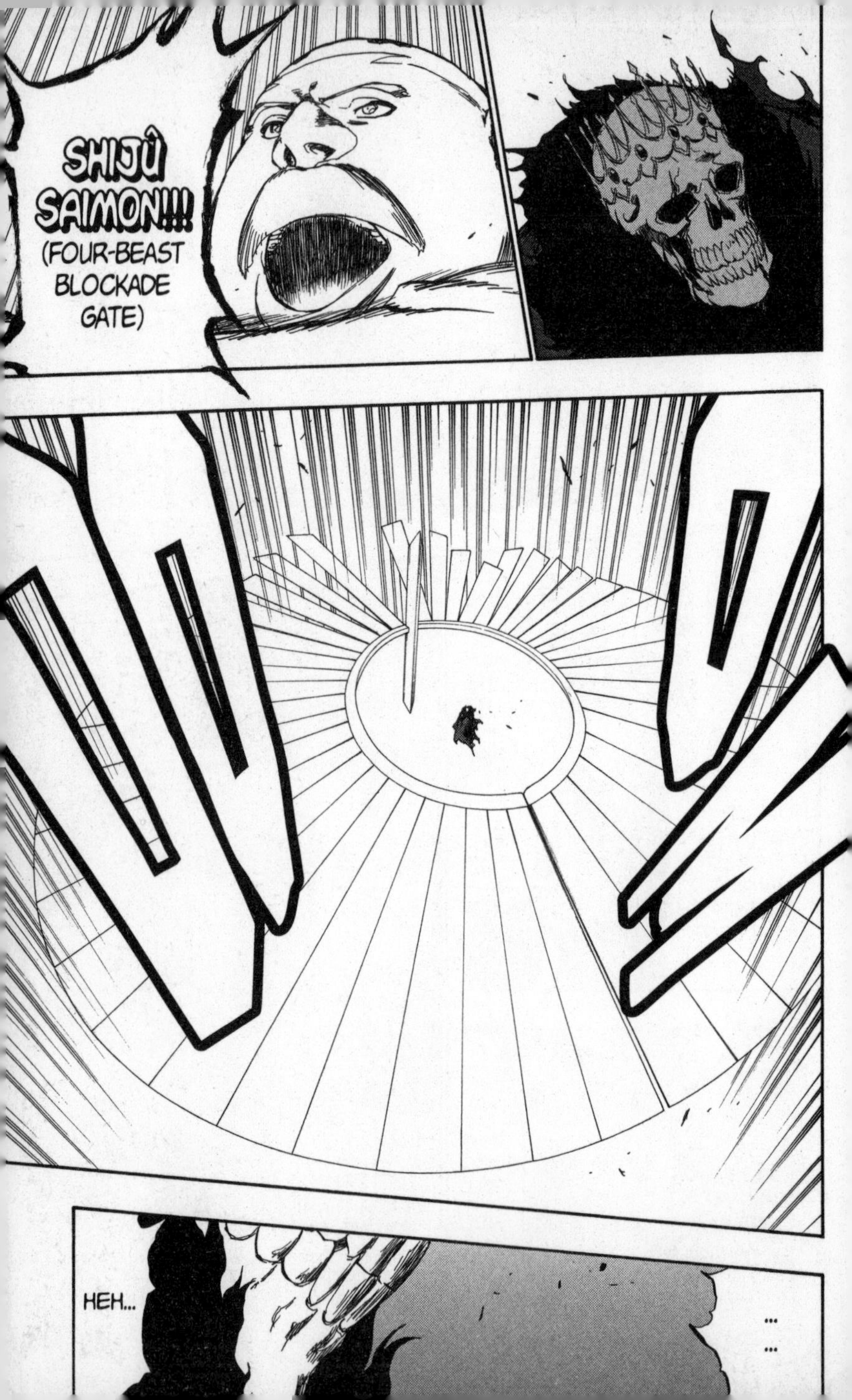
SHIJÛ SAIMON!!!
(FOUR-BEAST BLOCKADE GATE)
...
...
HEH...

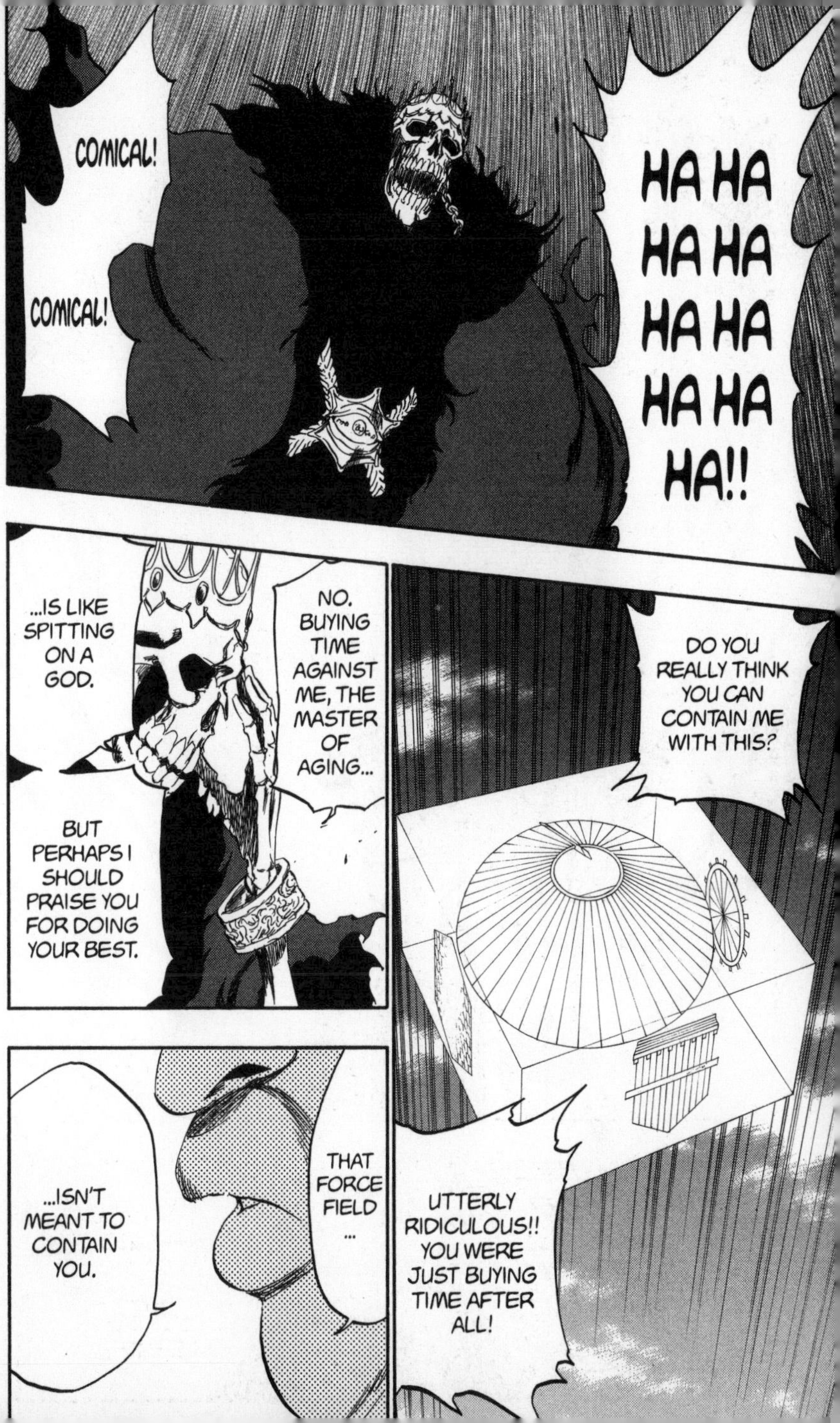
HA HA HA HA HA HA HA HA HA!!
COMICAL!
COMICAL!
DO YOU REALLY THINK YOU CAN CONTAIN ME WITH THIS?
UTTERLY RIDICULOUS!! YOU WERE JUST BUYING TIME AFTER ALL!
NO. BUYING TIME AGAINST ME, THE MASTER OF AGING...
...IS LIKE SPITTING ON A GOD.
BUT PERHAPS I SHOULD PRAISE YOU FOR DOING YOUR BEST.
THAT FORCE FIELD...
...ISN'T MEANT TO CONTAIN YOU.

READ THIS WAY

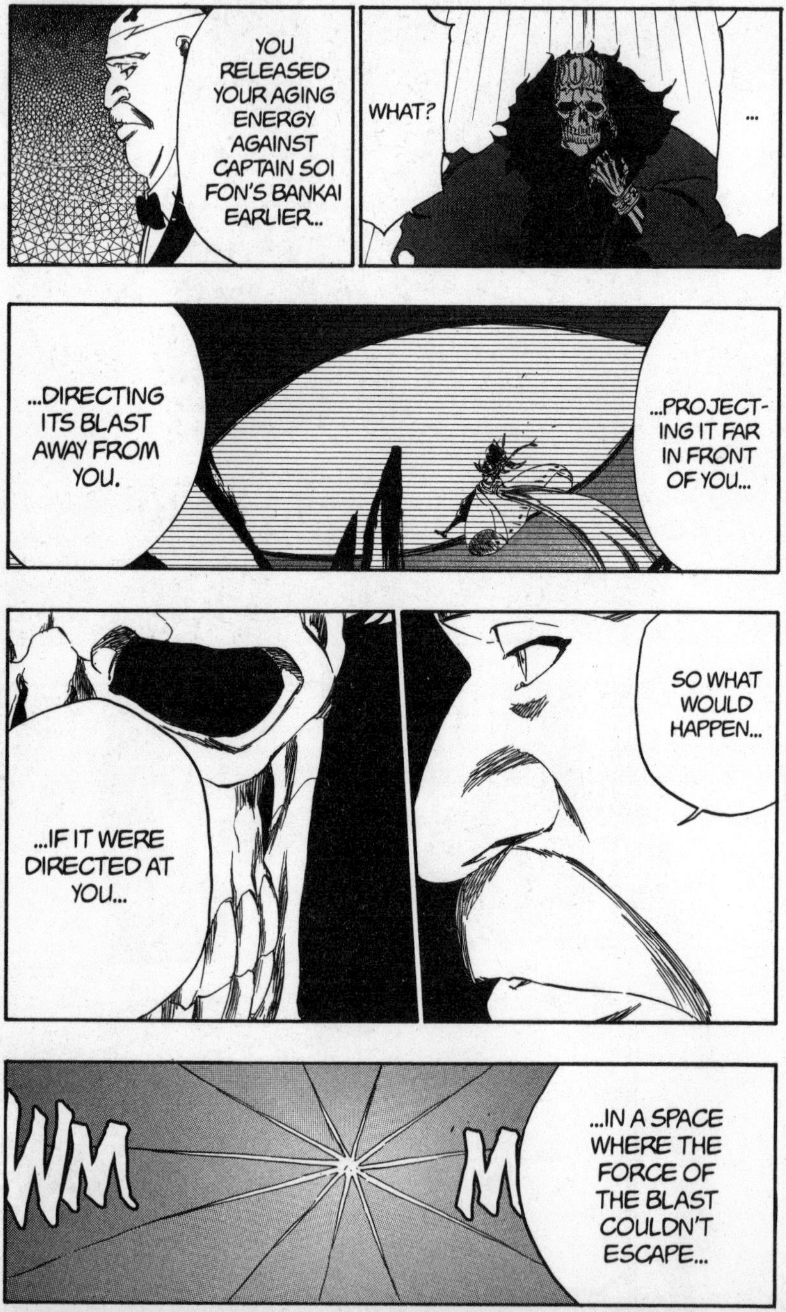
...
WHAT?
YOU RELEASED YOUR AGING ENERGY AGAINST CAPTAIN SOI FON'S BANKAI EARLIER...
...PROJECTING IT FAR IN FRONT OF YOU...
...DIRECTING ITS BLAST AWAY FROM YOU.
SO WHAT WOULD HAPPEN...
...IF IT WERE DIRECTED AT YOU...
...IN A SPACE WHERE THE FORCE OF THE BLAST COULDN'T ESCAPE...
M
WM

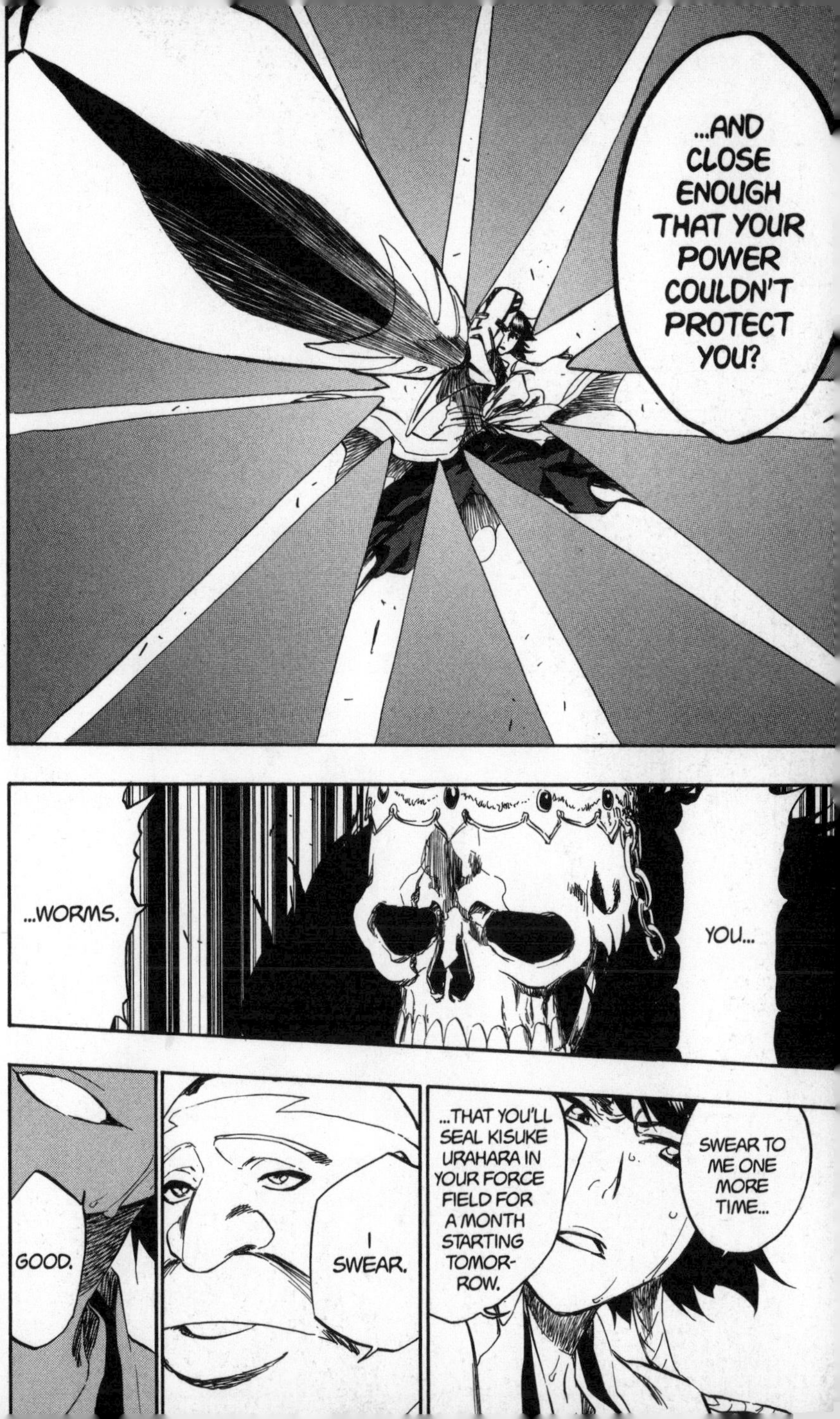
...AND CLOSE ENOUGH THAT YOUR POWER COULDN'T PROTECT YOU?
YOU...
...WORMS.
SWEAR TO ME ONE MORE TIME...
...THAT YOU'LL SEAL KISUKE URAHARA IN YOUR FORCE FIELD FOR A MONTH STARTING TOMOR-ROW.
I SWEAR.
GOOD.

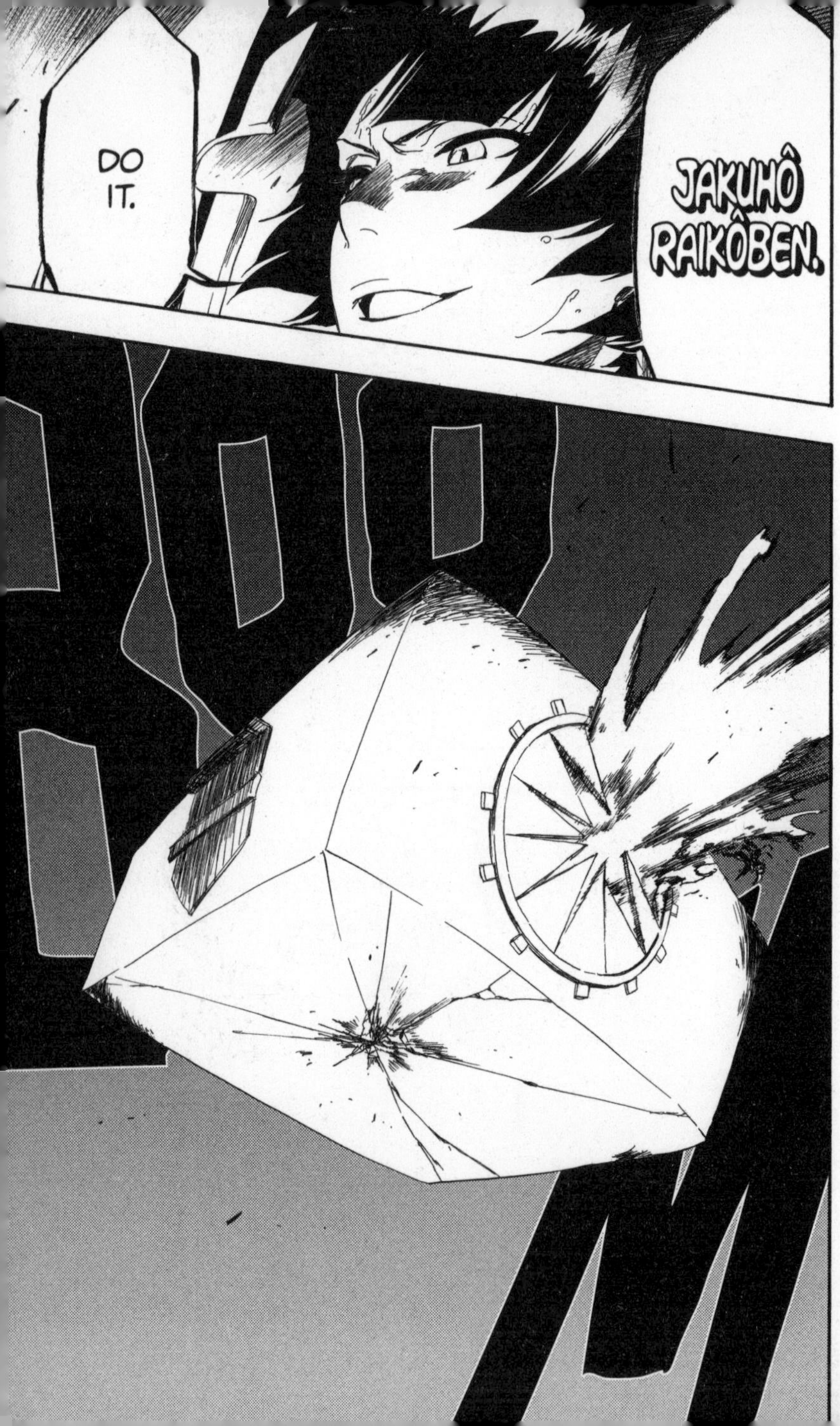
JAKUHÔ RAIKÔBEN.
DO IT.

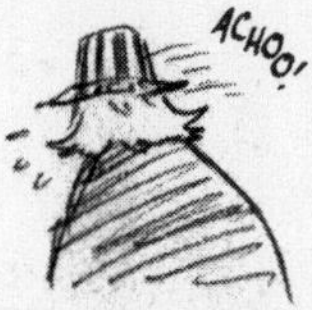
ACHOO!

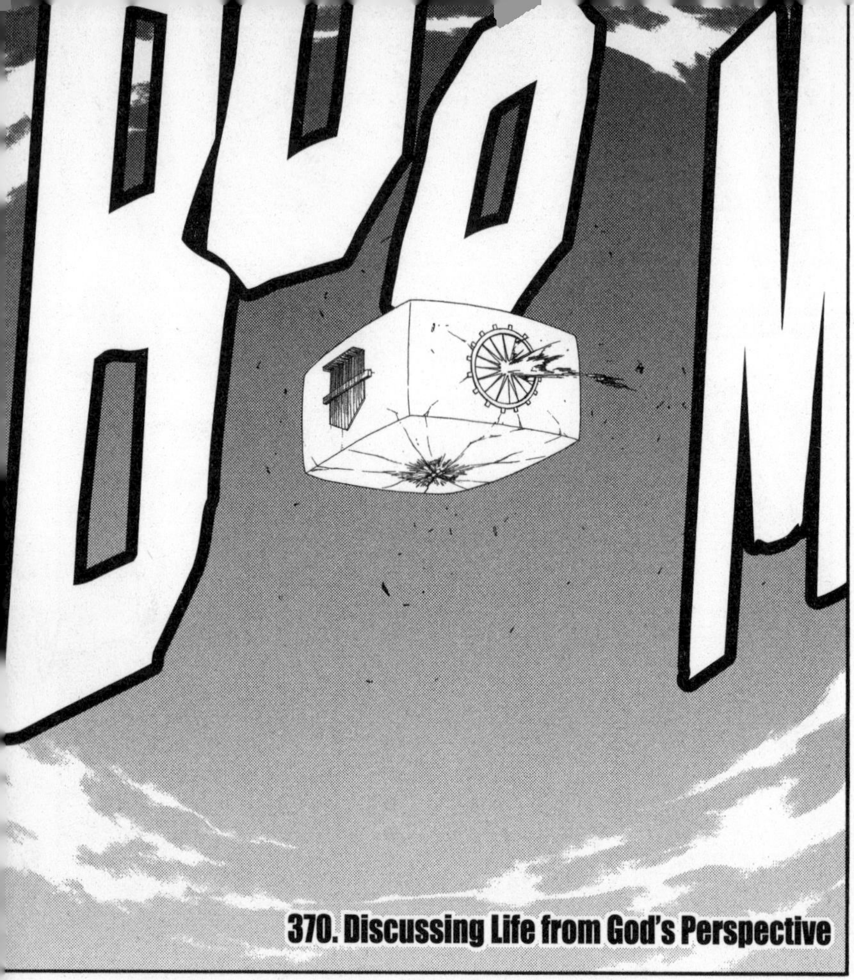
BOOM

370. Discussing Life from God's Perspective

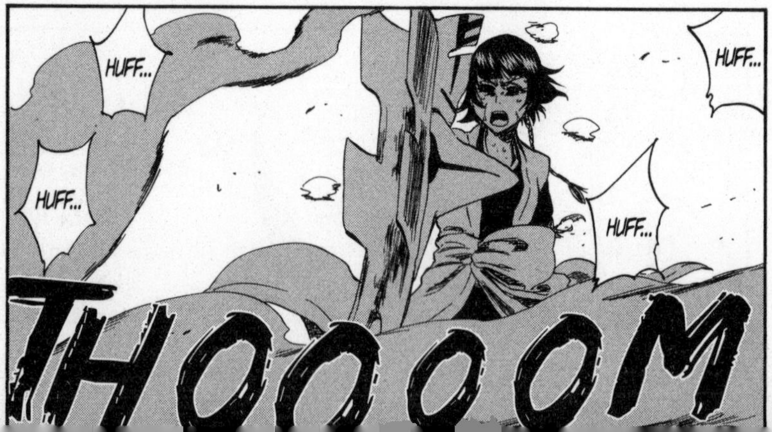
HUFF...
HUFF...
HUFF...
HUFF...
THOOOOM

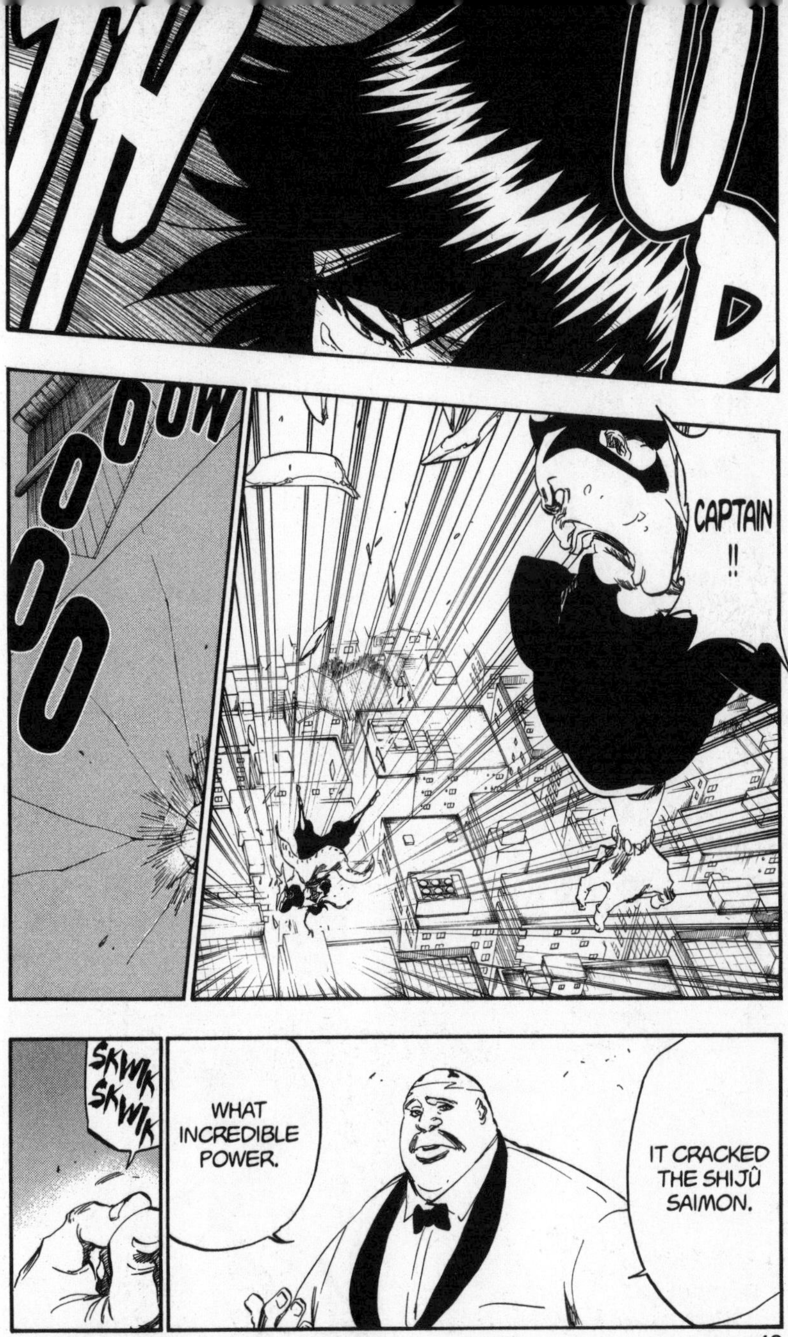
CAPTAIN !!
IT CRACKED THE SHIJÛ SAIMON.
WHAT INCREDIBLE POWER.
SKWIK SKWIK

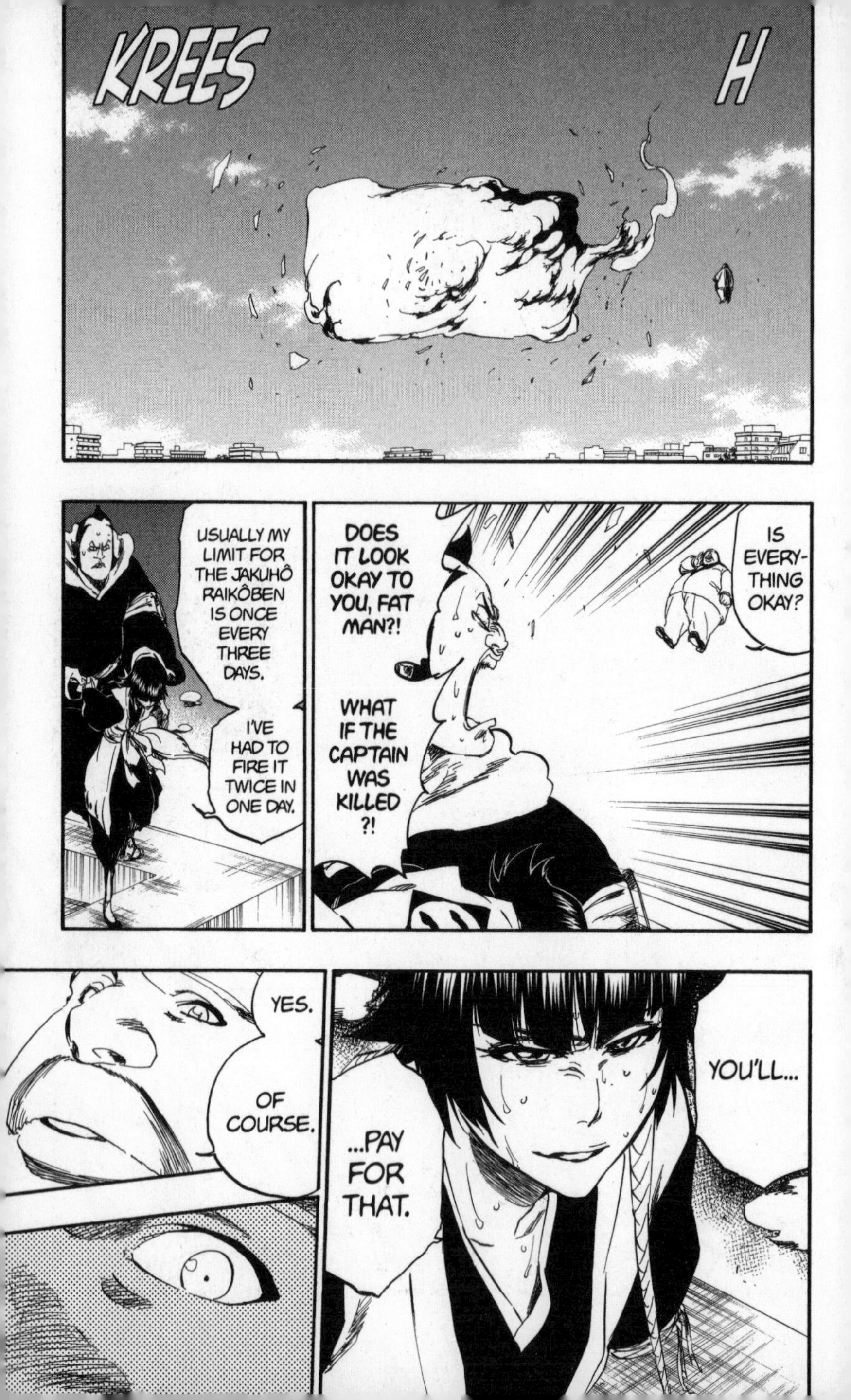
KREES H
IS EVERYTHING OKAY?
DOES IT LOOK OKAY TO YOU, FAT MAN?!
WHAT IF THE CAPTAIN WAS KILLED?!
USUALLY MY LIMIT FOR THE JAKUHÔ RAIKÔBEN IS ONCE EVERY THREE DAYS.
I'VE HAD TO FIRE IT TWICE IN ONE DAY.
YOU'LL...
...PAY FOR THAT.
YES.
OF COURSE.

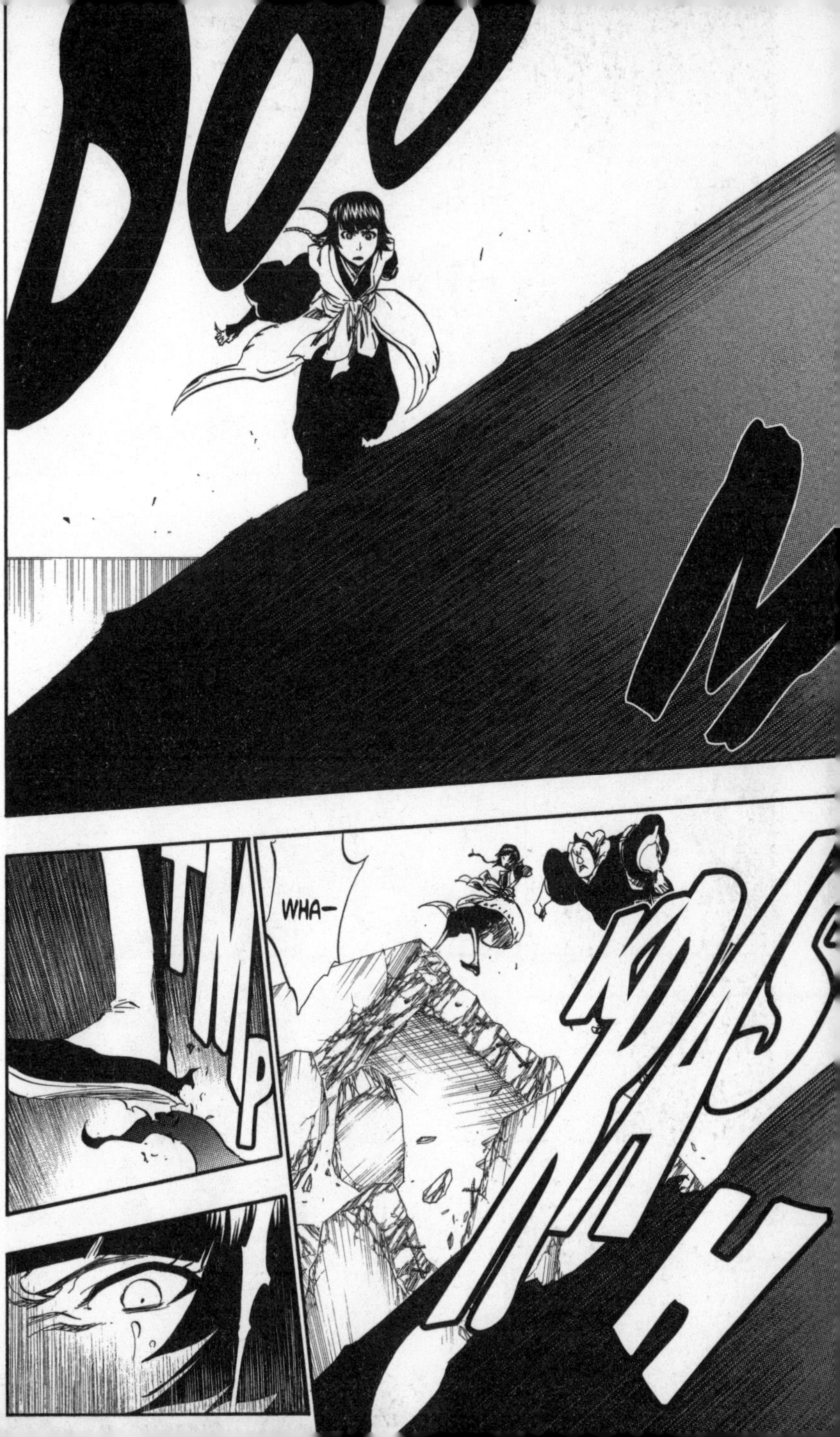
DOOM
WHA-
TMP

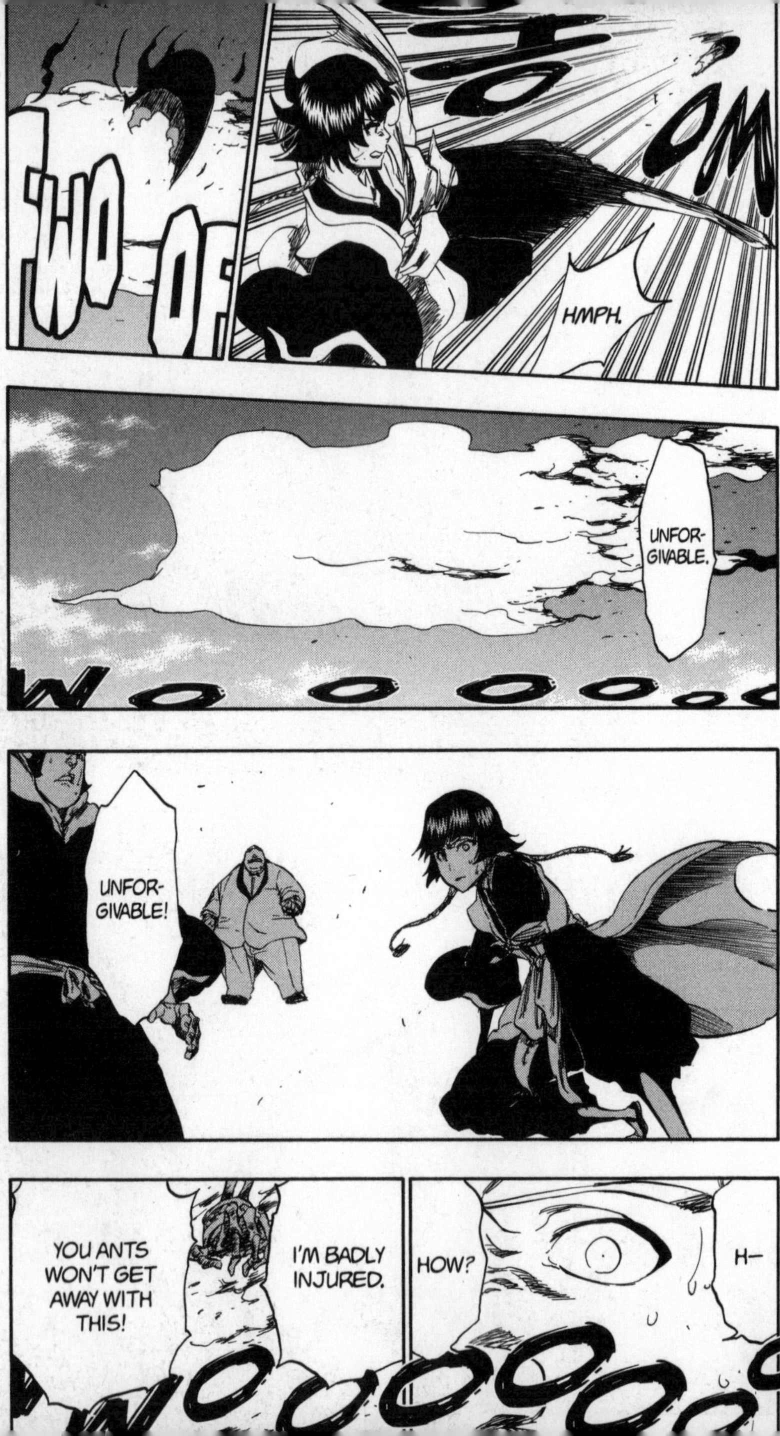

HMPH.
UNFOR-GIVABLE.
WOOOOO
UNFOR-GIVABLE!
H—
HOW?
I'M BADLY INJURED.
YOU ANTS WON'T GET AWAY WITH THIS!
WOOOOOOO

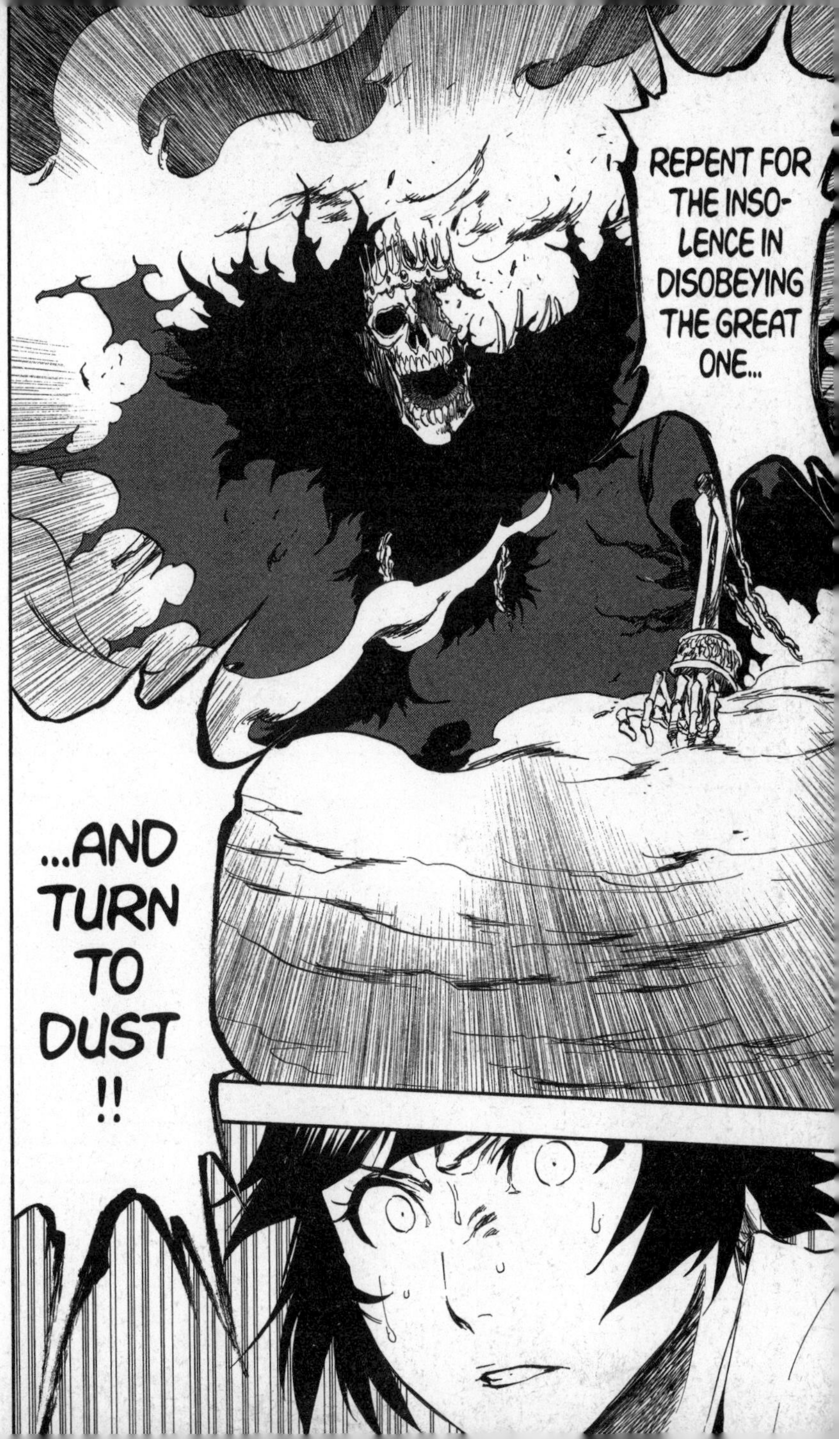
REPENT FOR THE INSO-LENCE IN DISOBEYING THE GREAT ONE...
...AND TURN TO DUST !!

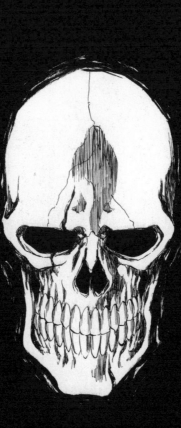

BLEACH370.

Discussing Life from God's Perspective

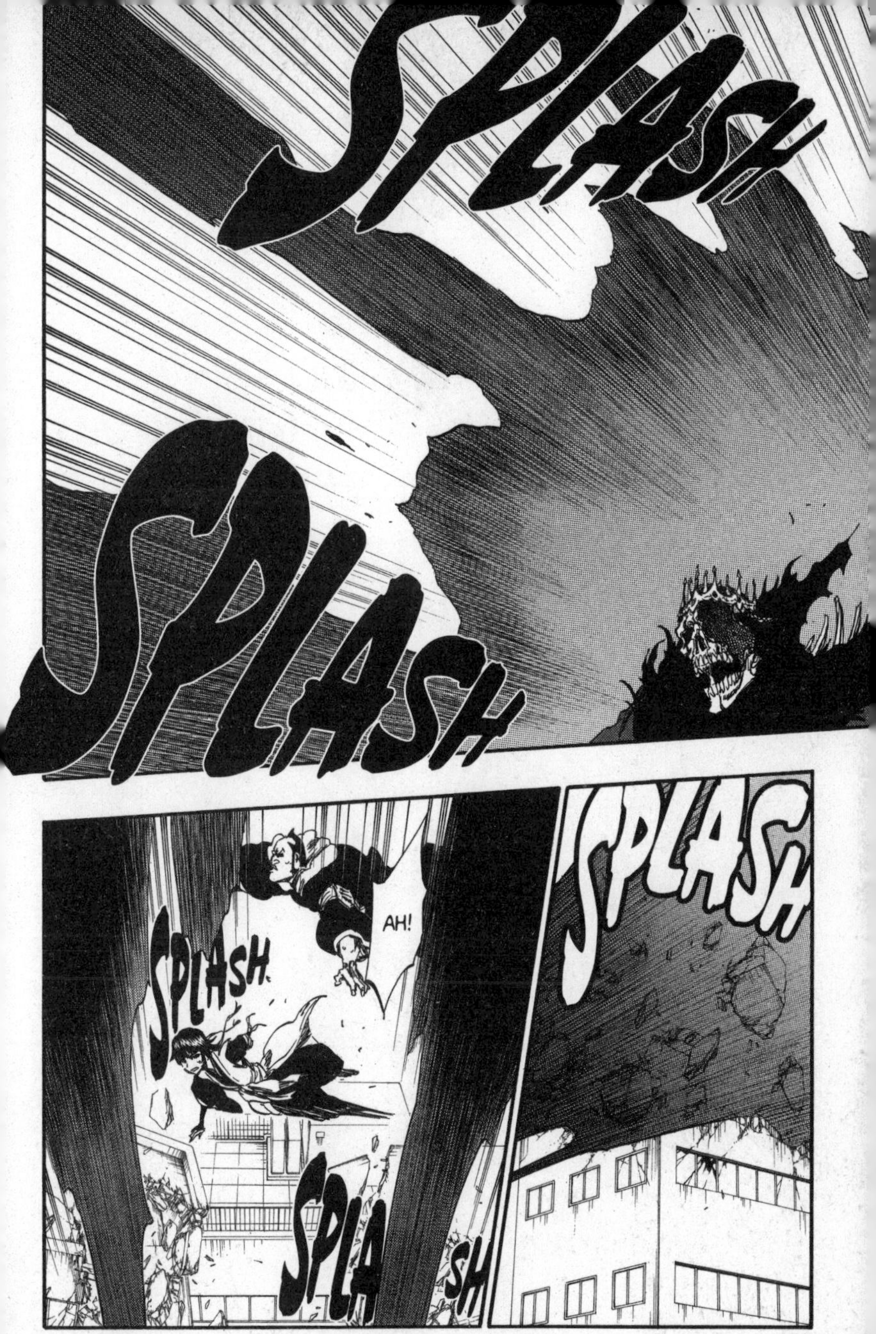
SPLASH
SPLASH
SPLASH
AH!
SPLASH
SPLASH

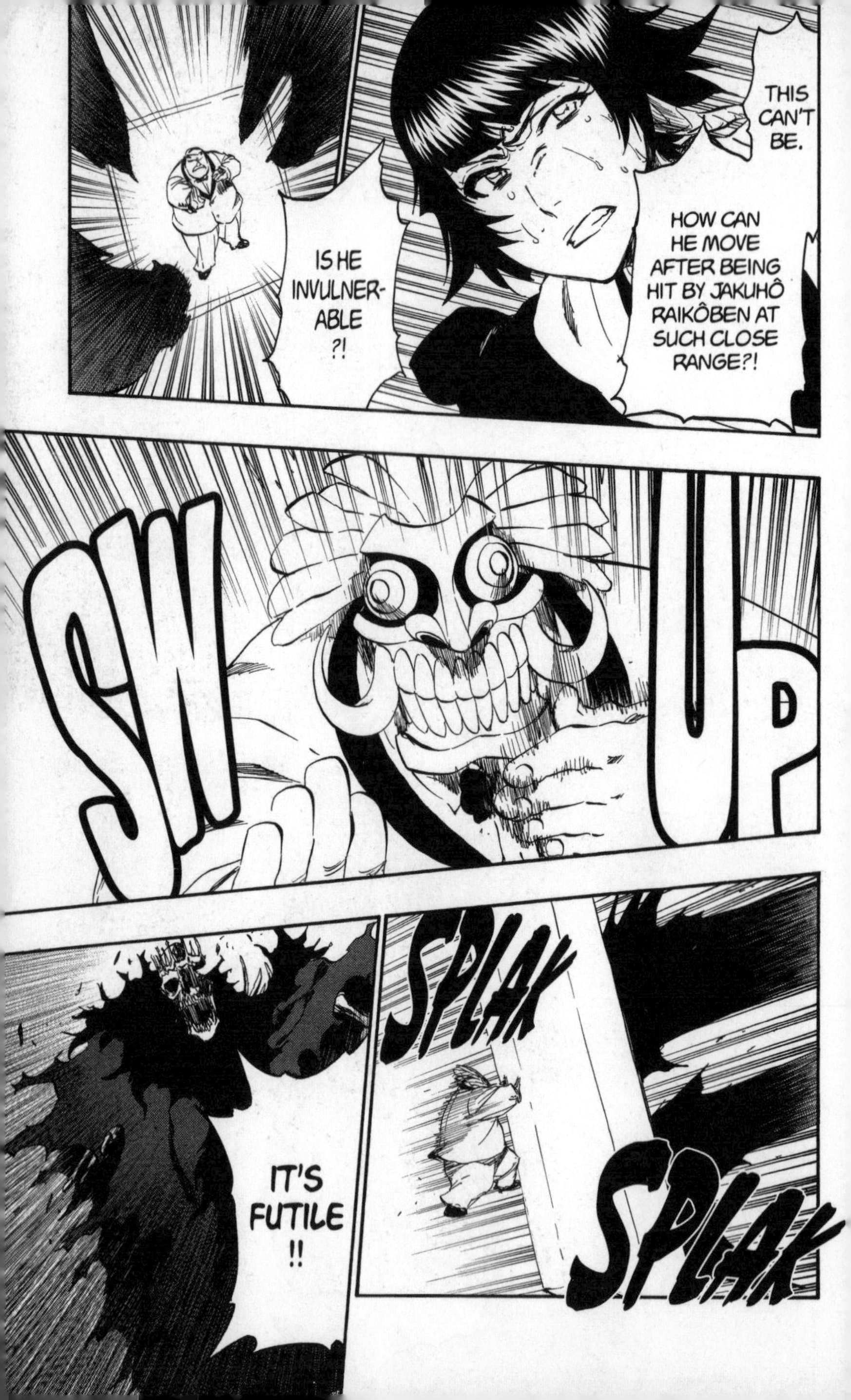
THIS CAN'T BE.
HOW CAN HE MOVE AFTER BEING HIT BY JAKUHÔ RAIKÔBEN AT SUCH CLOSE RANGE?!
IS HE INVULNER-ABLE ?!
SHWUP
SPLAK
SPLAK
IT'S FUTILE !!

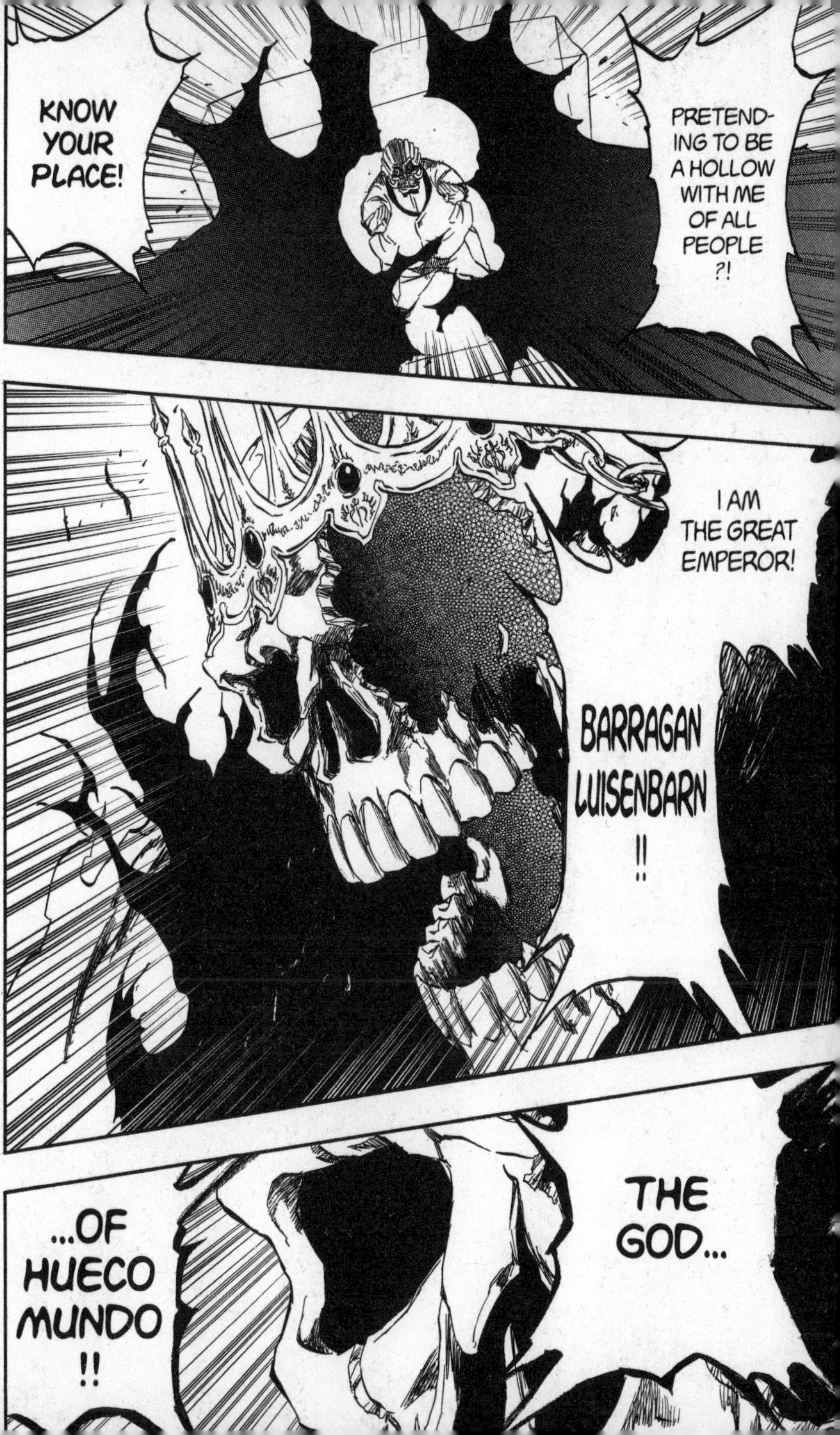
PRETENDING TO BE A HOLLOW WITH ME OF ALL PEOPLE?!
KNOW YOUR PLACE!
I AM THE GREAT EMPEROR!
BARRAGAN LUISENBARN!!
THE GOD...
...OF HUECO MUNDO!!

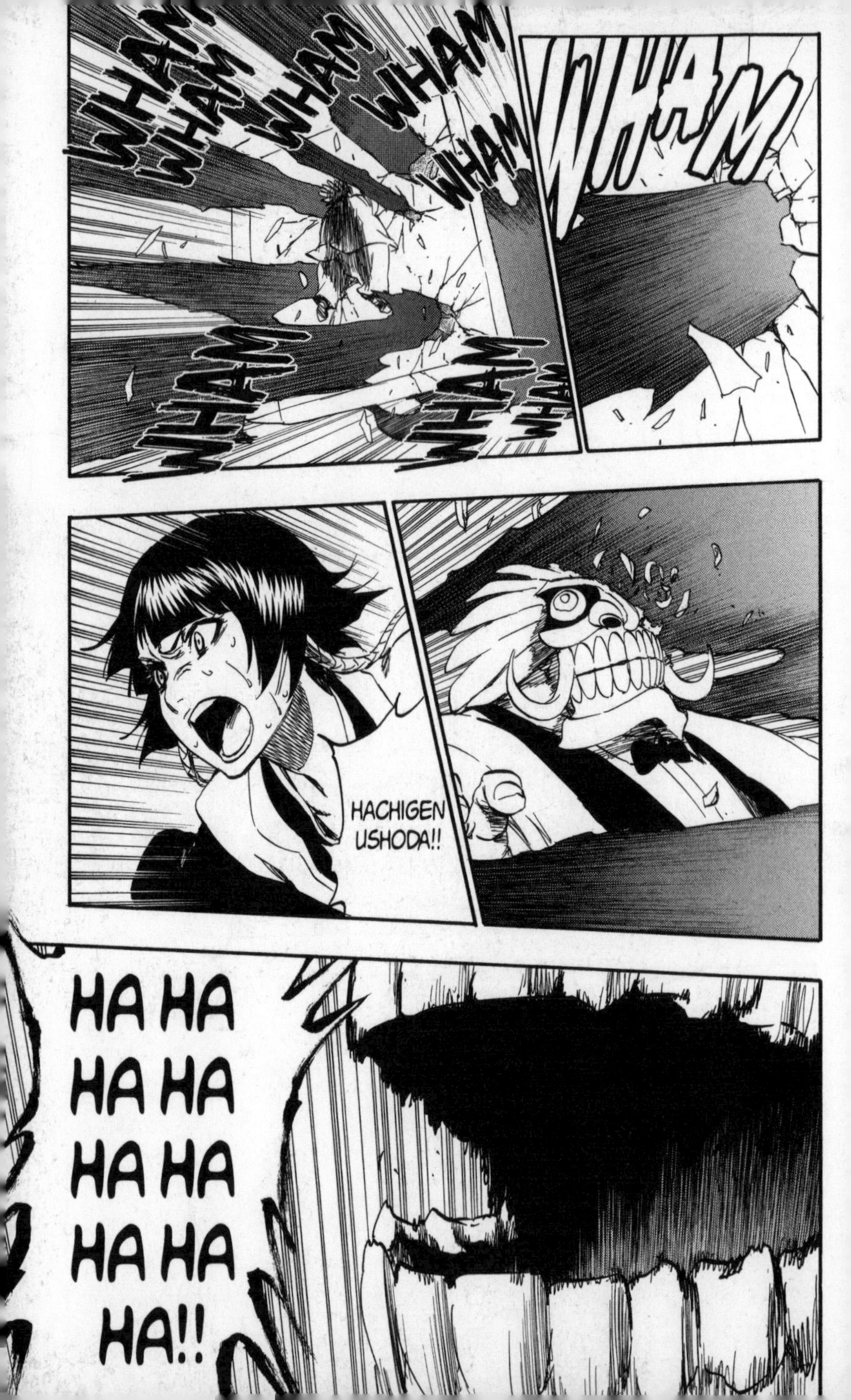
WHAM
WHAM
WHAM
WHAM
WHAM
WHAM
WHAM
WHAM
WHAM
HACHIGEN USHODA!!
HA HA HA HA HA HA HA HA HA!!

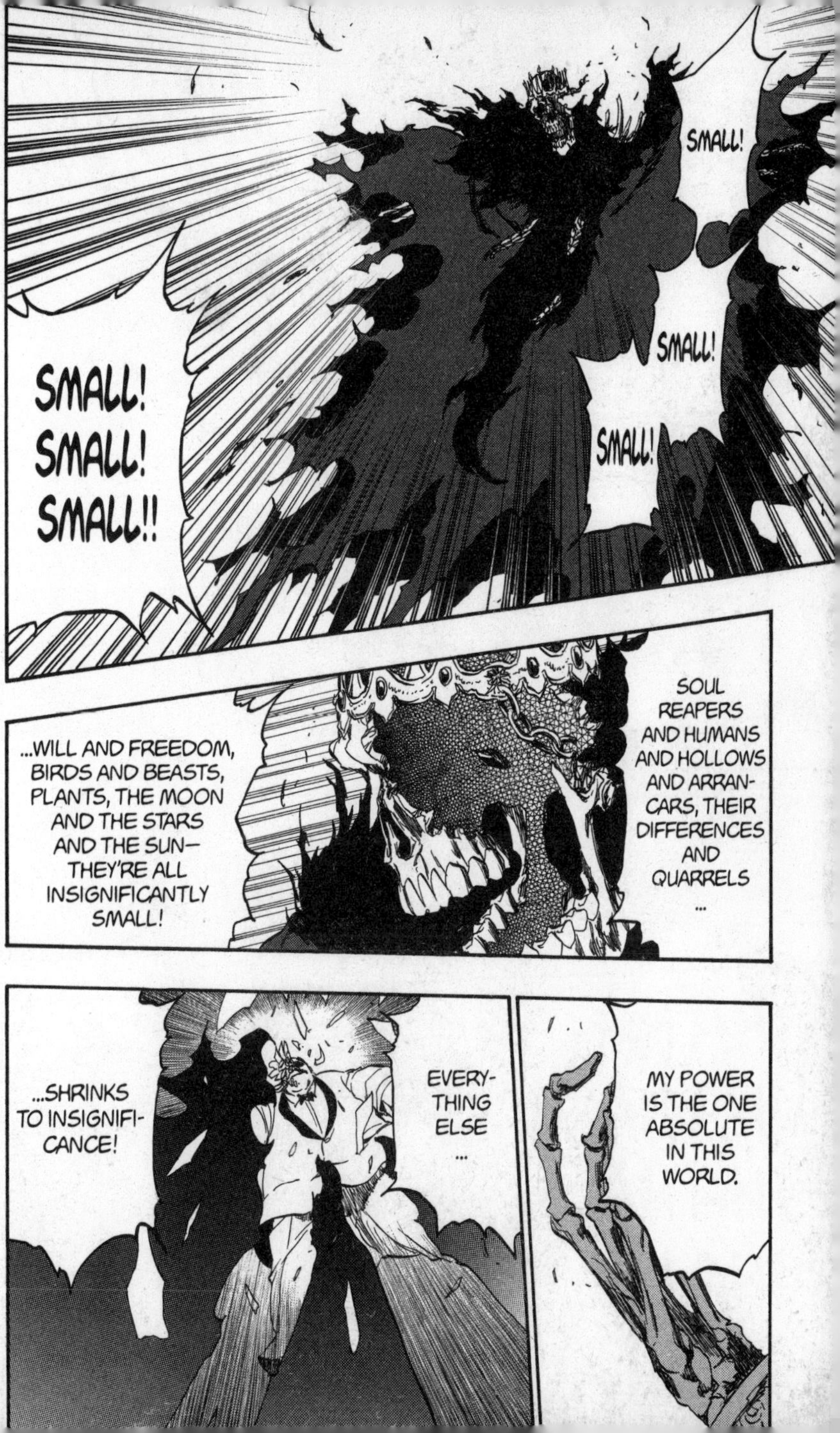
SMALL!
SMALL!
SMALL!
SMALL! SMALL! SMALL!!
SOUL REAPERS AND HUMANS AND HOLLOWS AND ARRANCARS, THEIR DIFFERENCES AND QUARRELS ...
...WILL AND FREEDOM, BIRDS AND BEASTS, PLANTS, THE MOON AND THE STARS AND THE SUN— THEY'RE ALL INSIGNIFICANTLY SMALL!
MY POWER IS THE ONE ABSOLUTE IN THIS WORLD.
EVERYTHING ELSE ...
...SHRINKS TO INSIGNIFICANCE!

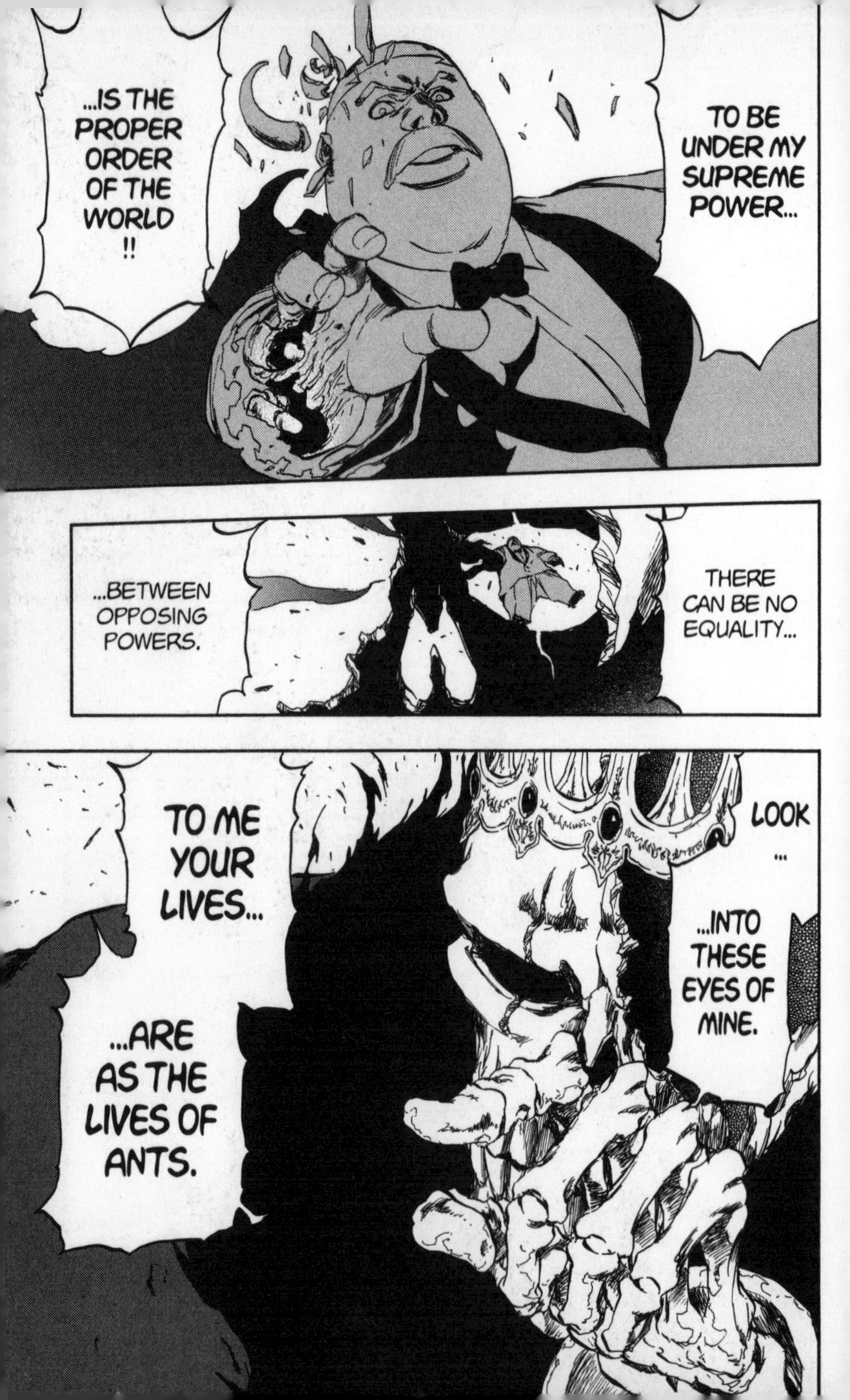
TO BE UNDER MY SUPREME POWER...
...IS THE PROPER ORDER OF THE WORLD !!
THERE CAN BE NO EQUALITY...
...BETWEEN OPPOSING POWERS.
LOOK ...
...INTO THESE EYES OF MINE.
TO ME YOUR LIVES...
...ARE AS THE LIVES OF ANTS.

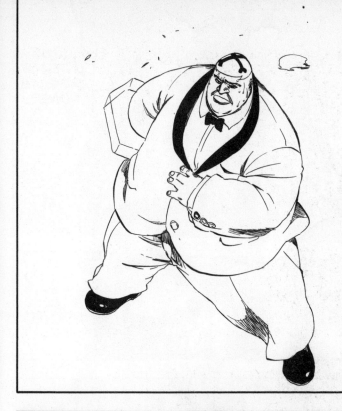

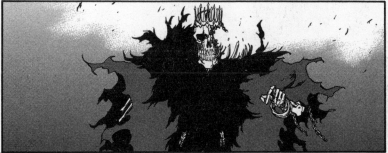

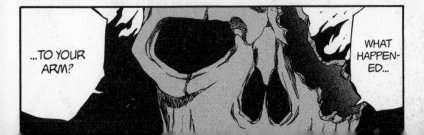

...TO YOUR ARM?

WHAT HAPPEN- ED...

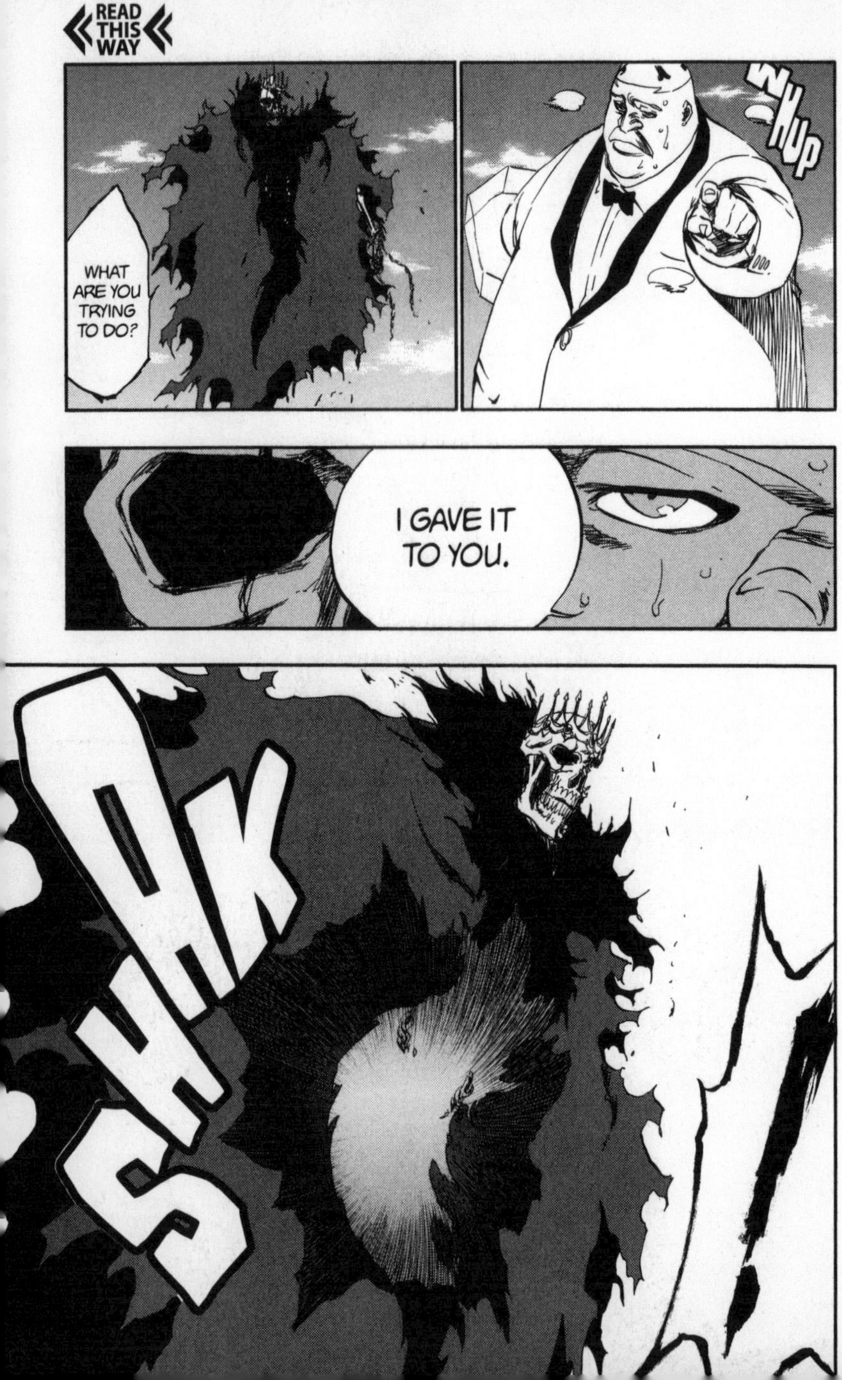
READ THIS WAY
WHUP
WHAT ARE YOU TRYING TO DO?
I GAVE IT TO YOU.
SHAK

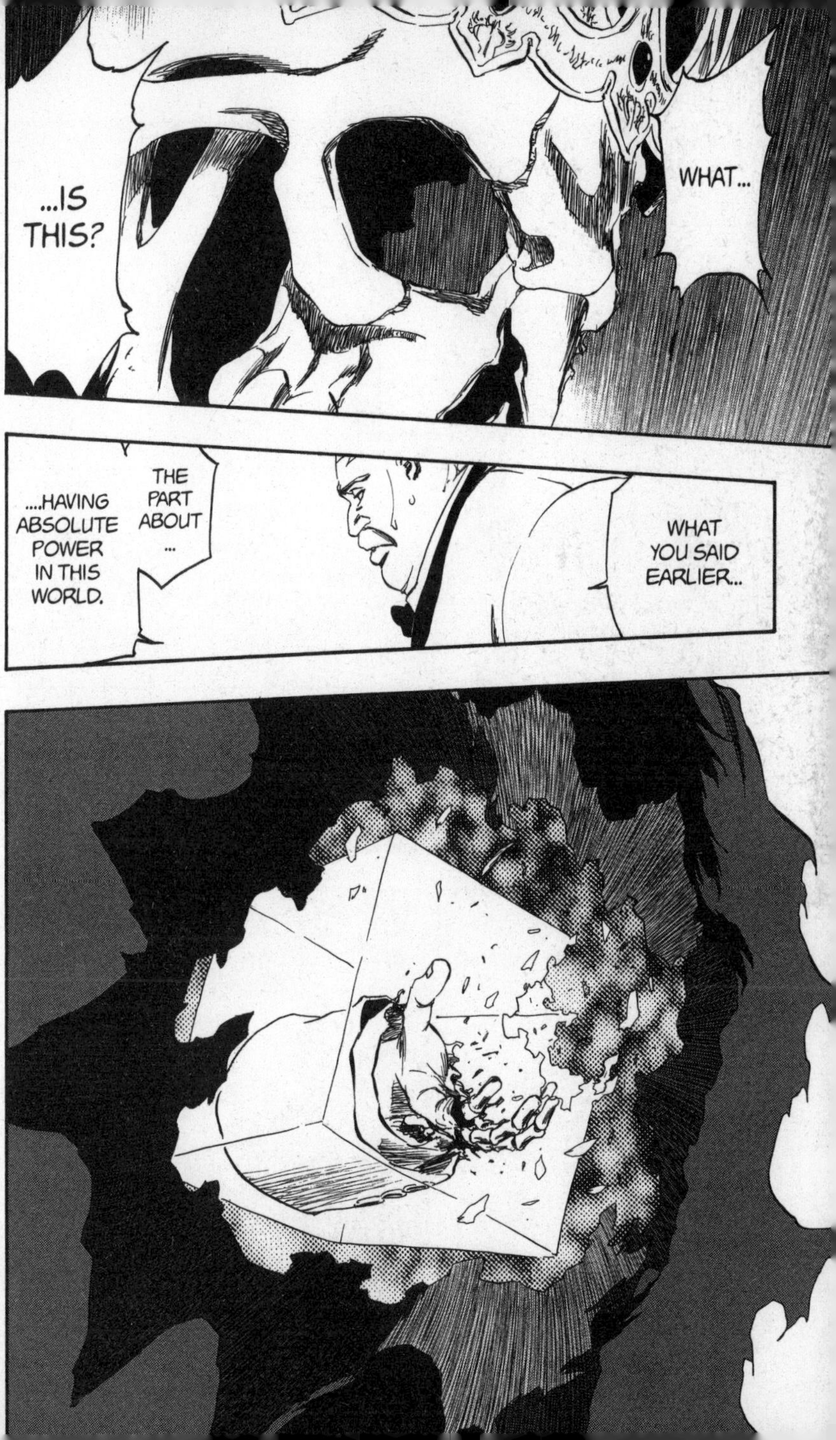
WHAT...
...IS THIS?
WHAT YOU SAID EARLIER...
THE PART ABOUT ...
....HAVING ABSOLUTE POWER IN THIS WORLD.

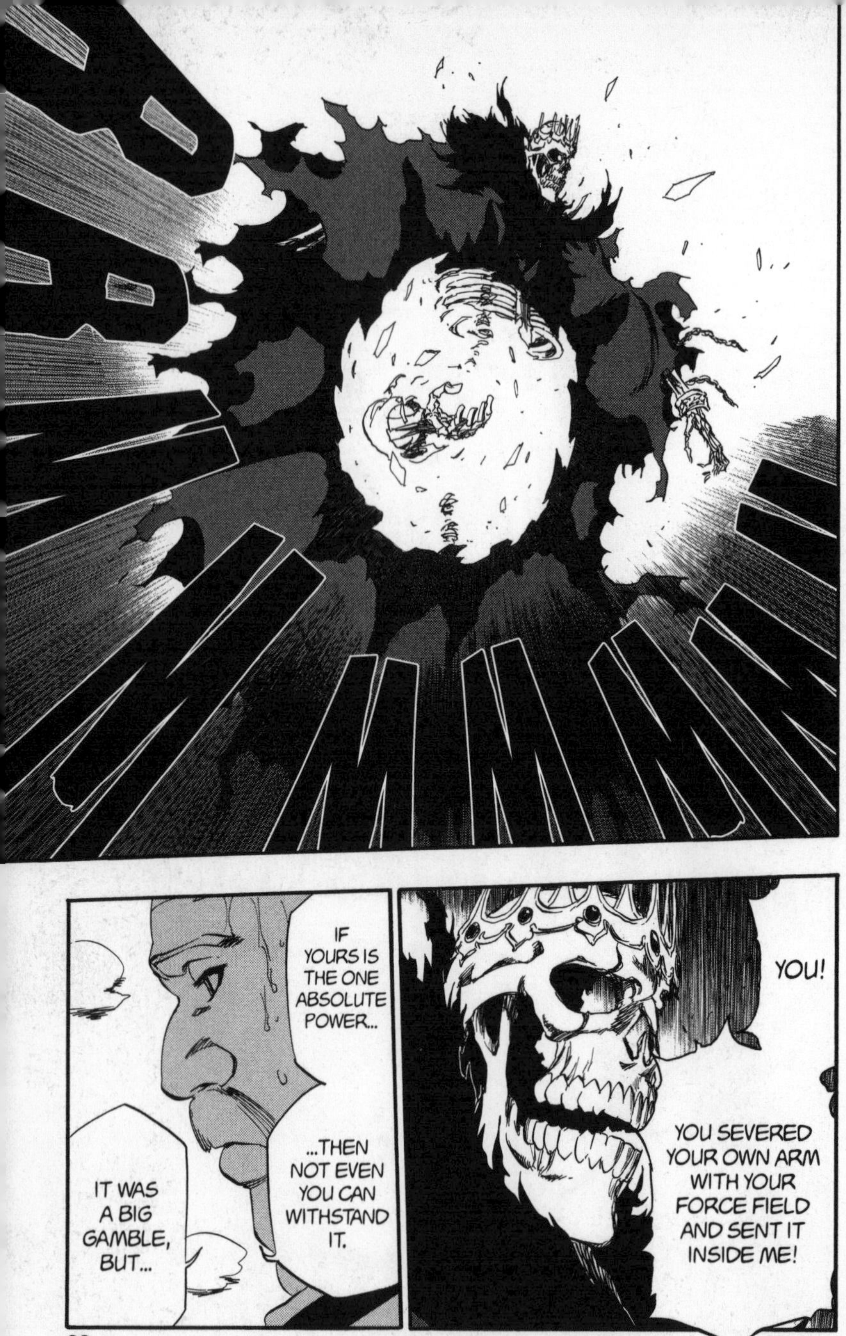
YOU!
YOU SEVERED YOUR OWN ARM WITH YOUR FORCE FIELD AND SENT IT INSIDE ME!
IF YOURS IS THE ONE ABSOLUTE POWER...
...THEN NOT EVEN YOU CAN WITHSTAND IT.
IT WAS A BIG GAMBLE, BUT...

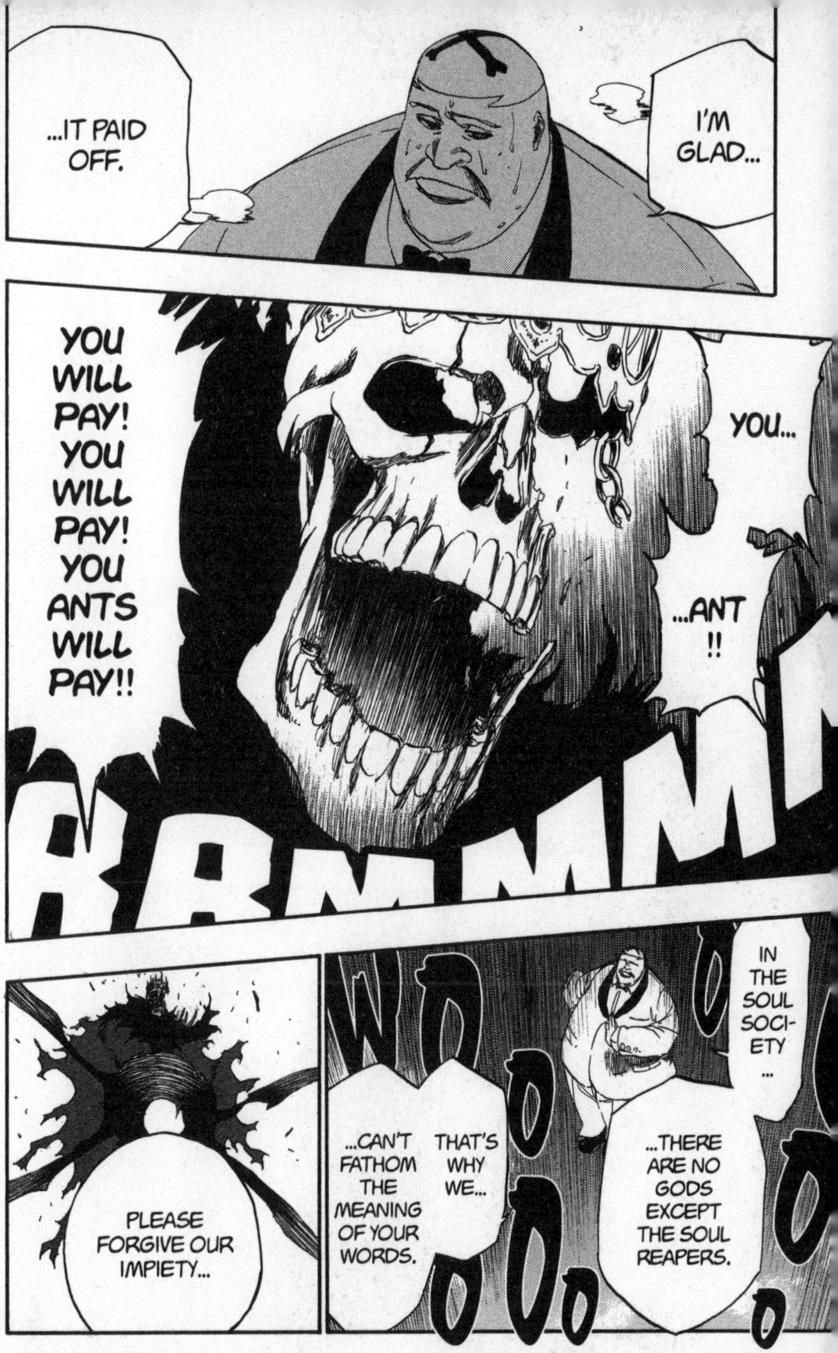

I'M GLAD...
...IT PAID OFF.
YOU...
...ANT !!
YOU WILL PAY! YOU WILL PAY! YOU ANTS WILL PAY!!
IN THE SOUL SOCIETY...
...THERE ARE NO GODS EXCEPT THE SOUL REAPERS.
THAT'S WHY WE...
...CAN'T FATHOM THE MEANING OF YOUR WORDS.
PLEASE FORGIVE OUR IMPIETY...

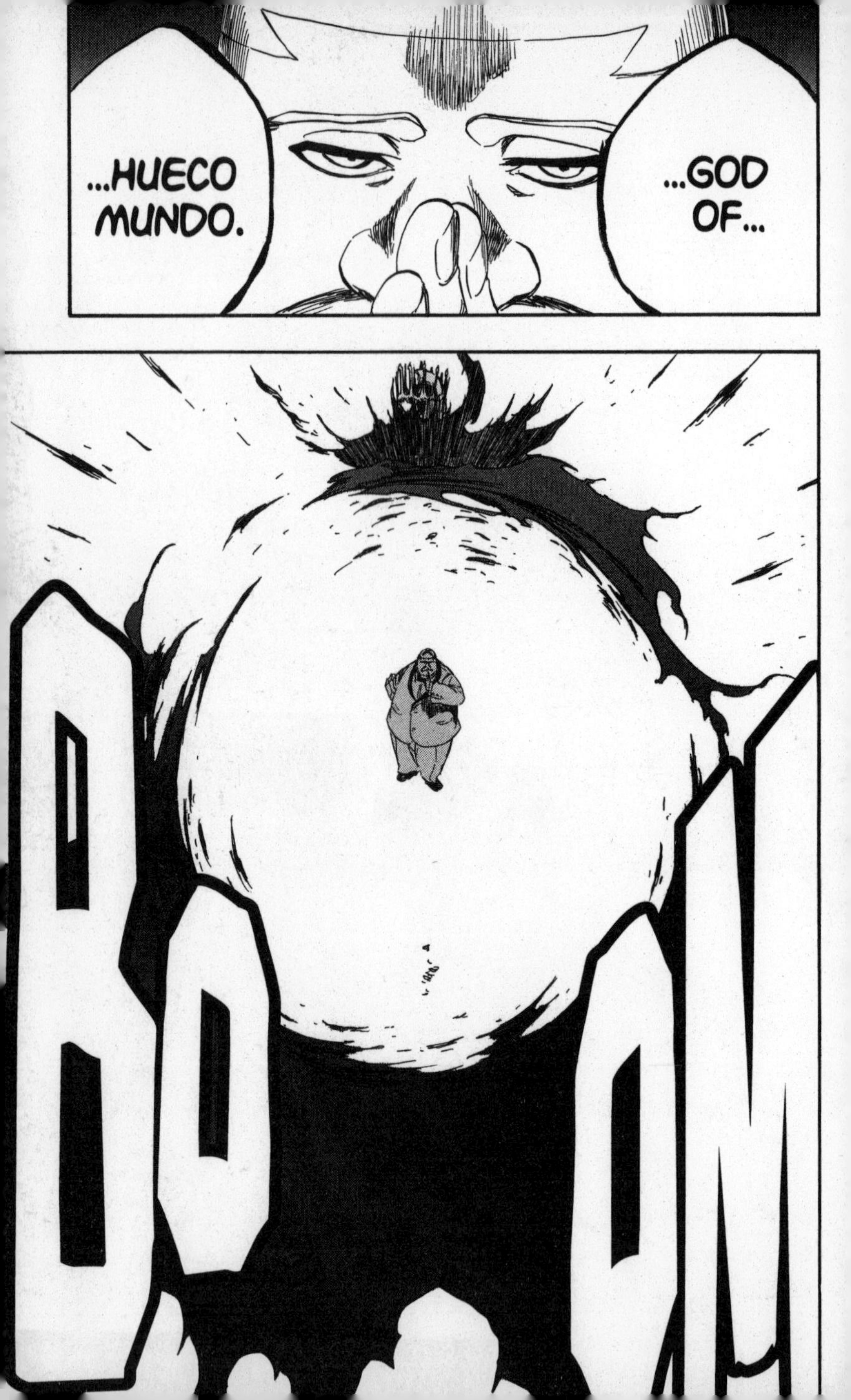
...GOD OF...
...HUECO MUNDO.
BOOM

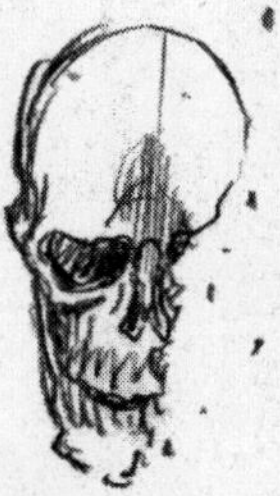

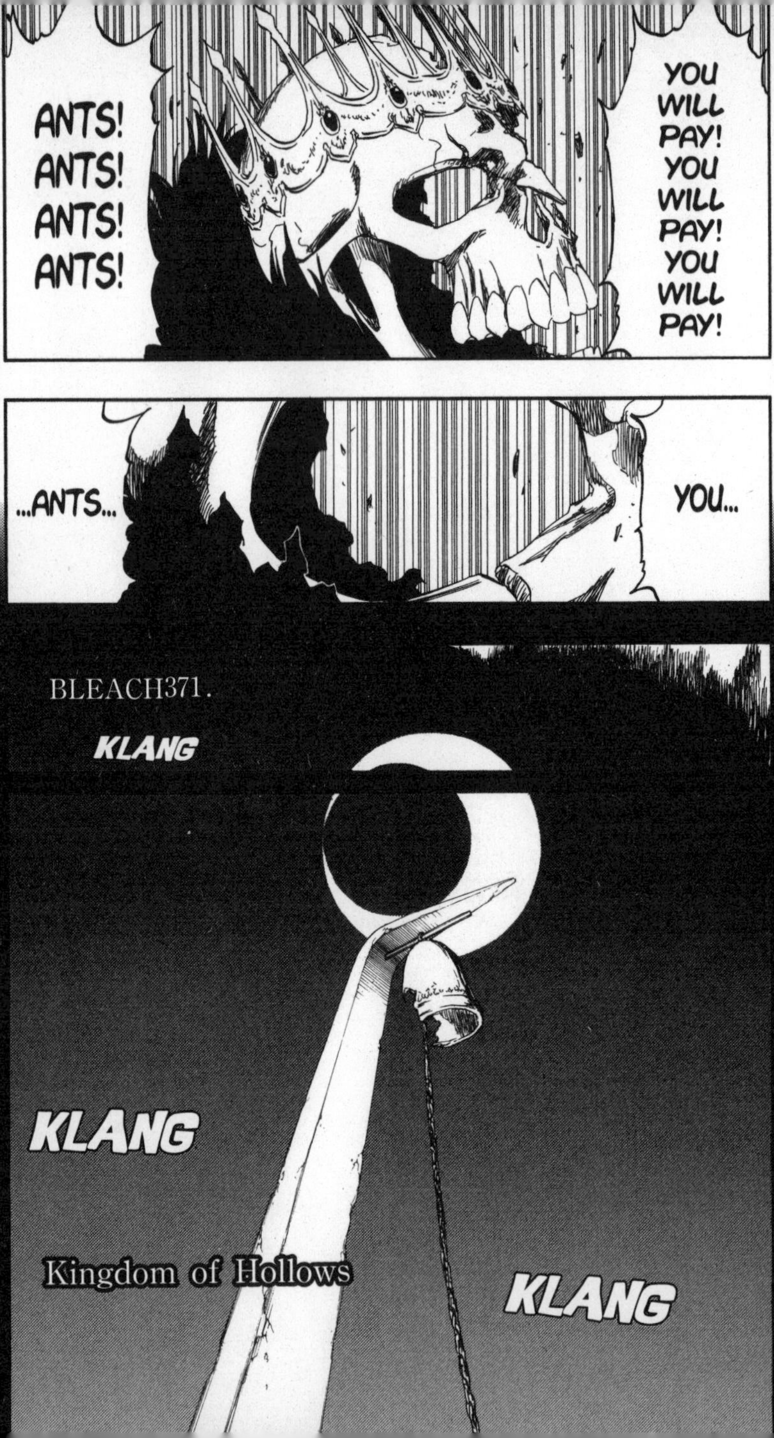
YOU WILL PAY! YOU WILL PAY! YOU WILL PAY!
ANTS! ANTS! ANTS! ANTS!
YOU...
...ANTS...
BLEACH371.
KLANG
KLANG
Kingdom of Hollows
KLANG

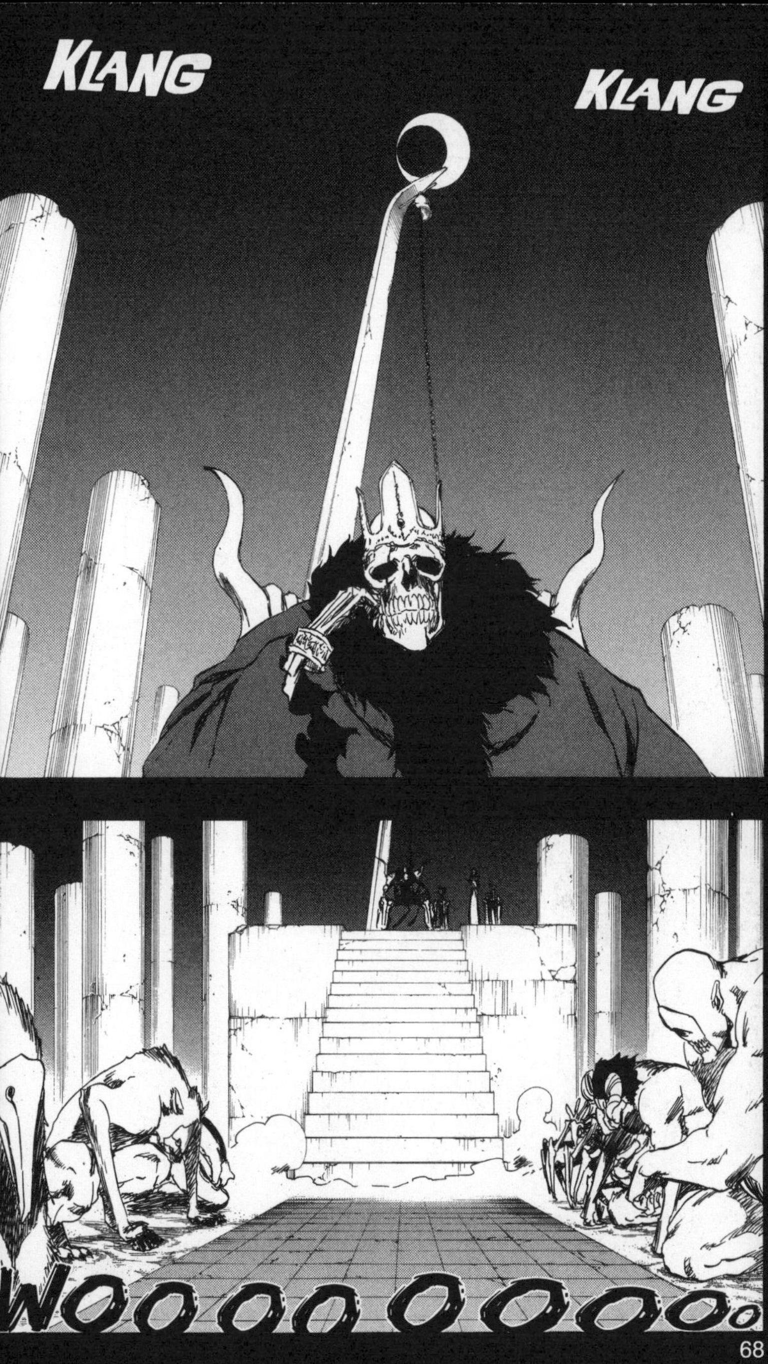
KLANG
KLANG
WOOOO OOOOO

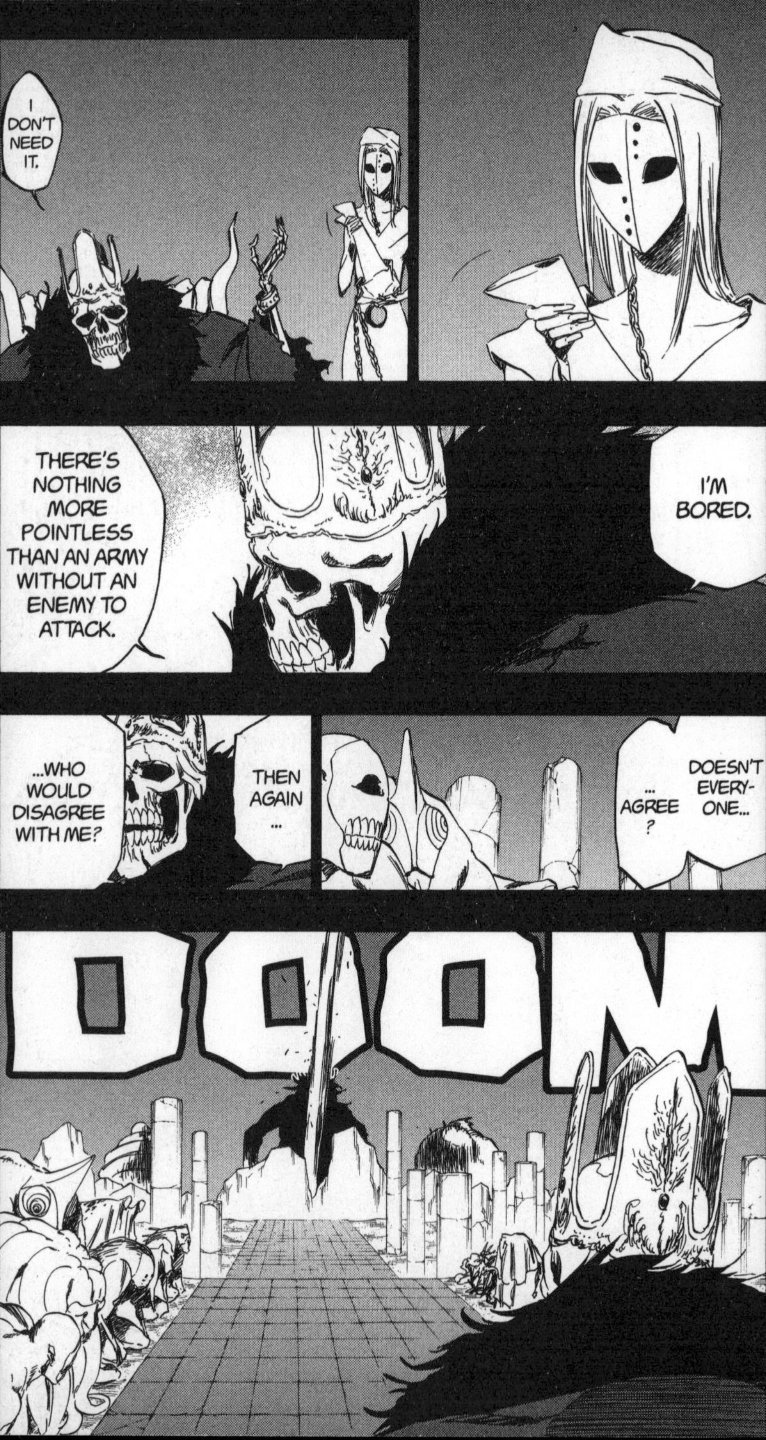
I DON'T NEED IT.
I'M BORED.
THERE'S NOTHING MORE POINTLESS THAN AN ARMY WITHOUT AN ENEMY TO ATTACK.
DOESN'T EVERY-ONE...
...AGREE?
THEN AGAIN...
...WHO WOULD DISAGREE WITH ME?
DOOM

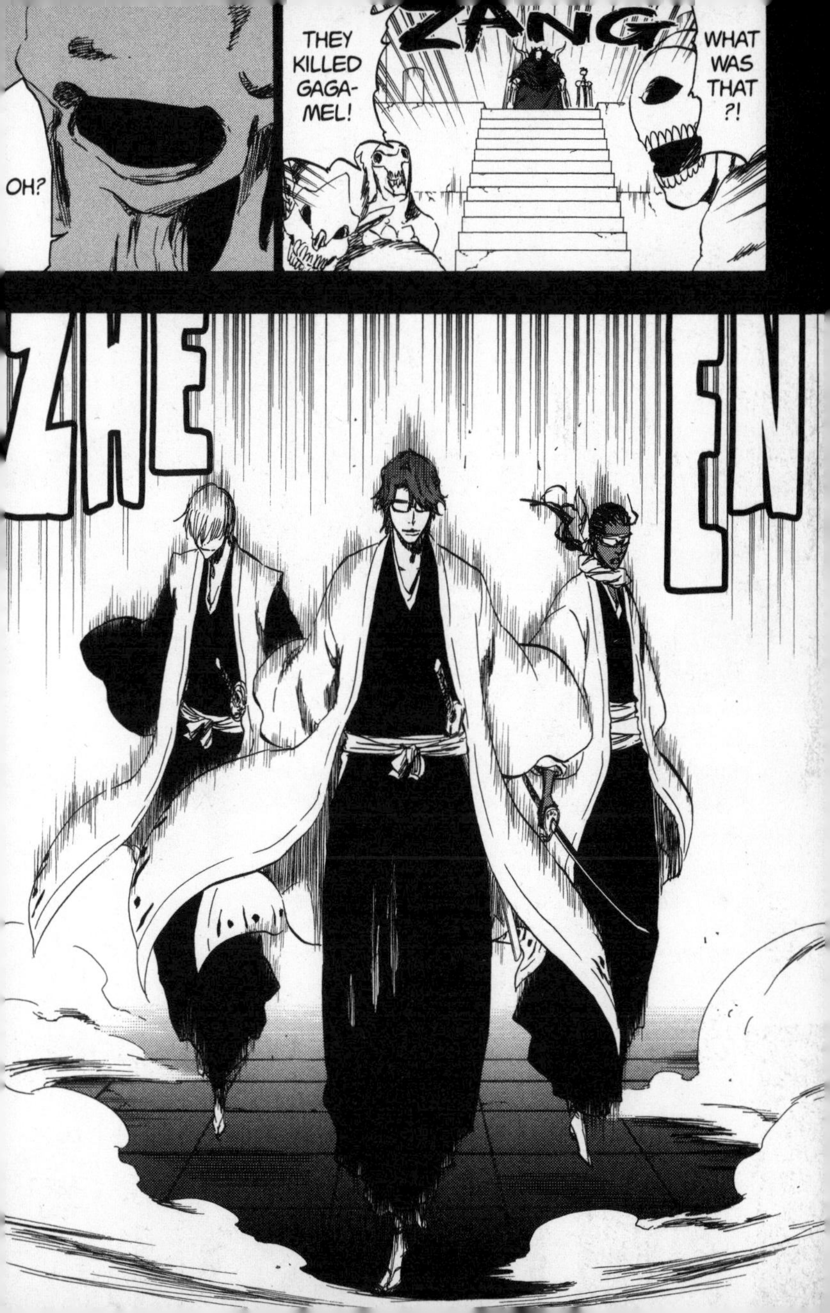
ZANG
WHAT WAS THAT?!
THEY KILLED GAGA-MEL!
OH?
ZHE
EN

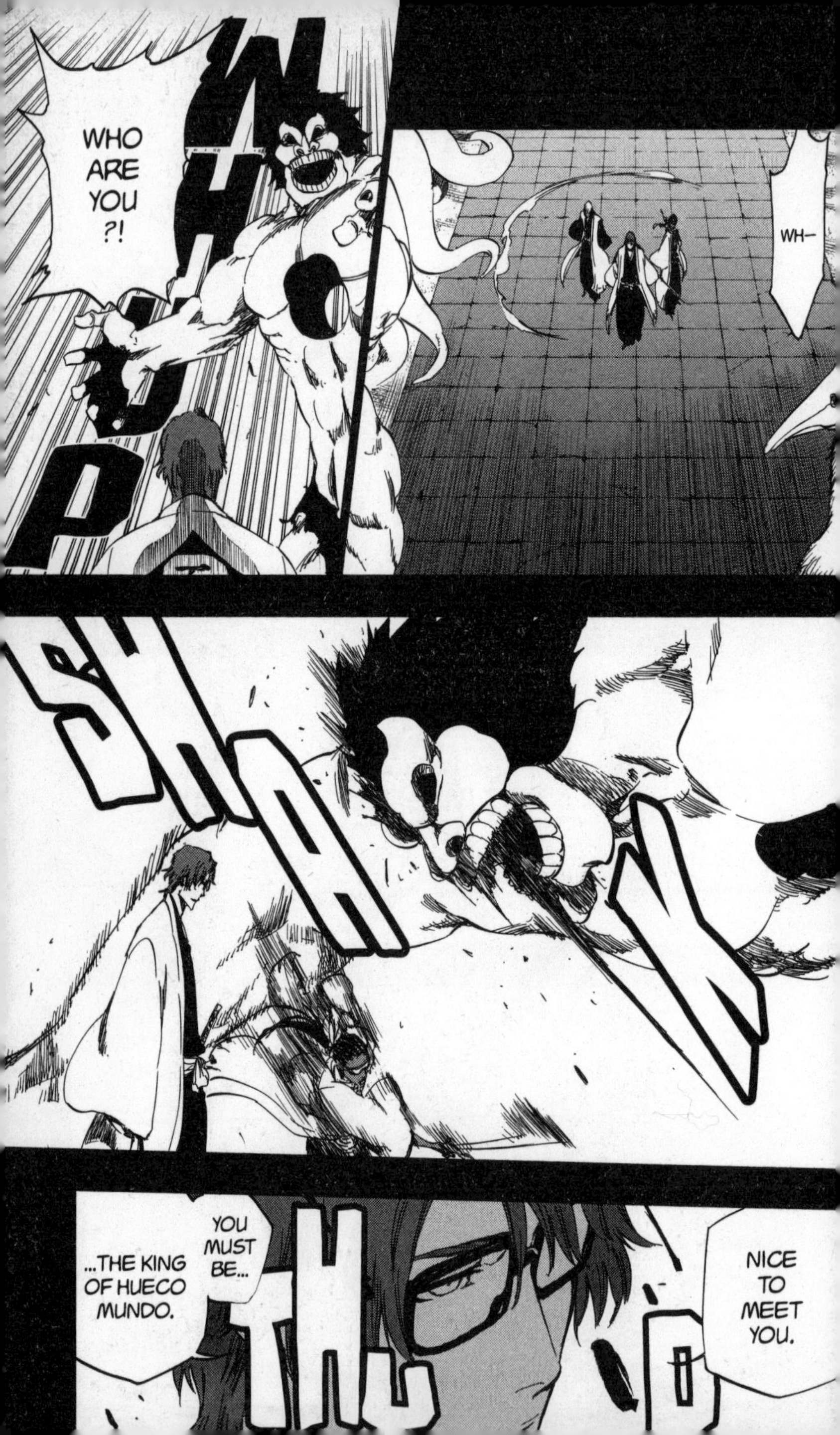
WH–
WHO ARE YOU ?!
NICE TO MEET YOU.
YOU MUST BE...
...THE KING OF HUECO MUNDO.

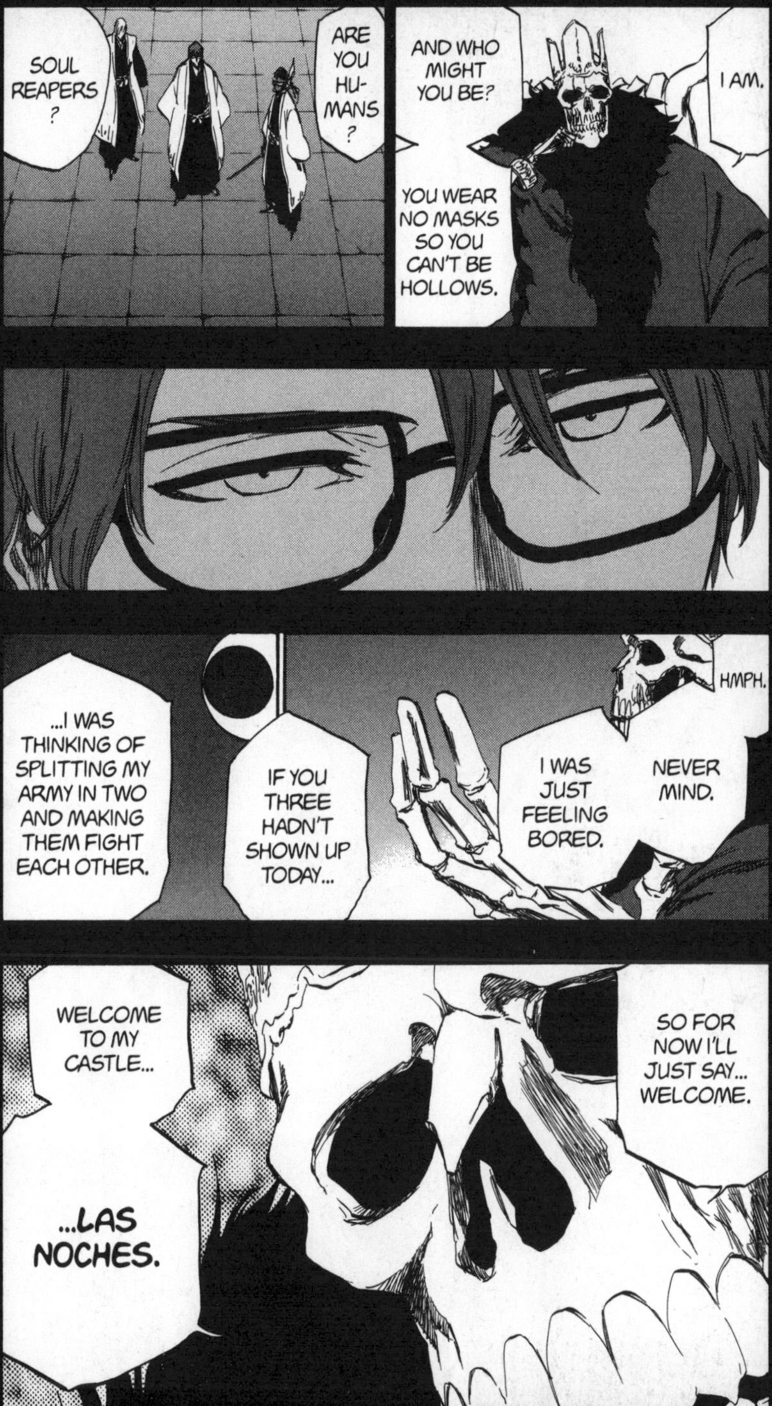
I AM.
AND WHO MIGHT YOU BE?
YOU WEAR NO MASKS SO YOU CAN'T BE HOLLOWS.
ARE YOU HU-MANS ?
SOUL REAPERS ?
HMPH.
NEVER MIND.
I WAS JUST FEELING BORED.
IF YOU THREE HADN'T SHOWN UP TODAY...
...I WAS THINKING OF SPLITTING MY ARMY IN TWO AND MAKING THEM FIGHT EACH OTHER.
SO FOR NOW I'LL JUST SAY... WELCOME.
WELCOME TO MY CASTLE...
...LAS NOCHES.

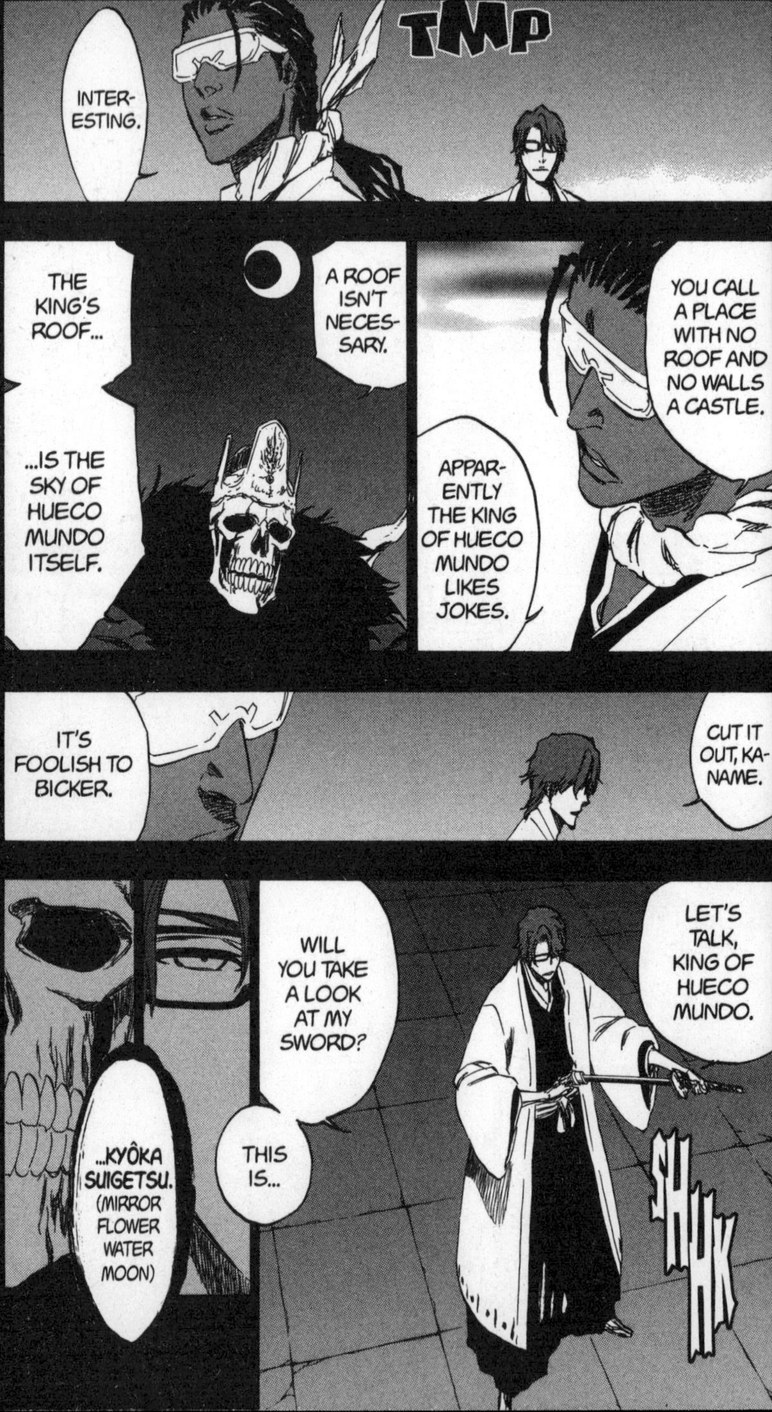
TMP
INTERESTING.
YOU CALL A PLACE WITH NO ROOF AND NO WALLS A CASTLE.
APPARENTLY THE KING OF HUECO MUNDO LIKES JOKES.
A ROOF ISN'T NECESSARY.
THE KING'S ROOF...
...IS THE SKY OF HUECO MUNDO ITSELF.
CUT IT OUT, KANAME.
IT'S FOOLISH TO BICKER.
LET'S TALK, KING OF HUECO MUNDO.
WILL YOU TAKE A LOOK AT MY SWORD?
SHHK
THIS IS...
...KYÔKA SUIGETSU. (MIRROR FLOWER WATER MOON)

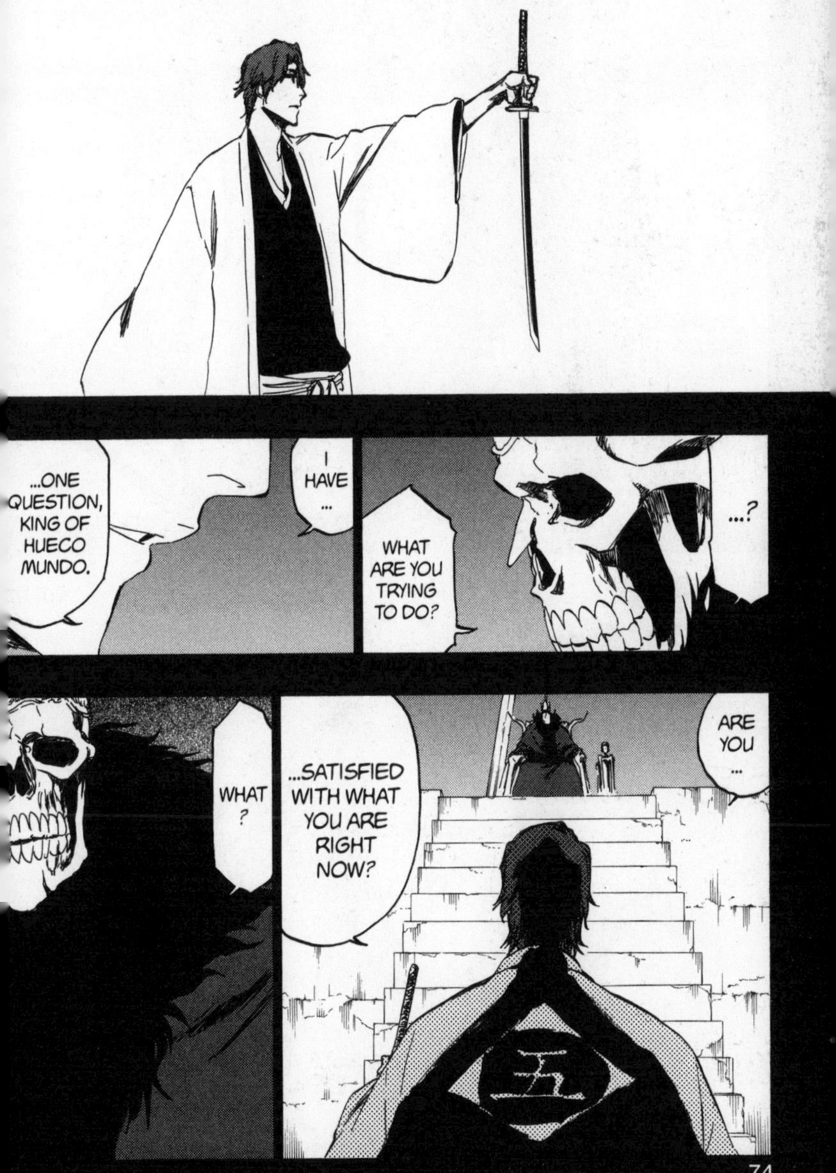
...?
WHAT ARE YOU TRYING TO DO?
I HAVE ...
...ONE QUESTION, KING OF HUECO MUNDO.
ARE YOU ...
...SATISFIED WITH WHAT YOU ARE RIGHT NOW?
WHAT?

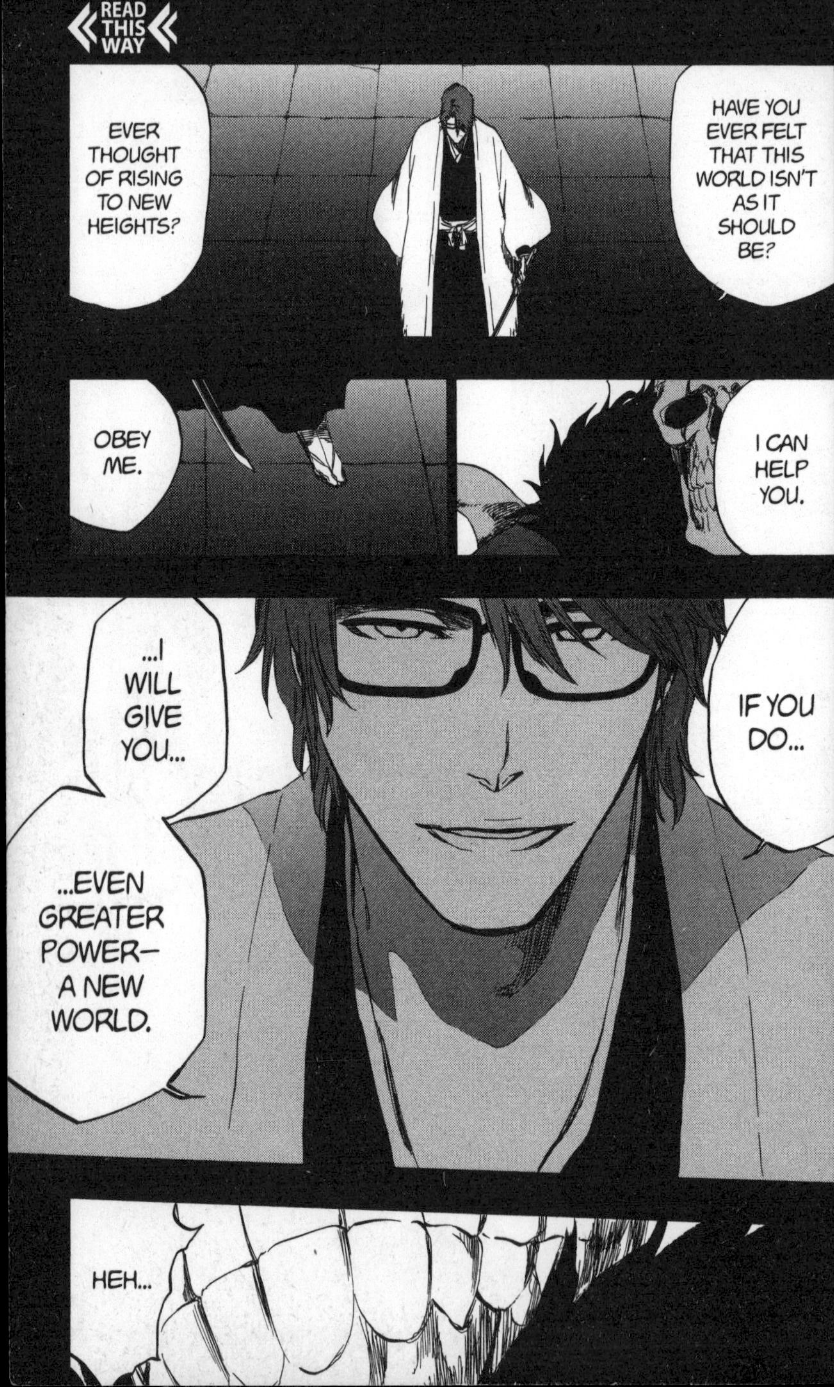
READ THIS WAY
HAVE YOU EVER FELT THAT THIS WORLD ISN'T AS IT SHOULD BE?
EVER THOUGHT OF RISING TO NEW HEIGHTS?
I CAN HELP YOU.
OBEY ME.
IF YOU DO...
...I WILL GIVE YOU...
...EVEN GREATER POWER— A NEW WORLD.
HEH...

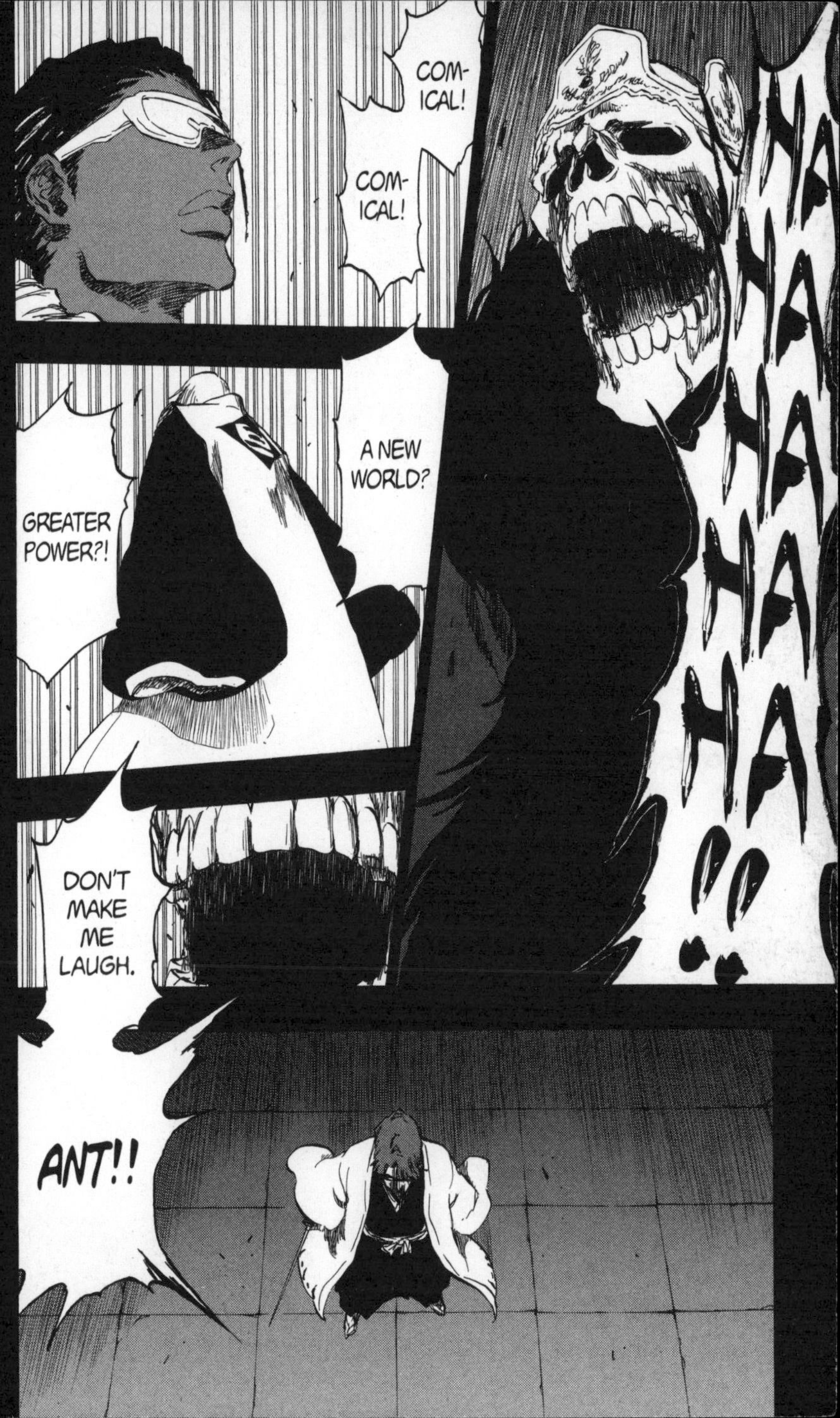
HA HA HA HA HA!!
COM-ICAL!
COM-ICAL!
A NEW WORLD?
GREATER POWER?!
DON'T MAKE ME LAUGH.
ANT!!

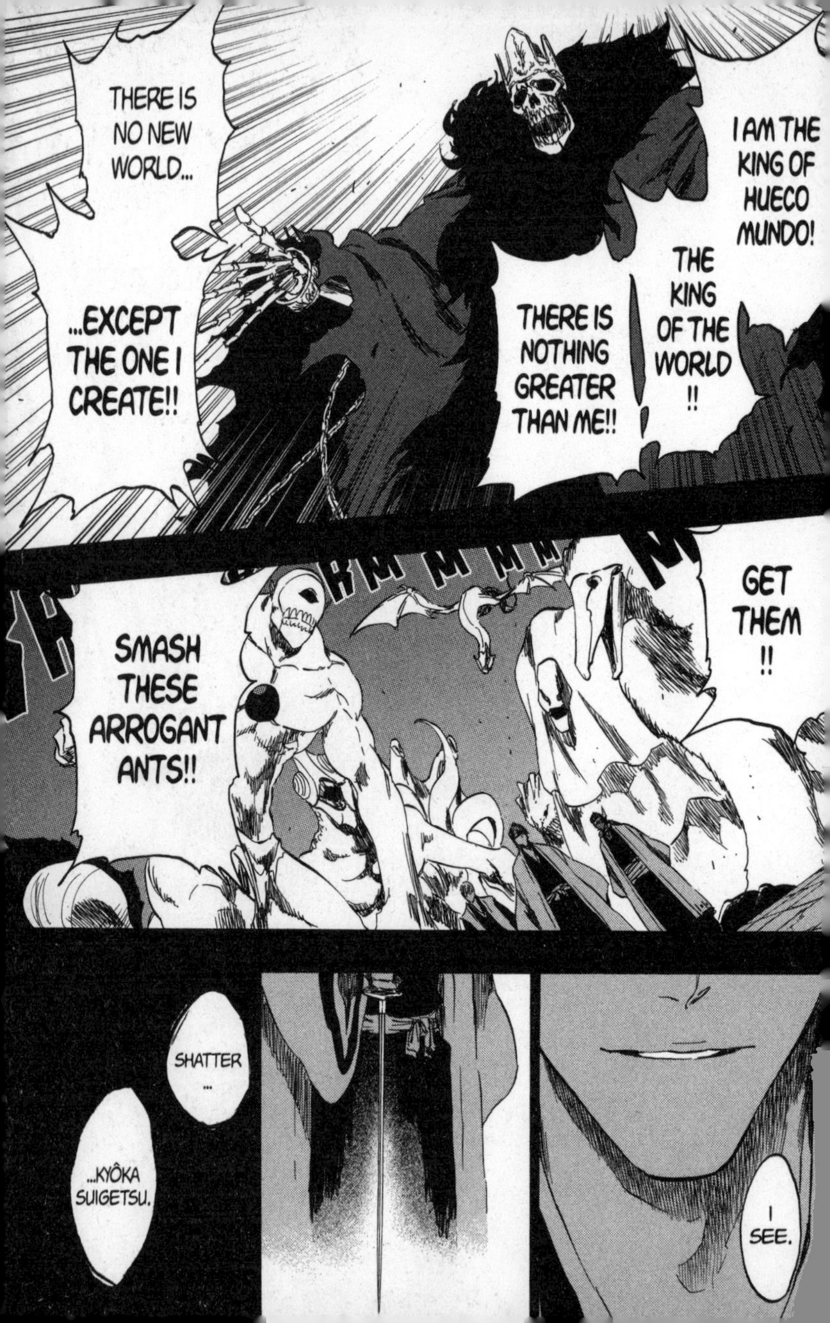
I AM THE KING OF HUECO MUNDO!
THE KING OF THE WORLD!!
THERE IS NOTHING GREATER THAN ME!!
THERE IS NO NEW WORLD...
...EXCEPT THE ONE I CREATE!!
GET THEM!!
SMASH THESE ARROGANT ANTS!!
I SEE.
SHATTER...
...KYÔKA SUIGETSU.

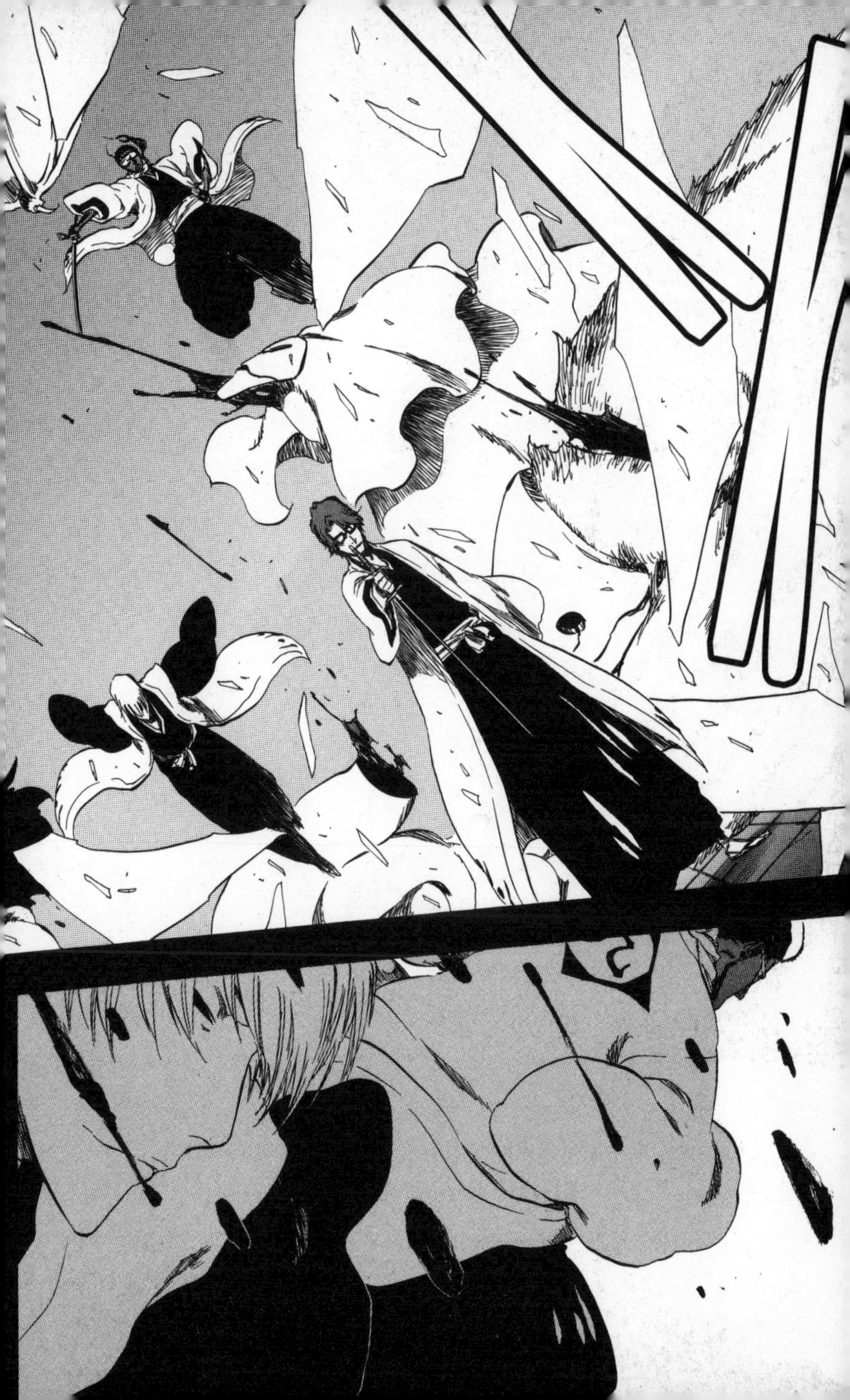

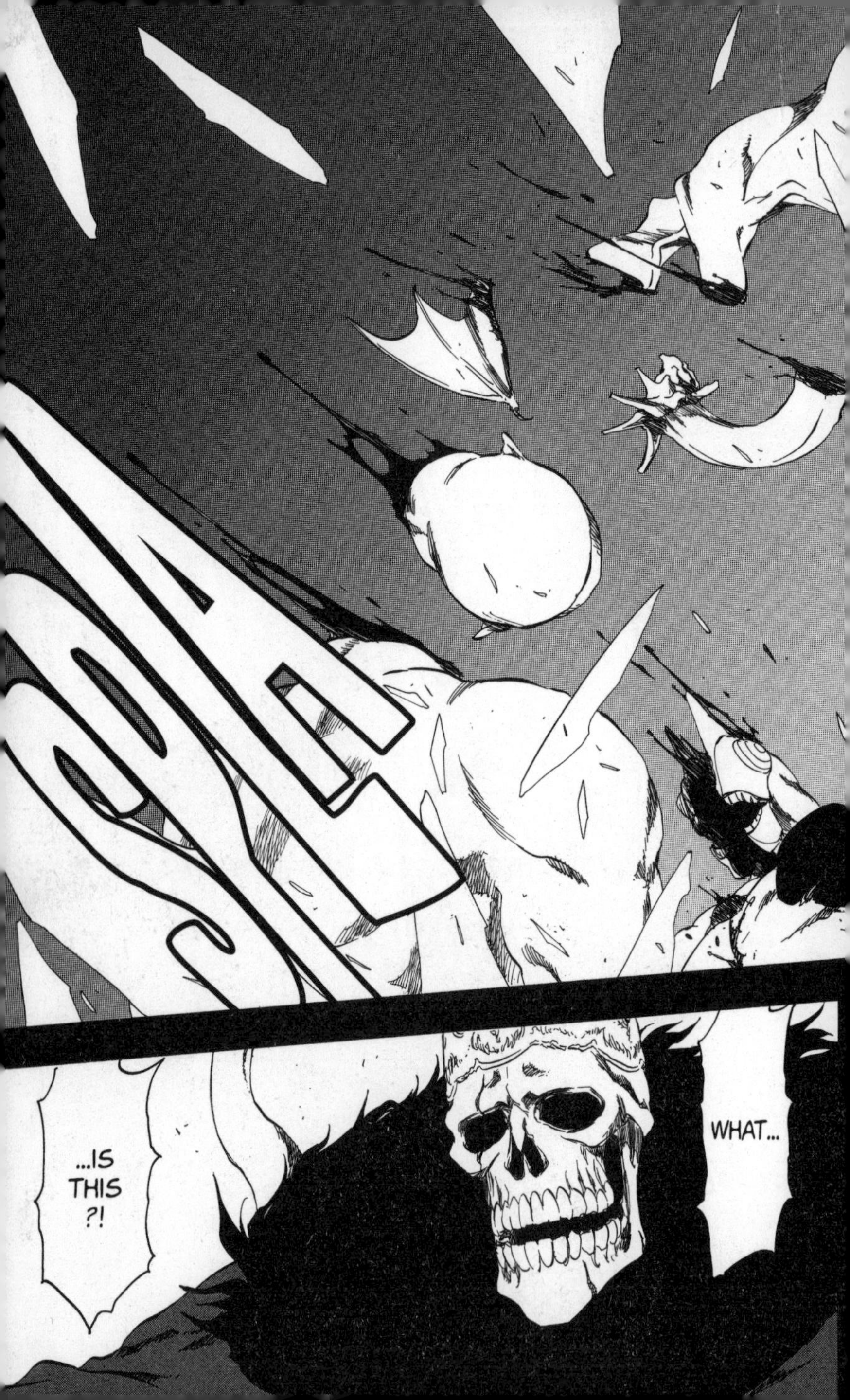
WHAT...
...IS THIS ?!

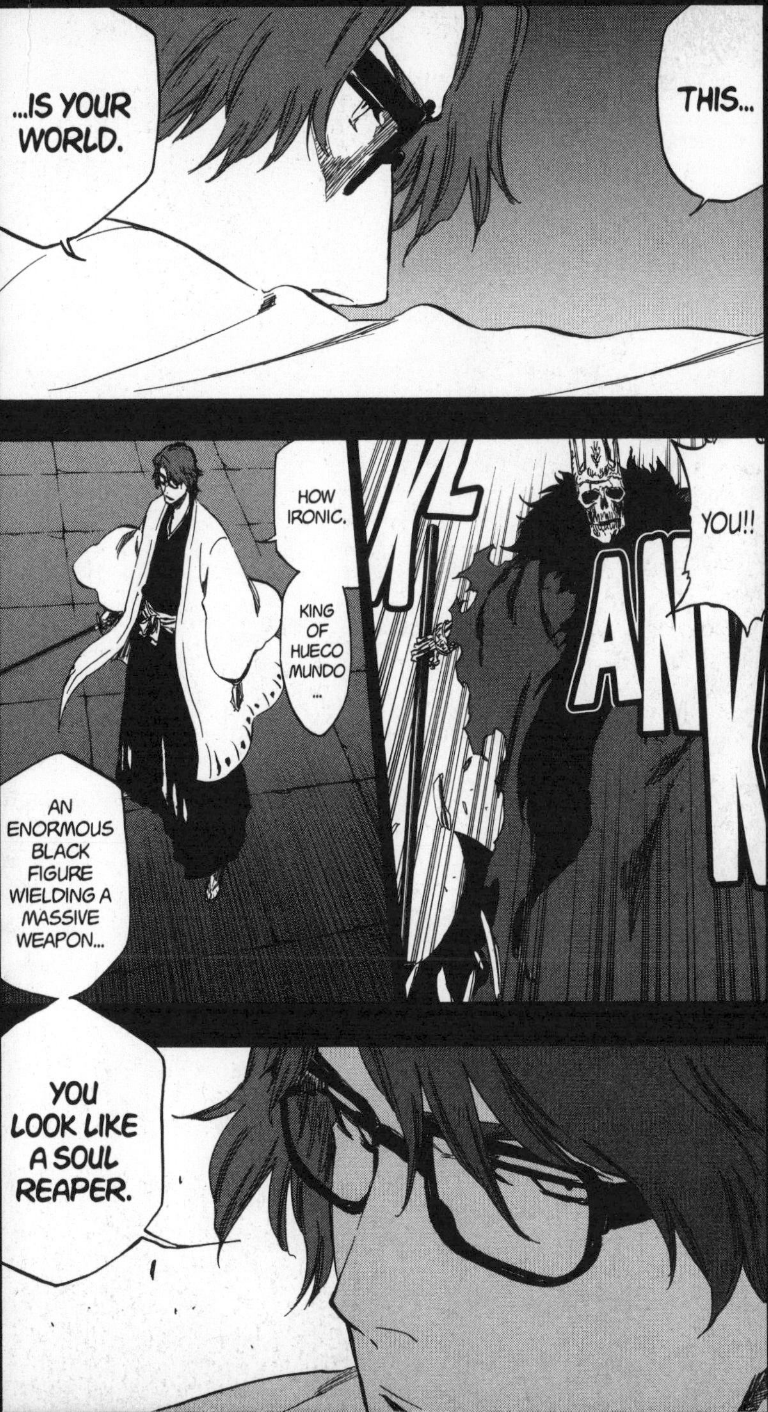
THIS...
...IS YOUR WORLD.
YOU!!
HOW IRONIC.
KING OF HUECO MUNDO...
AN ENORMOUS BLACK FIGURE WIELDING A MASSIVE WEAPON...
YOU LOOK LIKE A SOUL REAPER.

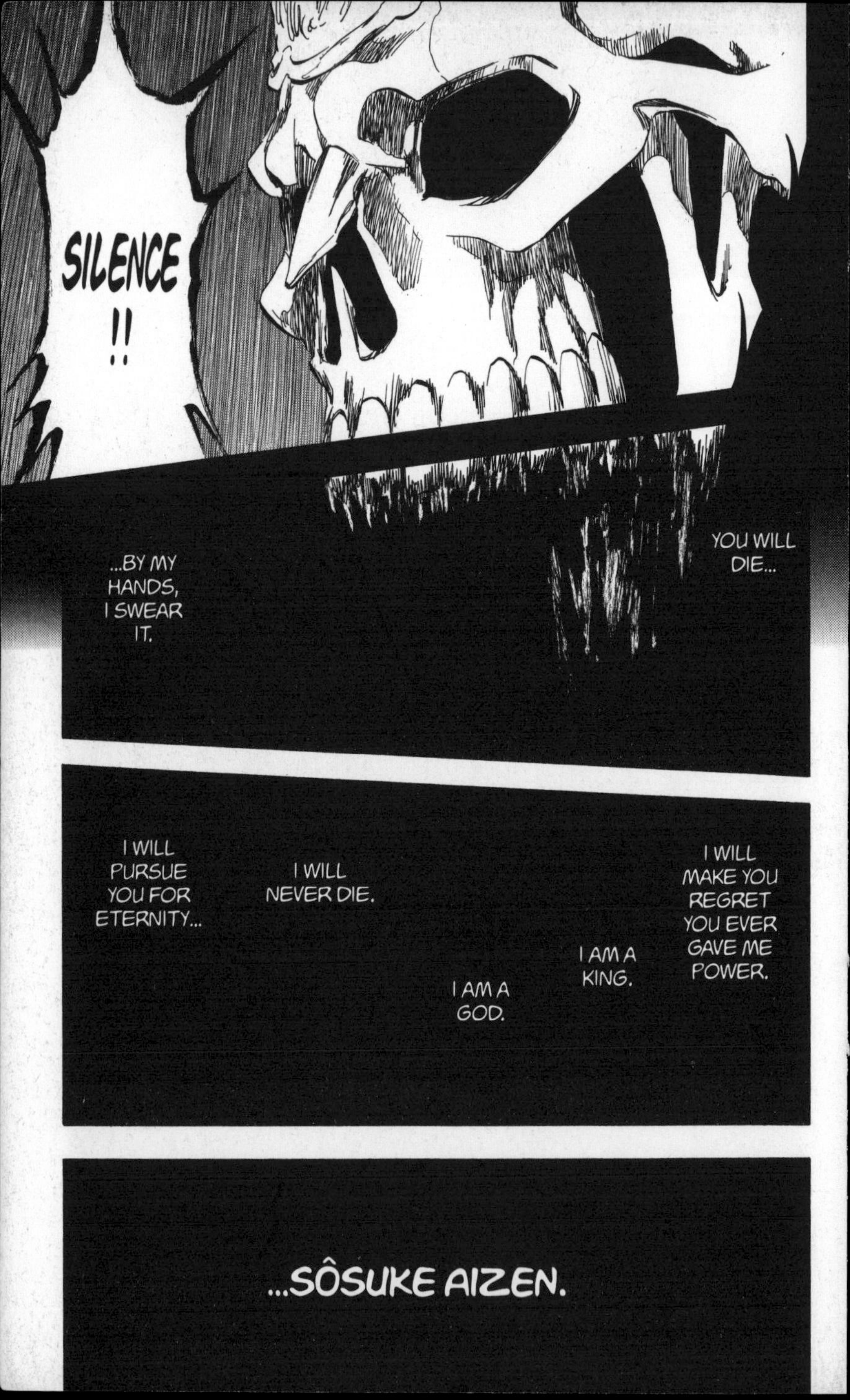
SILENCE!!
YOU WILL DIE...
...BY MY HANDS, I SWEAR IT.
I WILL MAKE YOU REGRET YOU EVER GAVE ME POWER.
I AM A KING.
I AM A GOD.
I WILL NEVER DIE.
I WILL PURSUE YOU FOR ETERNITY...
...SÔSUKE AIZEN.

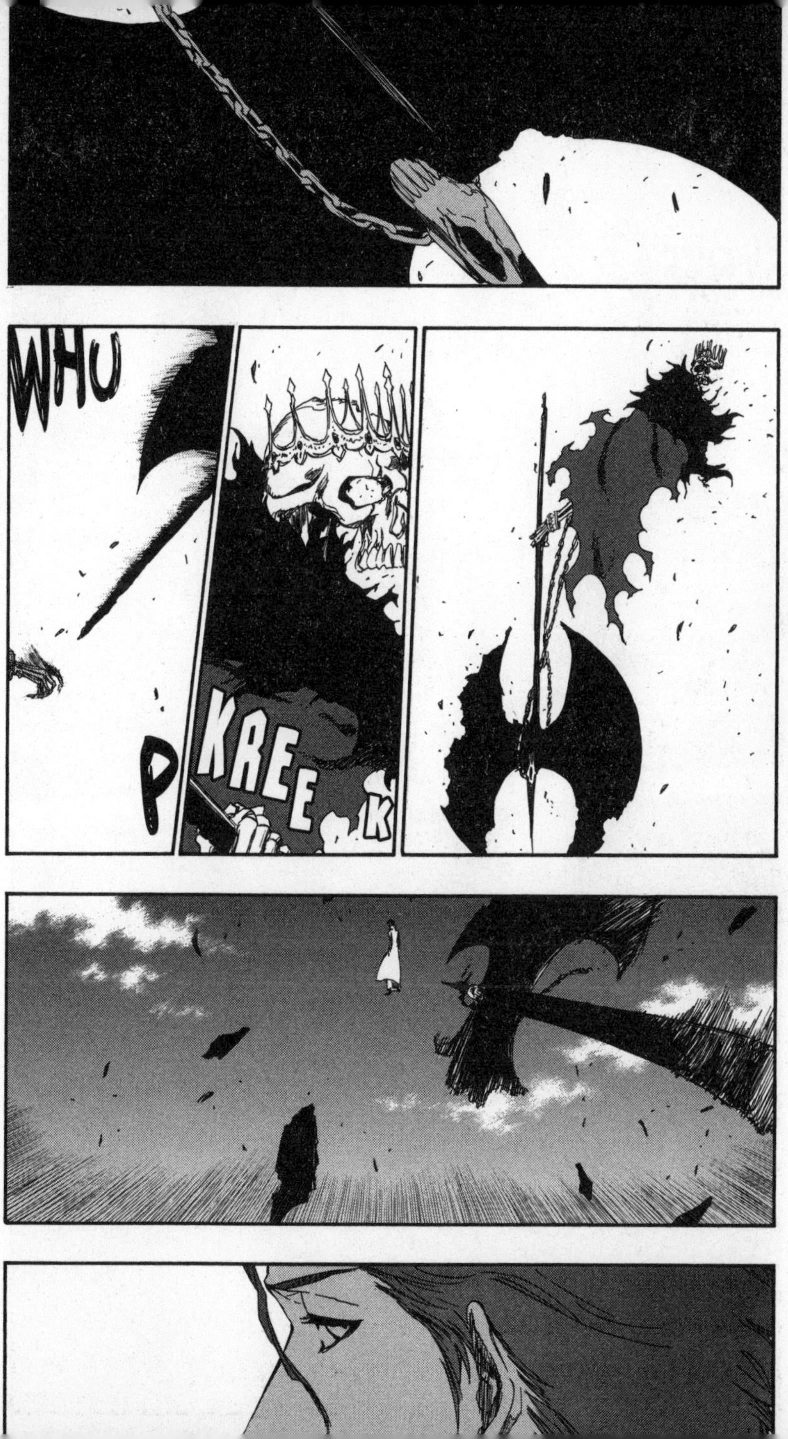
PKREEK
WHU

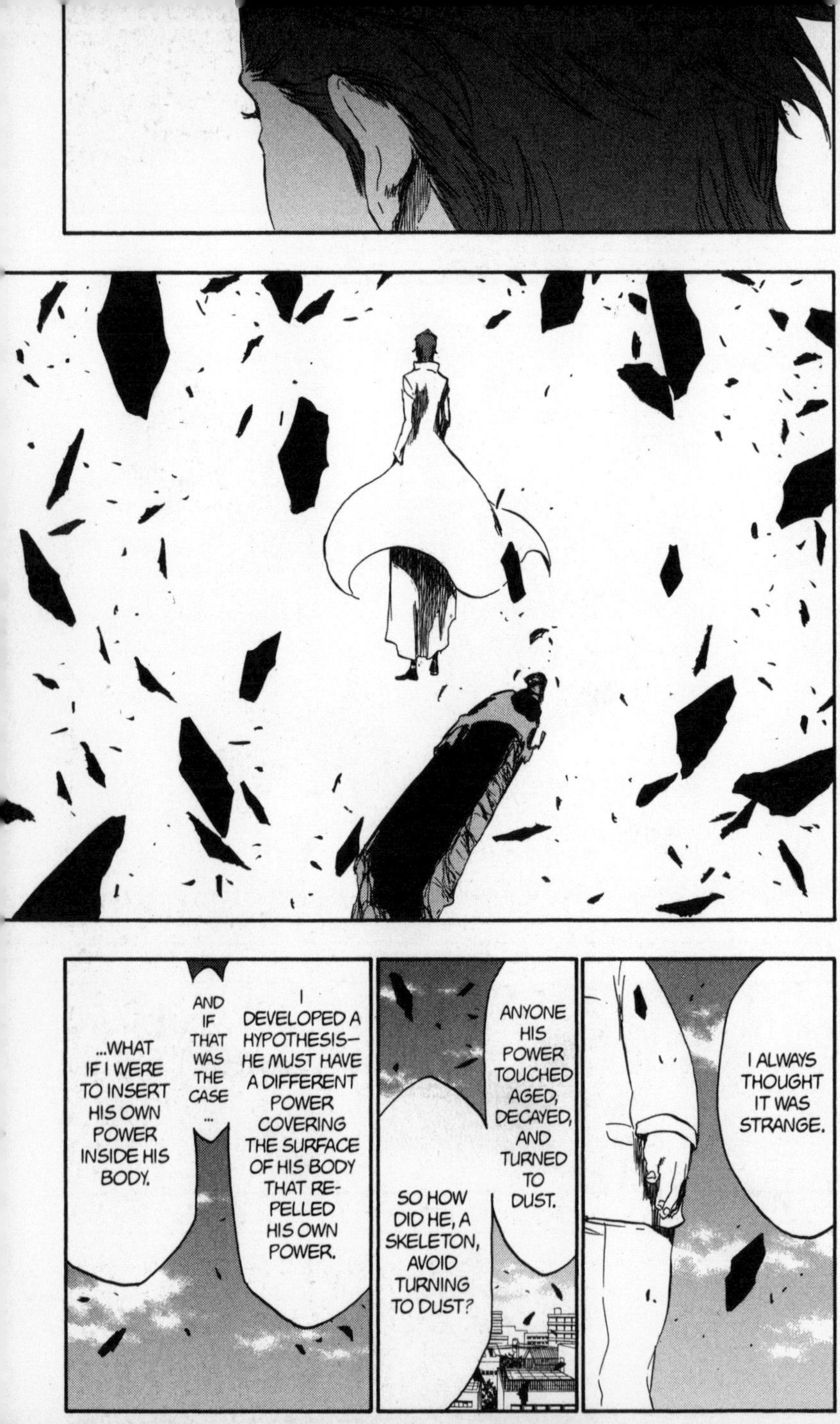
I ALWAYS THOUGHT IT WAS STRANGE.
ANYONE HIS POWER TOUCHED AGED, DECAYED, AND TURNED TO DUST.
SO HOW DID HE, A SKELETON, AVOID TURNING TO DUST?
I DEVELOPED A HYPOTHESIS— HE MUST HAVE A DIFFERENT POWER COVERING THE SURFACE OF HIS BODY THAT RE-PELLED HIS OWN POWER.
AND IF THAT WAS THE CASE...
...WHAT IF I WERE TO INSERT HIS OWN POWER INSIDE HIS BODY.

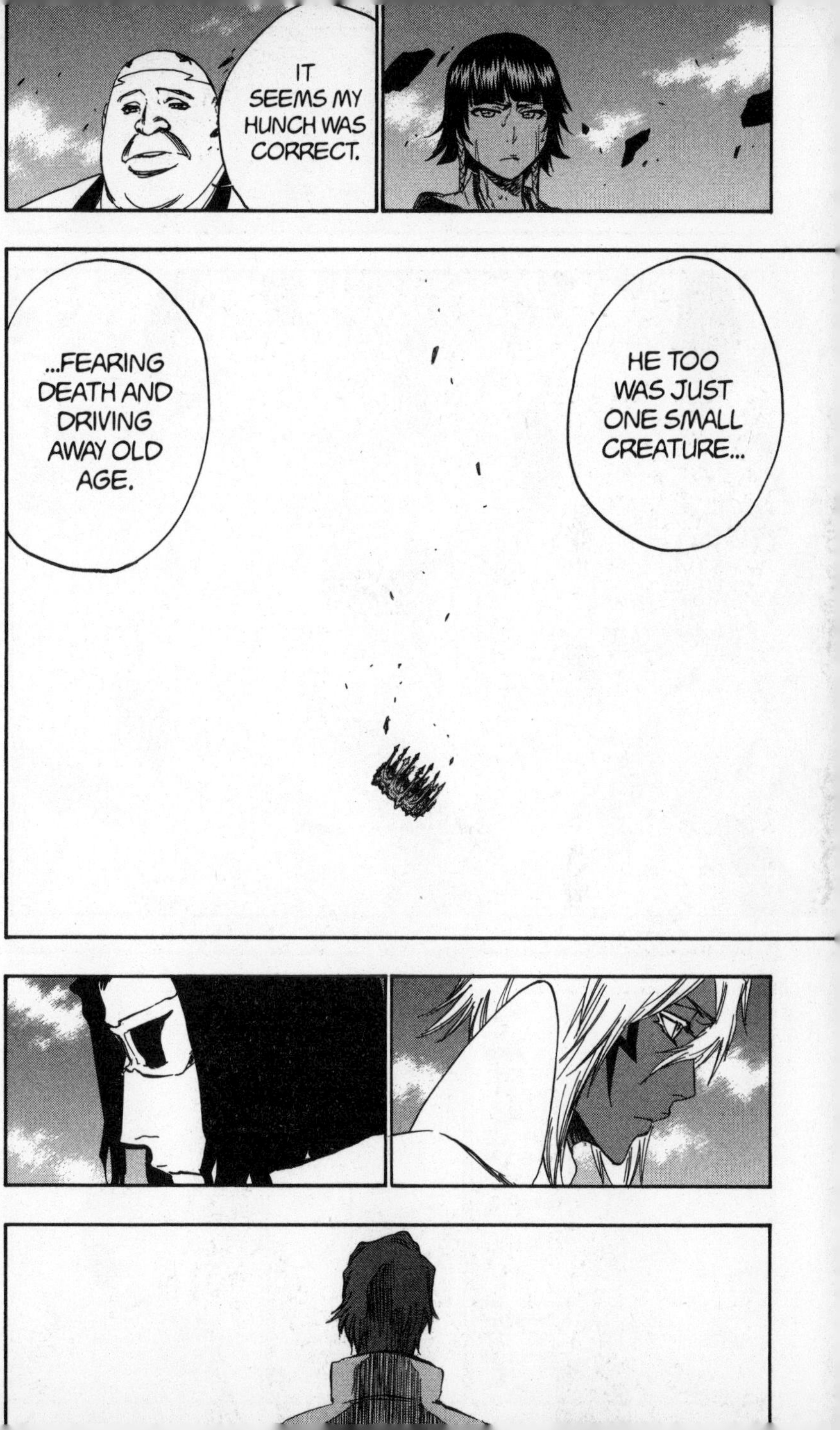
IT SEEMS MY HUNCH WAS CORRECT.
HE TOO WAS JUST ONE SMALL CREATURE...
...FEARING DEATH AND DRIVING AWAY OLD AGE.

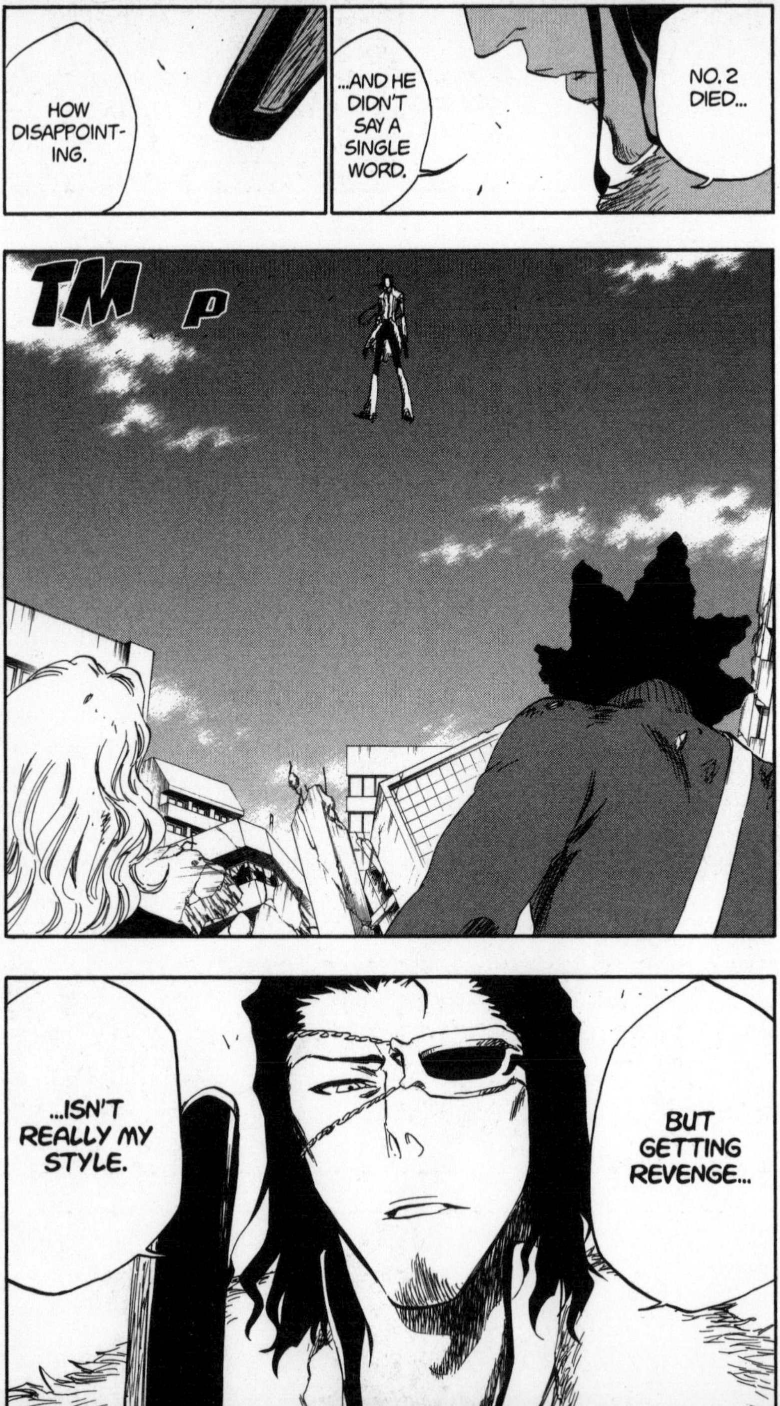
NO. 2 DIED...
...AND HE DIDN'T SAY A SINGLE WORD.
HOW DISAPPOINTING.
TMP
BUT GETTING REVENGE...
...ISN'T REALLY MY STYLE.

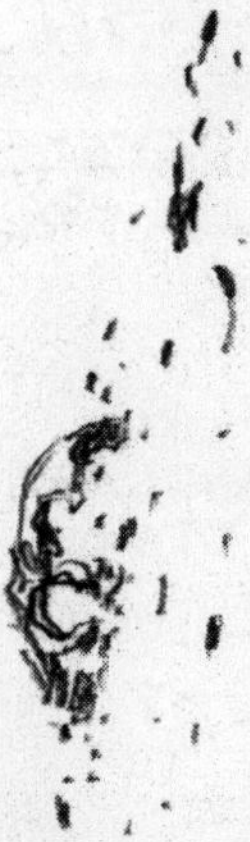

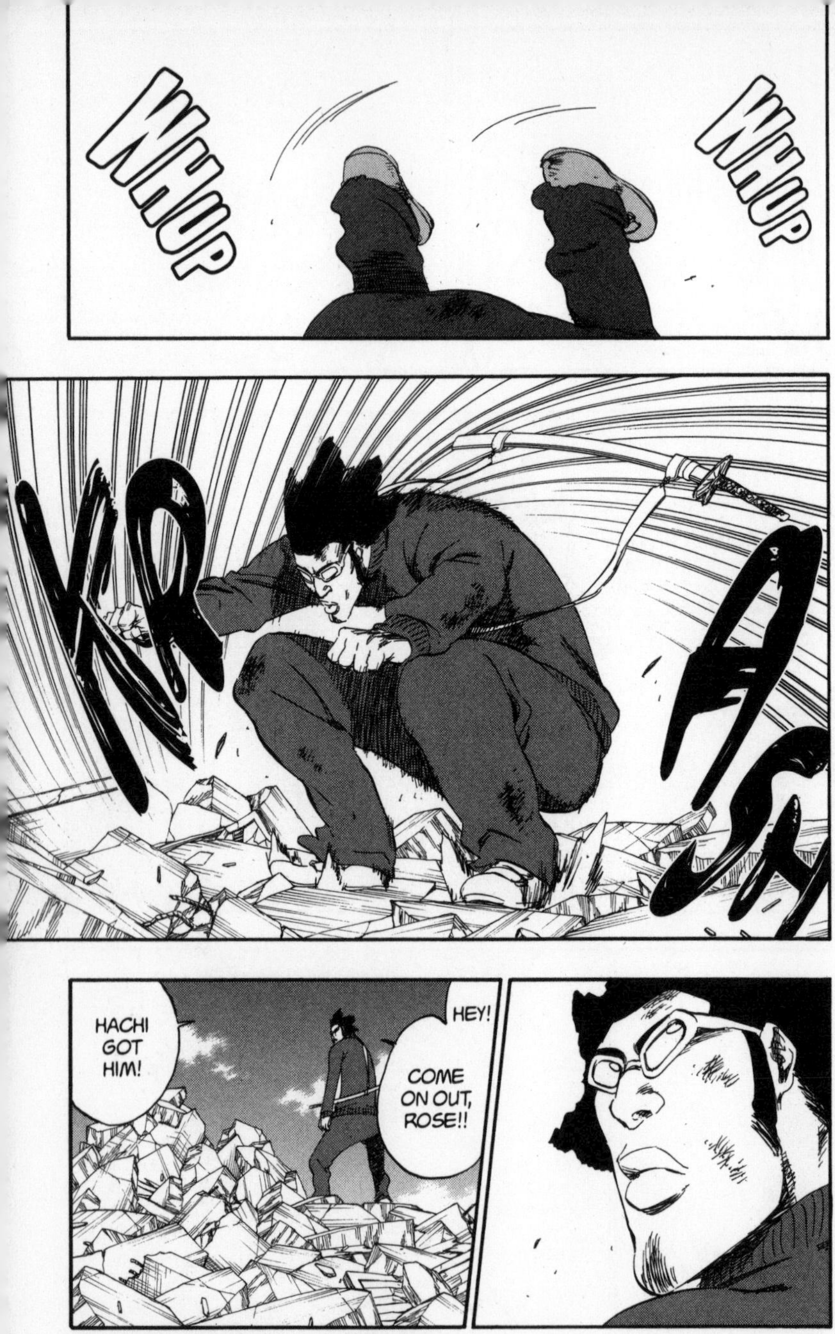
WHUP
WHUP
KRASH
HEY!
COME ON OUT, ROSE!!
HACHI GOT HIM!

372. The Metal Cudgel Flinger

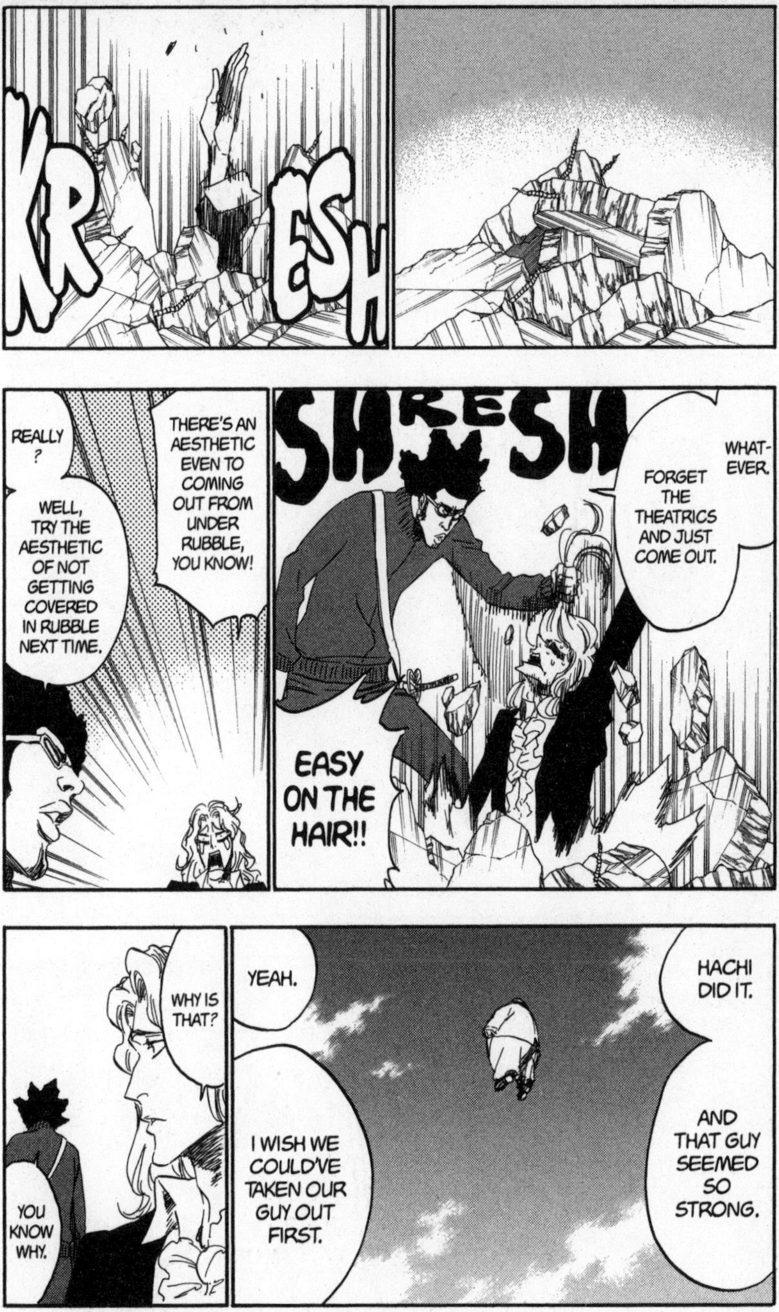
KRESH
SHRESH
WHAT-EVER.
FORGET THE THEATRICS AND JUST COME OUT.
EASY ON THE HAIR!!
THERE'S AN AESTHETIC EVEN TO COMING OUT FROM UNDER RUBBLE, YOU KNOW!
REALLY?
WELL, TRY THE AESTHETIC OF NOT GETTING COVERED IN RUBBLE NEXT TIME.
HACHI DID IT.
AND THAT GUY SEEMED SO STRONG.
YEAH.
I WISH WE COULD'VE TAKEN OUR GUY OUT FIRST.
WHY IS THAT?
YOU KNOW WHY.

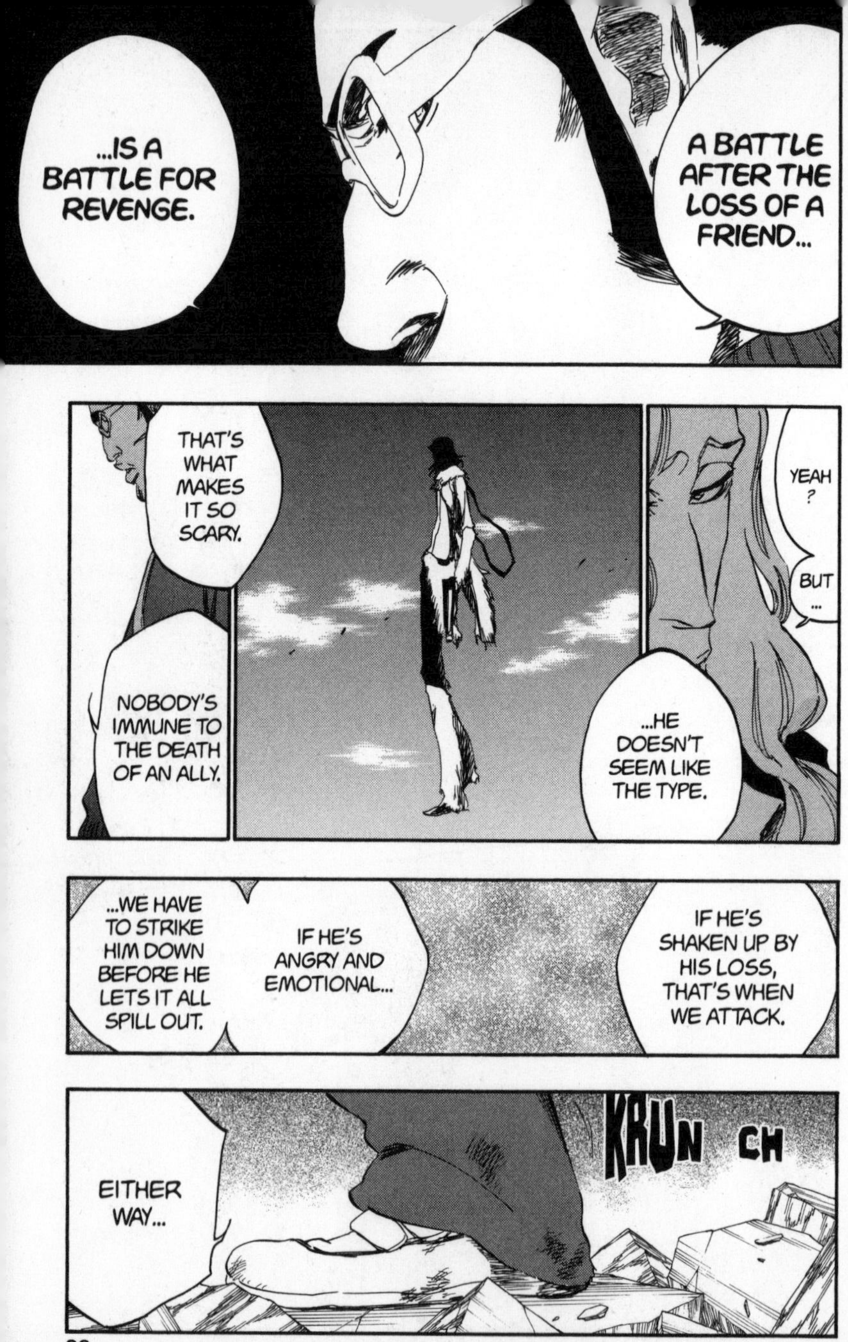
A BATTLE AFTER THE LOSS OF A FRIEND...
...IS A BATTLE FOR REVENGE.
YEAH?
BUT...
...HE DOESN'T SEEM LIKE THE TYPE.
THAT'S WHAT MAKES IT SO SCARY.
NOBODY'S IMMUNE TO THE DEATH OF AN ALLY.
IF HE'S SHAKEN UP BY HIS LOSS, THAT'S WHEN WE ATTACK.
IF HE'S ANGRY AND EMOTIONAL...
...WE HAVE TO STRIKE HIM DOWN BEFORE HE LETS IT ALL SPILL OUT.
KRUN CH
EITHER WAY...

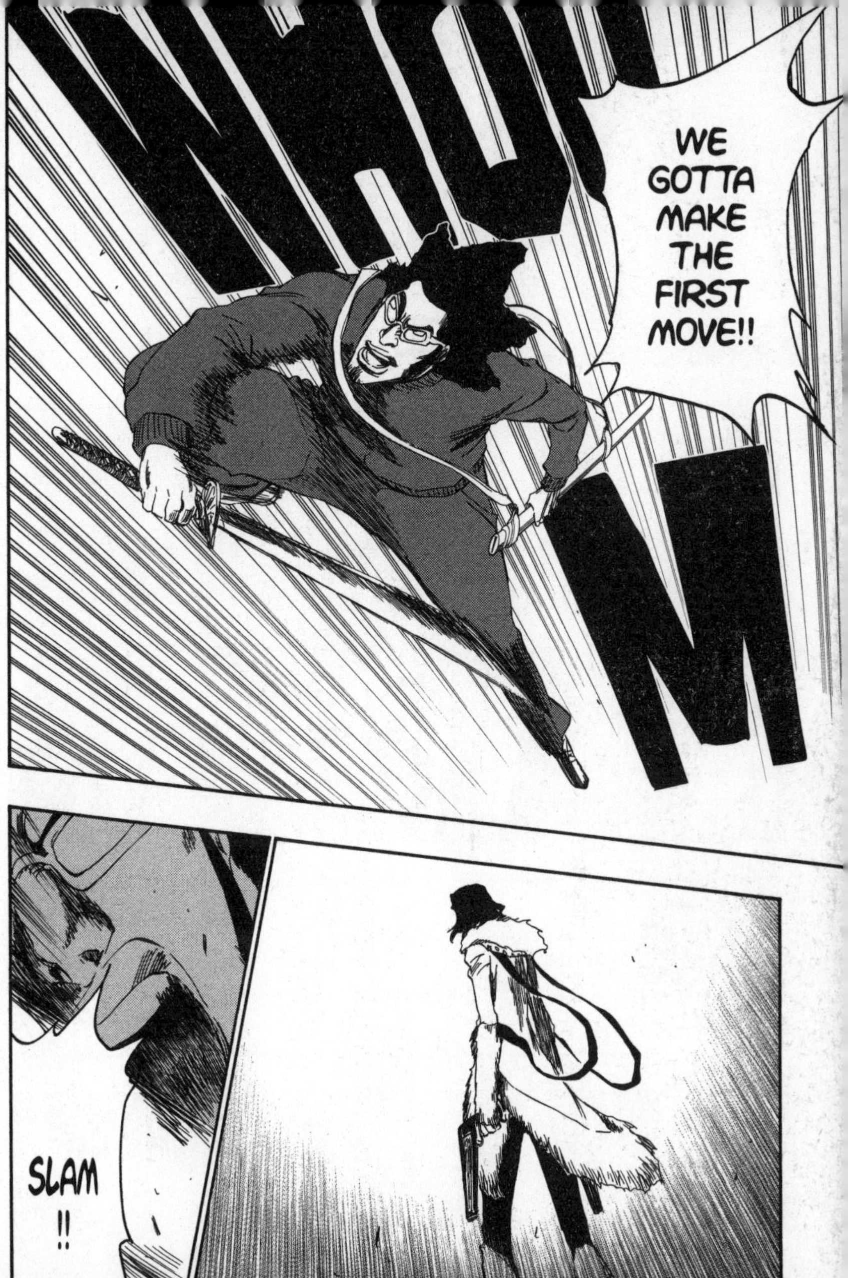
WE GOTTA MAKE THE FIRST MOVE!!
SLAM !!

BLEACH 372.

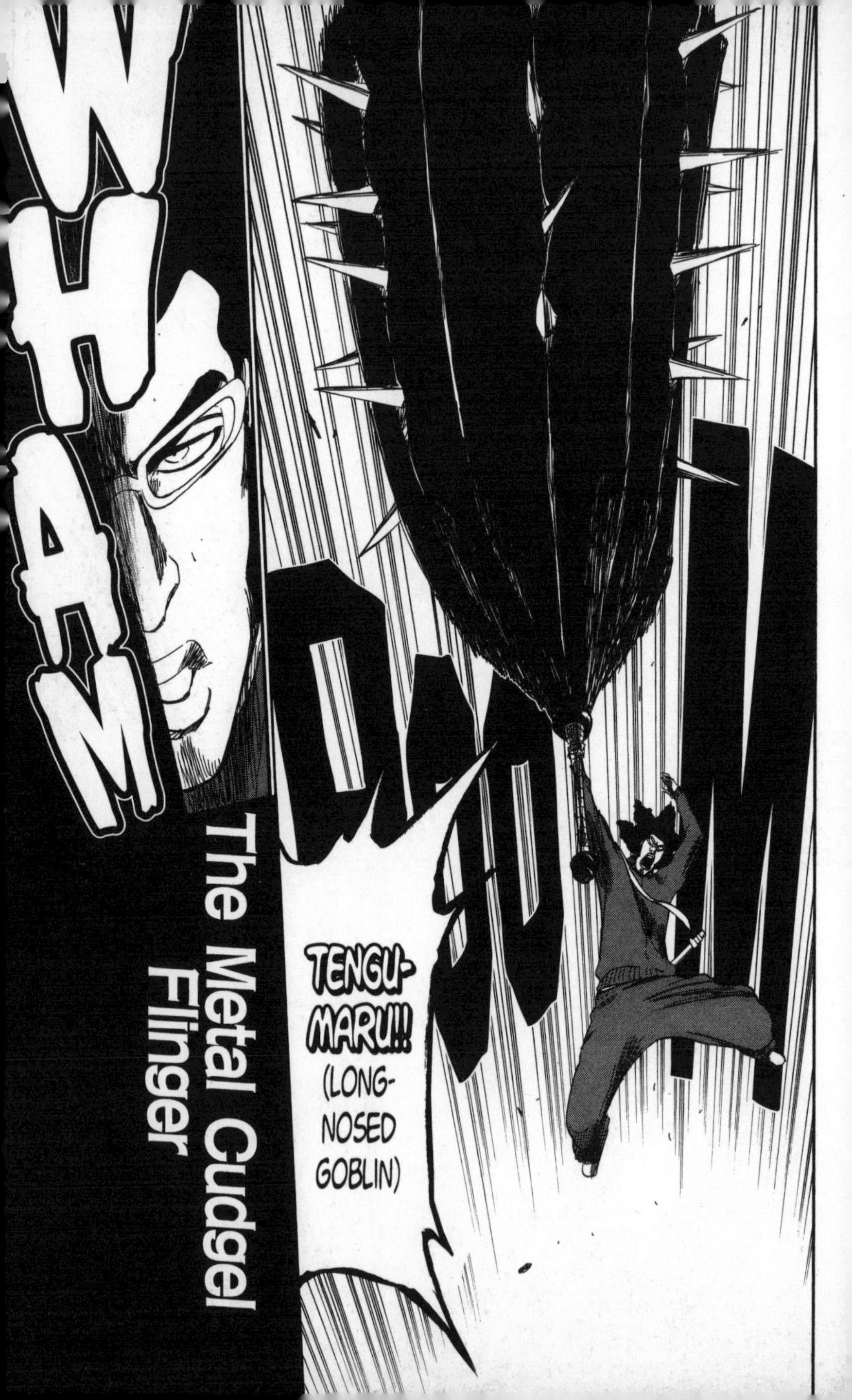
WHAM
DOOM
TENGU-MARU!!
(LONG-NOSED GOBLIN)
The Metal Cudgel Flinger

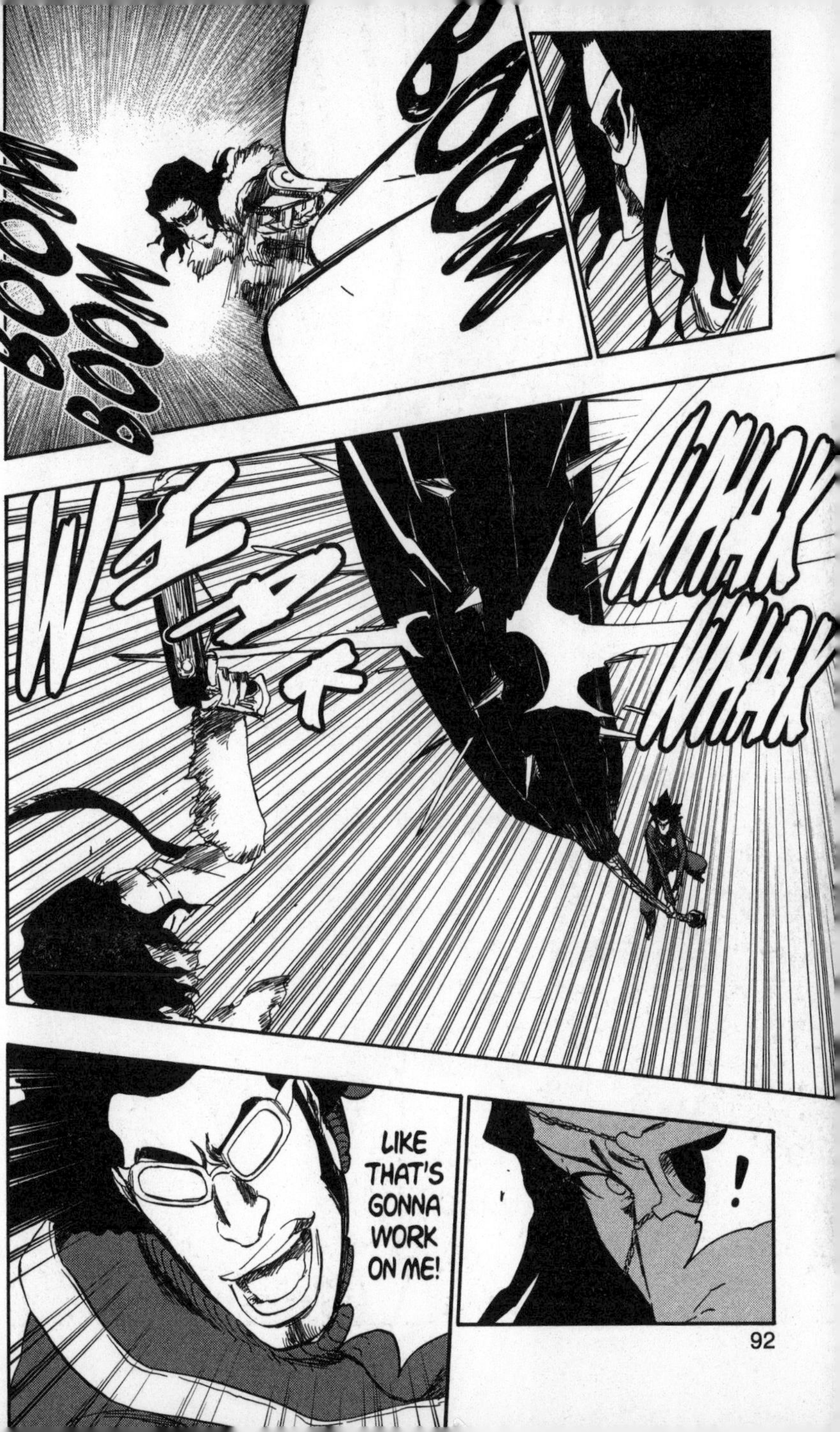
BOOM
BOOM BOOM
WHAK WHAK
WHAK
!
LIKE THAT'S GONNA WORK ON ME!

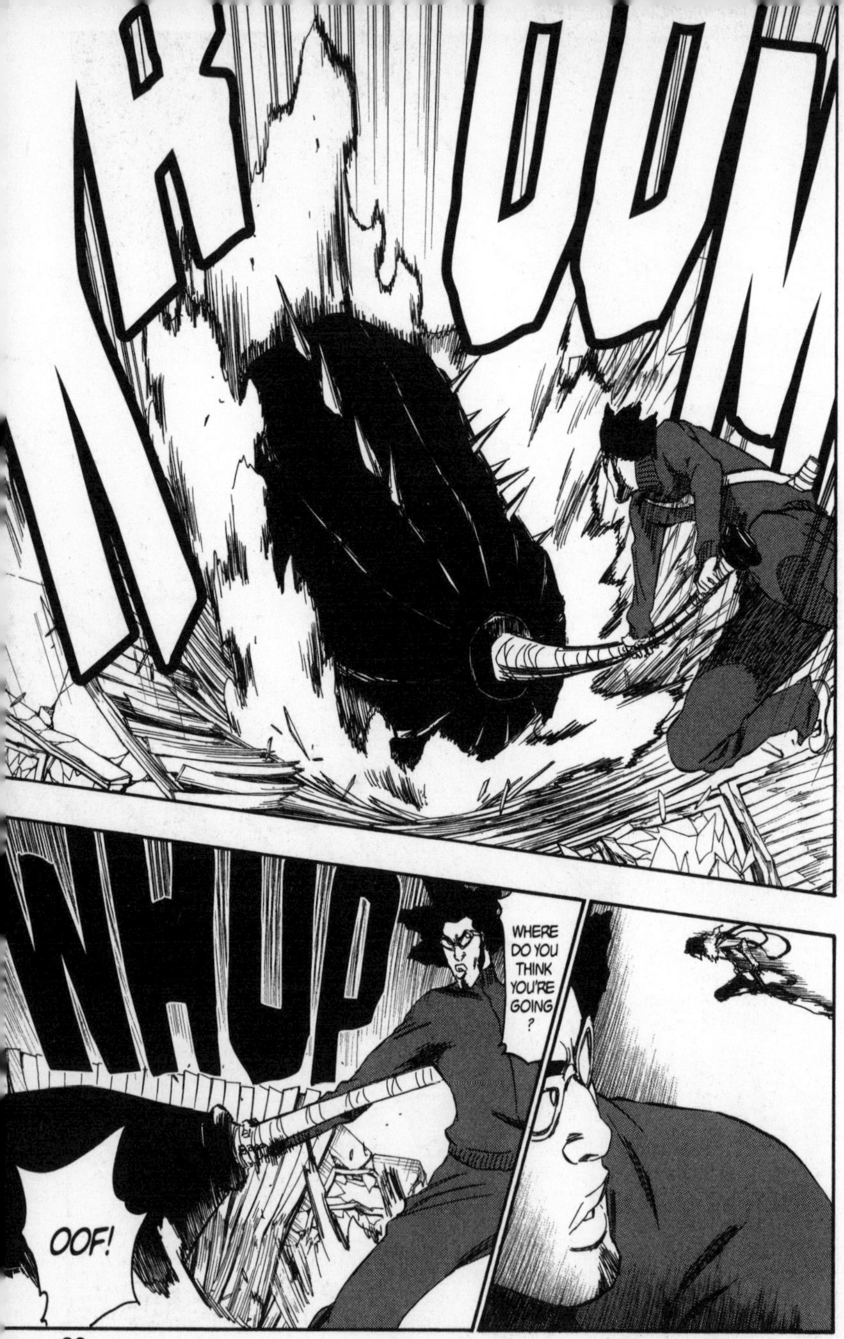
WHOOM
WHERE DO YOU THINK YOU'RE GOING?
WHUP
OOF!

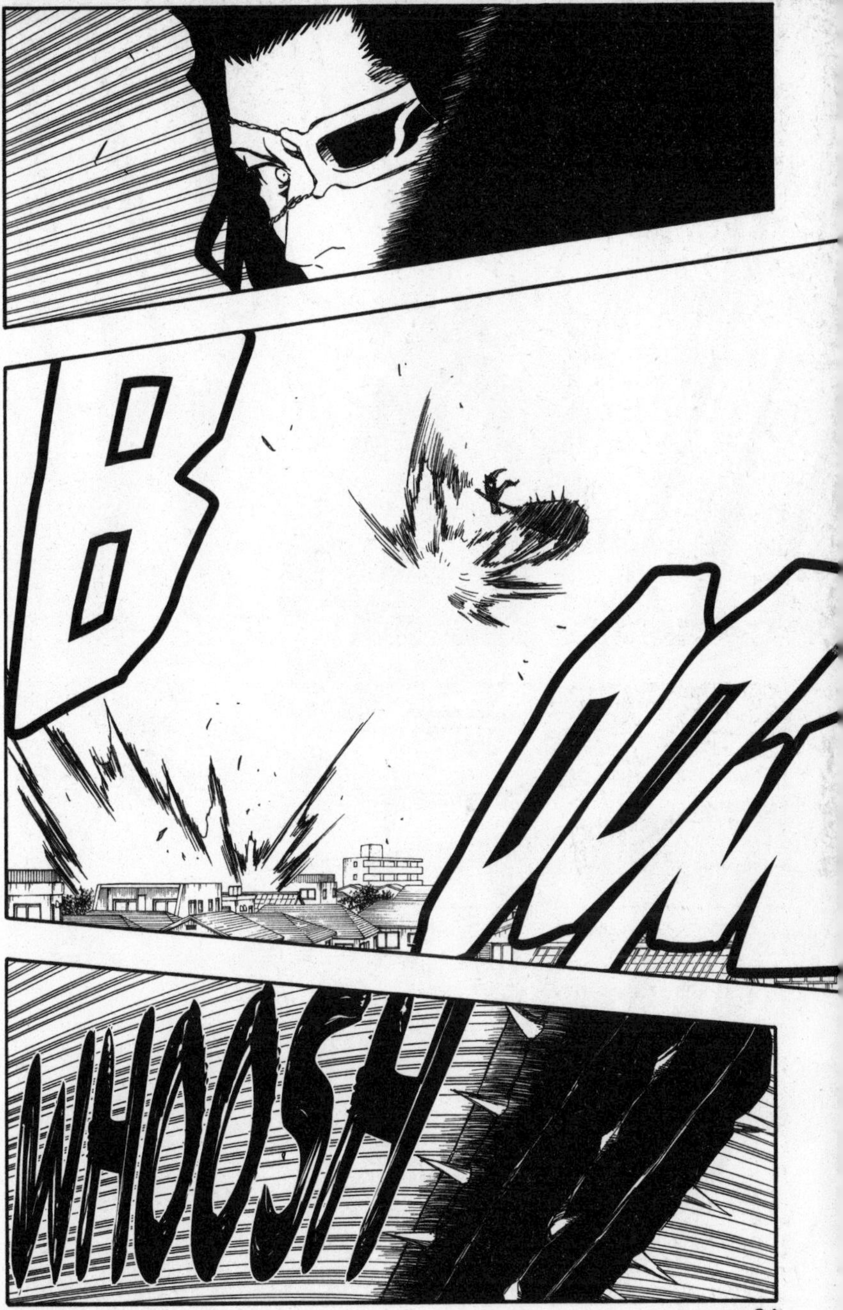
BUM
WHOOSH

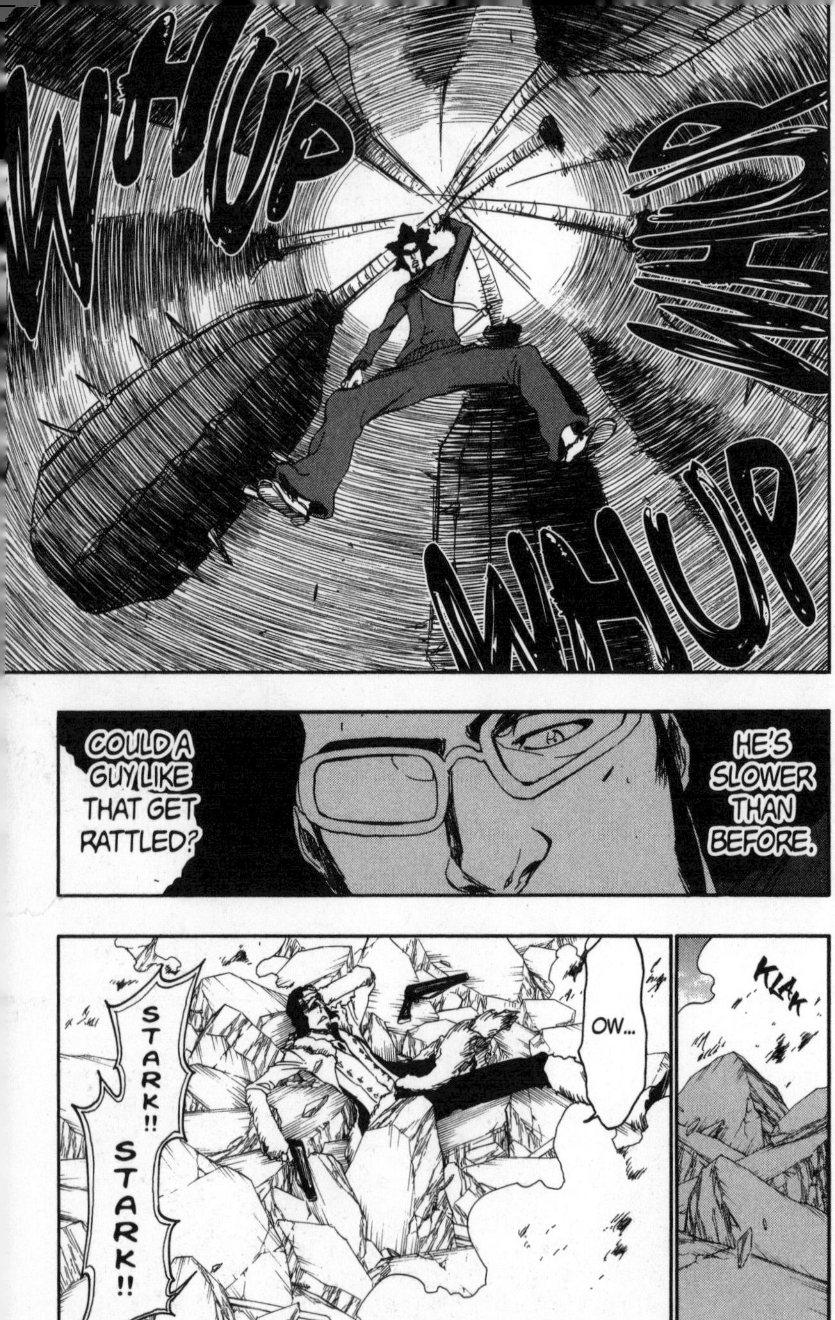
WHUP
WHUP
WHUP
HE'S SLOWER THAN BEFORE.
COULD A GUY LIKE THAT GET RATTLED?
KLAK
OW...
STARK!! STARK!!

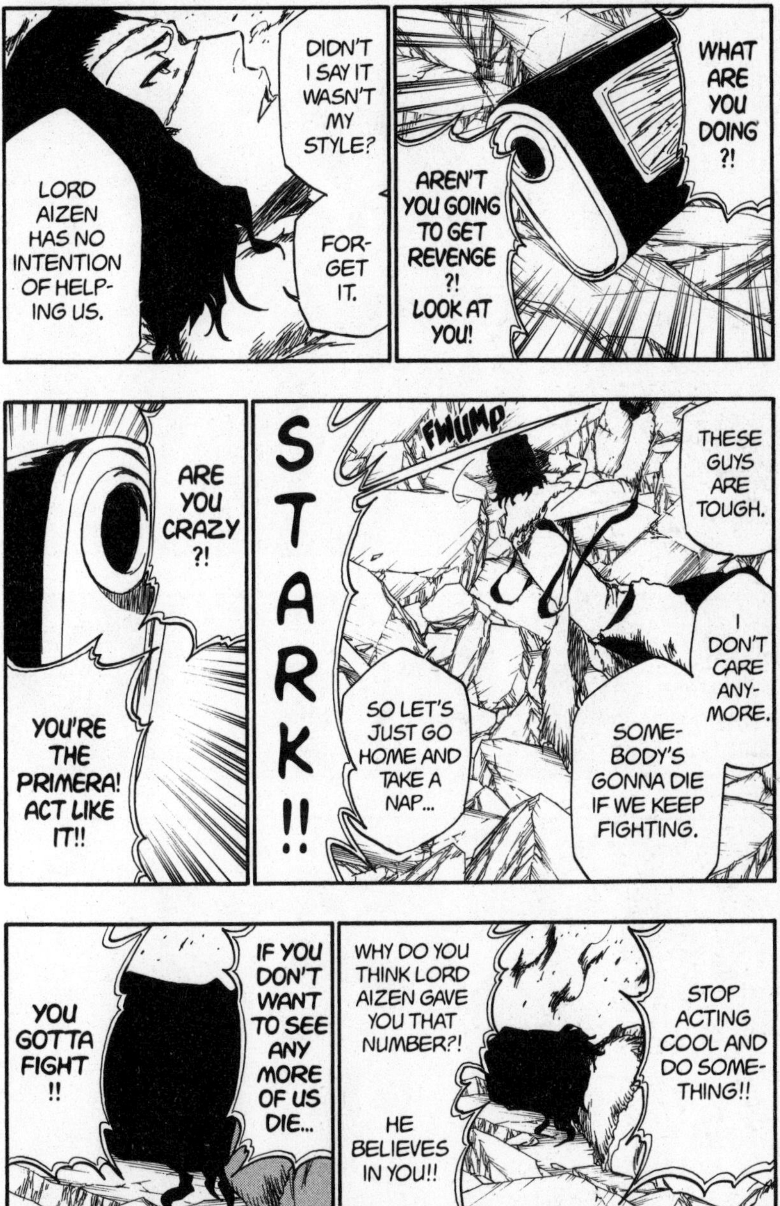
WHAT ARE YOU DOING?!
AREN'T YOU GOING TO GET REVENGE?! LOOK AT YOU!
DIDN'T I SAY IT WASN'T MY STYLE?
FORGET IT.
LORD AIZEN HAS NO INTENTION OF HELPING US.
FWUMP
THESE GUYS ARE TOUGH.
I DON'T CARE ANYMORE.
SOMEBODY'S GONNA DIE IF WE KEEP FIGHTING.
SO LET'S JUST GO HOME AND TAKE A NAP...
STARK!!
ARE YOU CRAZY?!
YOU'RE THE PRIMERA! ACT LIKE IT!!
STOP ACTING COOL AND DO SOMETHING!!
WHY DO YOU THINK LORD AIZEN GAVE YOU THAT NUMBER?!
HE BELIEVES IN YOU!!
IF YOU DON'T WANT TO SEE ANY MORE OF US DIE...
YOU GOTTA FIGHT!!

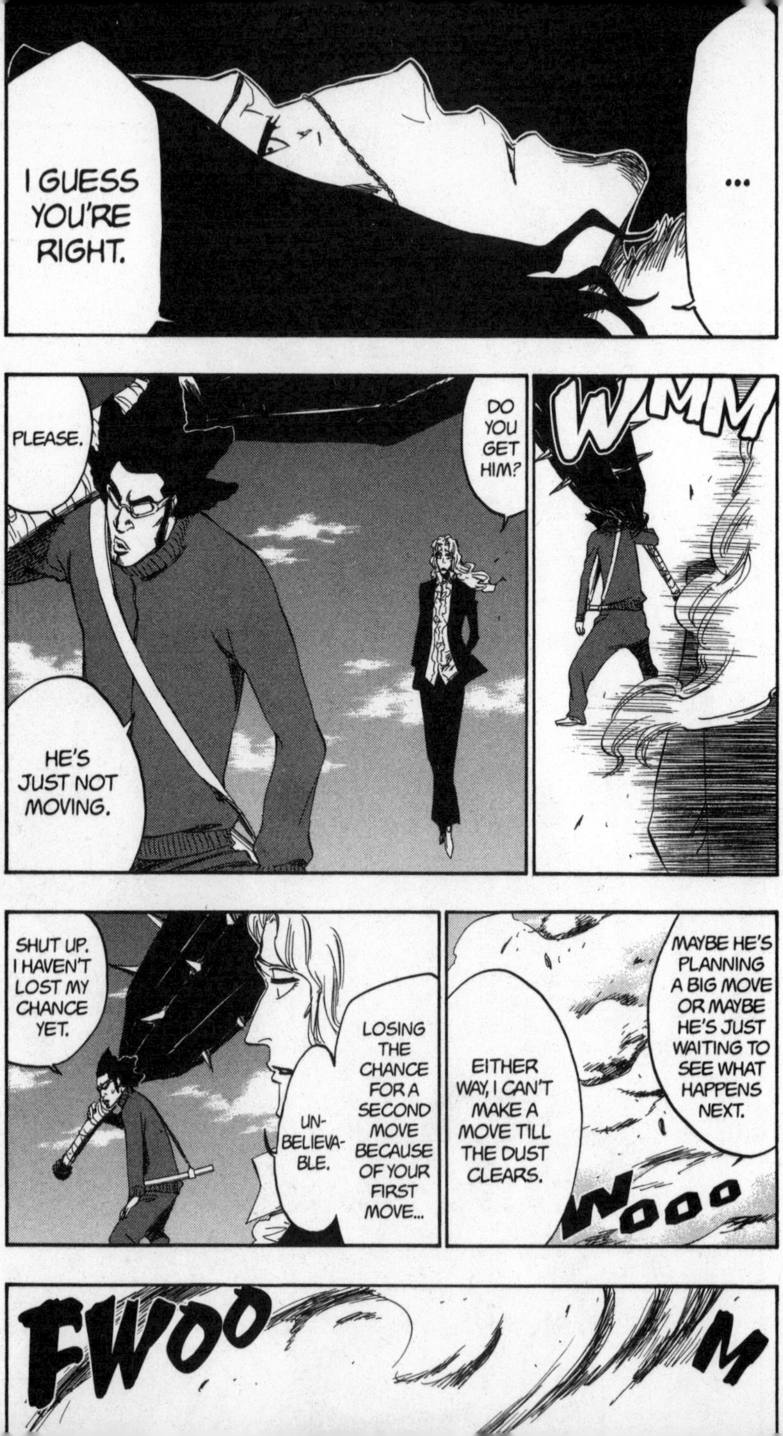
...
I GUESS YOU'RE RIGHT.
WMMM
DO YOU GET HIM?
PLEASE.
HE'S JUST NOT MOVING.
MAYBE HE'S PLANNING A BIG MOVE OR MAYBE HE'S JUST WAITING TO SEE WHAT HAPPENS NEXT.
EITHER WAY, I CAN'T MAKE A MOVE TILL THE DUST CLEARS.
WOOO
UN-BELIEVA-BLE.
LOSING THE CHANCE FOR A SECOND MOVE BECAUSE OF YOUR FIRST MOVE...
SHUT UP. I HAVEN'T LOST MY CHANCE YET.
FWOOM

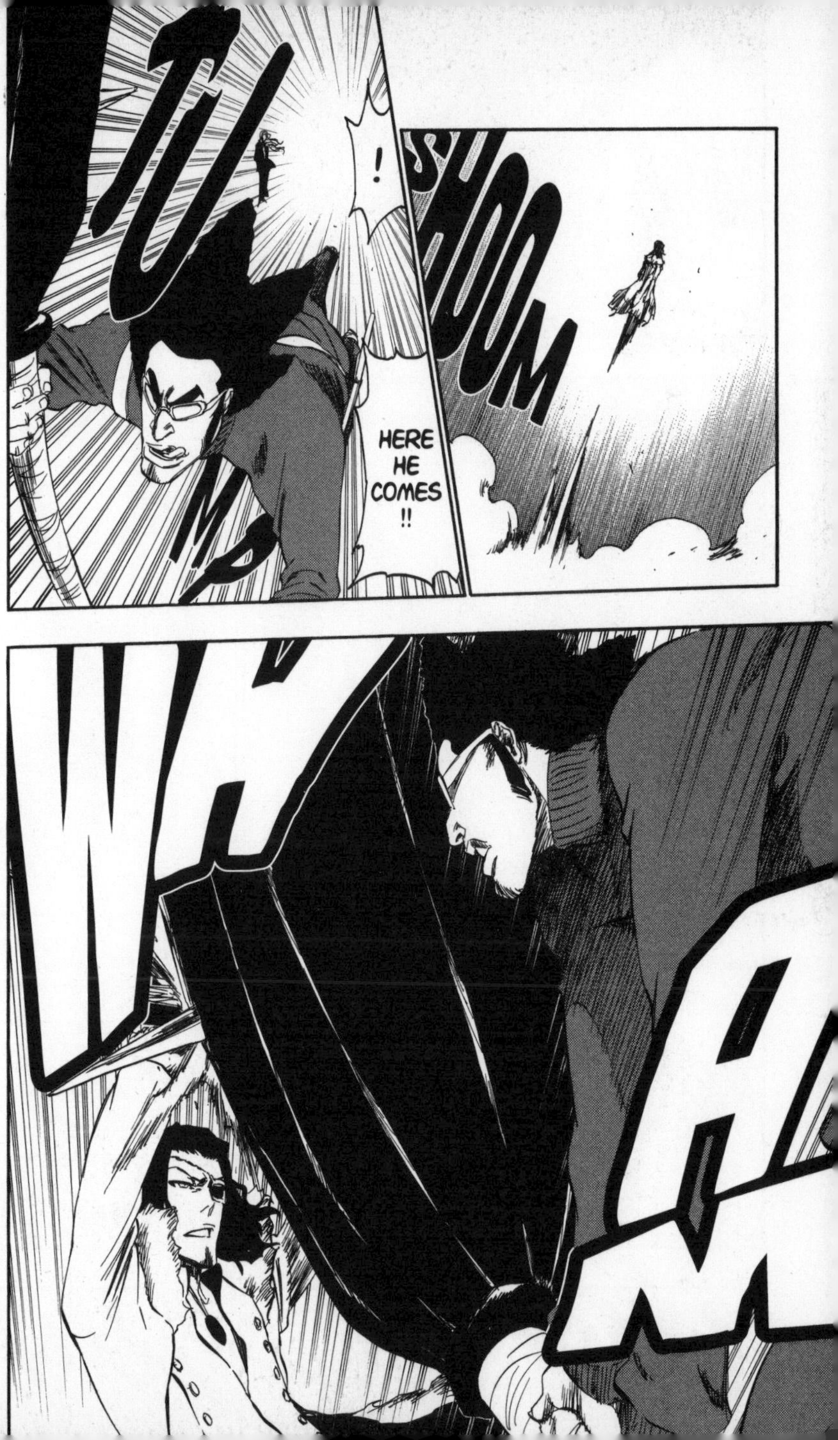
!
HERE HE COMES !!

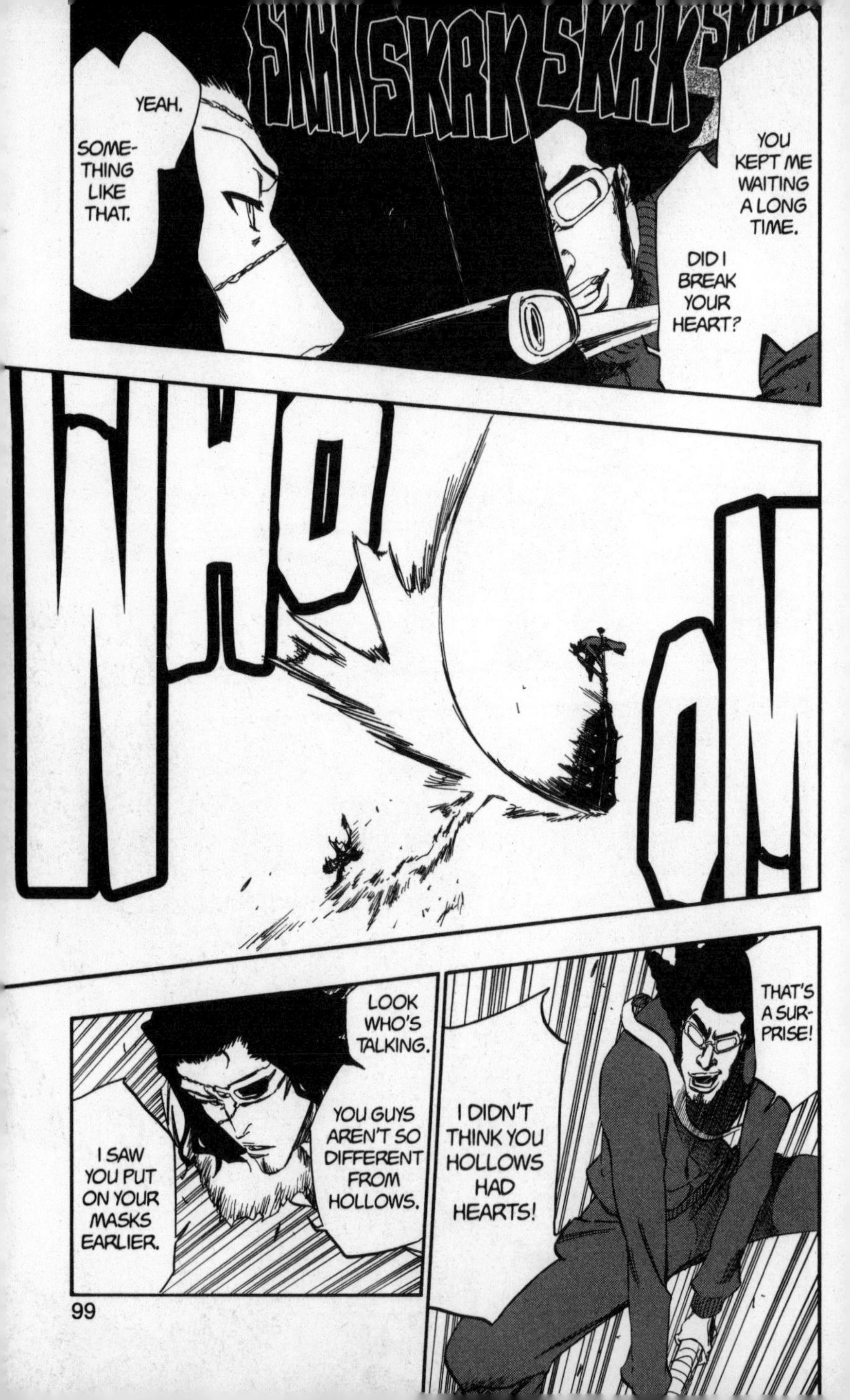
SKRK SKRK SKRK
YOU KEPT ME WAITING A LONG TIME.
DID I BREAK YOUR HEART?
YEAH.
SOME-THING LIKE THAT.
WHOOM
THAT'S A SUR-PRISE!
I DIDN'T THINK YOU HOLLOWS HAD HEARTS!
LOOK WHO'S TALKING.
YOU GUYS AREN'T SO DIFFERENT FROM HOLLOWS.
I SAW YOU PUT ON YOUR MASKS EARLIER.

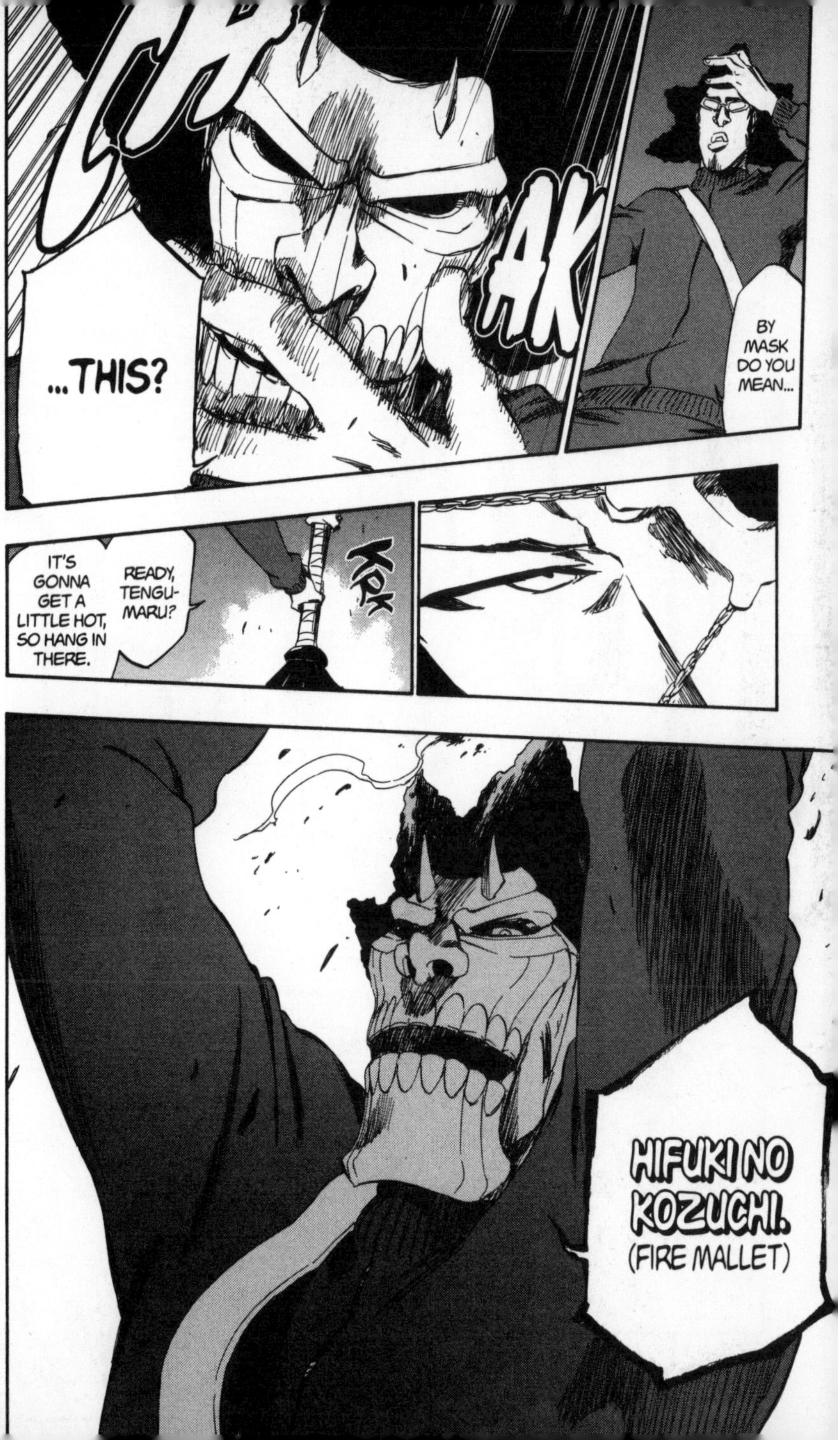
BY MASK DO YOU MEAN...
AK
...THIS?
KRK
READY, TENGU-MARU?
IT'S GONNA GET A LITTLE HOT, SO HANG IN THERE.
HIFUKI NO KOZUCHI. (FIRE MALLET)

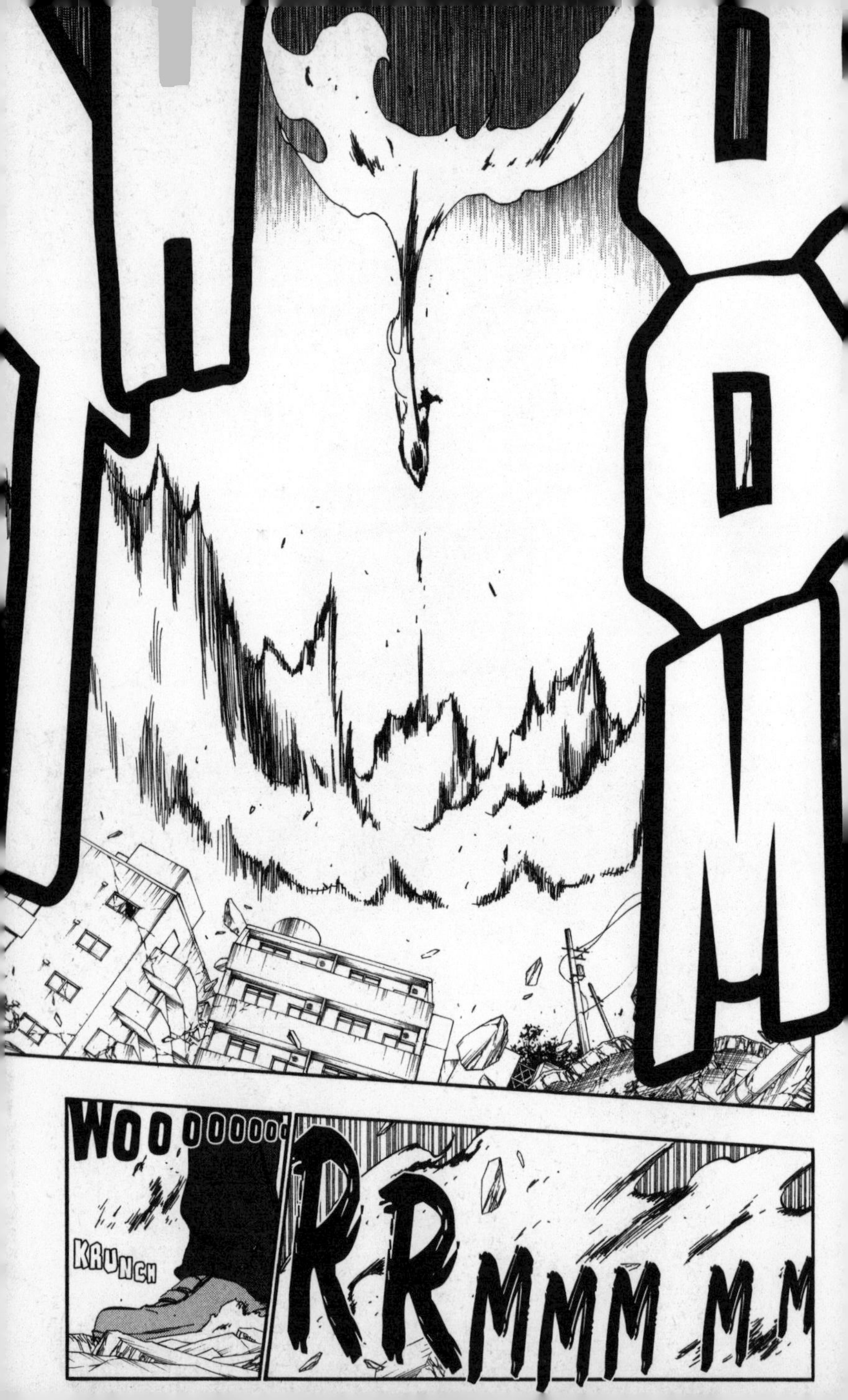
WOOOOOOOO
KRUNCH
RRMMM MM

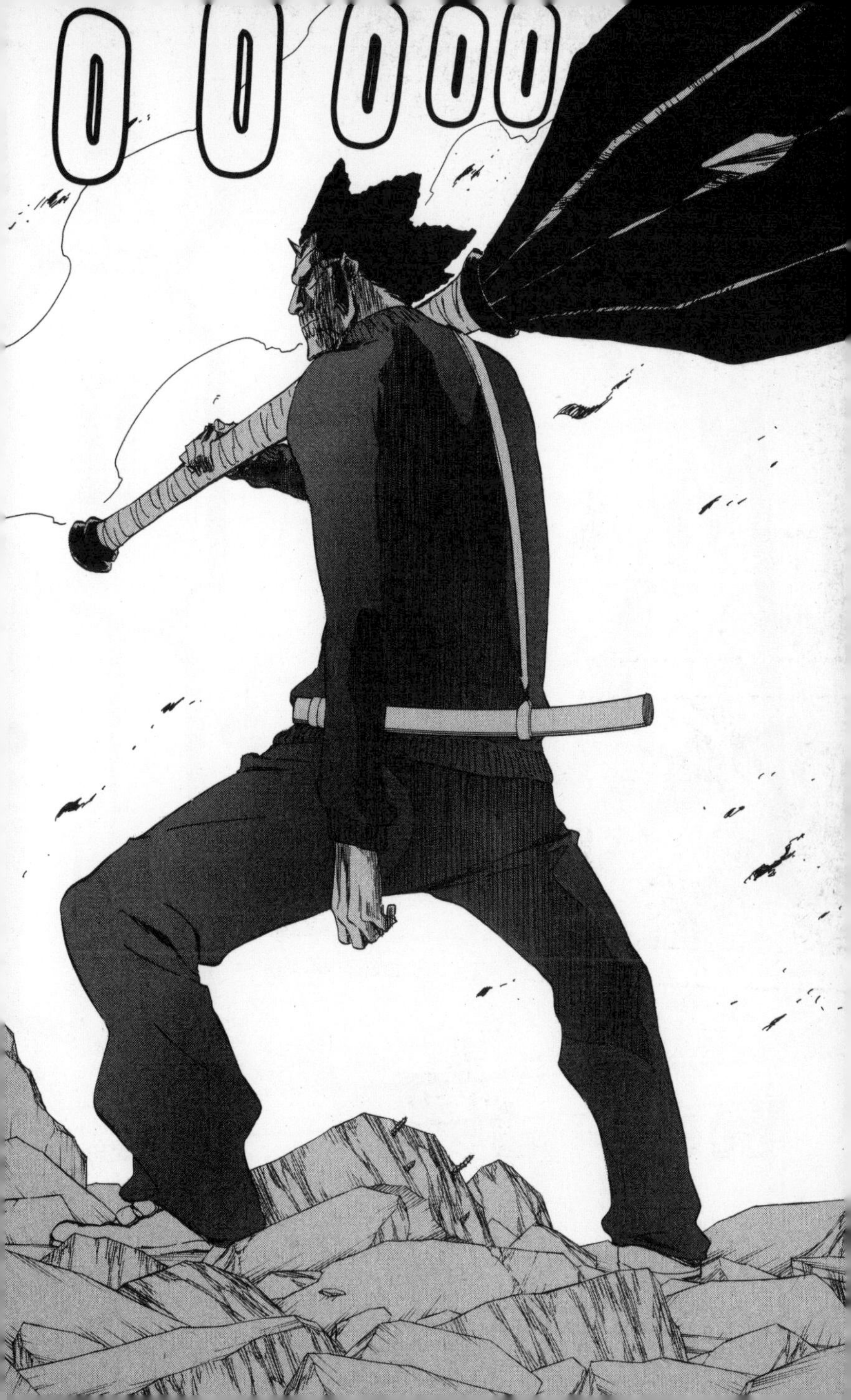
O O OOO

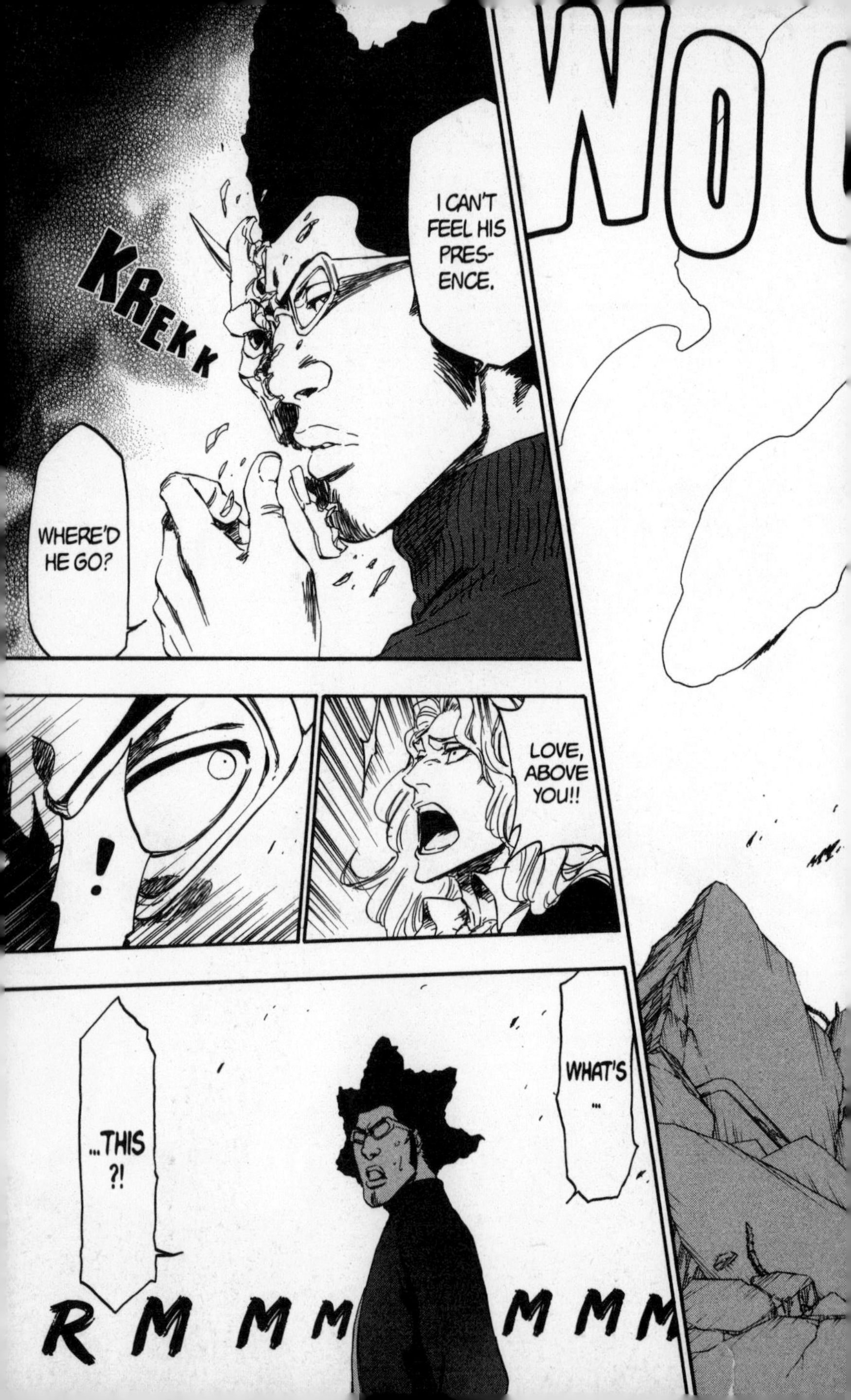
WOO
I CAN'T FEEL HIS PRES-ENCE.
KREKKK
WHERE'D HE GO?
LOVE, ABOVE YOU!!
!
WHAT'S ...
...THIS ?!
RMMMMMMMM

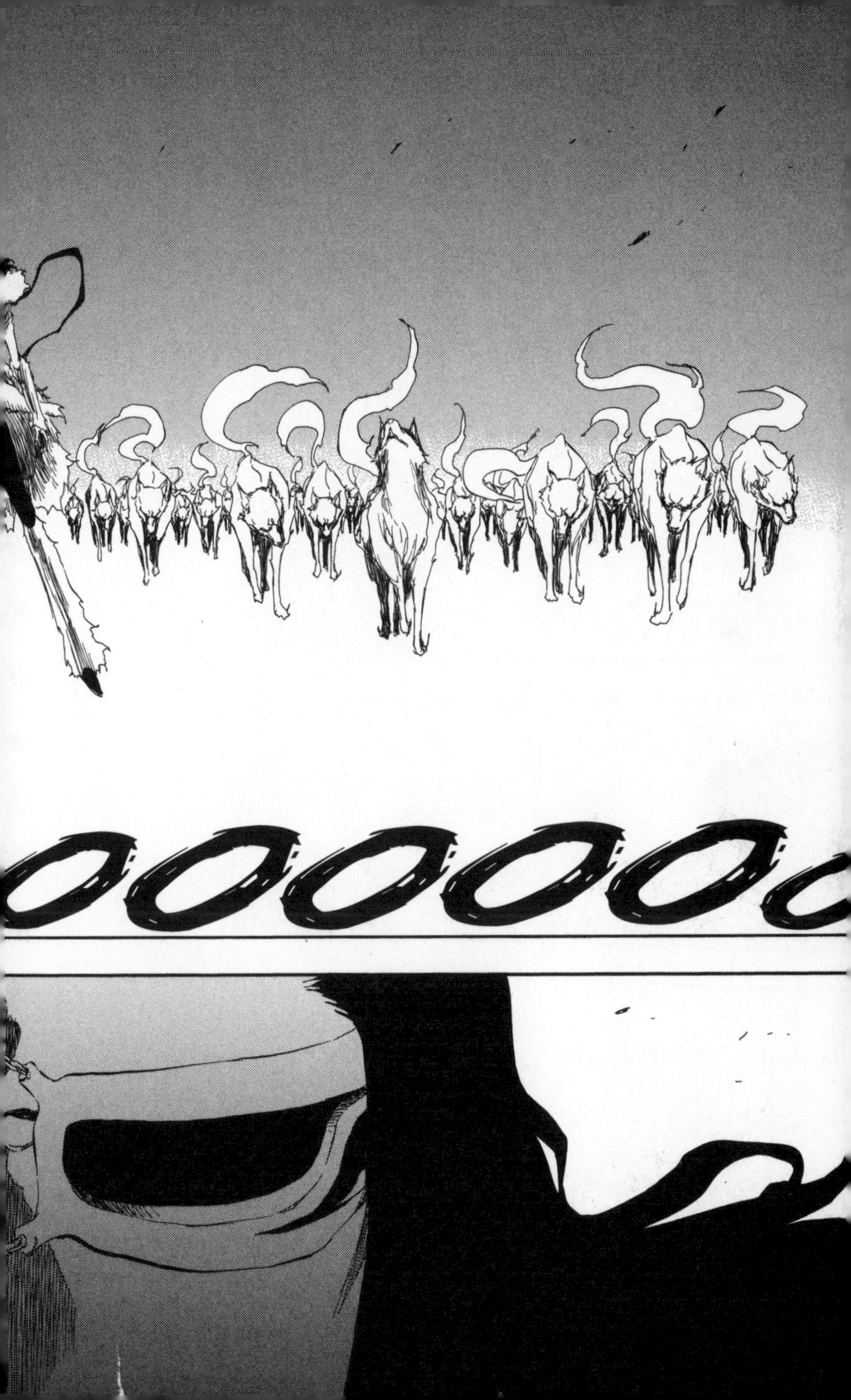
OOOOOO

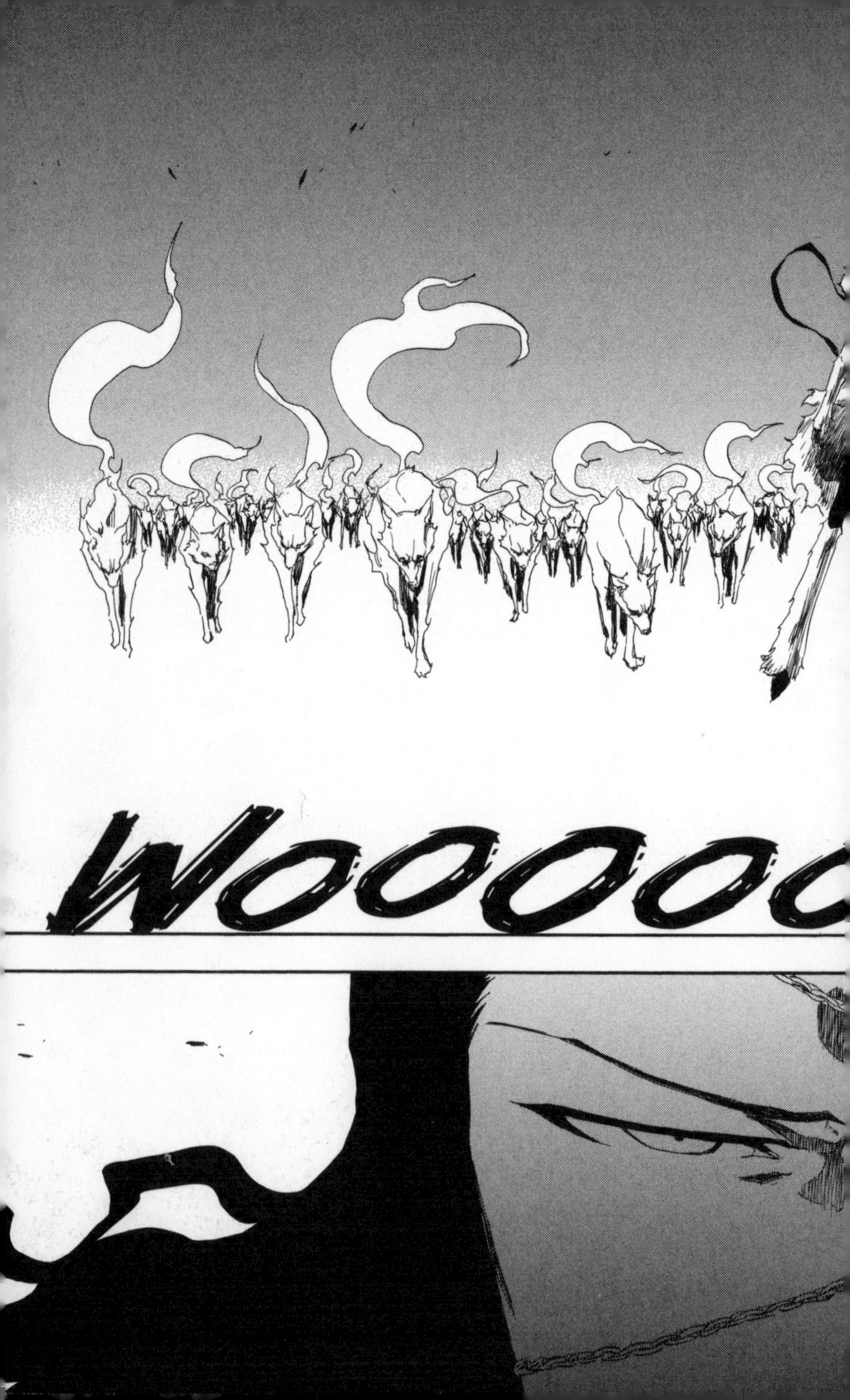
WOOOOO

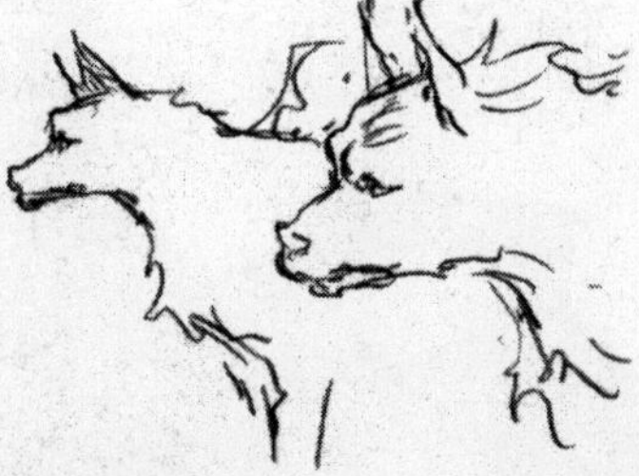

373. Wolves Ain't Howl Alone

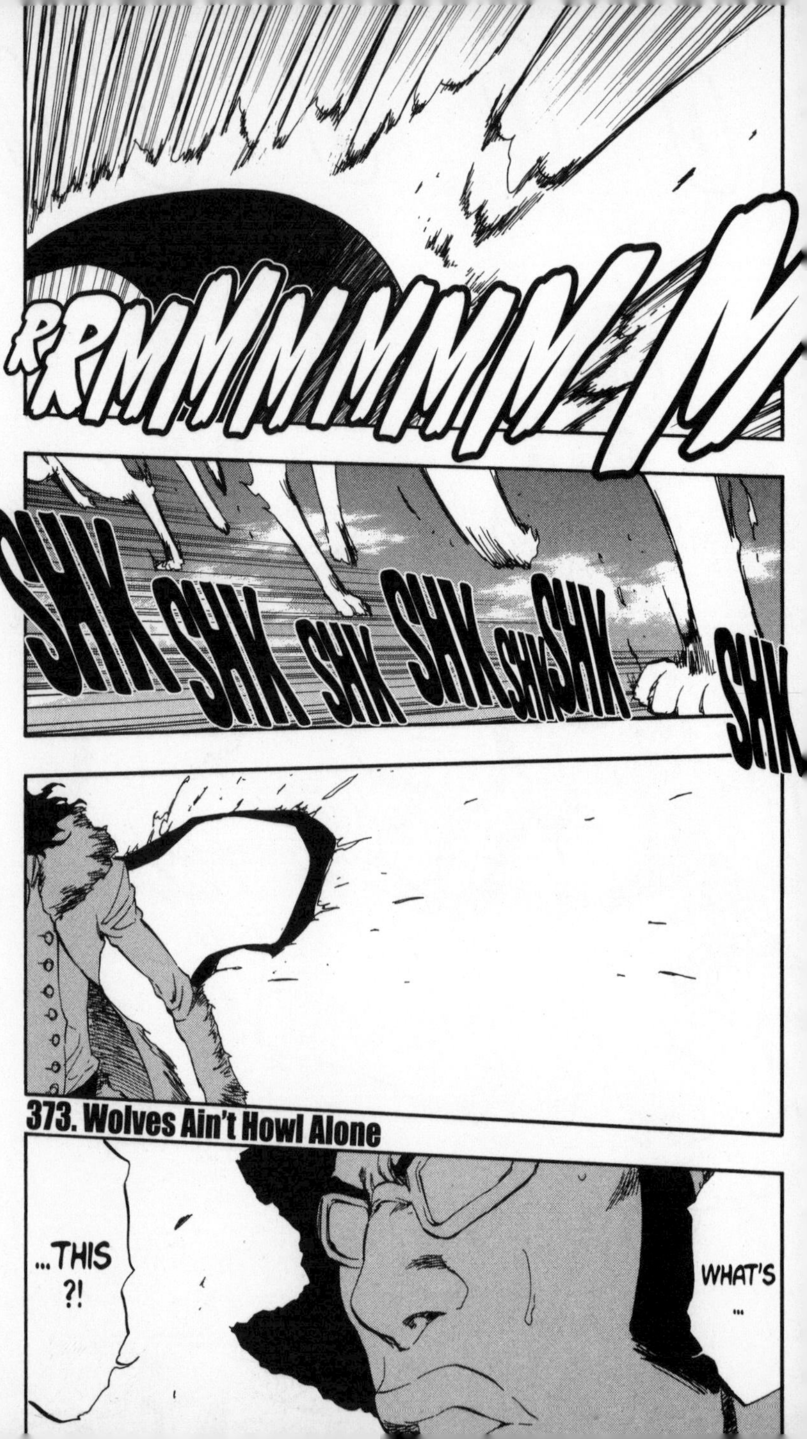
RRMMMMMMMMMMM
SHK SHK SHK SHK SHK SHK SHK
WHAT'S ...
...THIS ?!

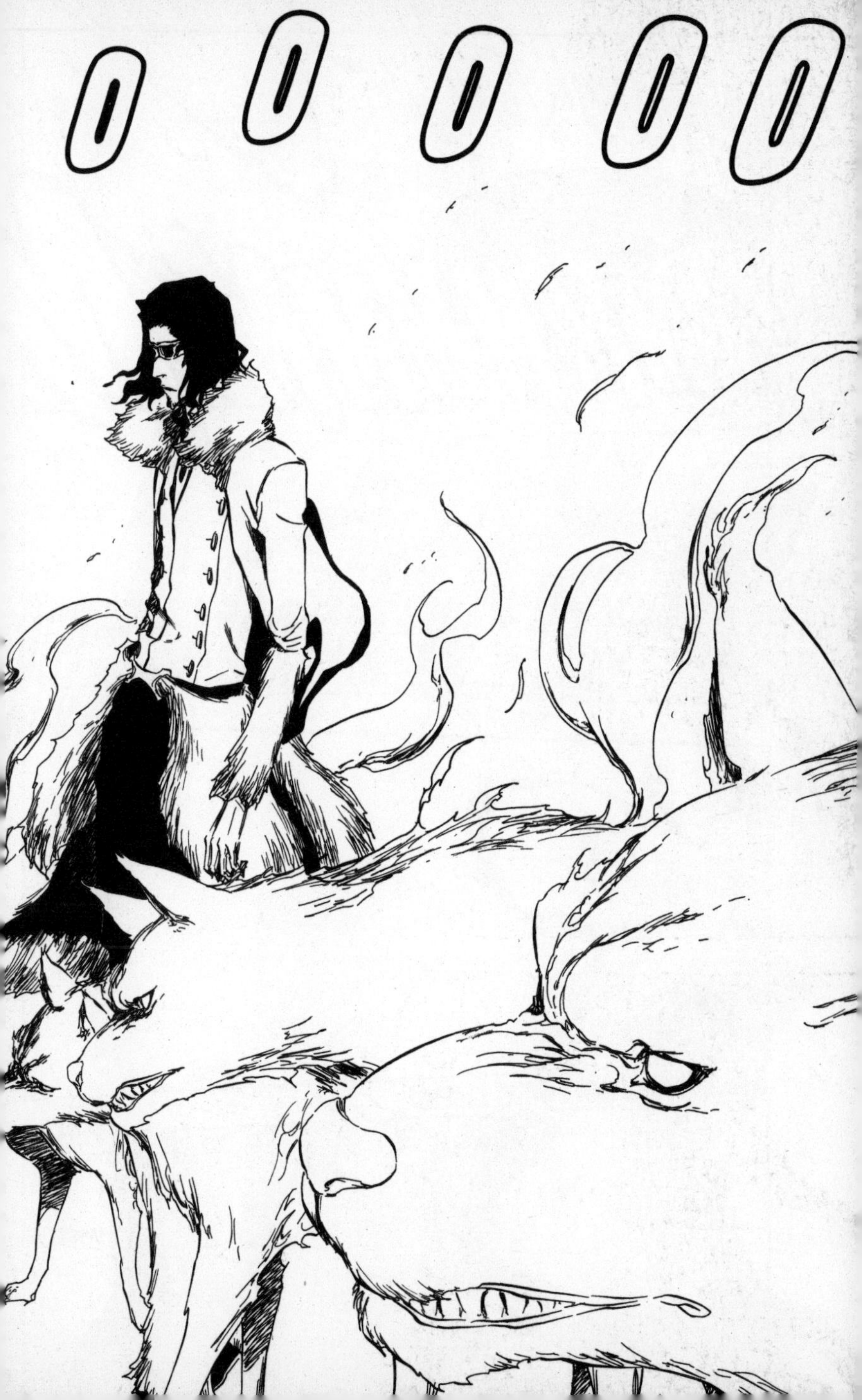
OOOOO

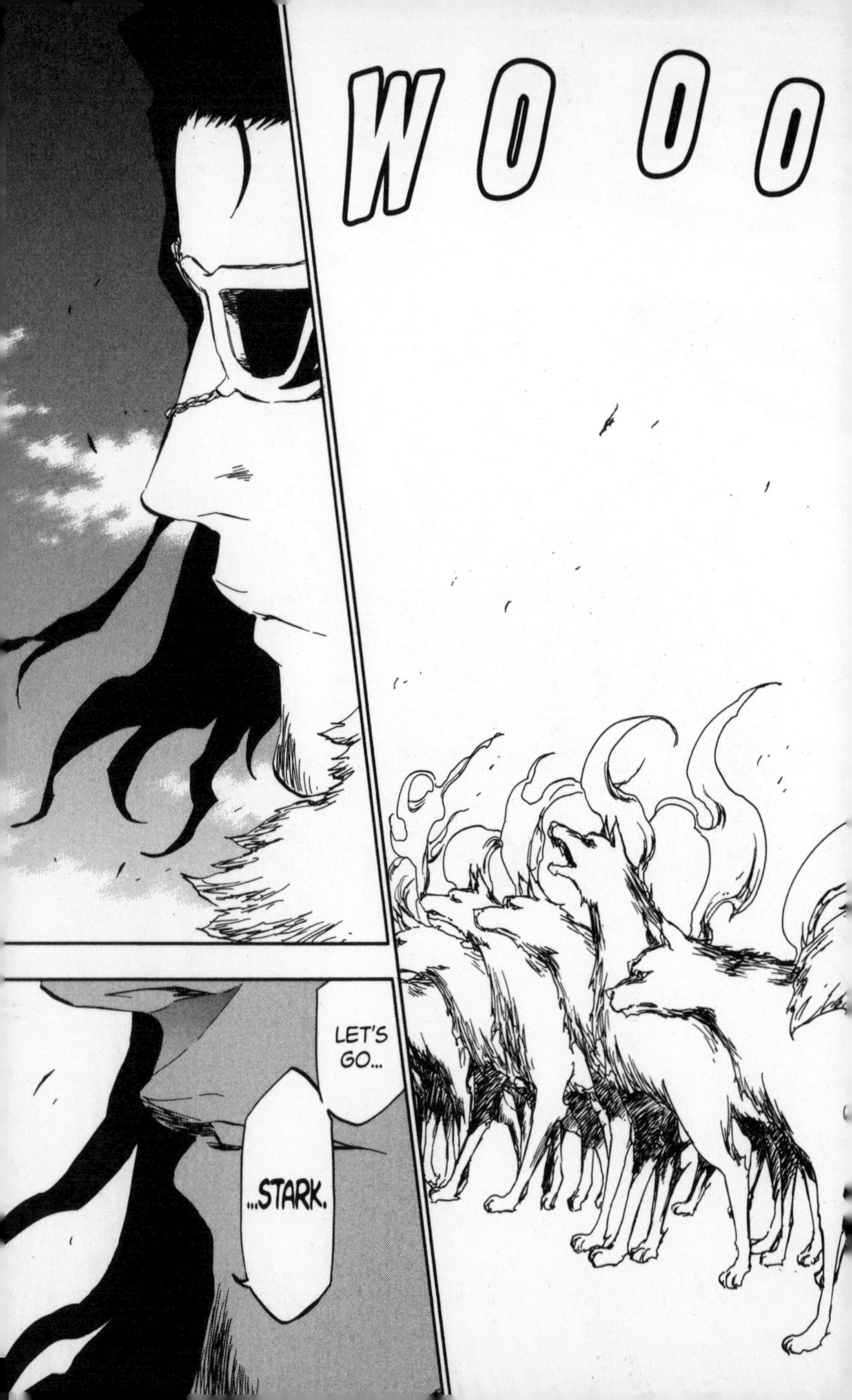
WOOO
LET'S GO...
...STARK.

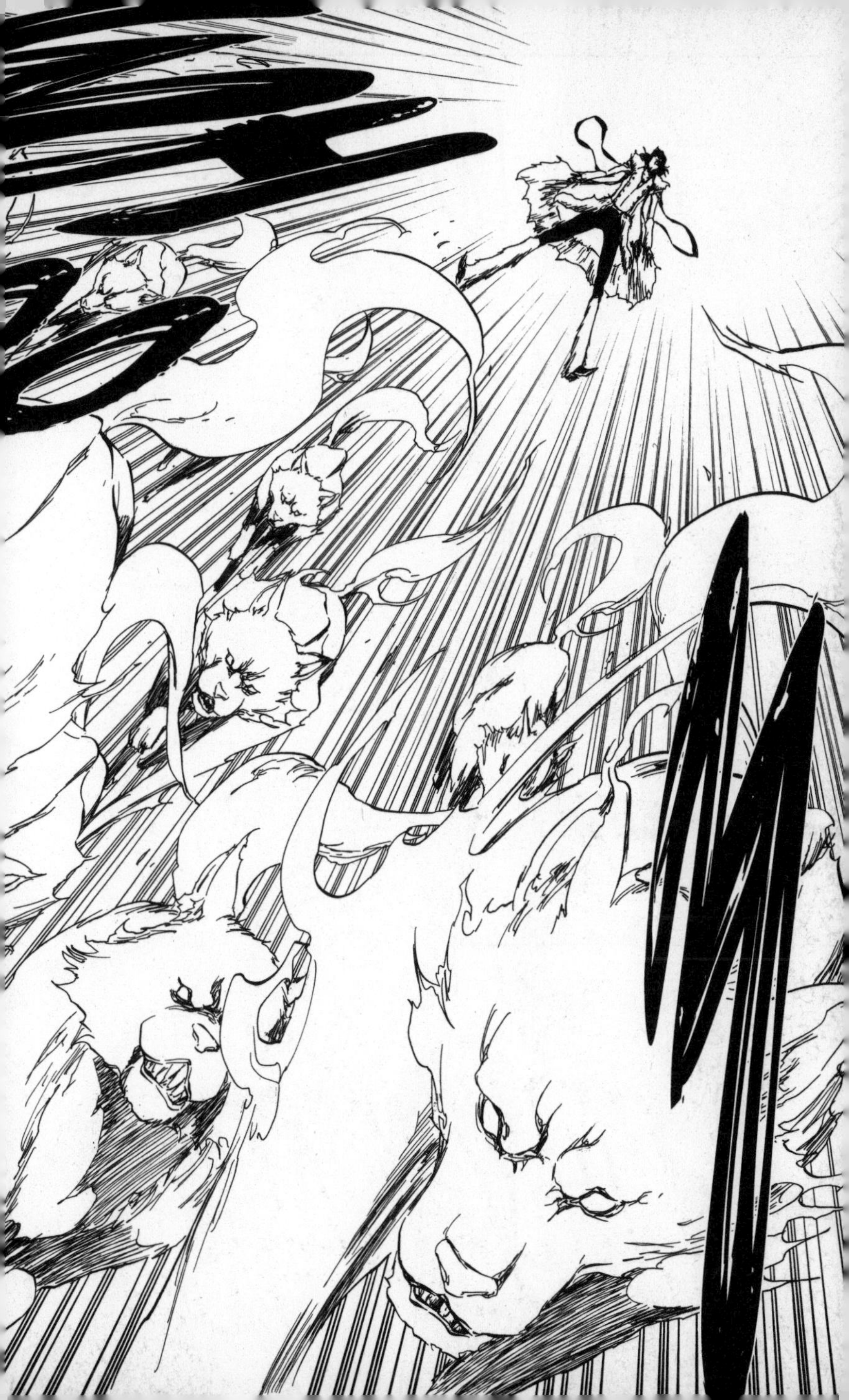

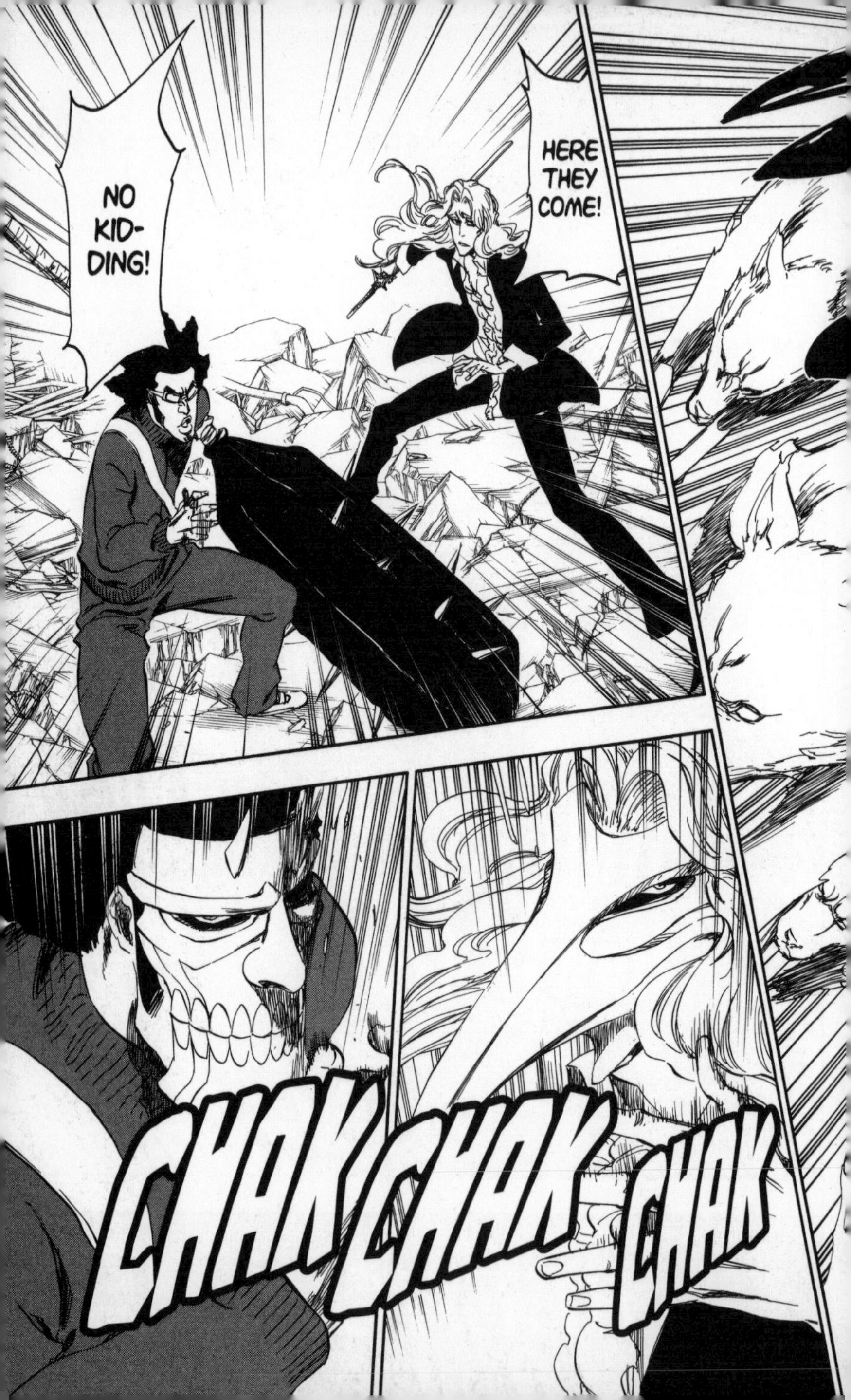
HERE THEY COME!
NO KID-DING!
CHAK CHAK CHAK

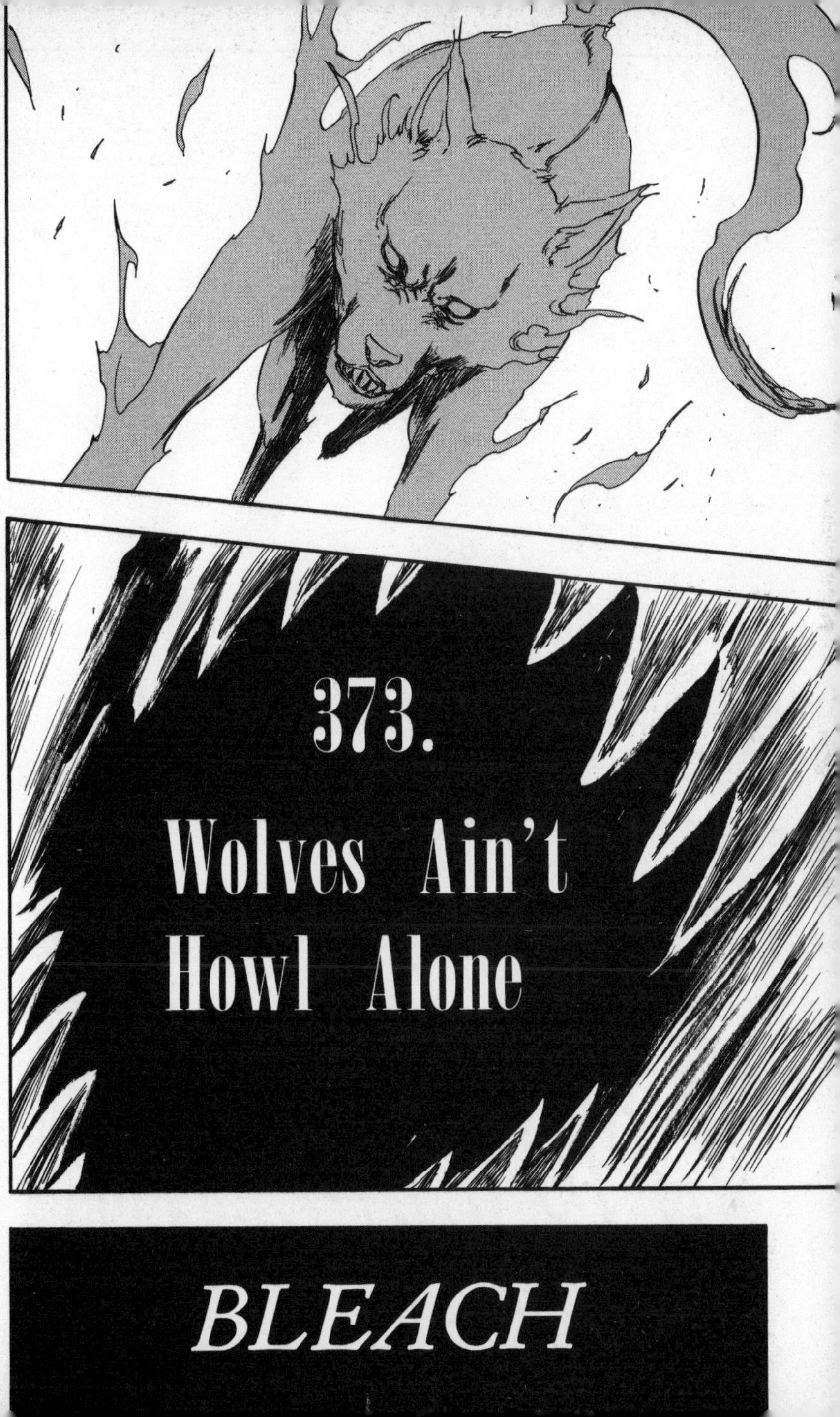
373.
Wolves Ain't Howl Alone
BLEACH

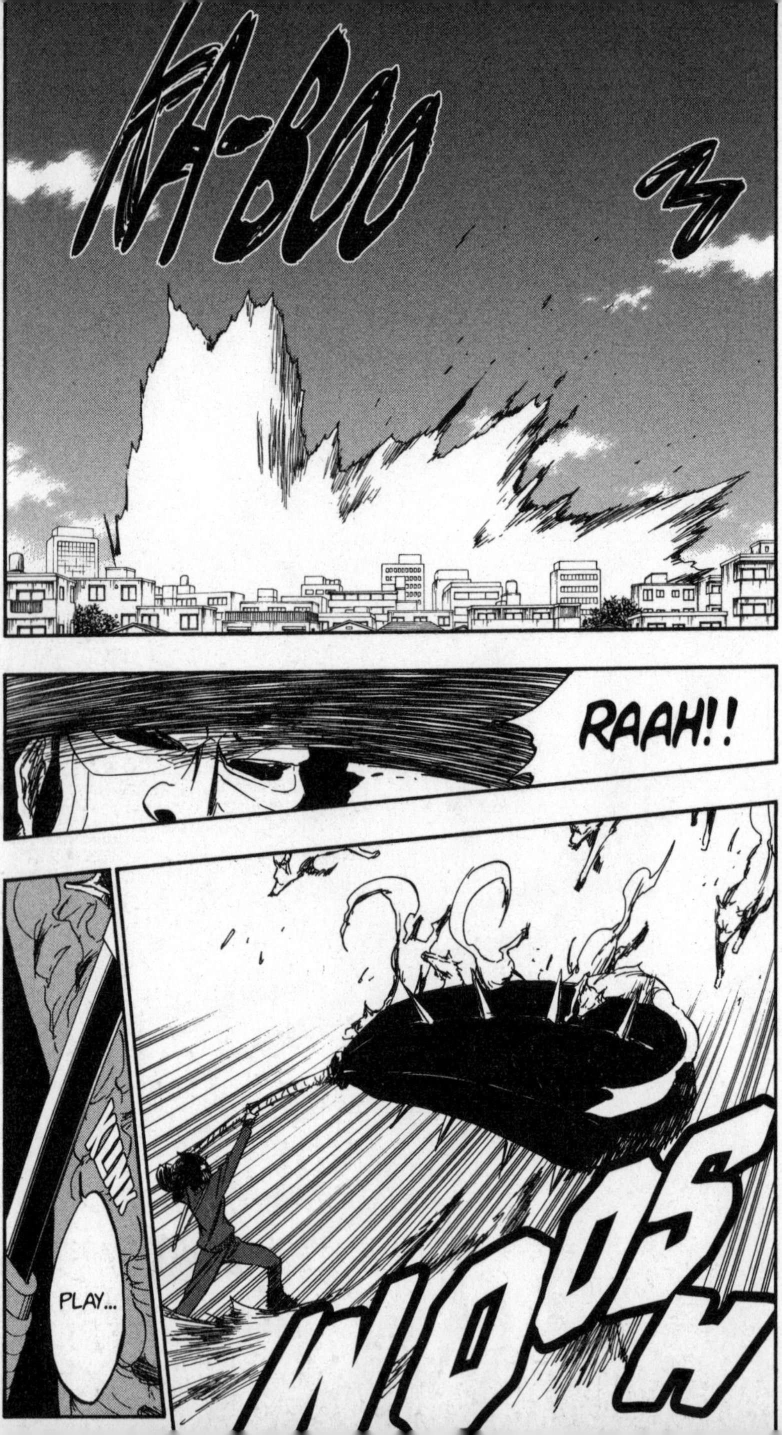
KA-BOOM
RAAH!!
KLINK
PLAY...

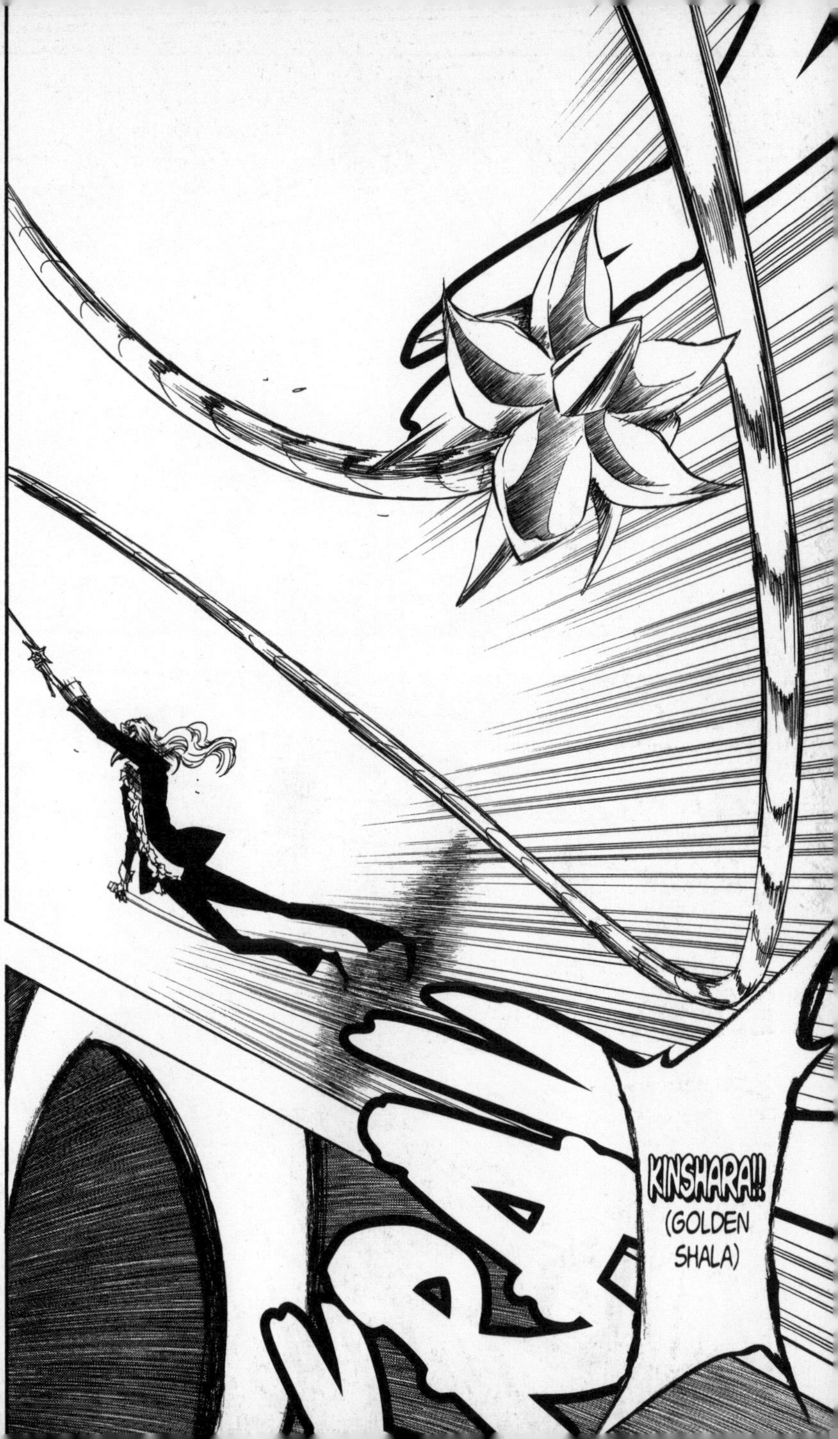
KINSHARA!!
(GOLDEN
SHALA)

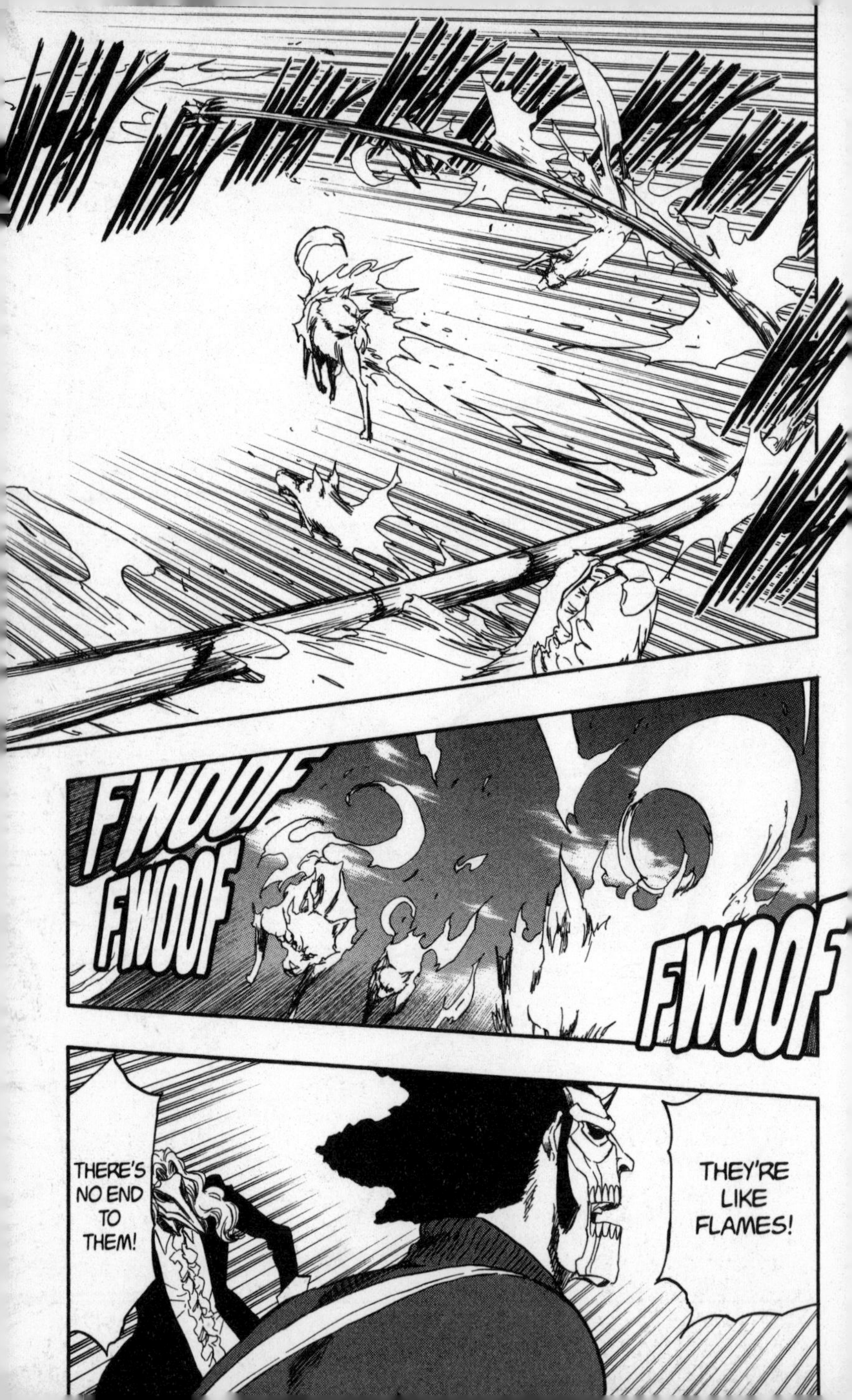

FWOOF
FWOOF
FWOOF
THEY'RE LIKE FLAMES!
THERE'S NO END TO THEM!

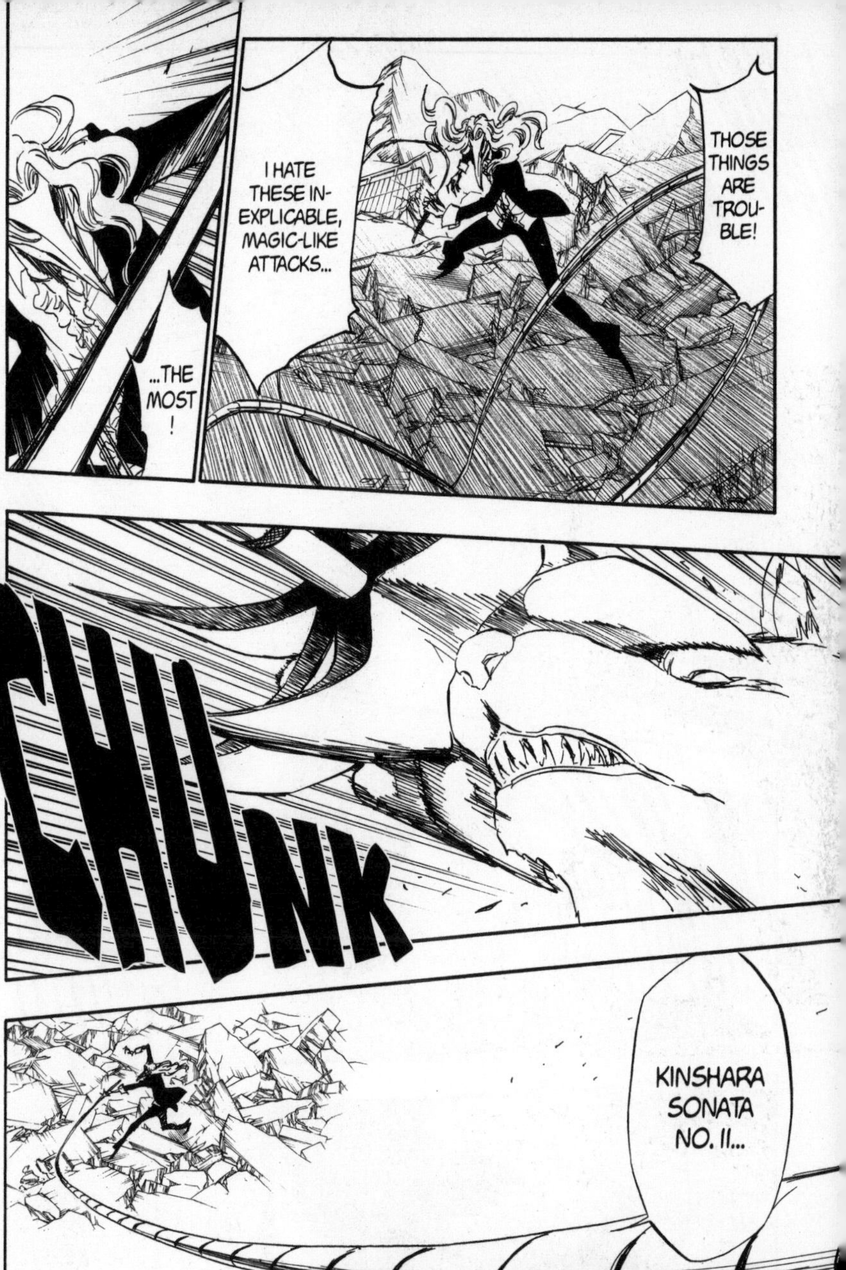
THOSE THINGS ARE TROUBLE!
I HATE THESE INEXPLICABLE, MAGIC-LIKE ATTACKS...
...THE MOST!
CHUNK
KINSHARA SONATA NO. II...

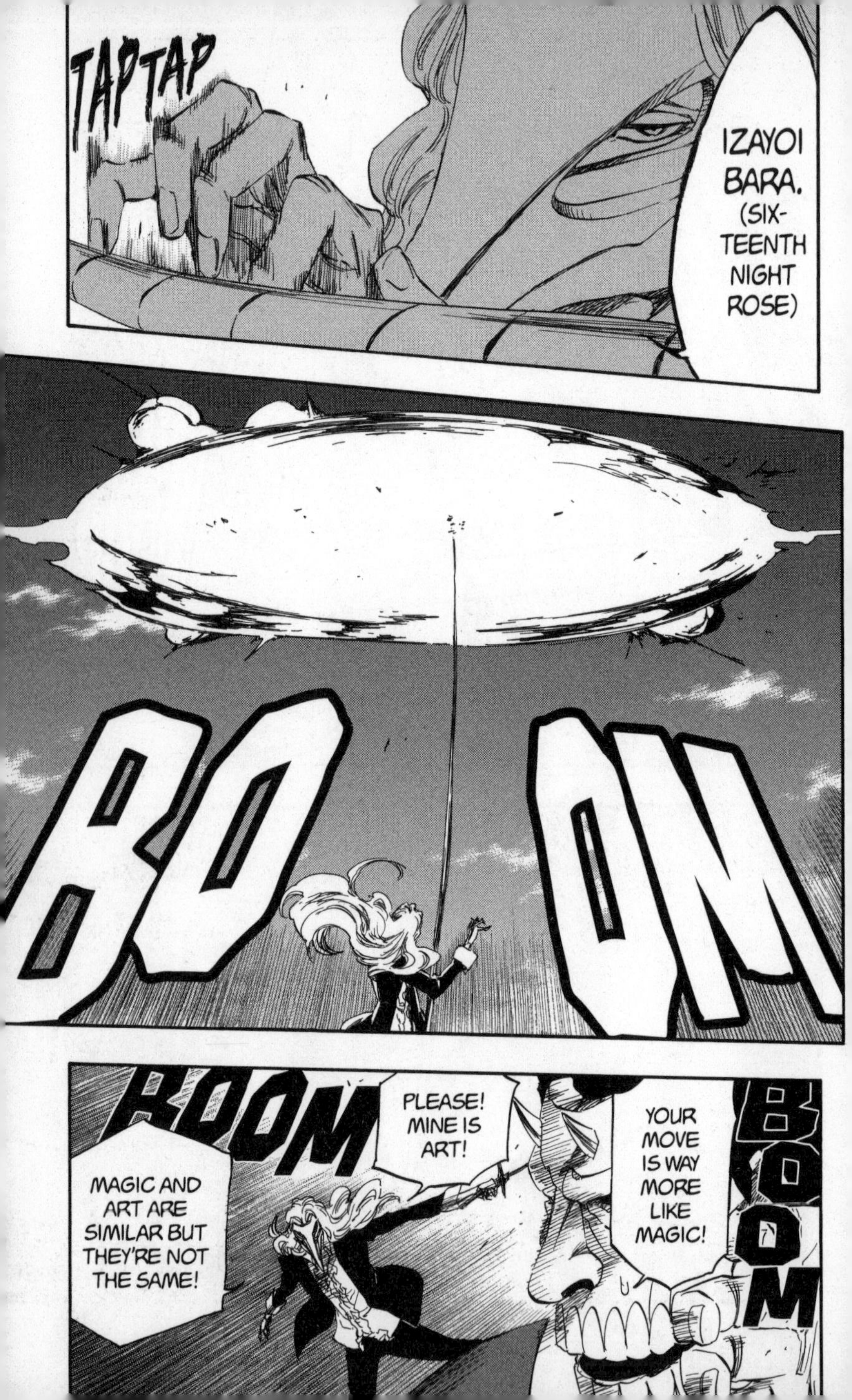
IZAYOI BARA. (SIXTEENTH NIGHT ROSE)
TAPTAP
BOOM
BOOM
YOUR MOVE IS WAY MORE LIKE MAGIC!
PLEASE! MINE IS ART!
BOOM
MAGIC AND ART ARE SIMILAR BUT THEY'RE NOT THE SAME!

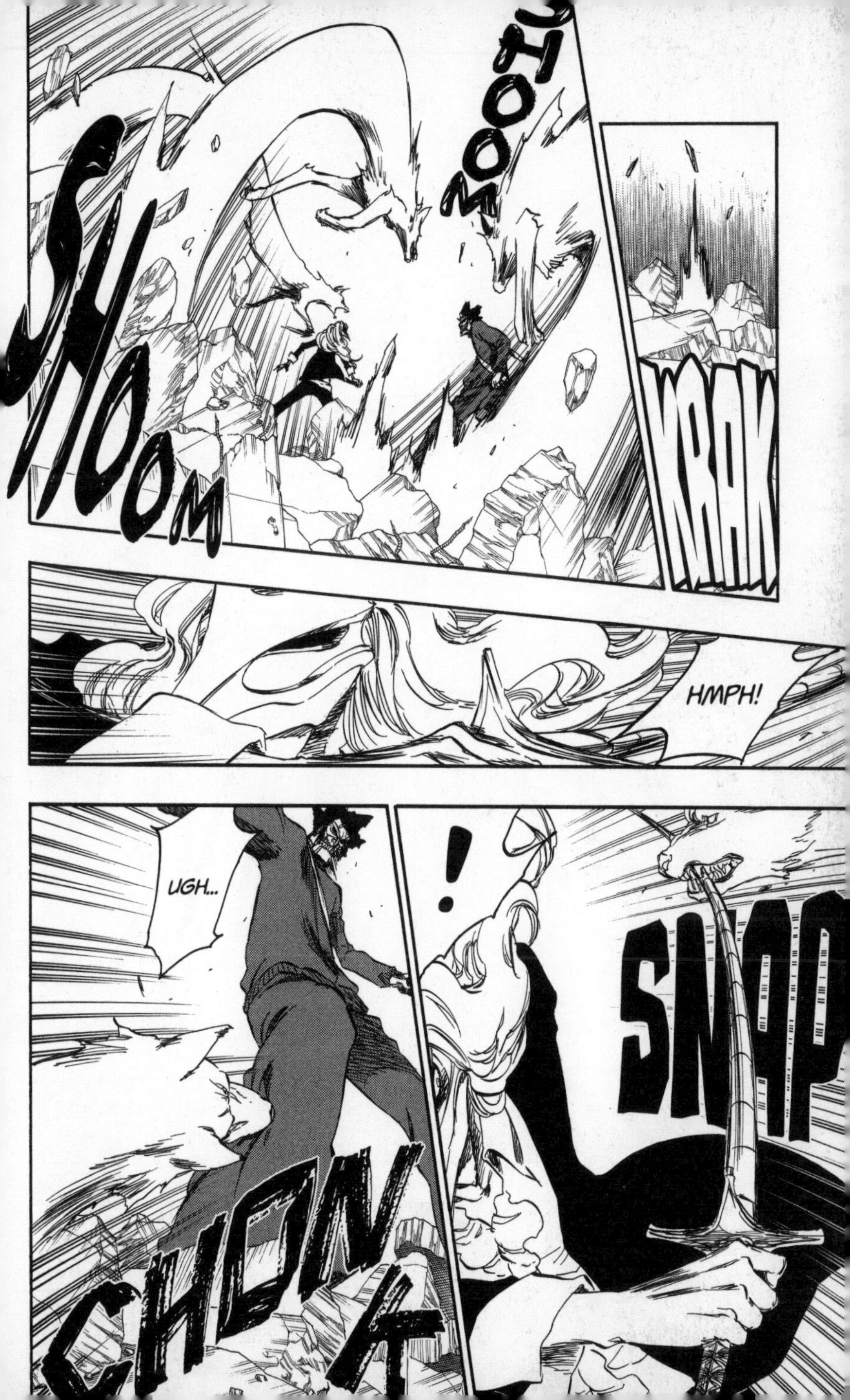
KRAK
SHOOM
SHOOM
HMPH!
!
SNAP
UGH...
CHOMK

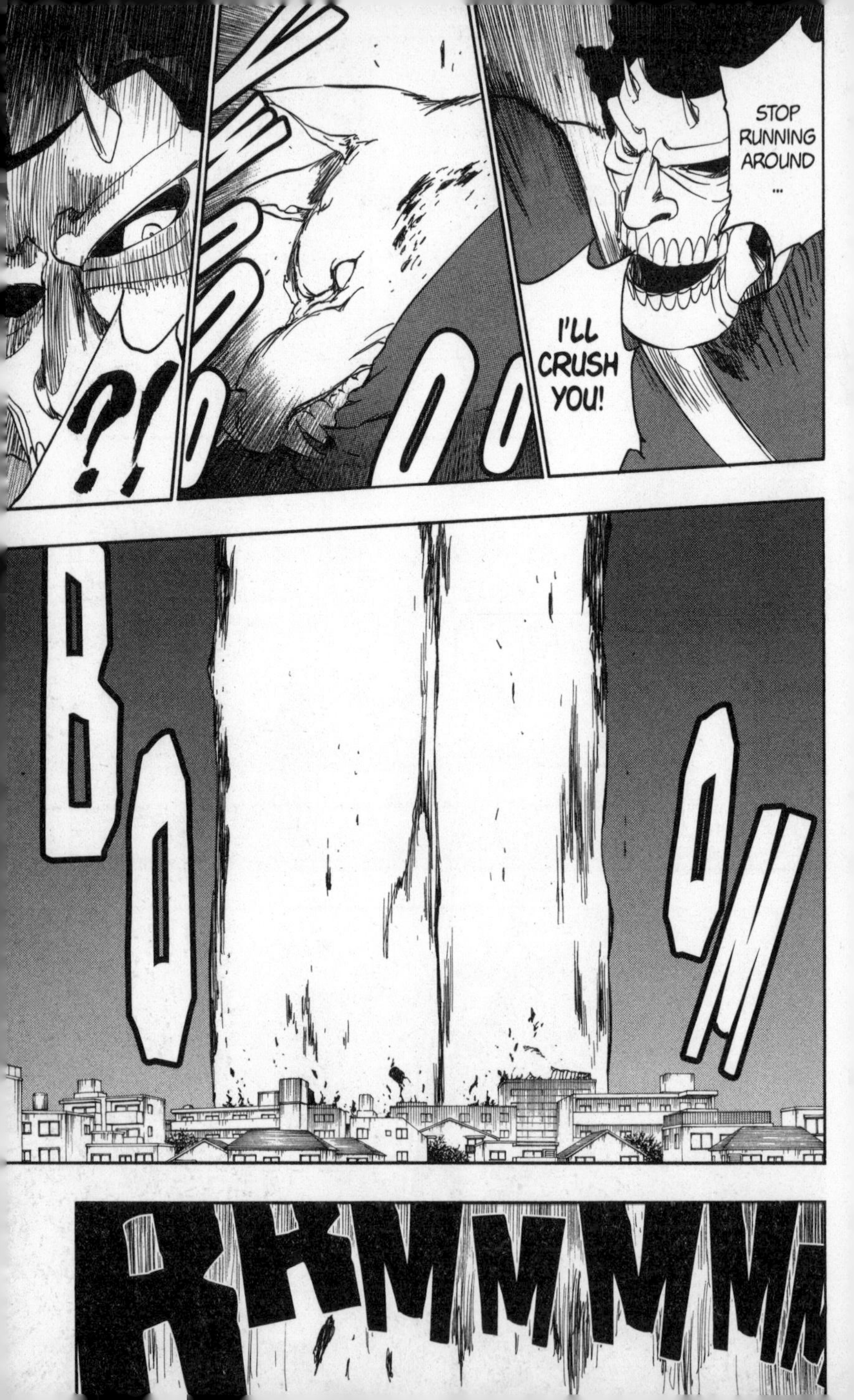
STOP RUNNING AROUND ...
I'LL CRUSH YOU!
BOOM

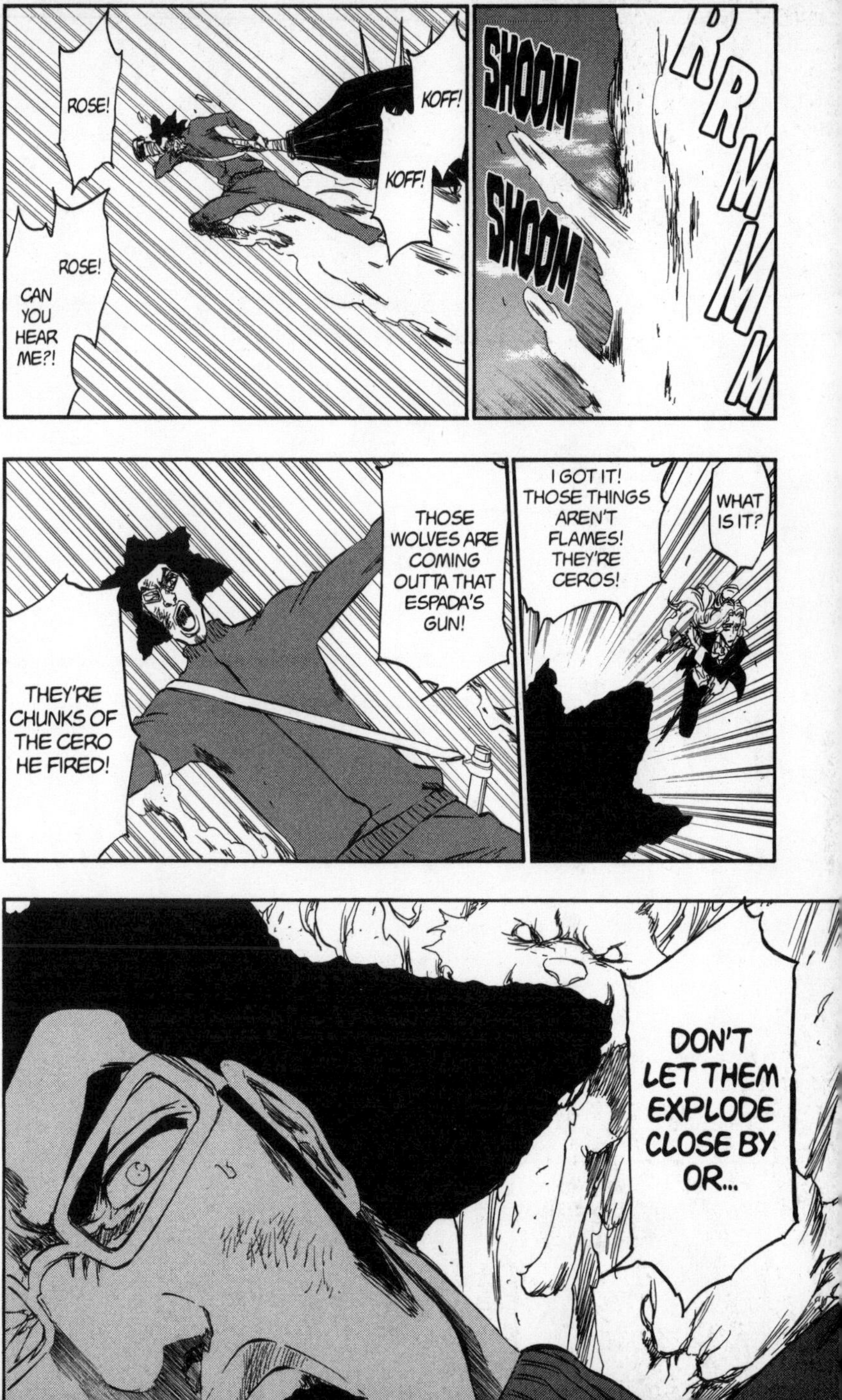
RRMMMM
SHOOM
SHOOM
KOFF!
KOFF!
ROSE!
ROSE! CAN YOU HEAR ME?!
WHAT IS IT?
I GOT IT! THOSE THINGS AREN'T FLAMES! THEY'RE CEROS!
THOSE WOLVES ARE COMING OUTTA THAT ESPADA'S GUN!
THEY'RE CHUNKS OF THE CERO HE FIRED!
DON'T LET THEM EXPLODE CLOSE BY OR...

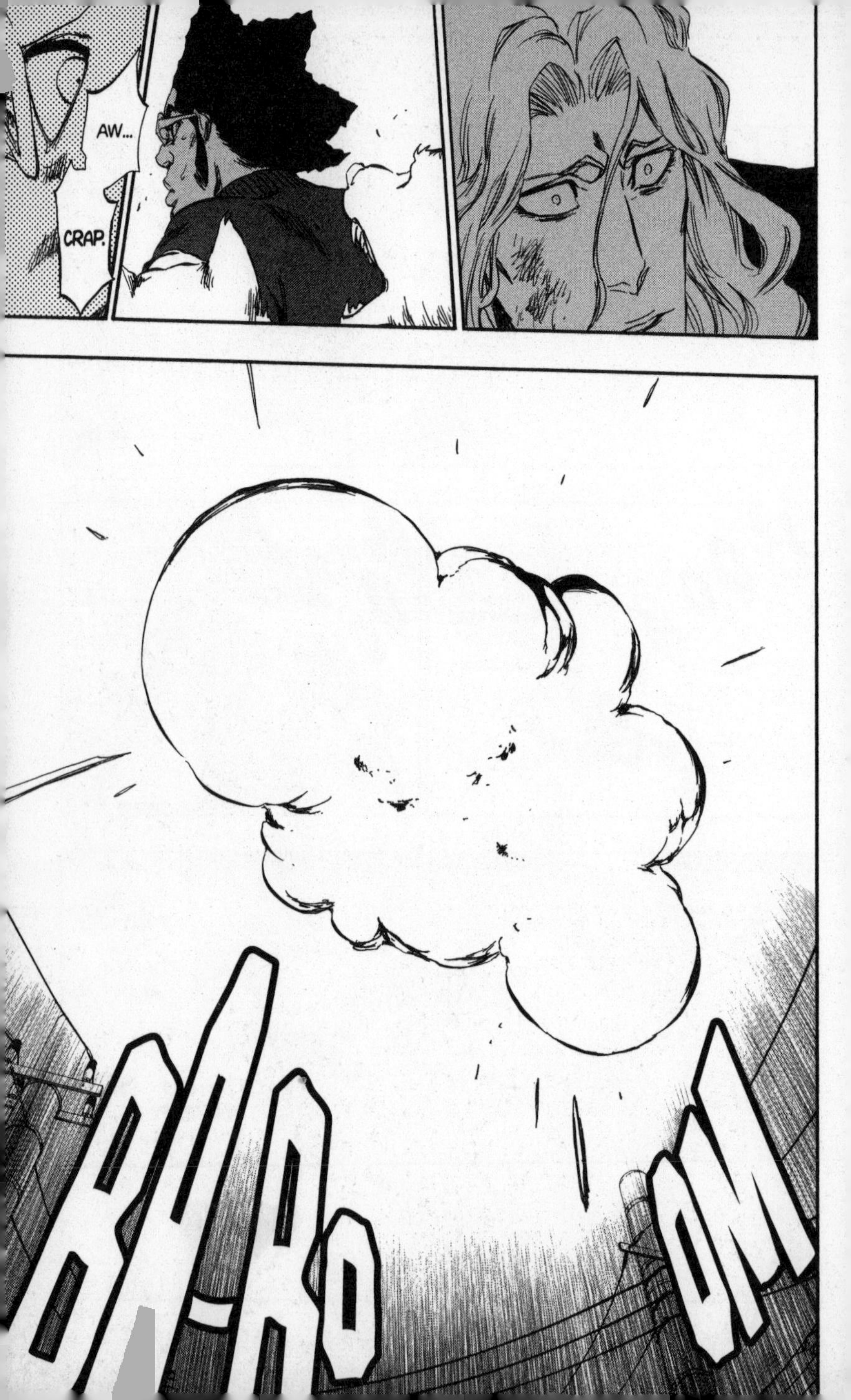
AW...
CRAP.
BAB-ROOM

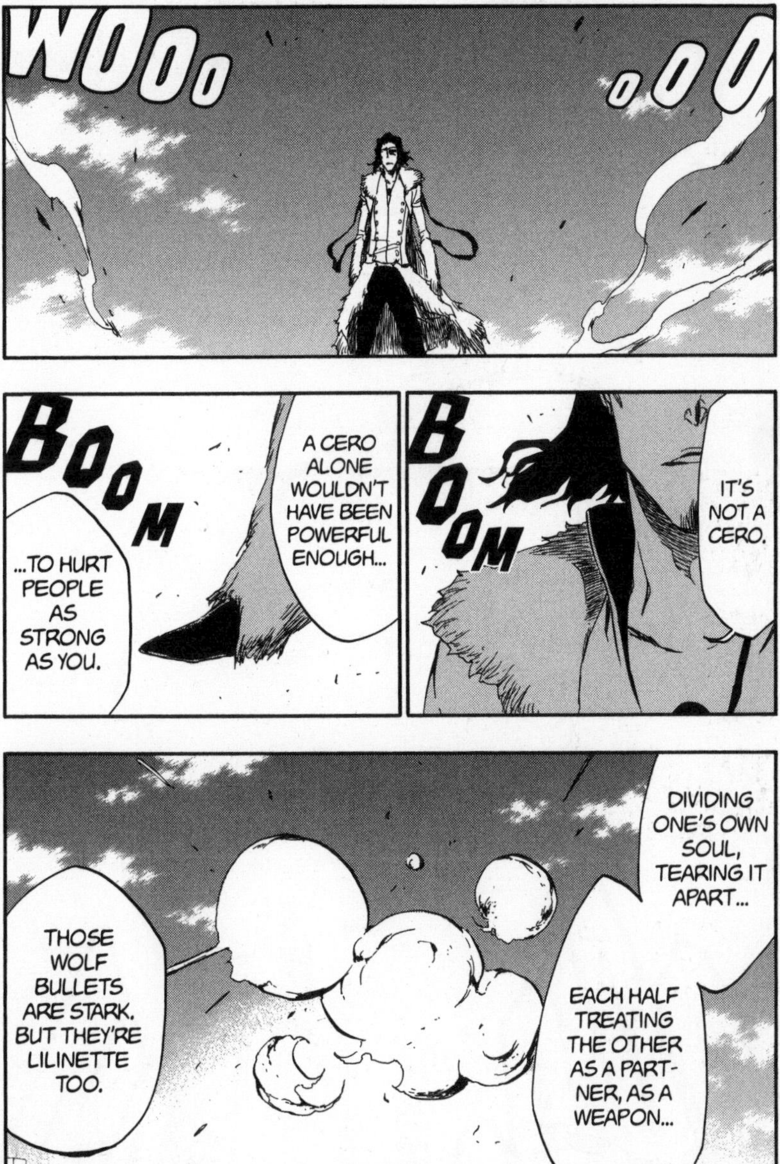
WOOo
oOO
IT'S NOT A CERO.
BOOM
A CERO ALONE WOULDN'T HAVE BEEN POWERFUL ENOUGH...
BOOM
...TO HURT PEOPLE AS STRONG AS YOU.
DIVIDING ONE'S OWN SOUL, TEARING IT APART...
EACH HALF TREATING THE OTHER AS A PART-NER, AS A WEAPON...
THOSE WOLF BULLETS ARE STARK. BUT THEY'RE LILINETTE TOO.

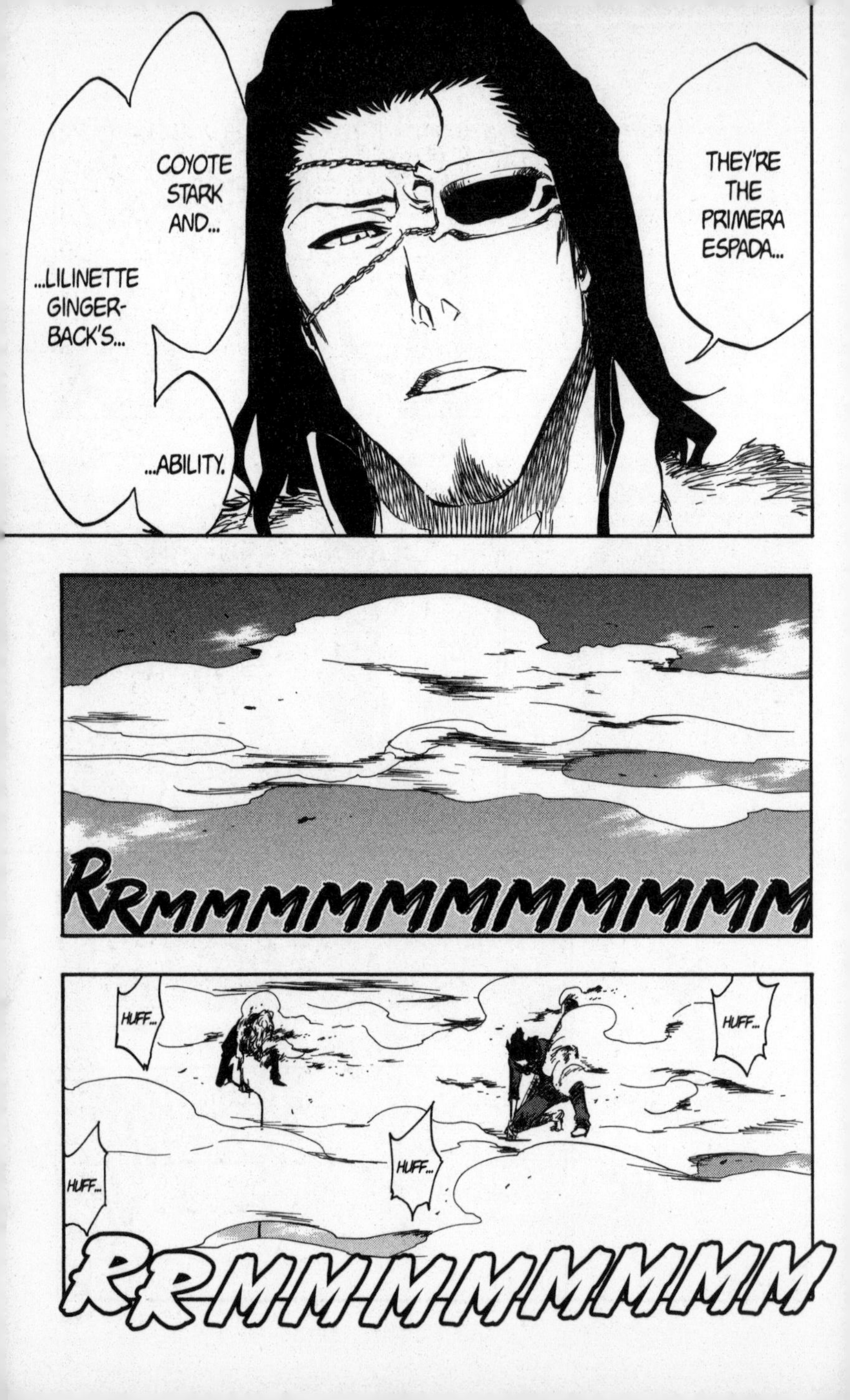
THEY'RE THE PRIMERA ESPADA...
COYOTE STARK AND...
...LILINETTE GINGER-BACK'S...
...ABILITY.
RRMMMMMMMMMMMMMM
HUFF...
HUFF...
HUFF...
HUFF...
RRMMMMMMMMMMMM

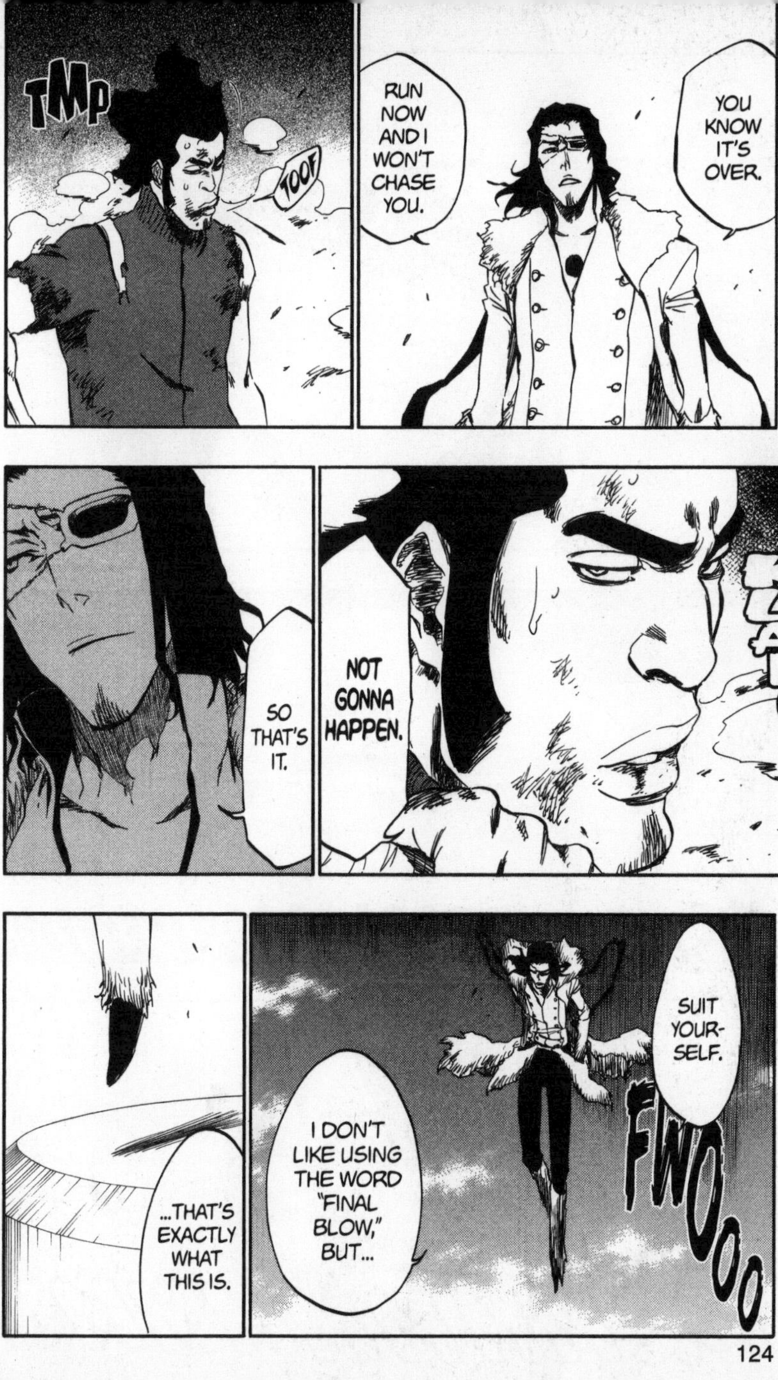
YOU KNOW IT'S OVER.
RUN NOW AND I WON'T CHASE YOU.
TMP
TOOF
KLANG
NOT GONNA HAPPEN.
SO THAT'S IT.
SUIT YOUR-SELF.
FWOOOO
I DON'T LIKE USING THE WORD "FINAL BLOW," BUT...
...THAT'S EXACTLY WHAT THIS IS.

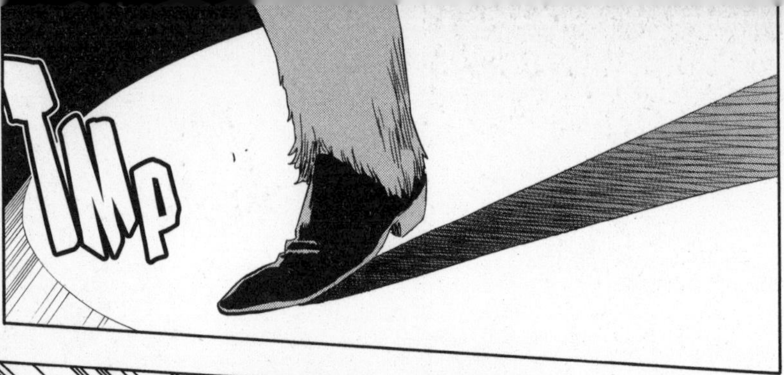
TMP

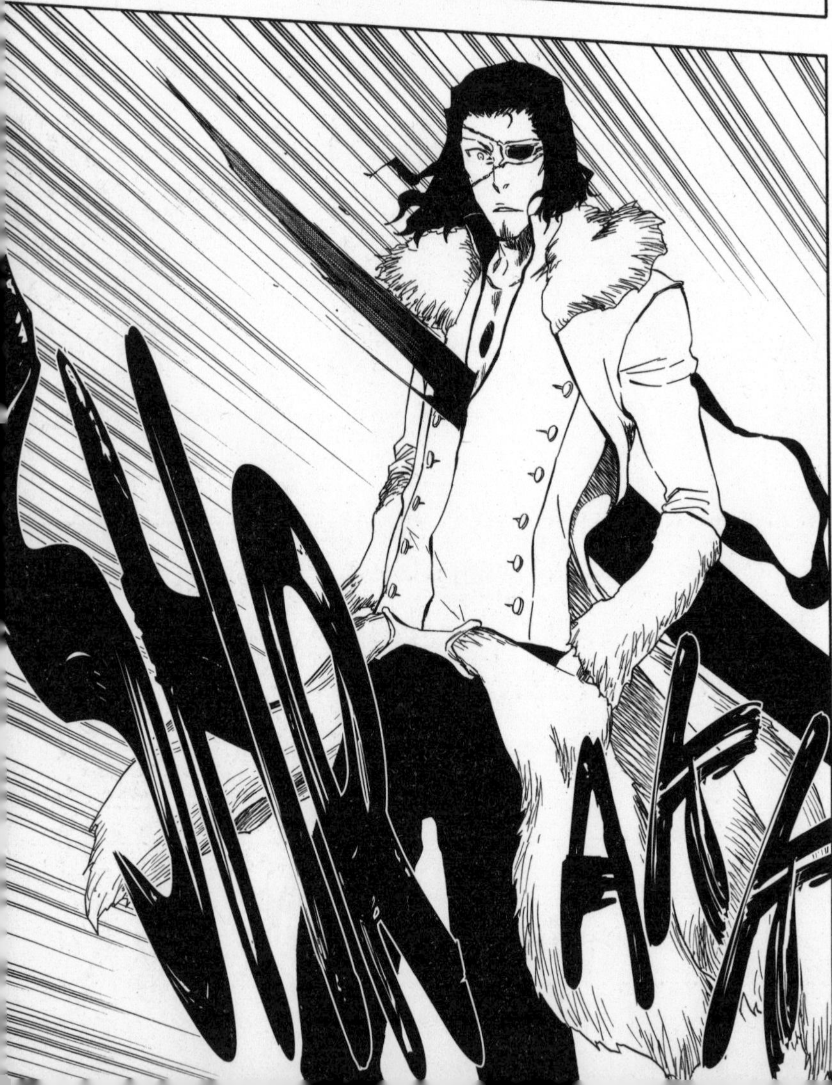
SHRAKK

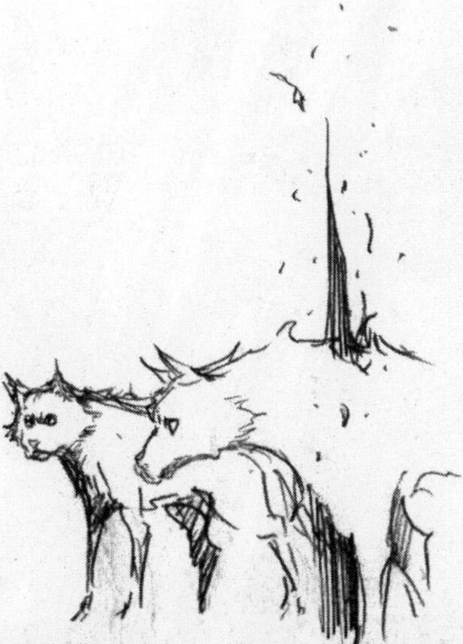

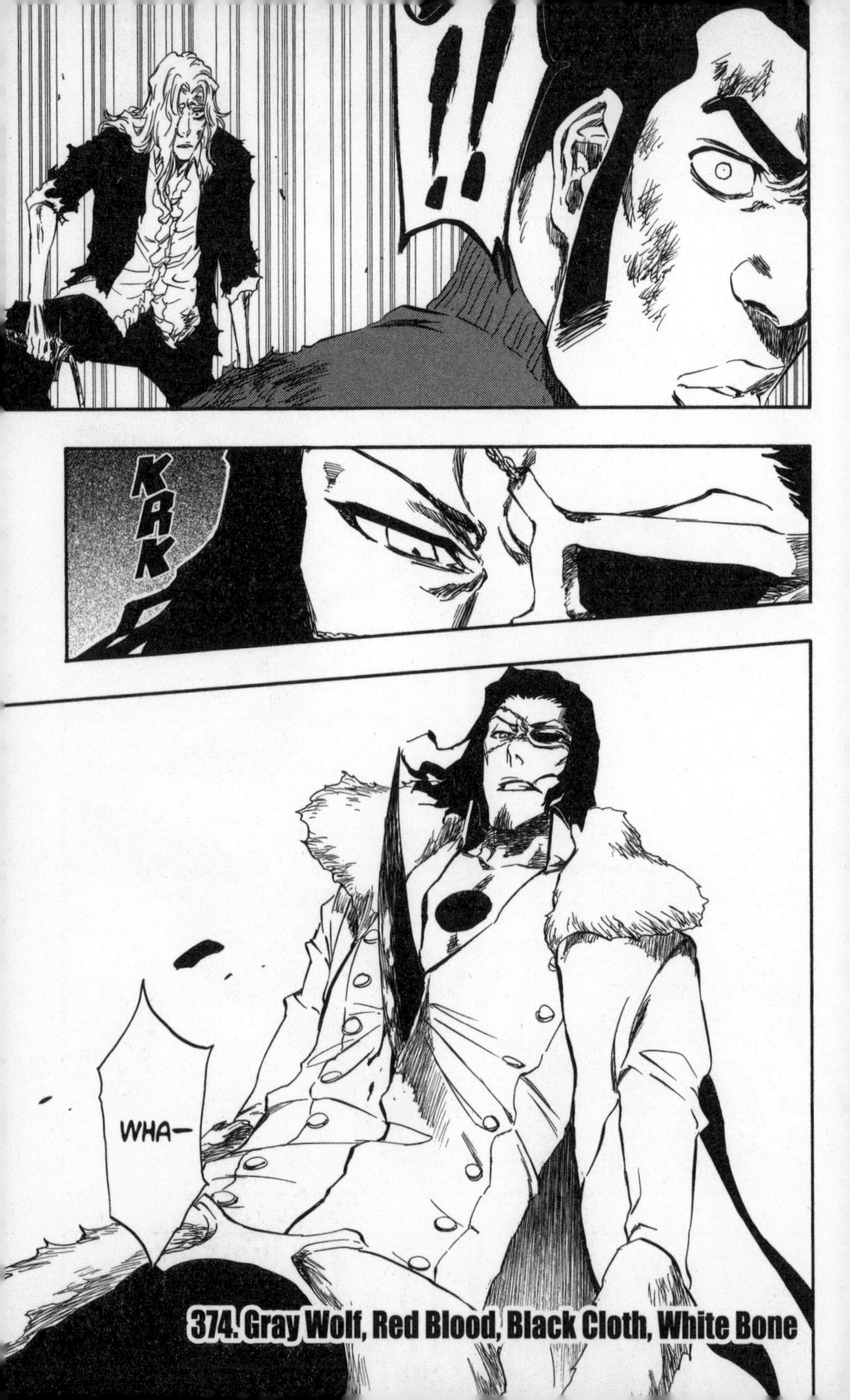
!!
KRK
WHA-
374. Gray Wolf, Red Blood, Black Cloth, White Bone

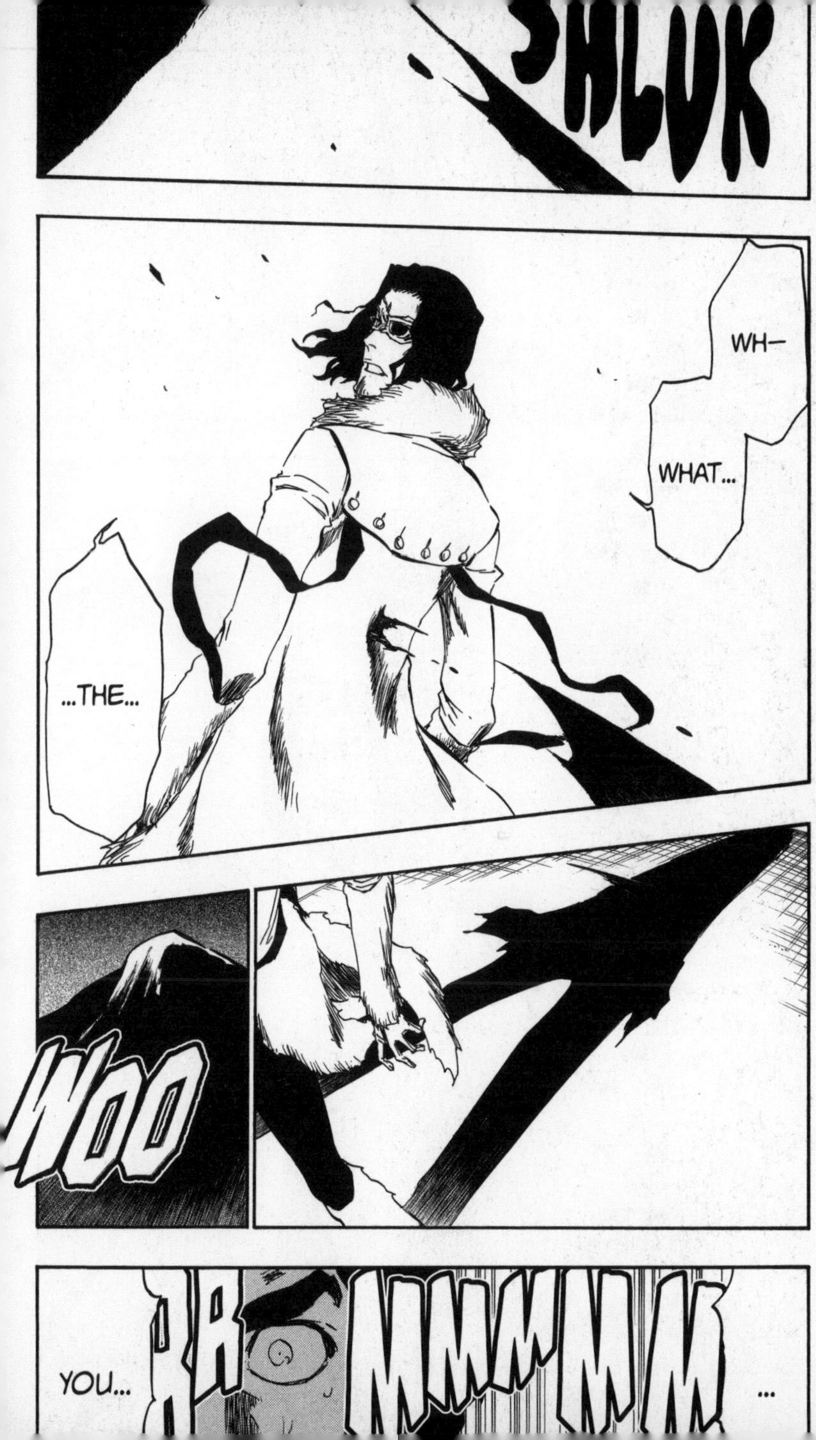
SHLUK
WH—
WHAT...
...THE...
WOO
...
RAMMMMMM
YOU...

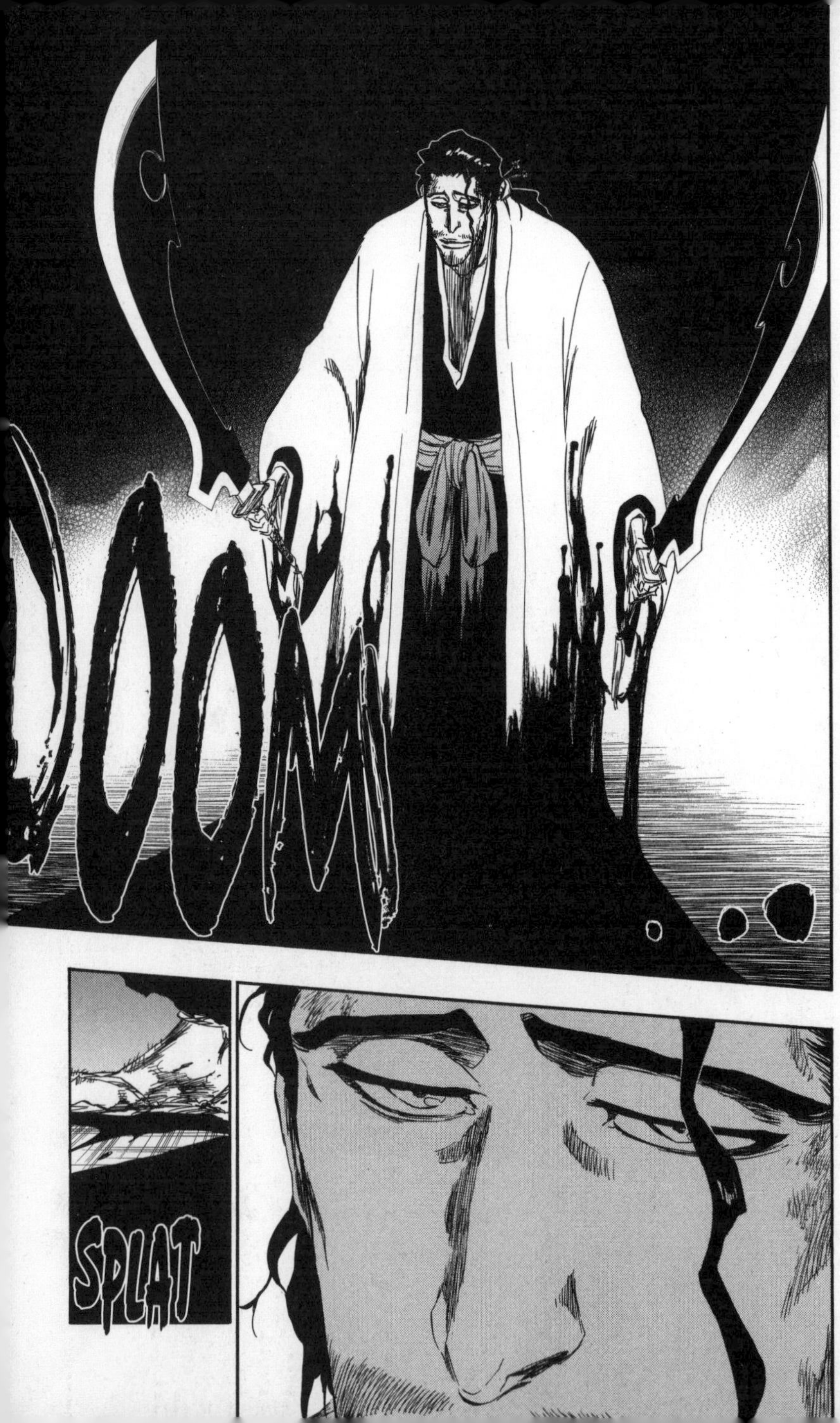
DOOM...
SPLAT

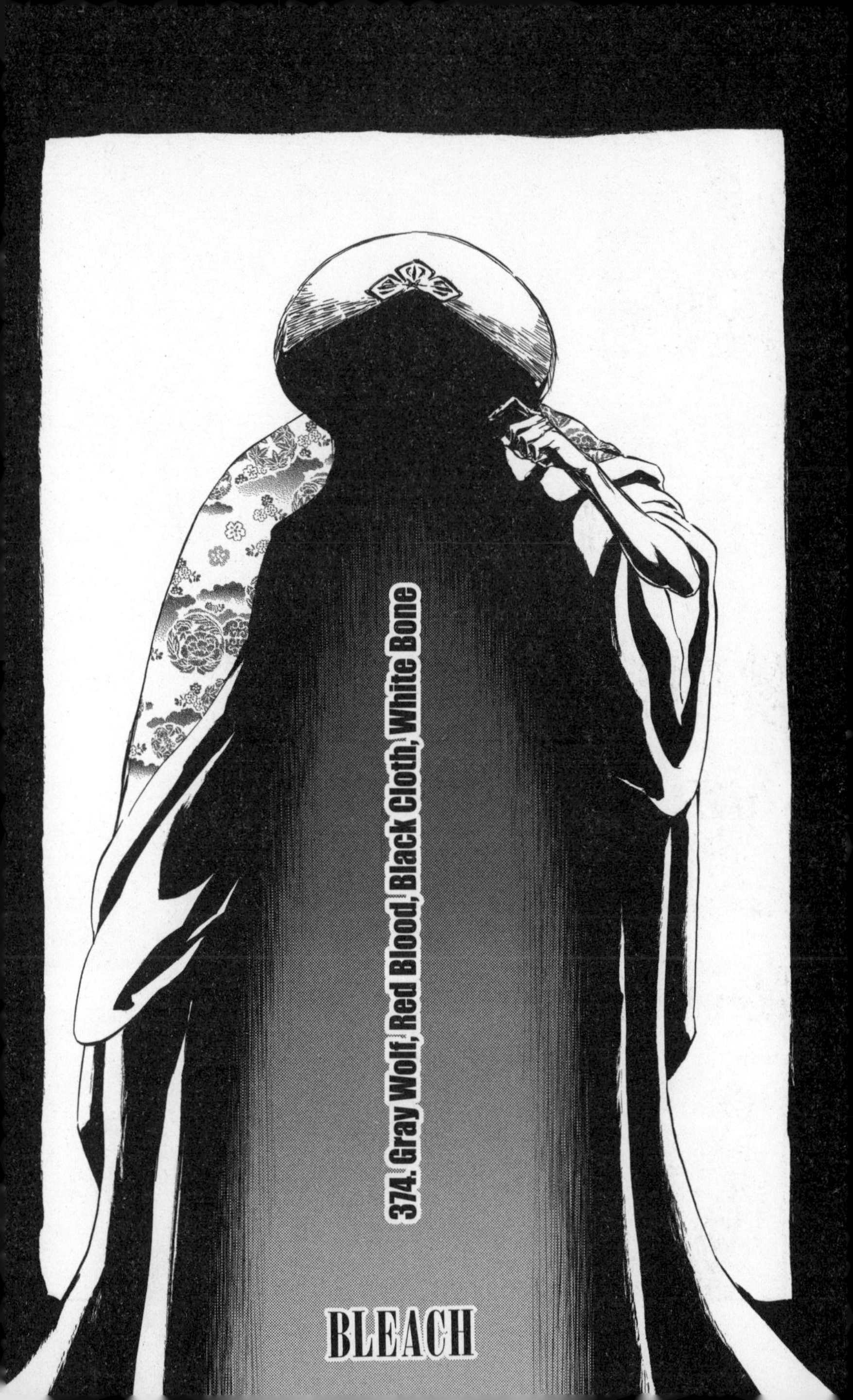
374. Gray Wolf, Red Blood, Black Cloth, White Bone
BLEACH

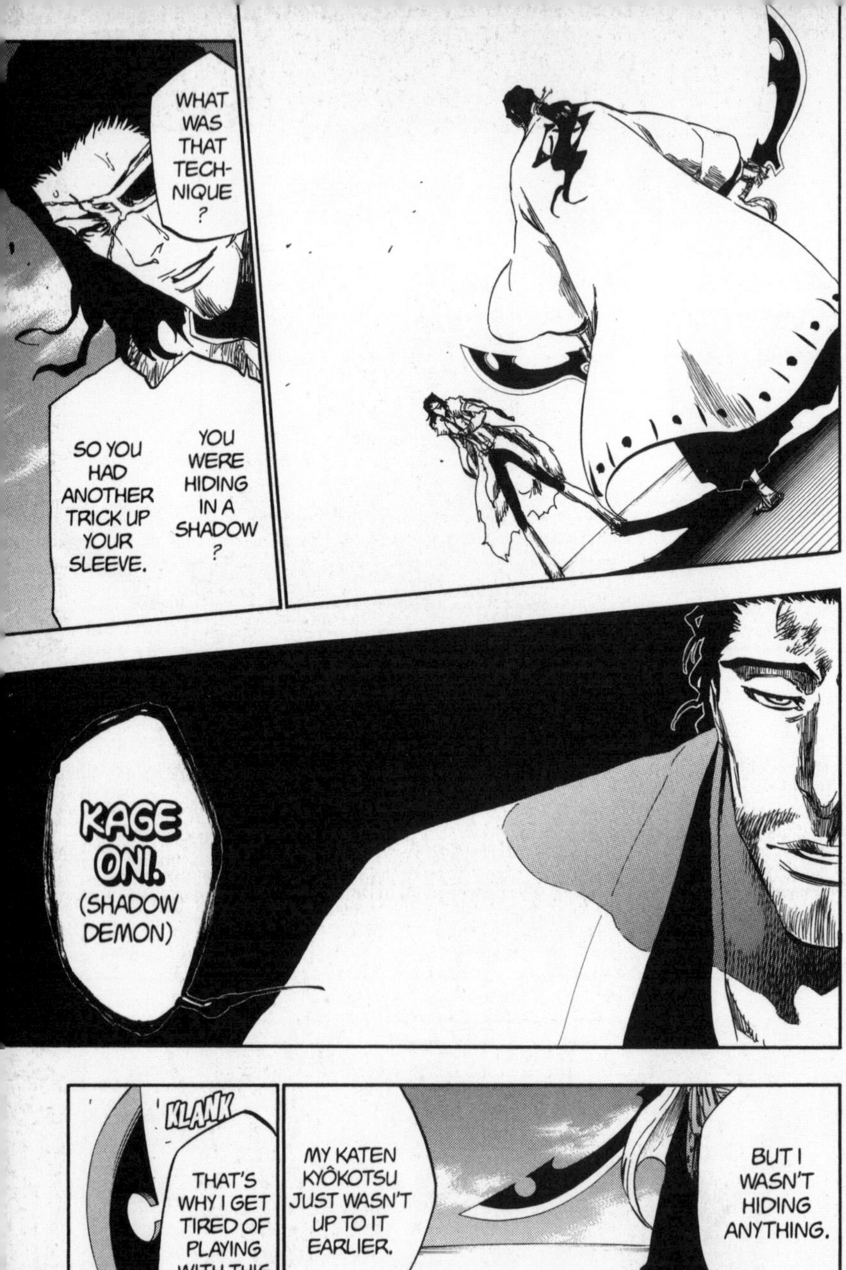
WHAT WAS THAT TECHNIQUE?
YOU WERE HIDING IN A SHADOW?
SO YOU HAD ANOTHER TRICK UP YOUR SLEEVE.
KAGE ONI. (SHADOW DEMON)
BUT I WASN'T HIDING ANYTHING.
MY KATEN KYÔKOTSU JUST WASN'T UP TO IT EARLIER.
KLANK
THAT'S WHY I GET TIRED OF PLAYING WITH THIS CHILD.

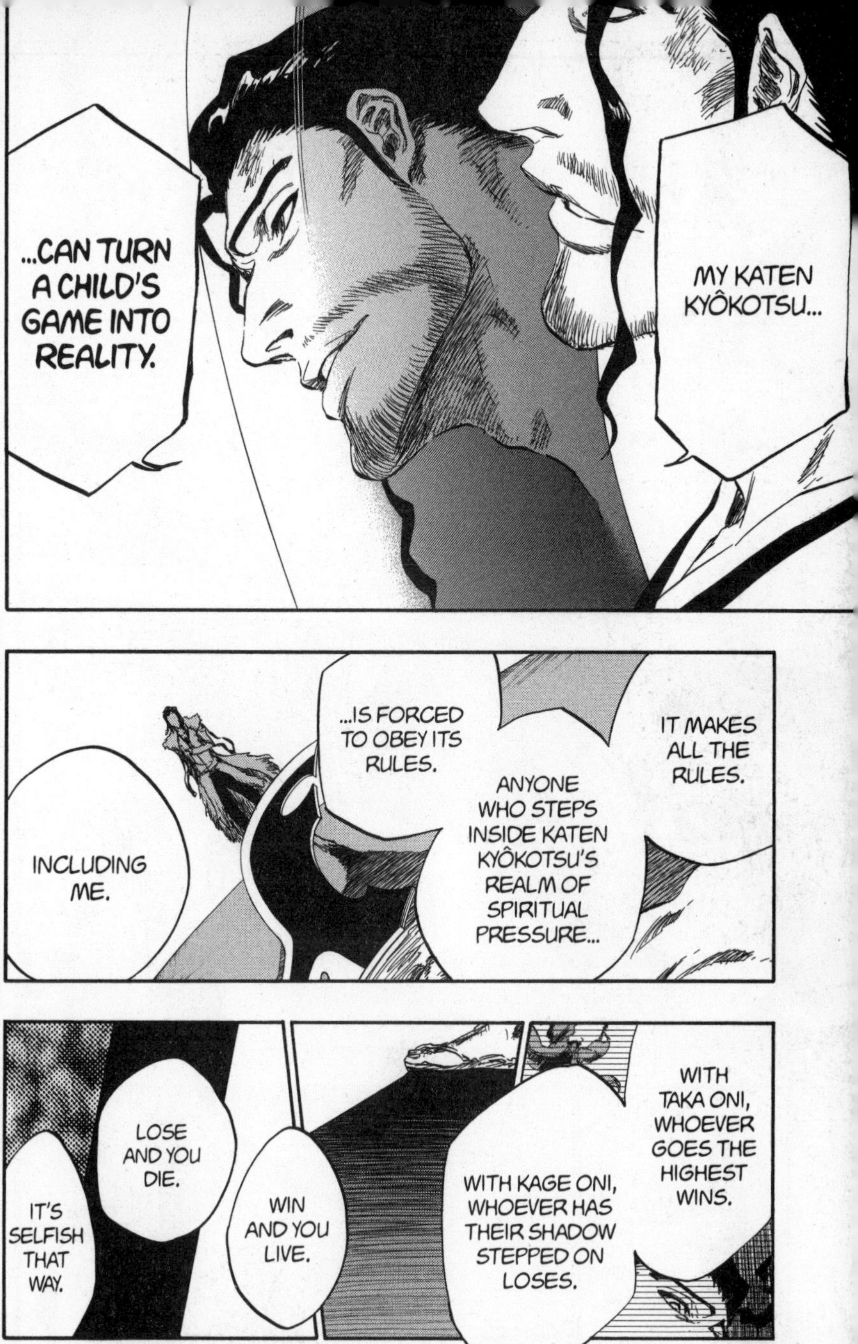

MY KATEN KYÔKOTSU...
...CAN TURN A CHILD'S GAME INTO REALITY.
IT MAKES ALL THE RULES.
ANYONE WHO STEPS INSIDE KATEN KYÔKOTSU'S REALM OF SPIRITUAL PRESSURE...
...IS FORCED TO OBEY ITS RULES.
INCLUDING ME.
WITH TAKA ONI, WHOEVER GOES THE HIGHEST WINS.
WITH KAGE ONI, WHOEVER HAS THEIR SHADOW STEPPED ON LOSES.
WIN AND YOU LIVE.
LOSE AND YOU DIE.
IT'S SELFISH THAT WAY.

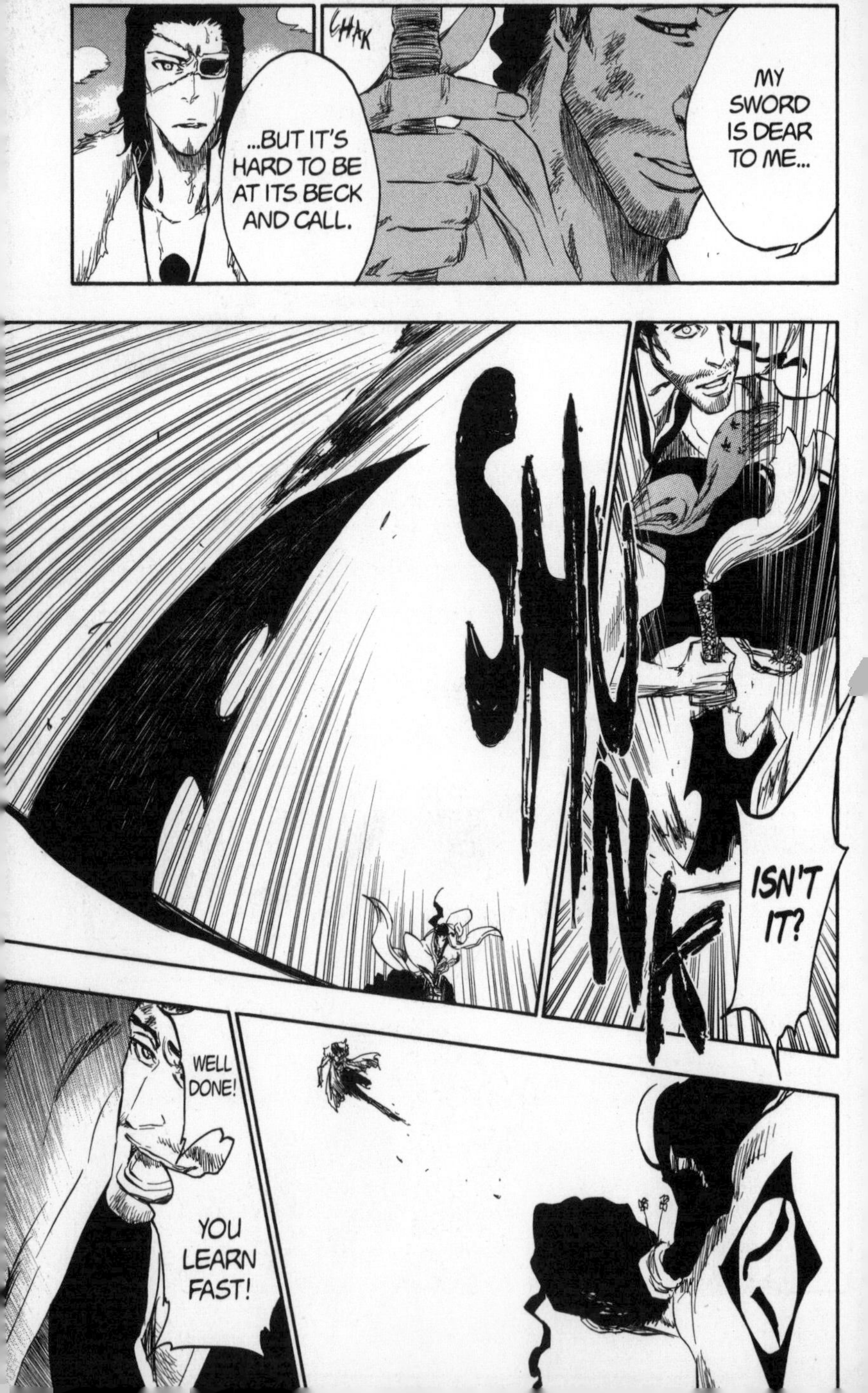
CHAK
MY SWORD IS DEAR TO ME...
...BUT IT'S HARD TO BE AT ITS BECK AND CALL.
ISN'T IT?
SHUNK
WELL DONE!
YOU LEARN FAST!

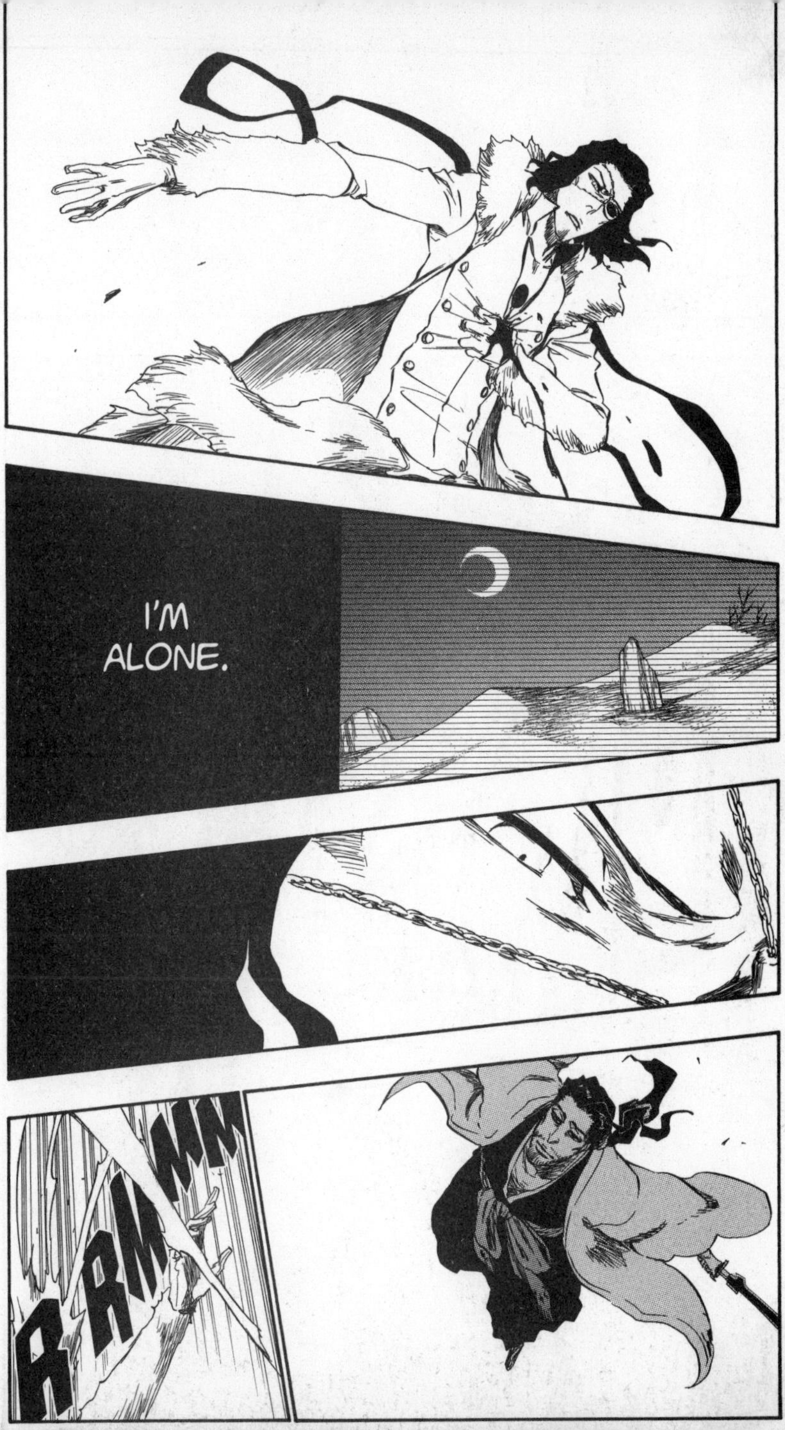
I'M
ALONE.
RRMMM

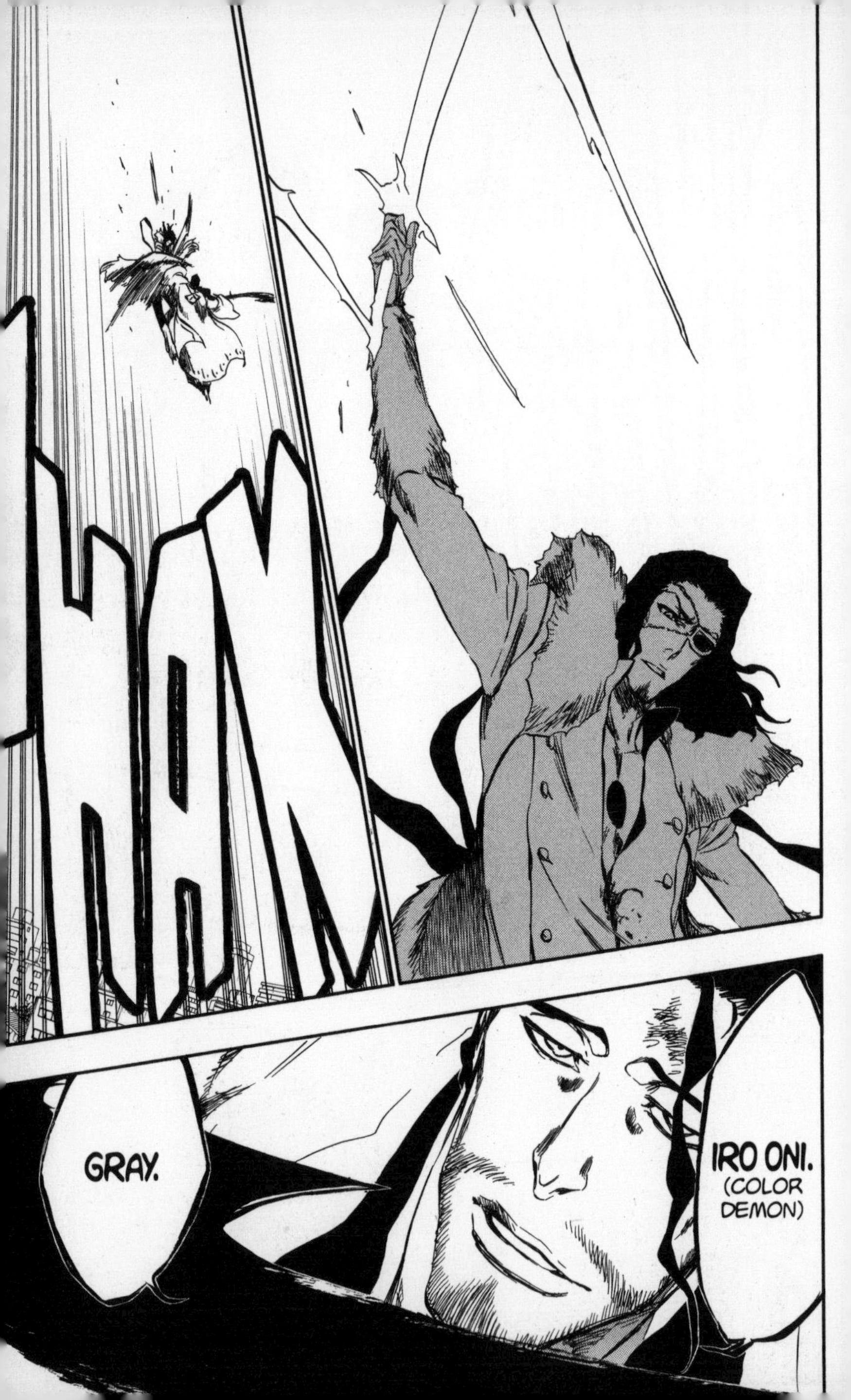
IRO ONI.
(COLOR DEMON)
GRAY.

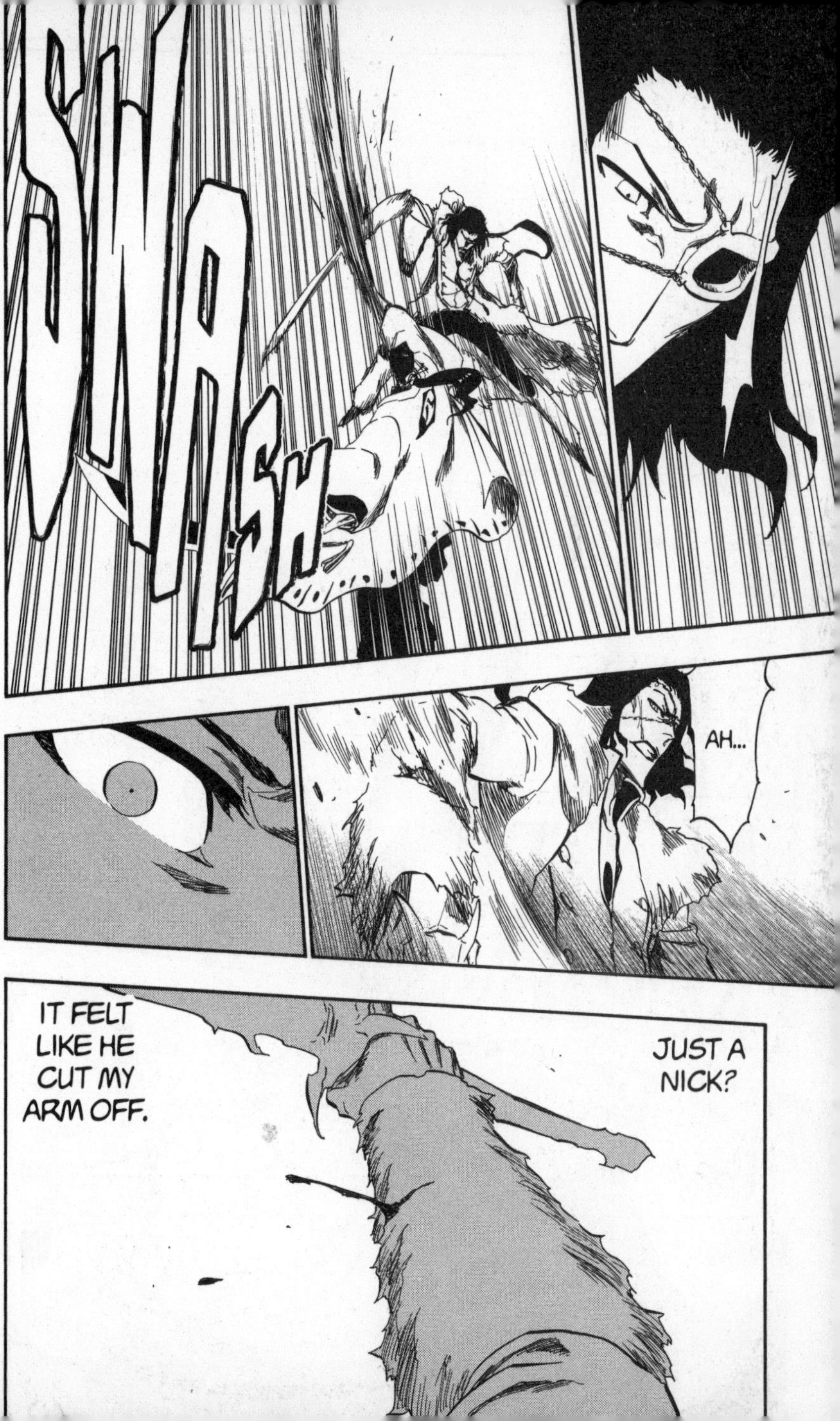
SWASH
AH...
JUST A NICK?
IT FELT LIKE HE CUT MY ARM OFF.

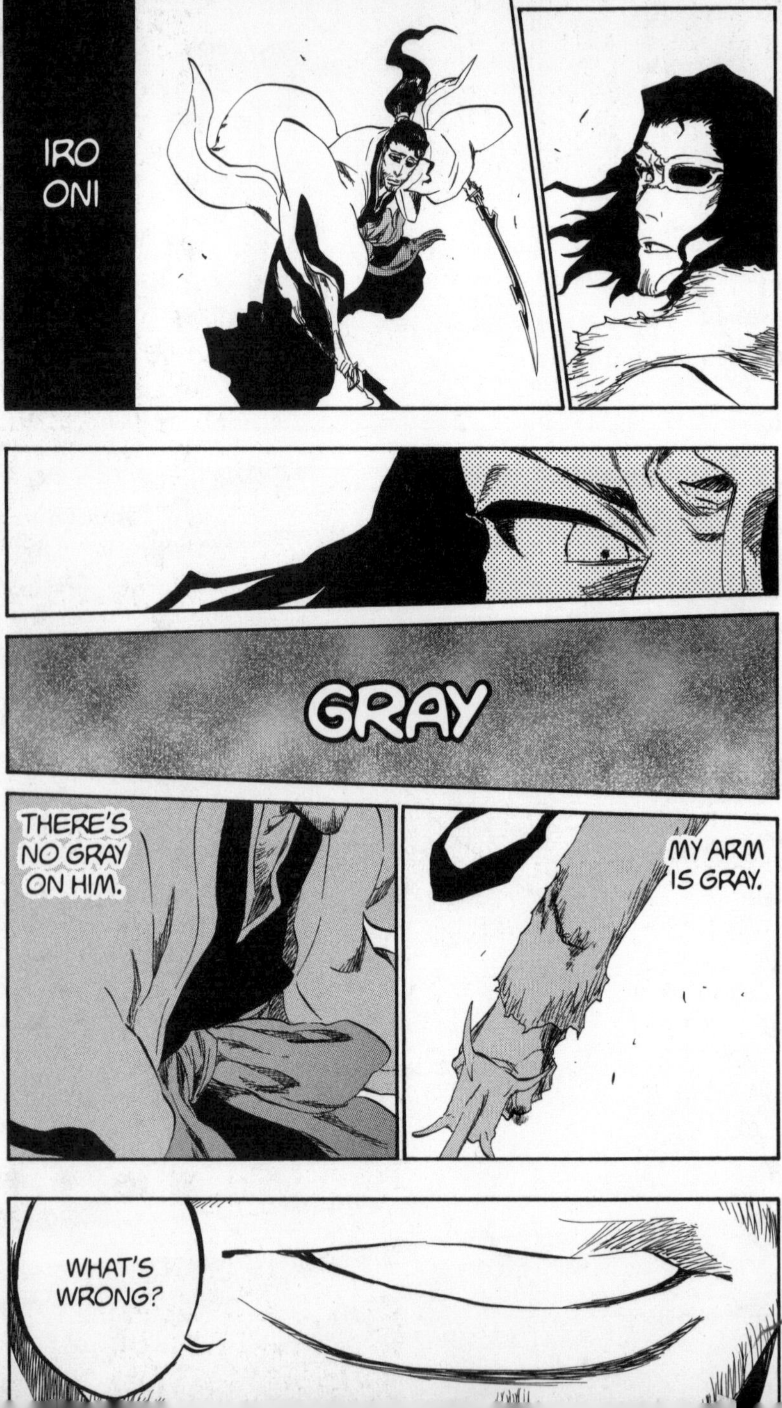
IRO ONI
GRAY
MY ARM IS GRAY.
THERE'S NO GRAY ON HIM.
WHAT'S WRONG?

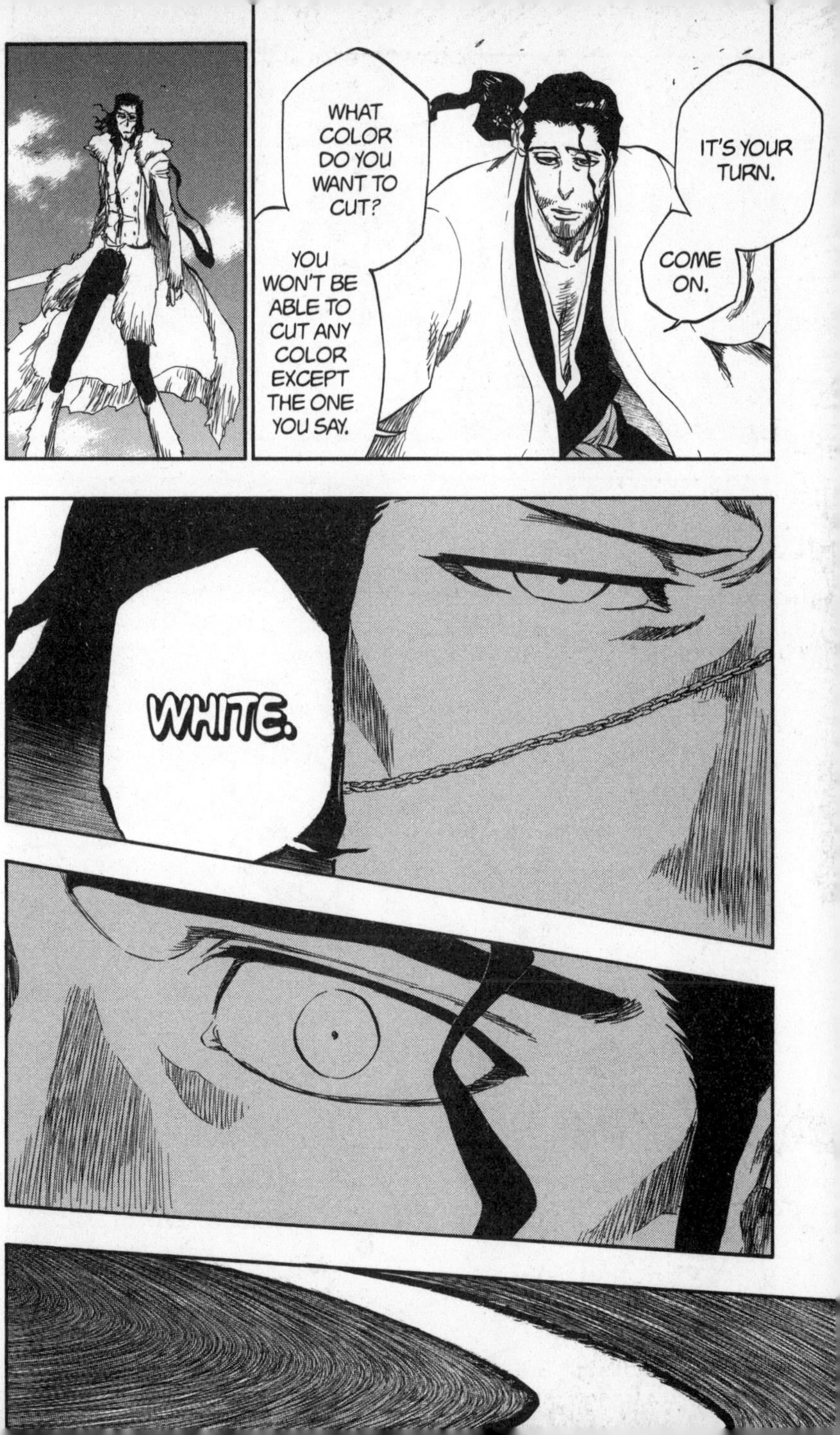
IT'S YOUR TURN.
COME ON.
WHAT COLOR DO YOU WANT TO CUT?
YOU WON'T BE ABLE TO CUT ANY COLOR EXCEPT THE ONE YOU SAY.
WHITE.

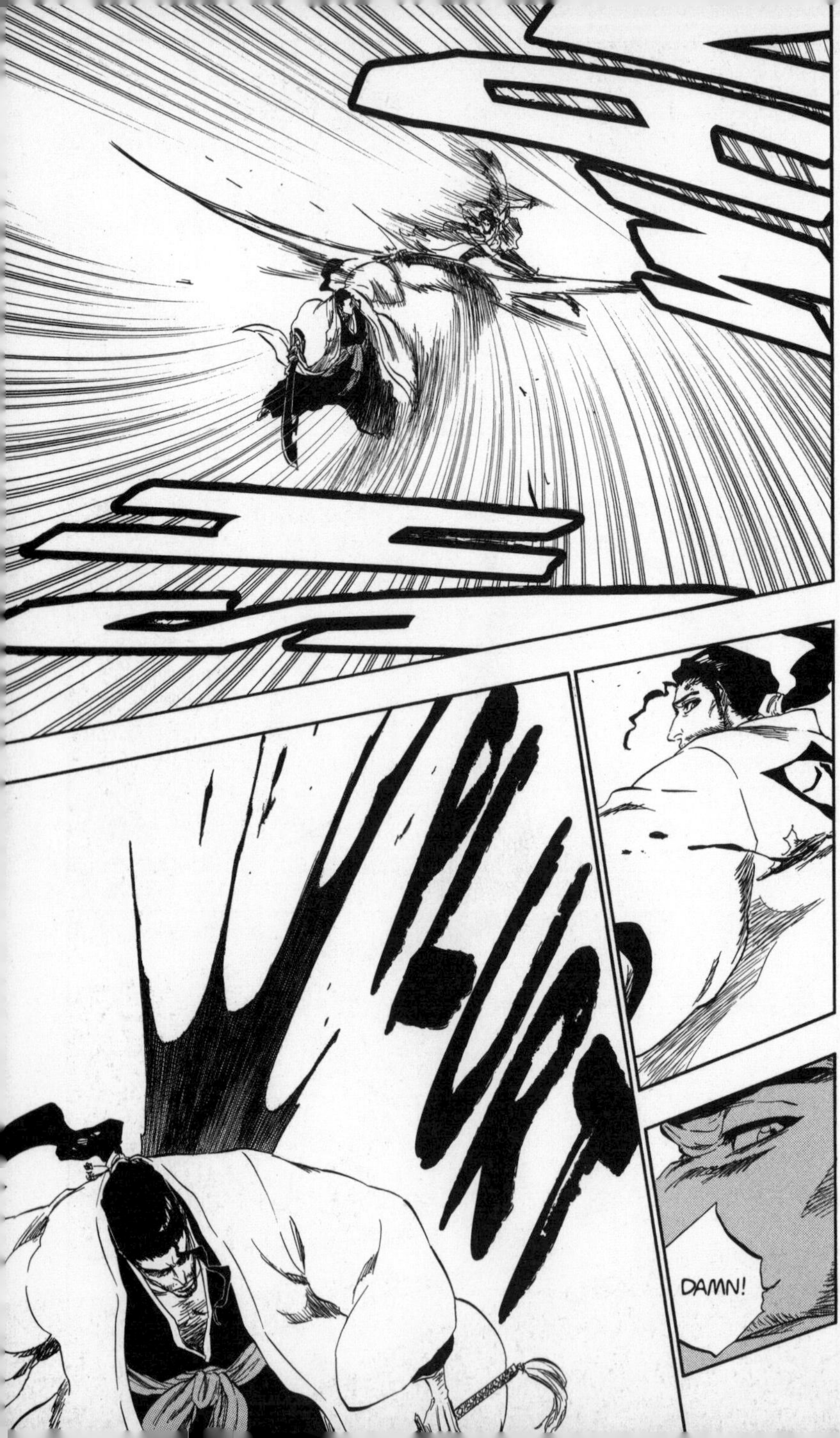
DAMN!

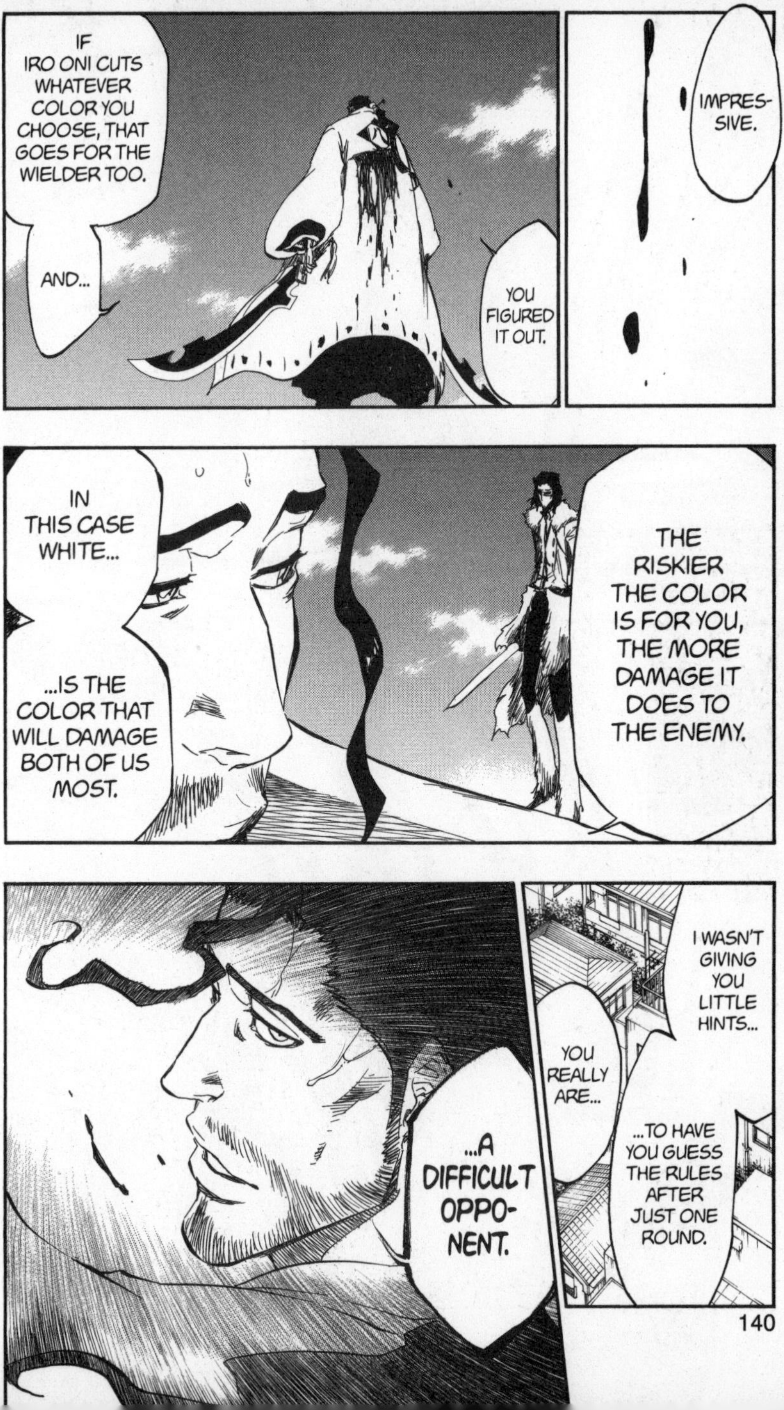
IMPRESSIVE.
YOU FIGURED IT OUT.
IF IRO ONI CUTS WHATEVER COLOR YOU CHOOSE, THAT GOES FOR THE WIELDER TOO.
AND...
THE RISKIER THE COLOR IS FOR YOU, THE MORE DAMAGE IT DOES TO THE ENEMY.
IN THIS CASE WHITE...
...IS THE COLOR THAT WILL DAMAGE BOTH OF US MOST.
I WASN'T GIVING YOU LITTLE HINTS...
...TO HAVE YOU GUESS THE RULES AFTER JUST ONE ROUND.
YOU REALLY ARE...
...A DIFFICULT OPPONENT.

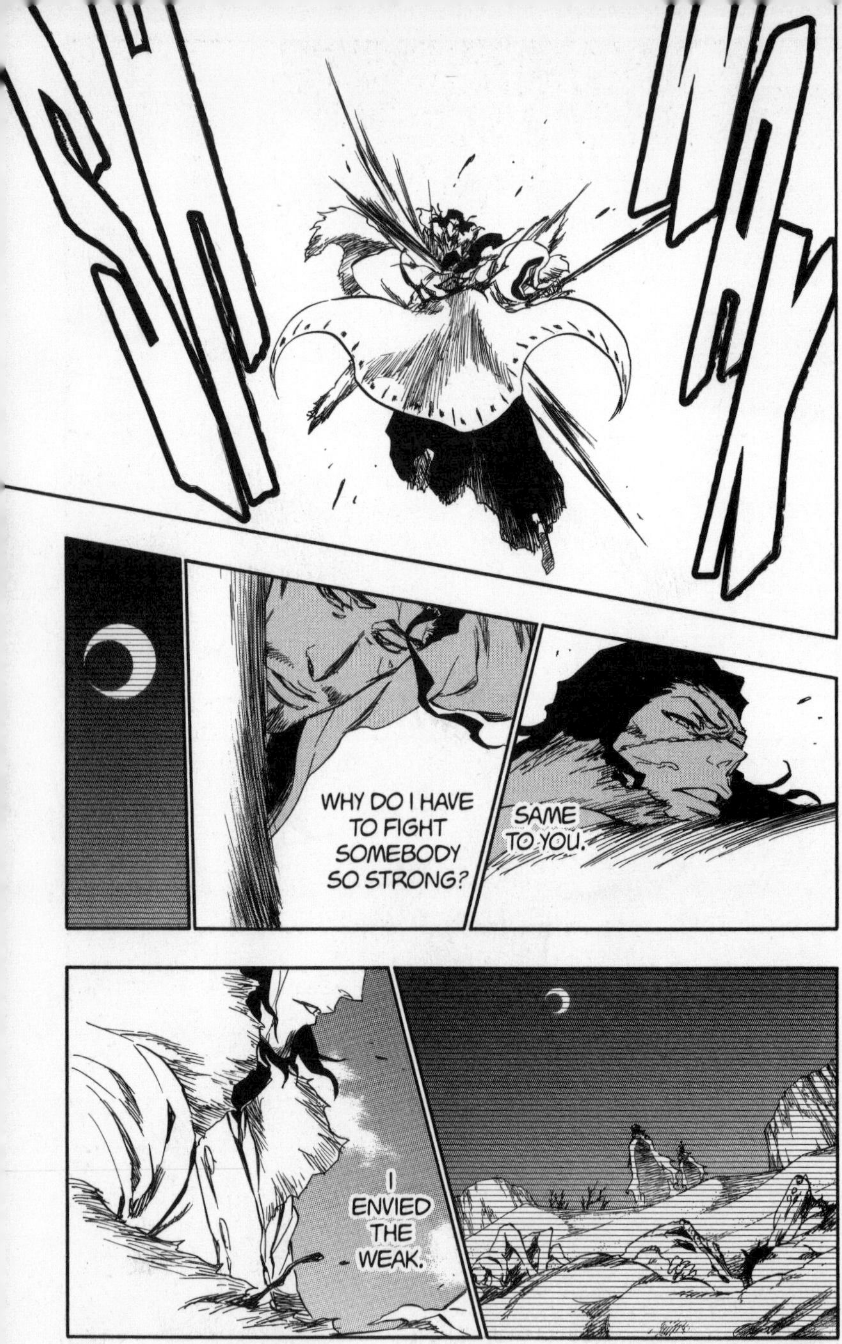
SAME TO YOU.
WHY DO I HAVE TO FIGHT SOMEBODY SO STRONG?
I ENVIED THE WEAK.

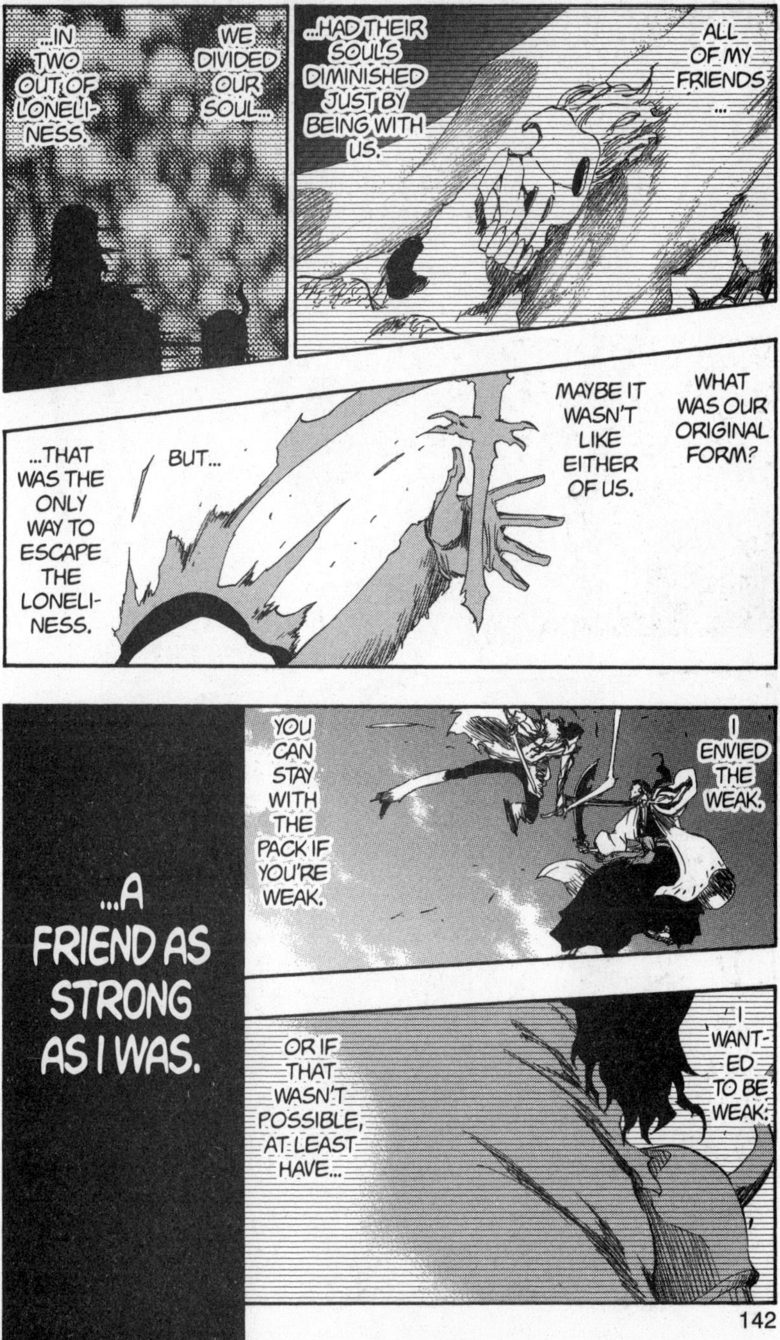
ALL OF MY FRIENDS...
...HAD THEIR SOULS DIMINISHED JUST BY BEING WITH US.
WE DIVIDED OUR SOUL...
...IN TWO OUT OF LONELI-NESS.
WHAT WAS OUR ORIGINAL FORM?
MAYBE IT WASN'T LIKE EITHER OF US.
BUT...
...THAT WAS THE ONLY WAY TO ESCAPE THE LONELI-NESS.
I ENVIED THE WEAK.
YOU CAN STAY WITH THE PACK IF YOU'RE WEAK.
I WANT-ED TO BE WEAK.
OR IF THAT WASN'T POSSIBLE, AT LEAST HAVE...
...A FRIEND AS STRONG AS I WAS.

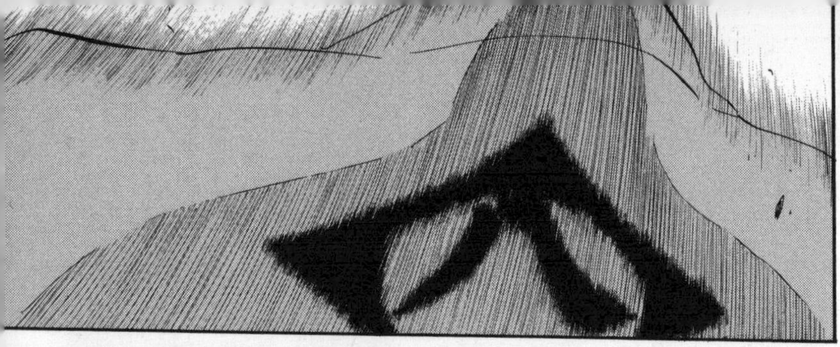

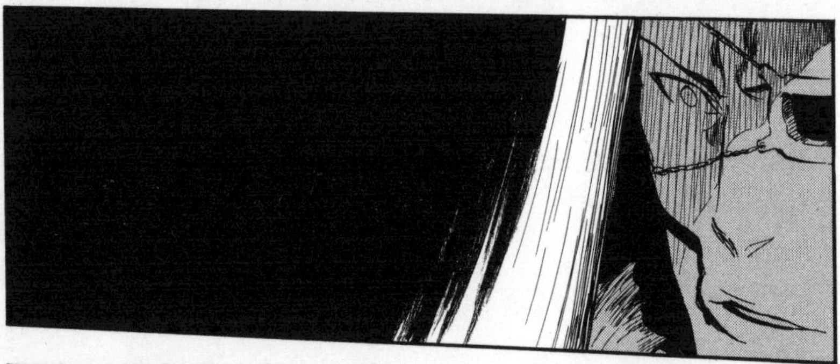

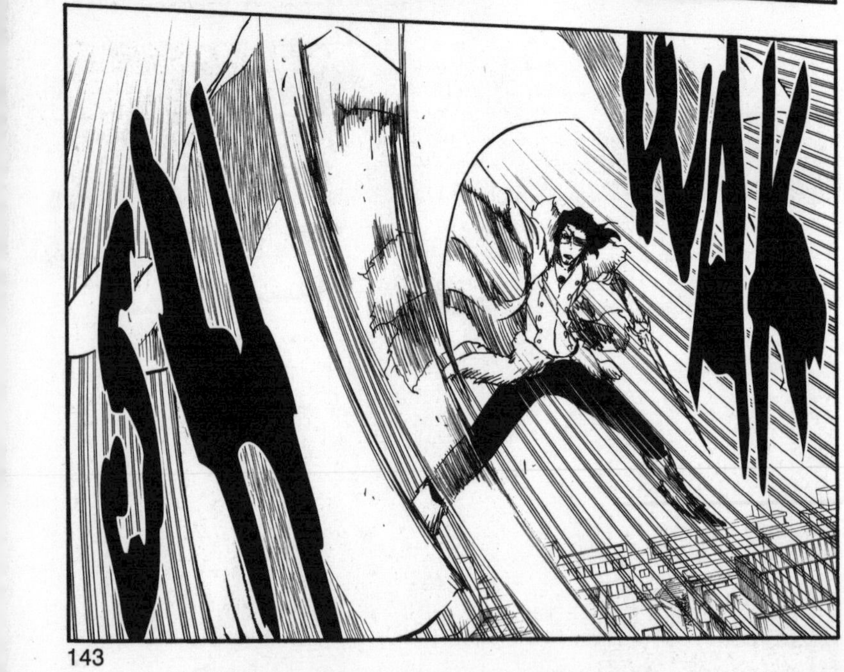
SHWAK

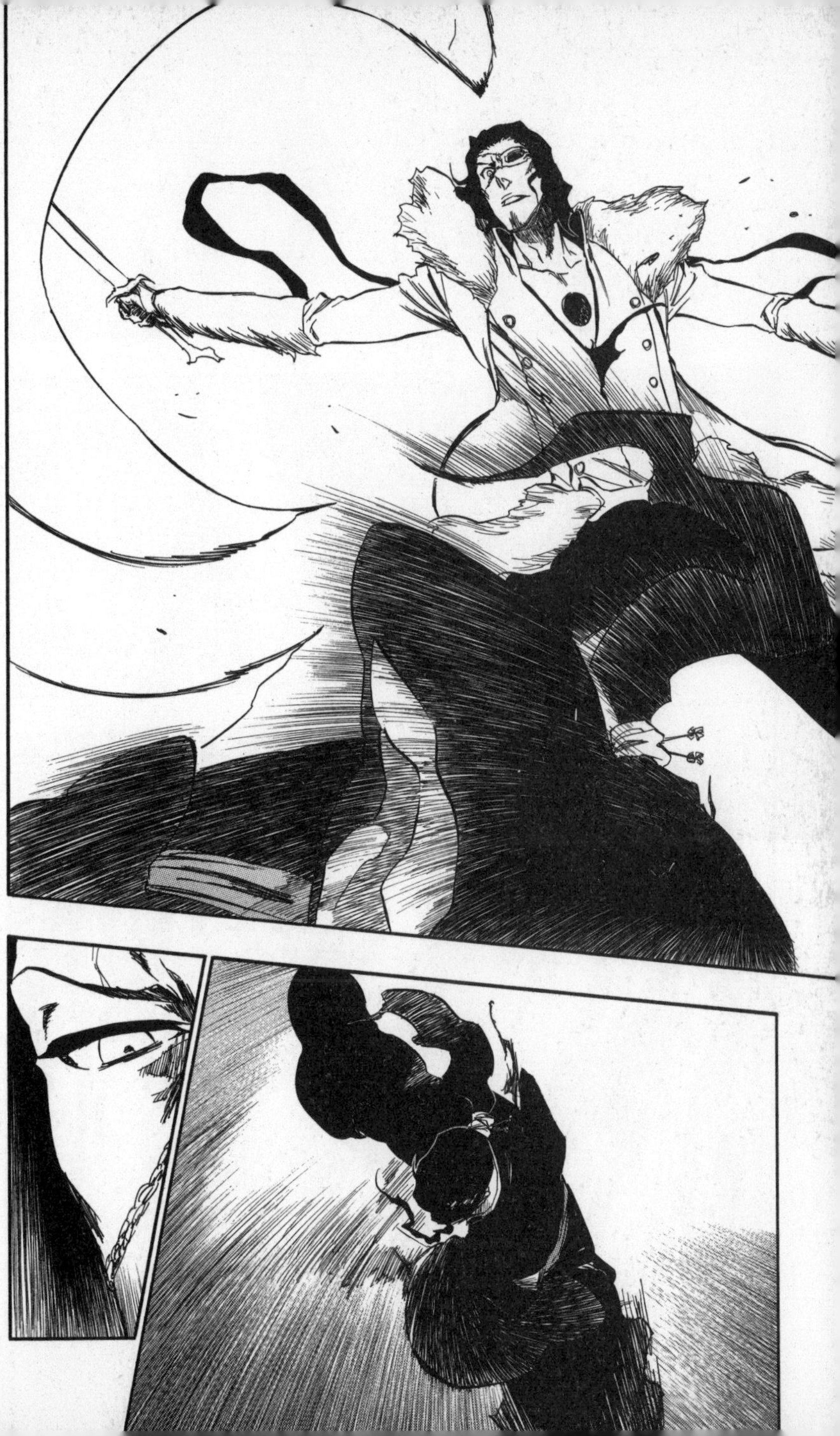

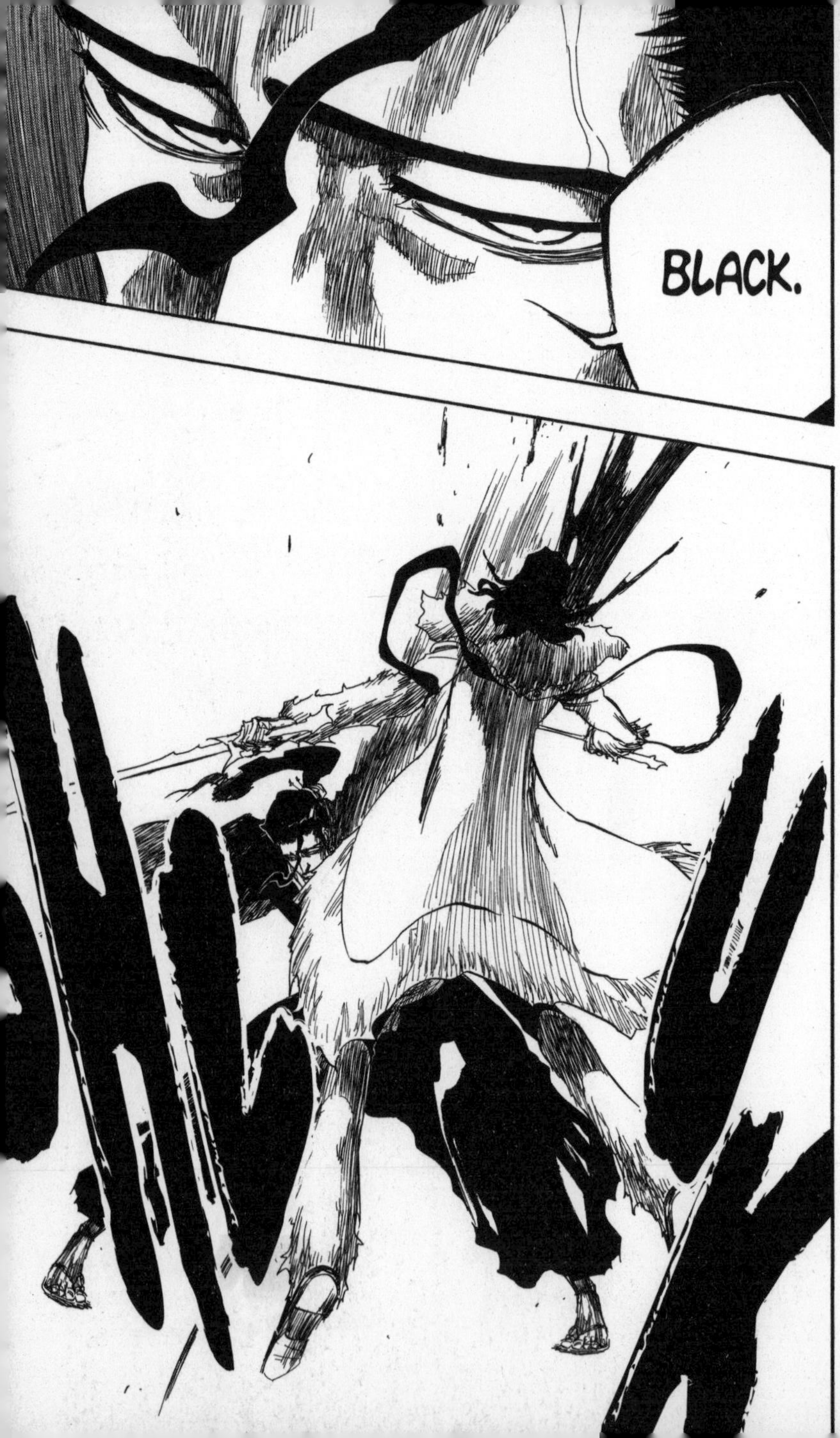
BLACK.

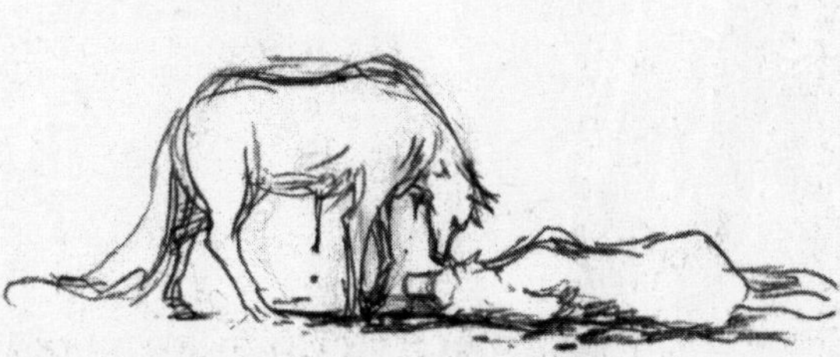

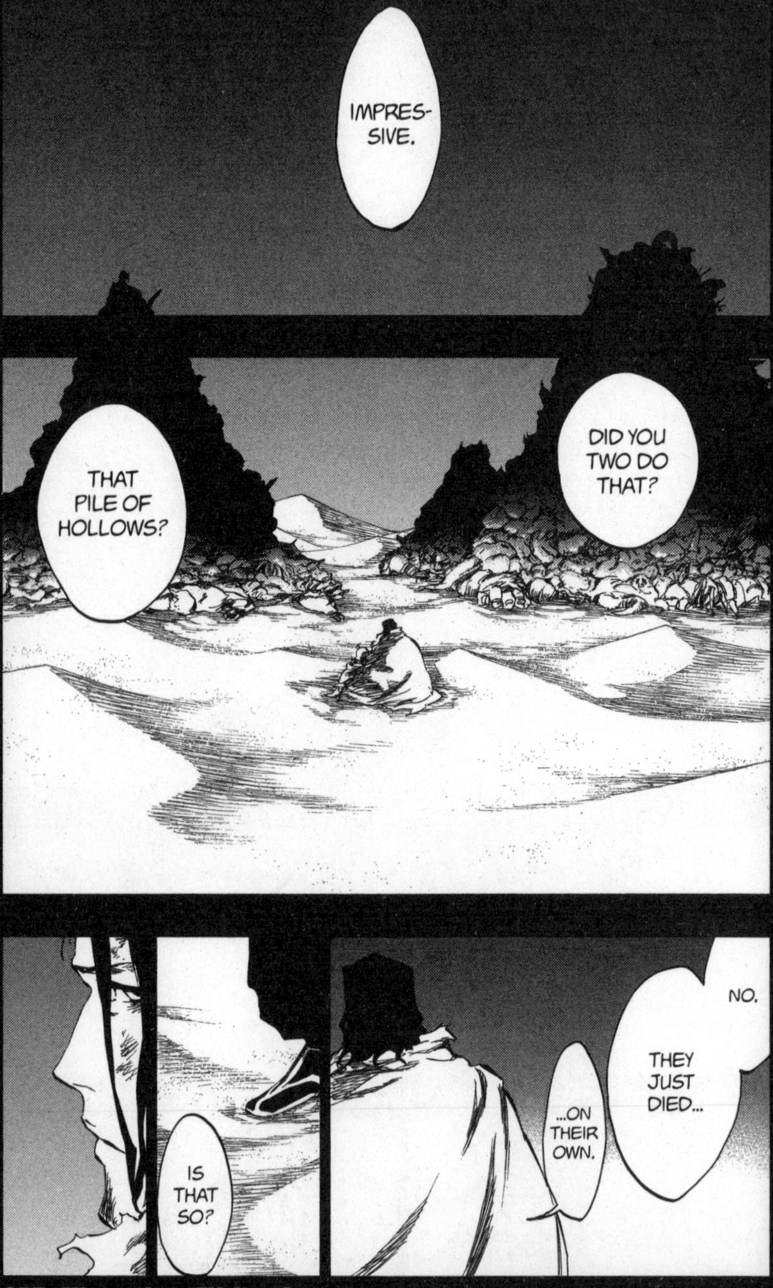
IMPRES-
SIVE.
DID YOU TWO DO THAT?
THAT PILE OF HOLLOWS?
NO.
THEY JUST DIED...
...ON THEIR OWN.
IS THAT SO?

375. EXecution, EXtinction

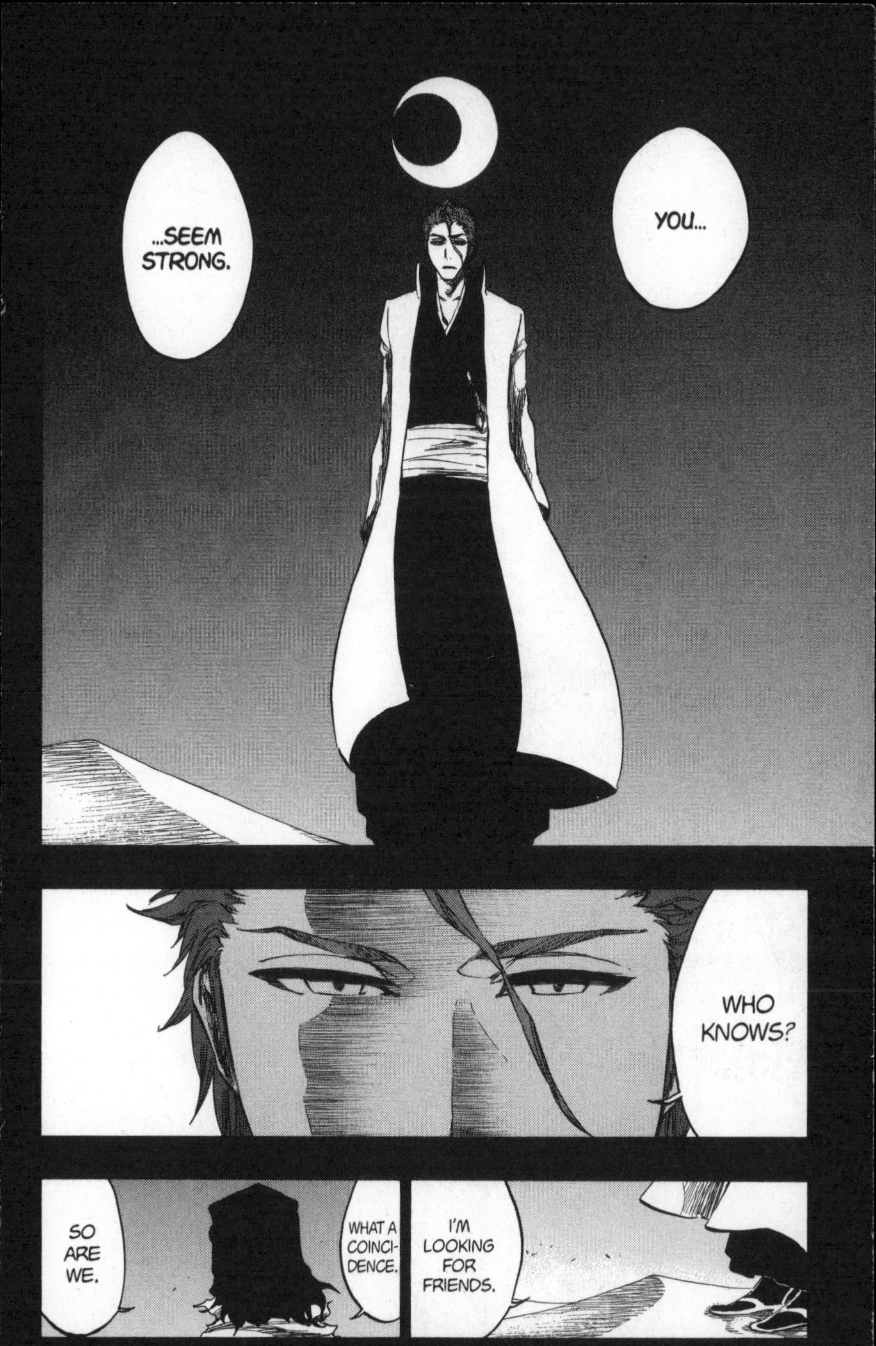
YOU...
...SEEM STRONG.
WHO KNOWS?
I'M LOOKING FOR FRIENDS.
WHAT A COINCI-DENCE.
SO ARE WE.

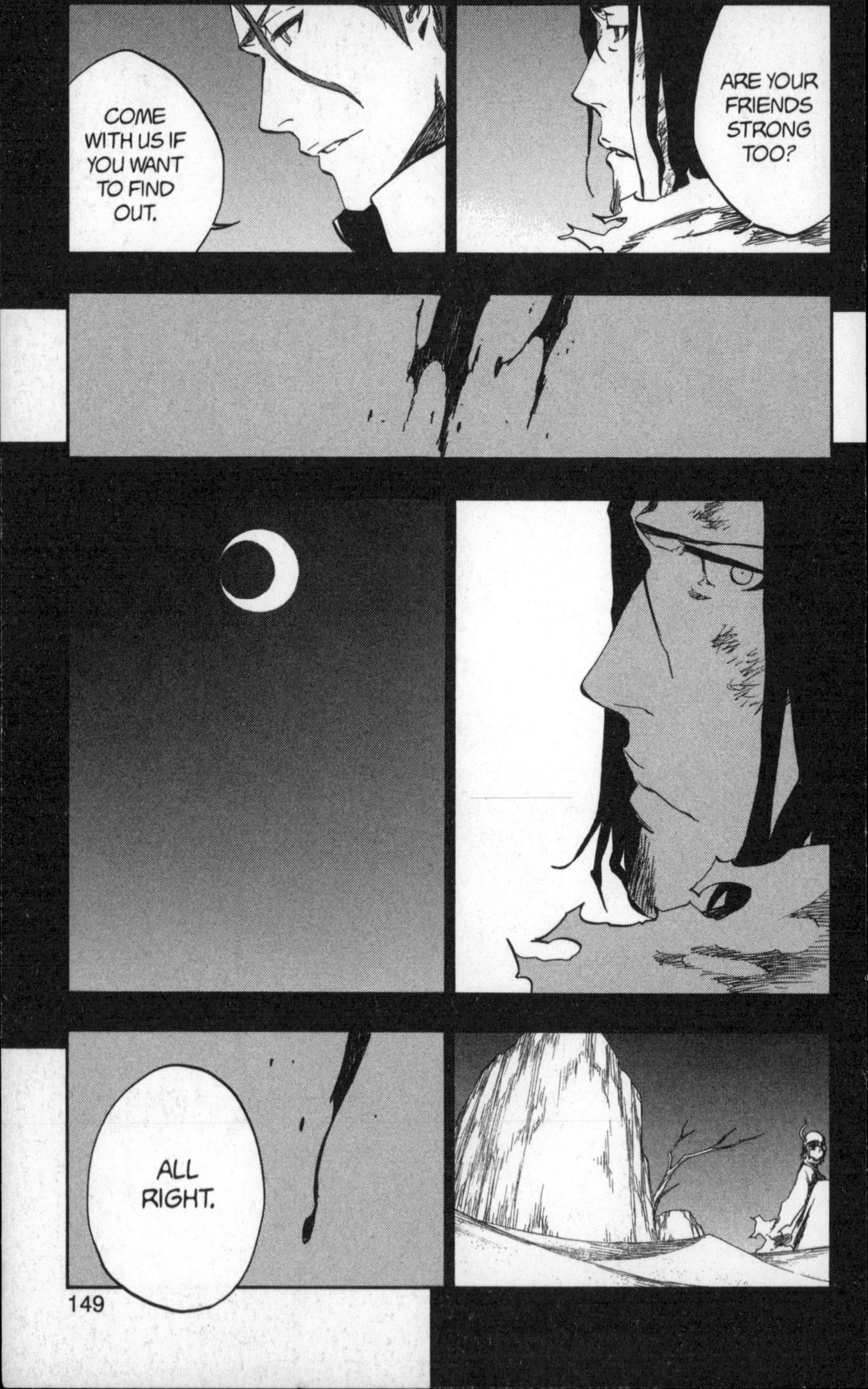
ARE YOUR FRIENDS STRONG TOO?
COME WITH US IF YOU WANT TO FIND OUT.
ALL RIGHT.

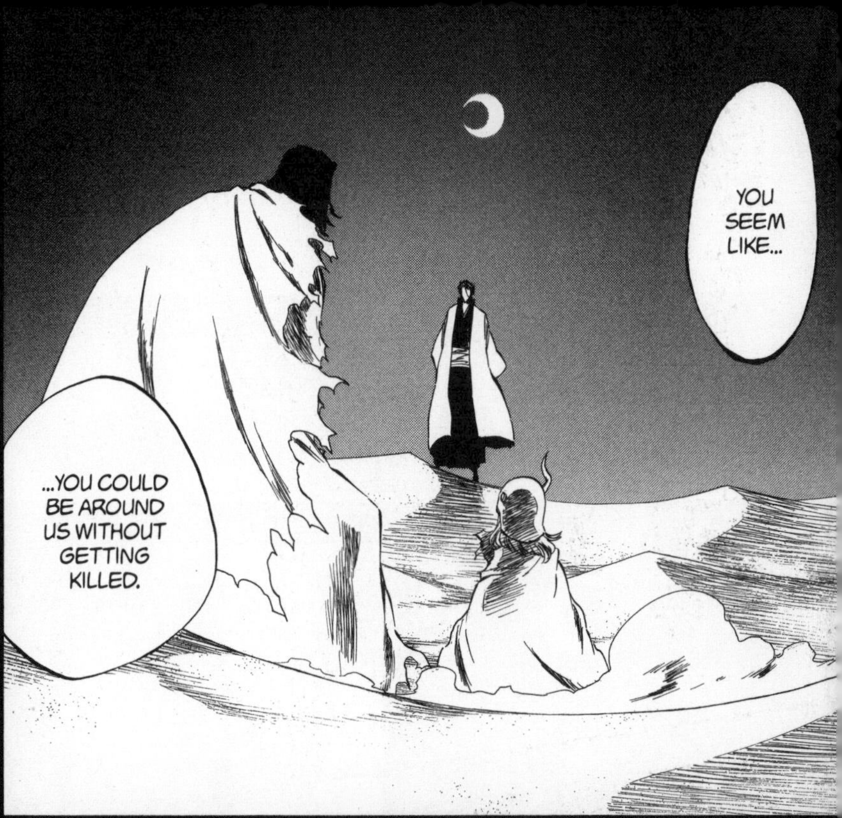
YOU SEEM LIKE...
...YOU COULD BE AROUND US WITHOUT GETTING KILLED.

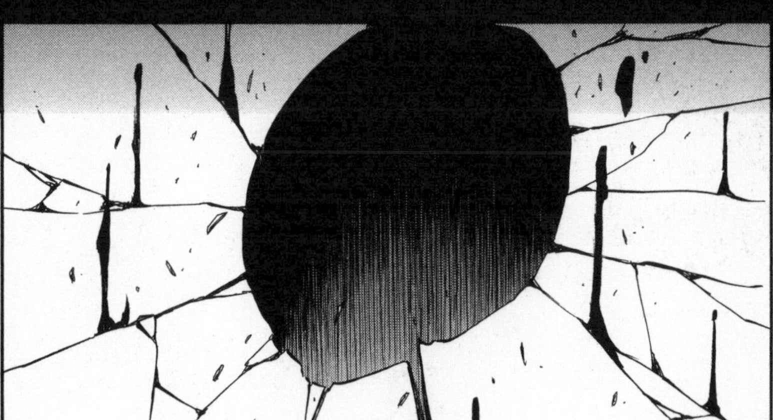

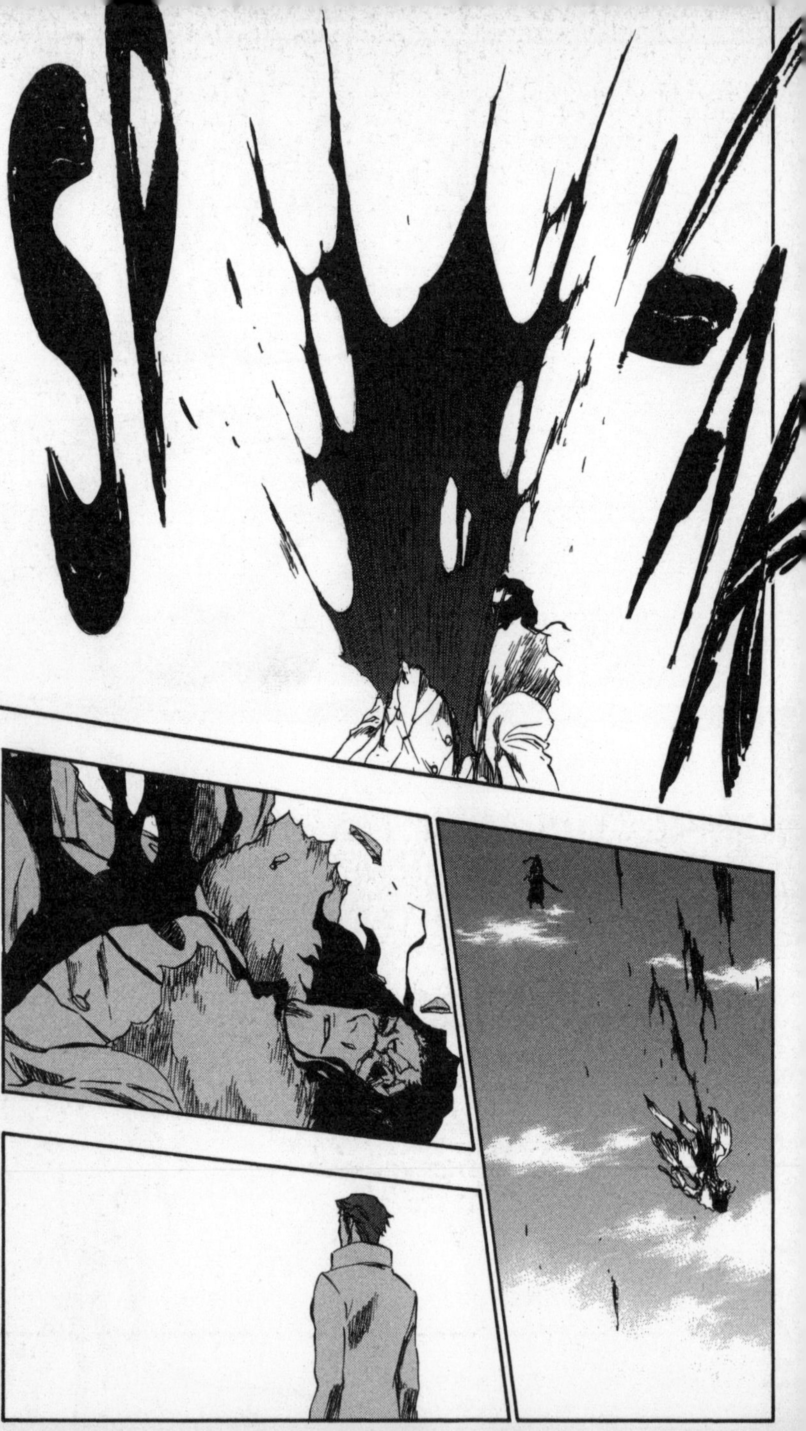
SPLAK

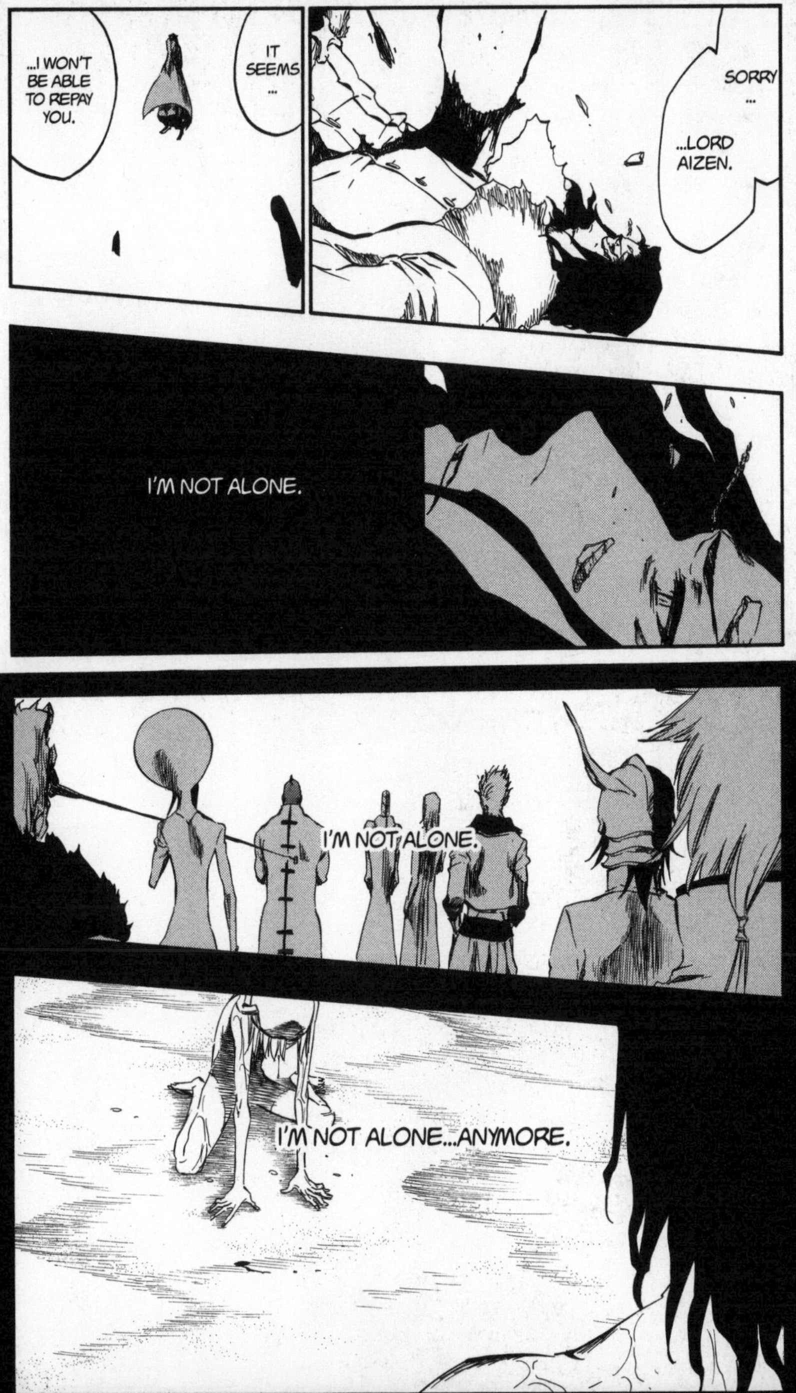
SORRY ... ...LORD AIZEN.
IT SEEMS ...
...I WON'T BE ABLE TO REPAY YOU.
I'M NOT ALONE.
I'M NOT ALONE.
I'M NOT ALONE...ANYMORE.

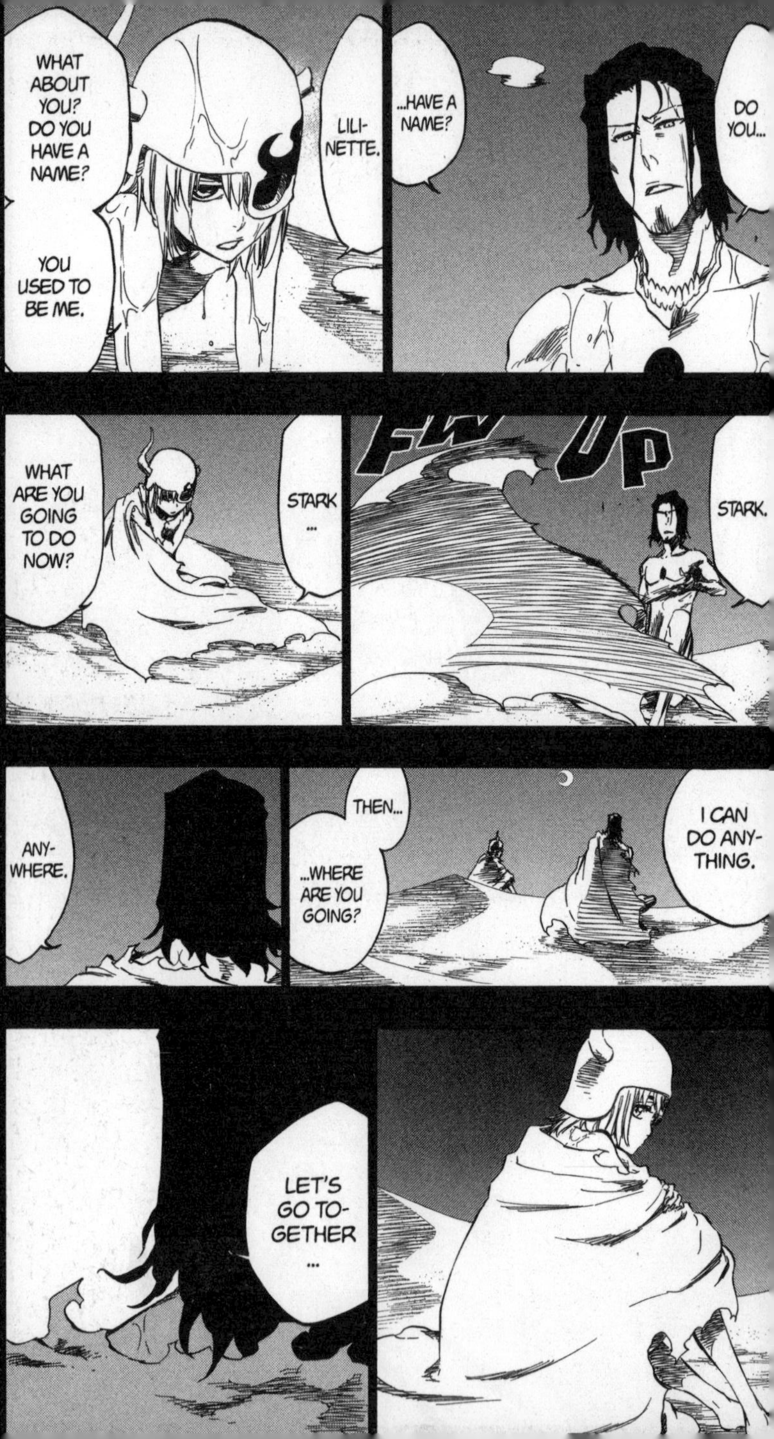
DO YOU...
...HAVE A NAME?
LILI-NETTE.
WHAT ABOUT YOU? DO YOU HAVE A NAME?
YOU USED TO BE ME.
STARK.
FWUP
STARK...
WHAT ARE YOU GOING TO DO NOW?
I CAN DO ANY-THING.
THEN...
...WHERE ARE YOU GOING?
ANY-WHERE.
LET'S GO TO-GETHER...

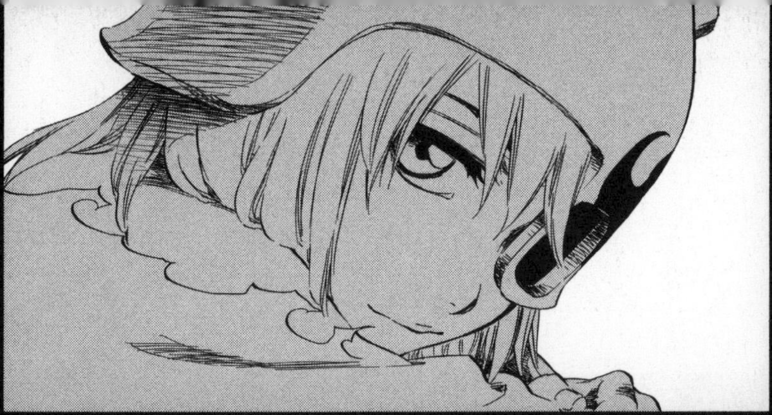

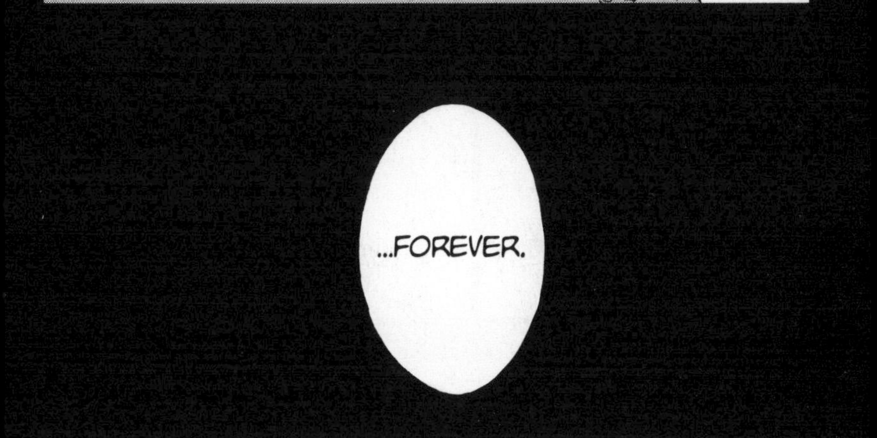
...FOREVER.

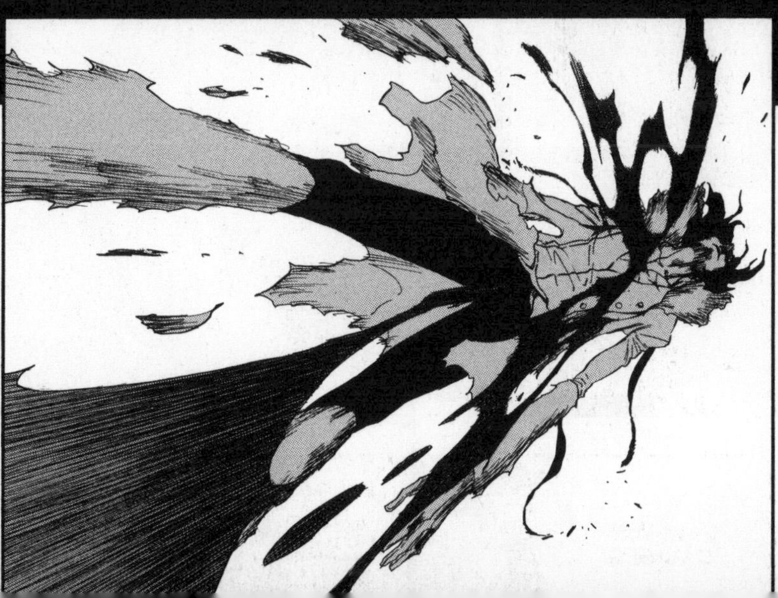

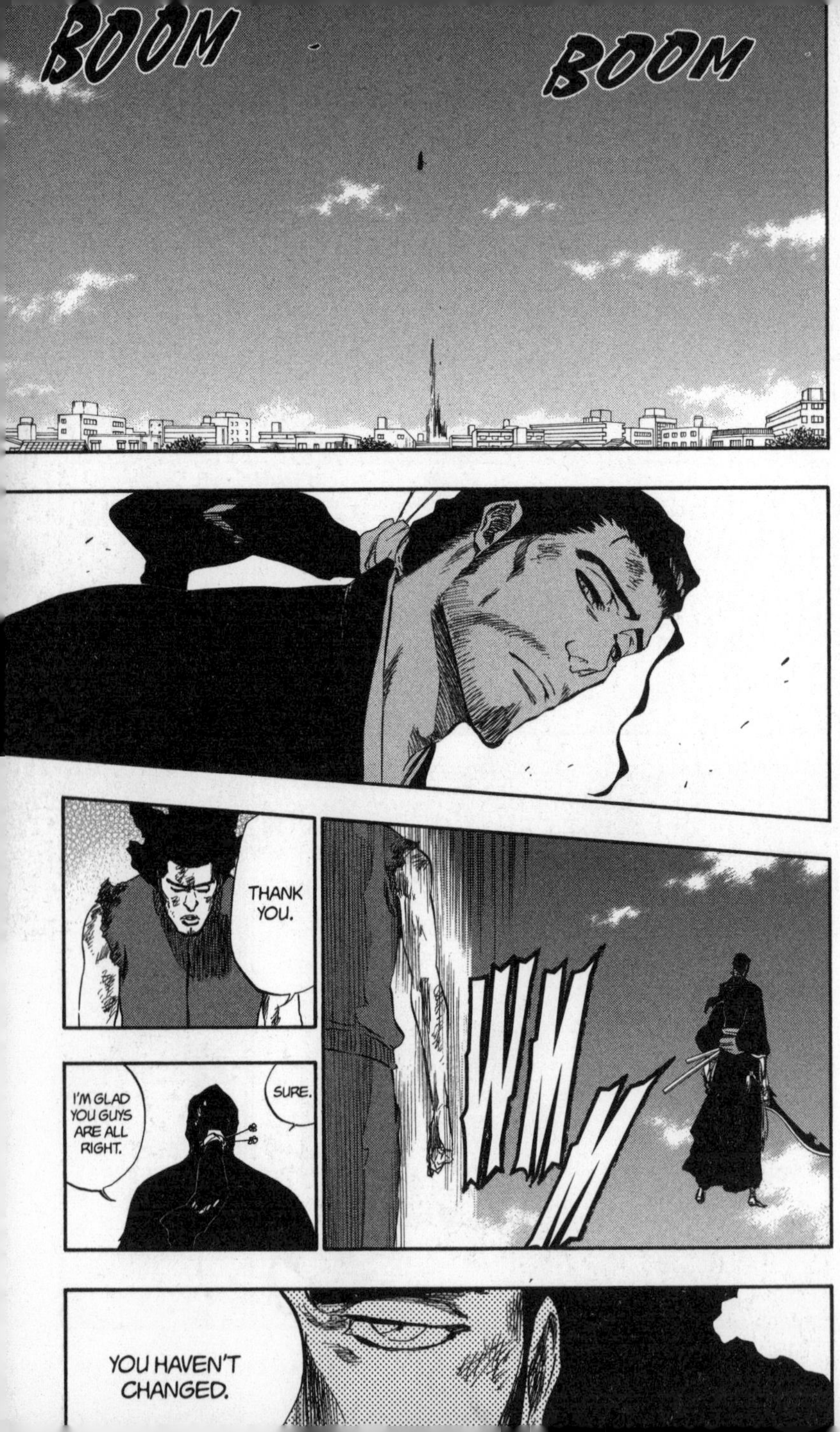

BOOM
BOOM
THANK YOU.
WM
SURE.
I'M GLAD YOU GUYS ARE ALL RIGHT.
YOU HAVEN'T CHANGED.

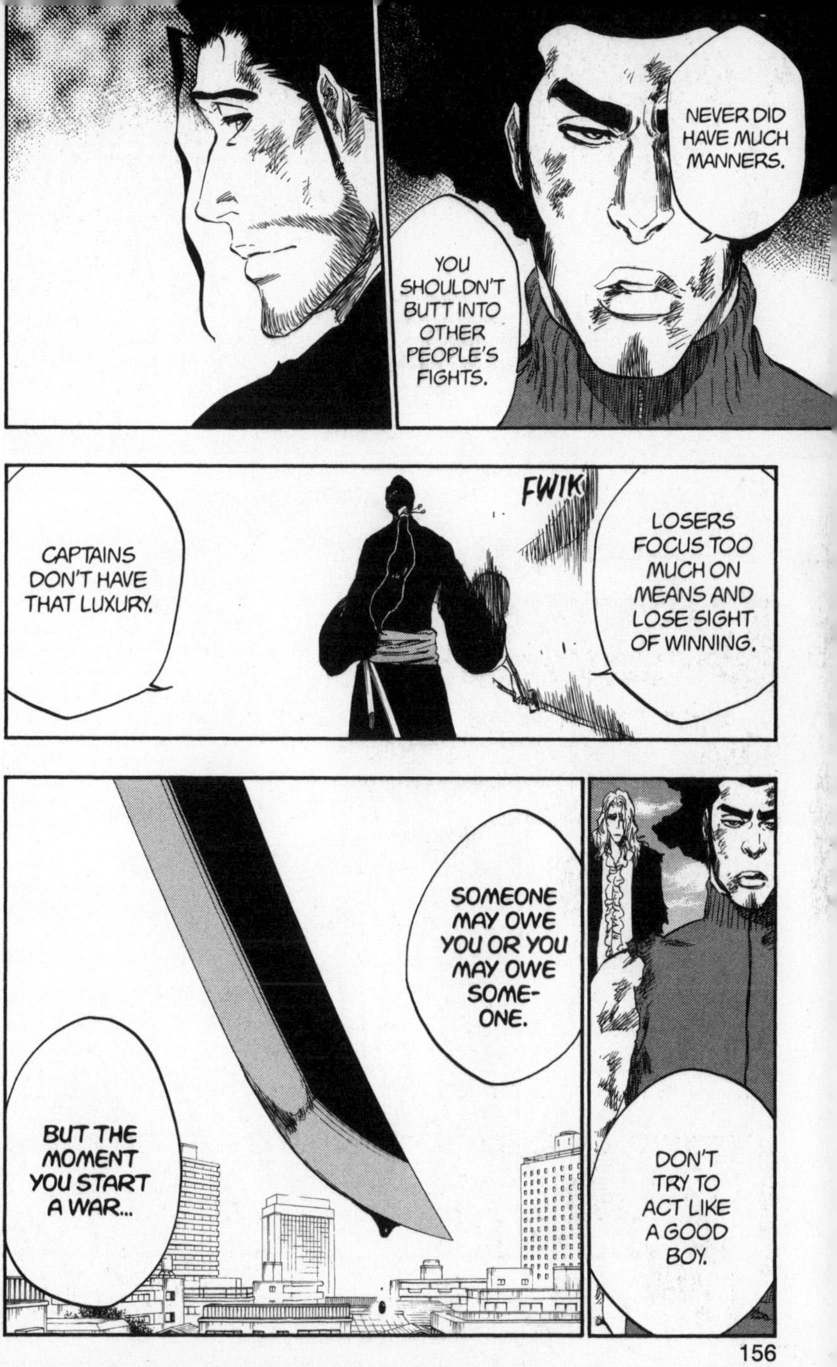
NEVER DID HAVE MUCH MANNERS.
YOU SHOULDN'T BUTT INTO OTHER PEOPLE'S FIGHTS.
FWIK
LOSERS FOCUS TOO MUCH ON MEANS AND LOSE SIGHT OF WINNING.
CAPTAINS DON'T HAVE THAT LUXURY.
DON'T TRY TO ACT LIKE A GOOD BOY.
SOMEONE MAY OWE YOU OR YOU MAY OWE SOME-ONE.
BUT THE MOMENT YOU START A WAR...

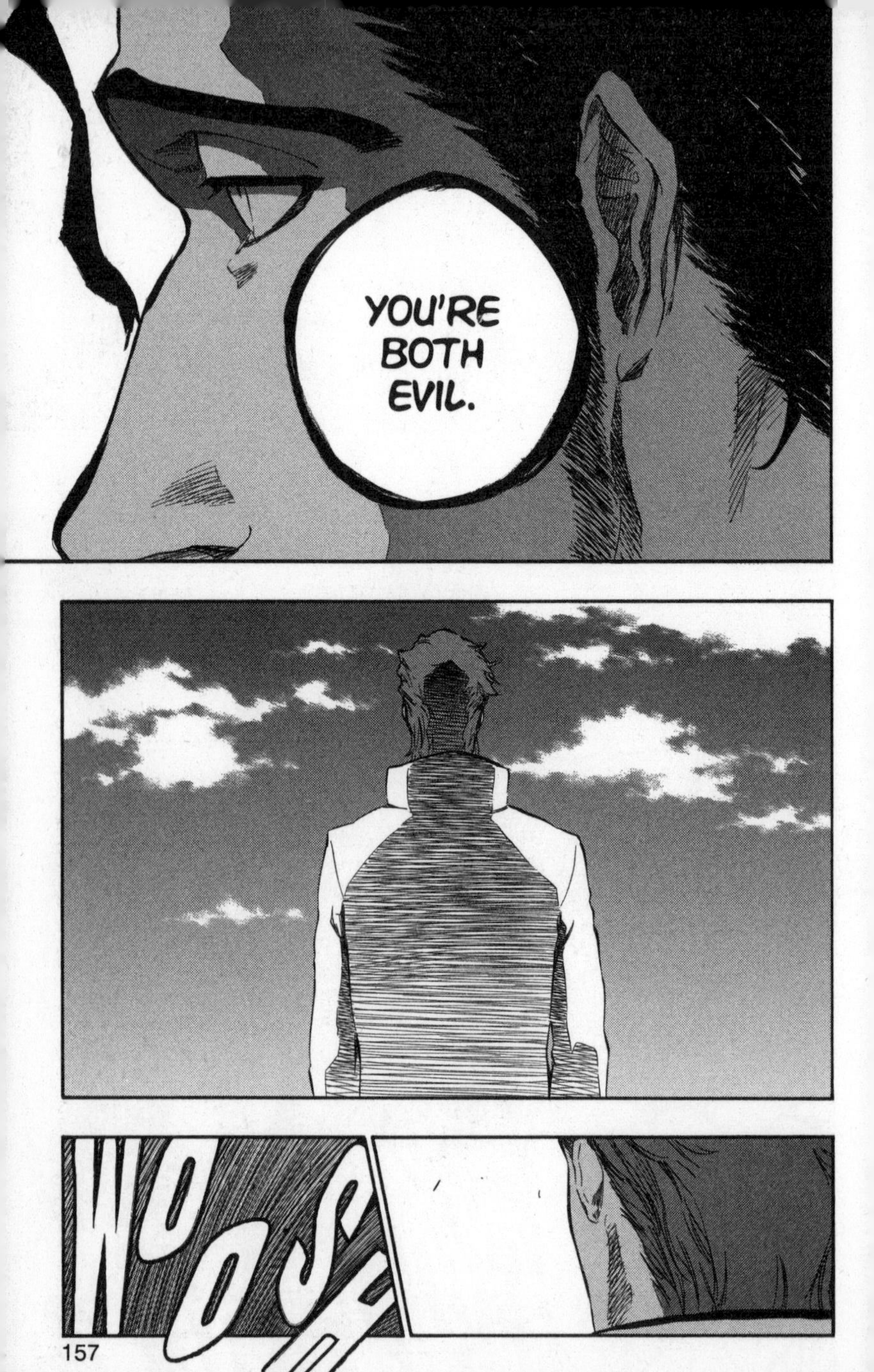
YOU'RE BOTH EVIL.
WOOSH

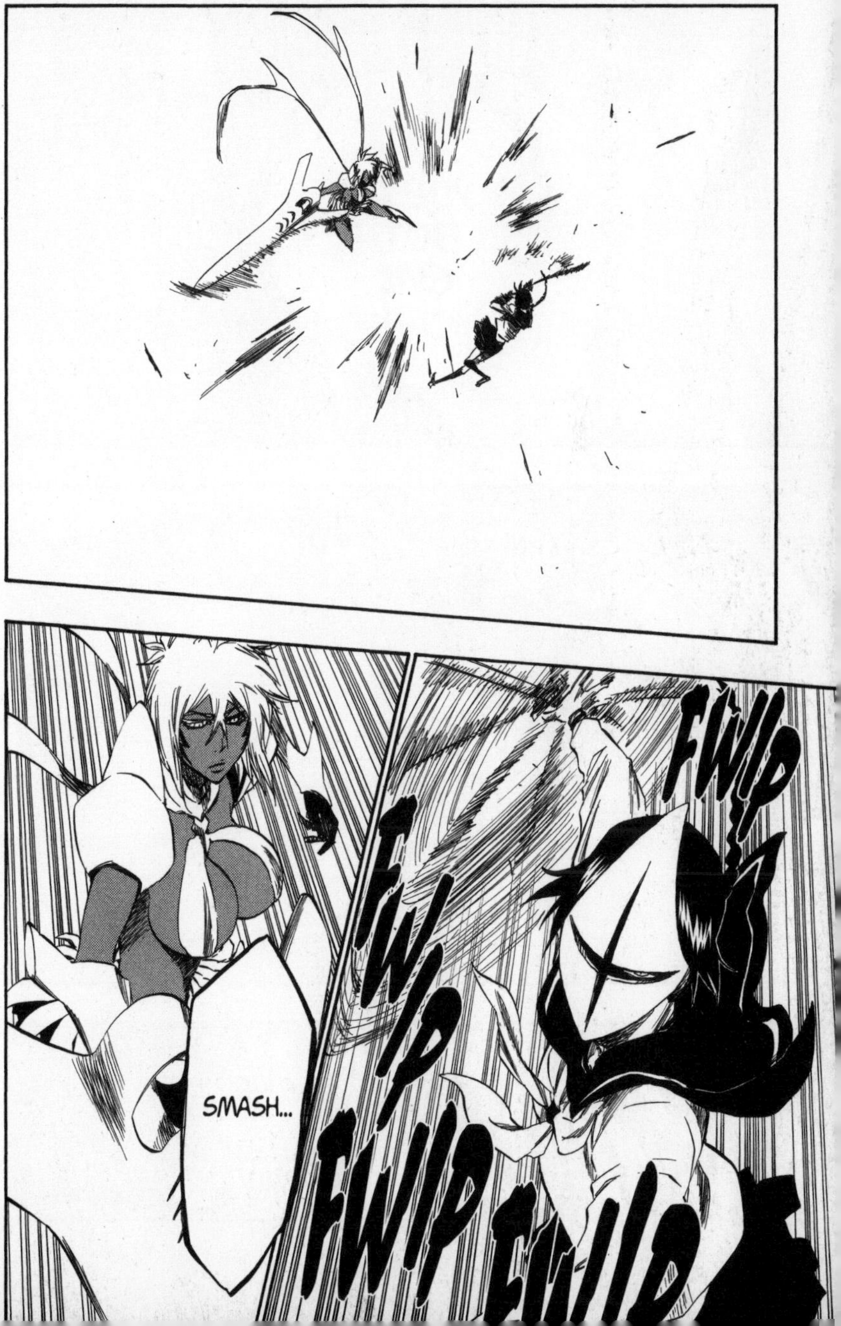
FWIP!
FWIP
FWIP
FWIP
SMASH...

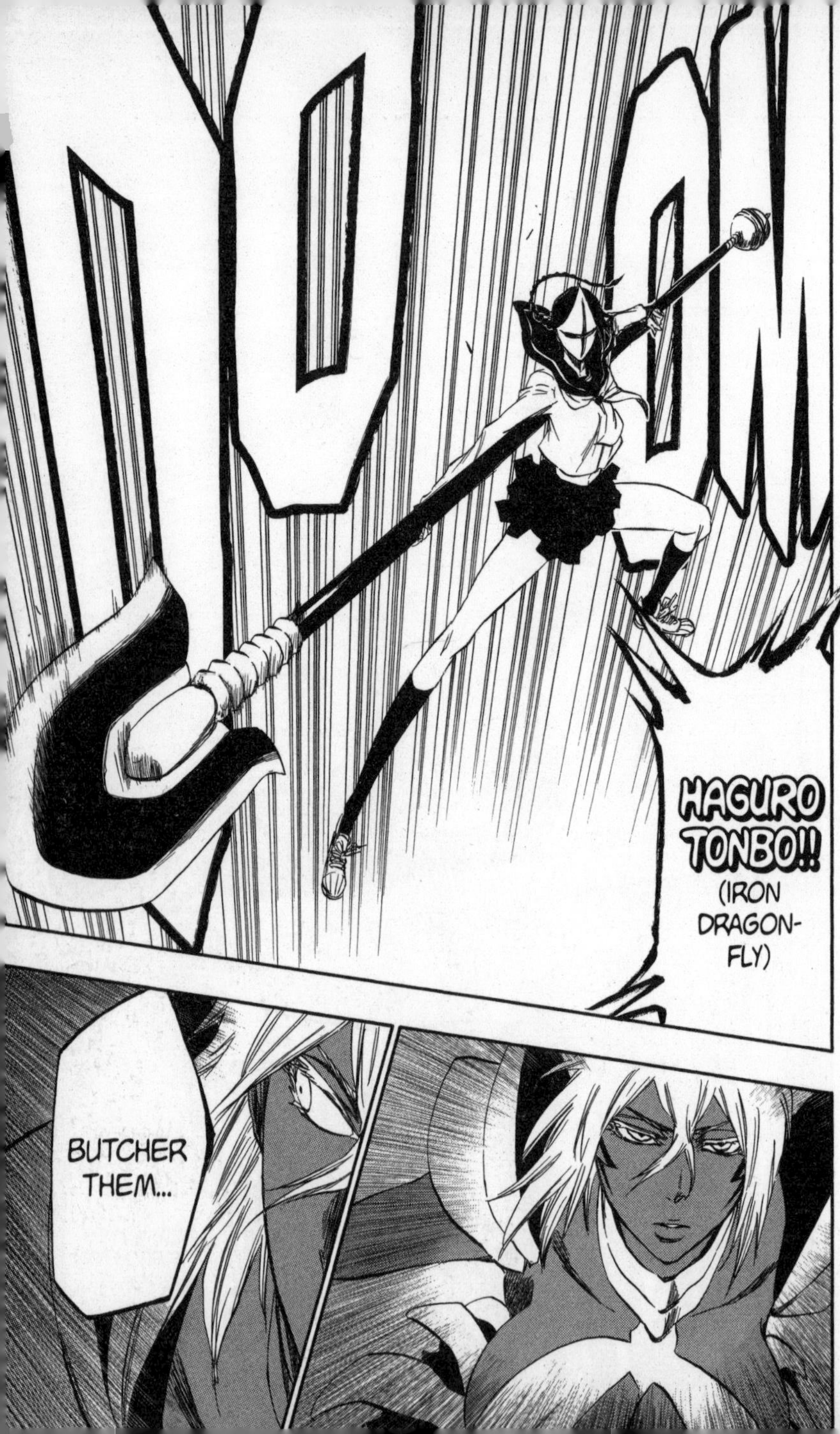
HAGURO TONBO!!
(IRON DRAGON-FLY)
BUTCHER THEM...

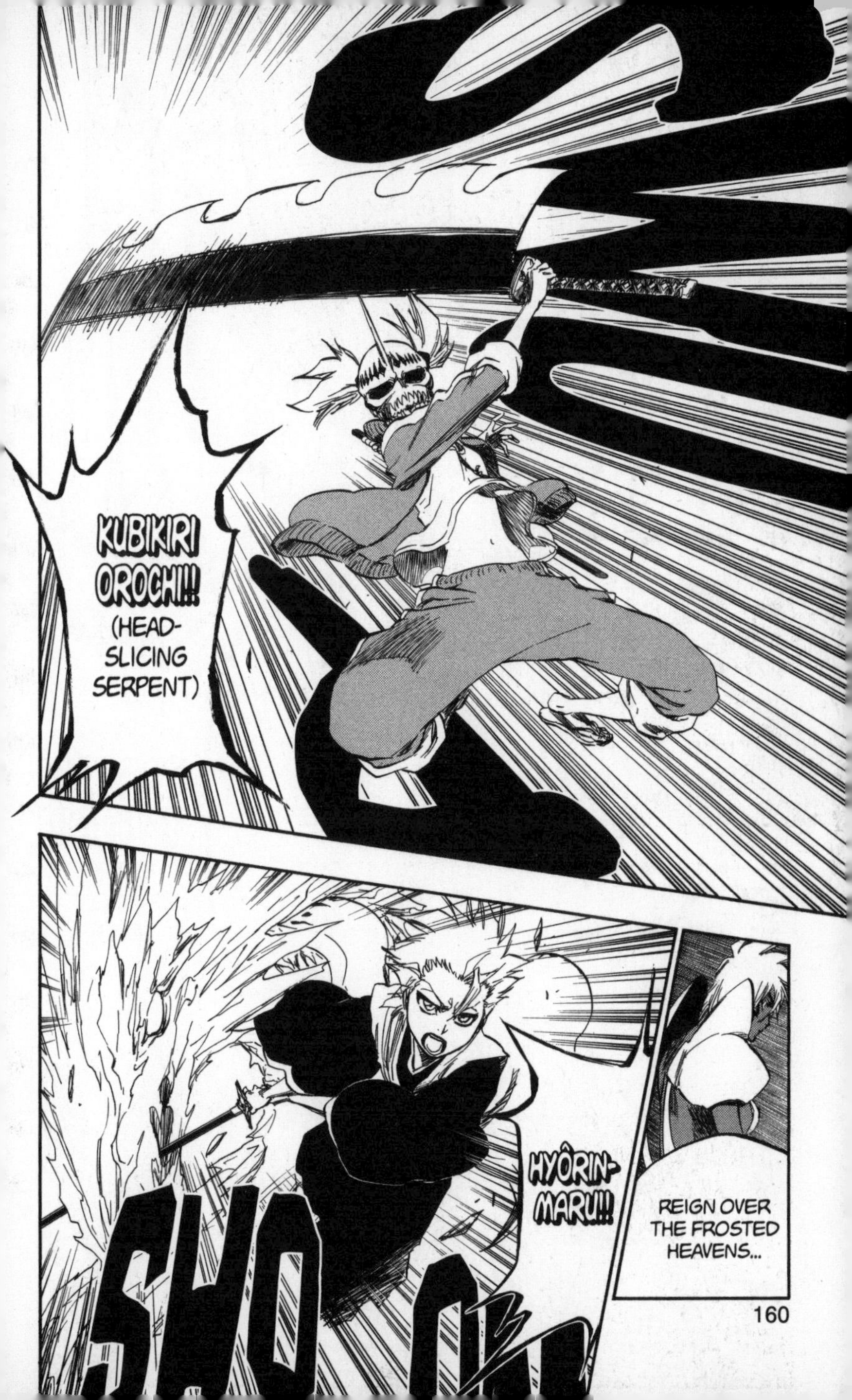
KUBIKIRI OROCHI!!! (HEAD-SLICING SERPENT)
REIGN OVER THE FROSTED HEAVENS...
HYÔRINMARU!!!
SHOOM

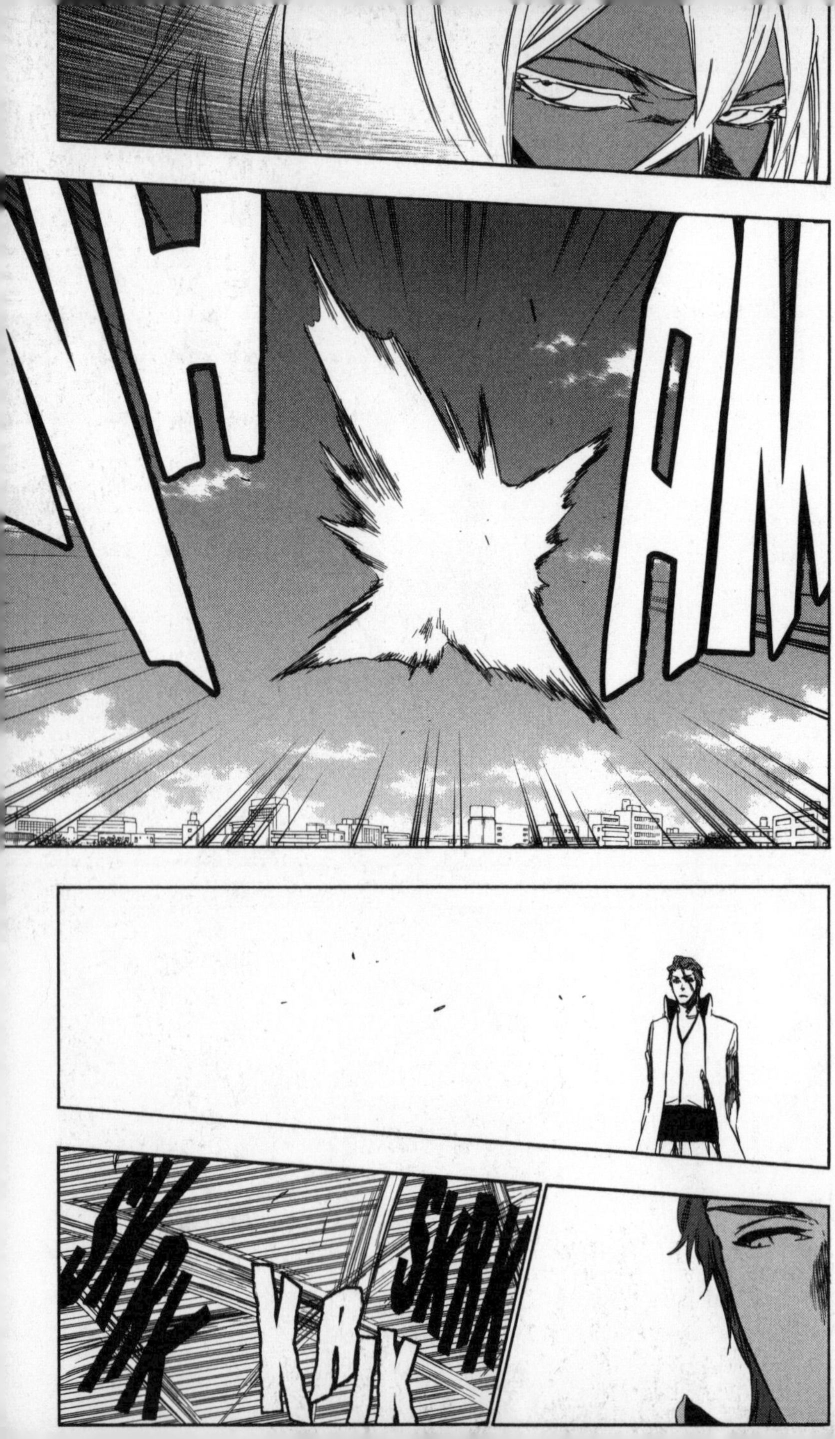
WHAM
SKRK
KRIK
SKRK

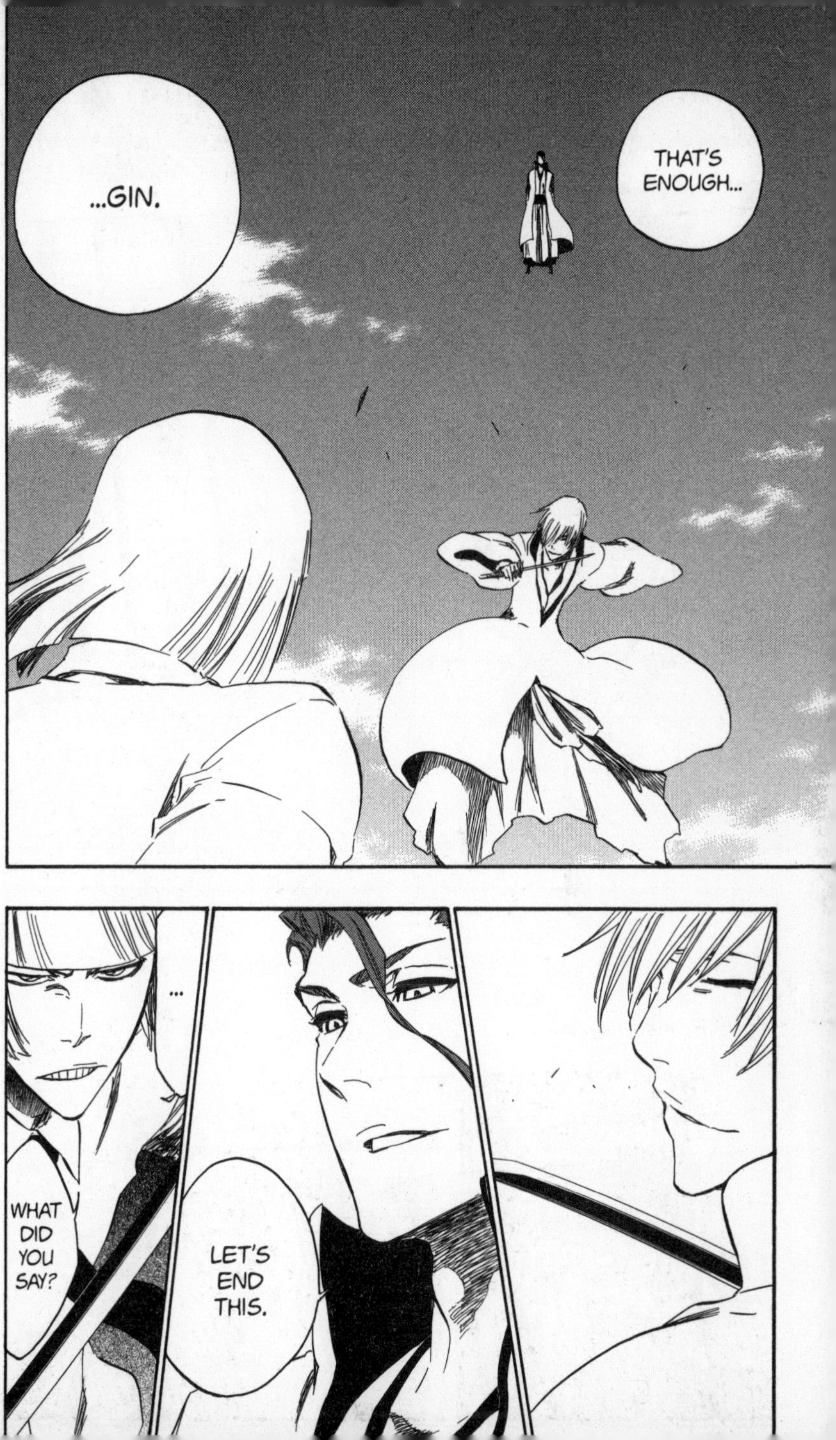
THAT'S ENOUGH...
...GIN.
LET'S END THIS.
...
WHAT DID YOU SAY?

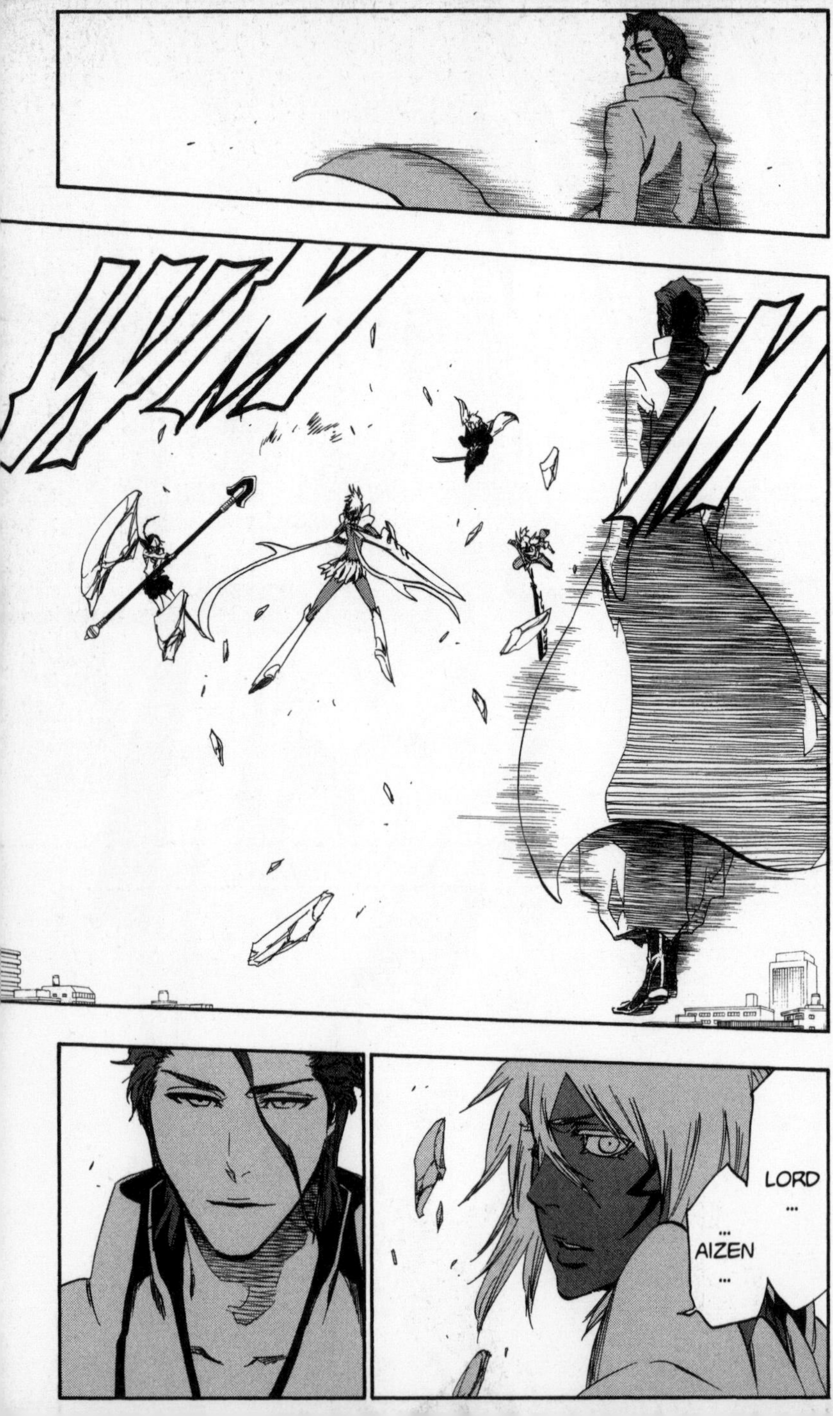
LORD
...
...
AIZEN
...

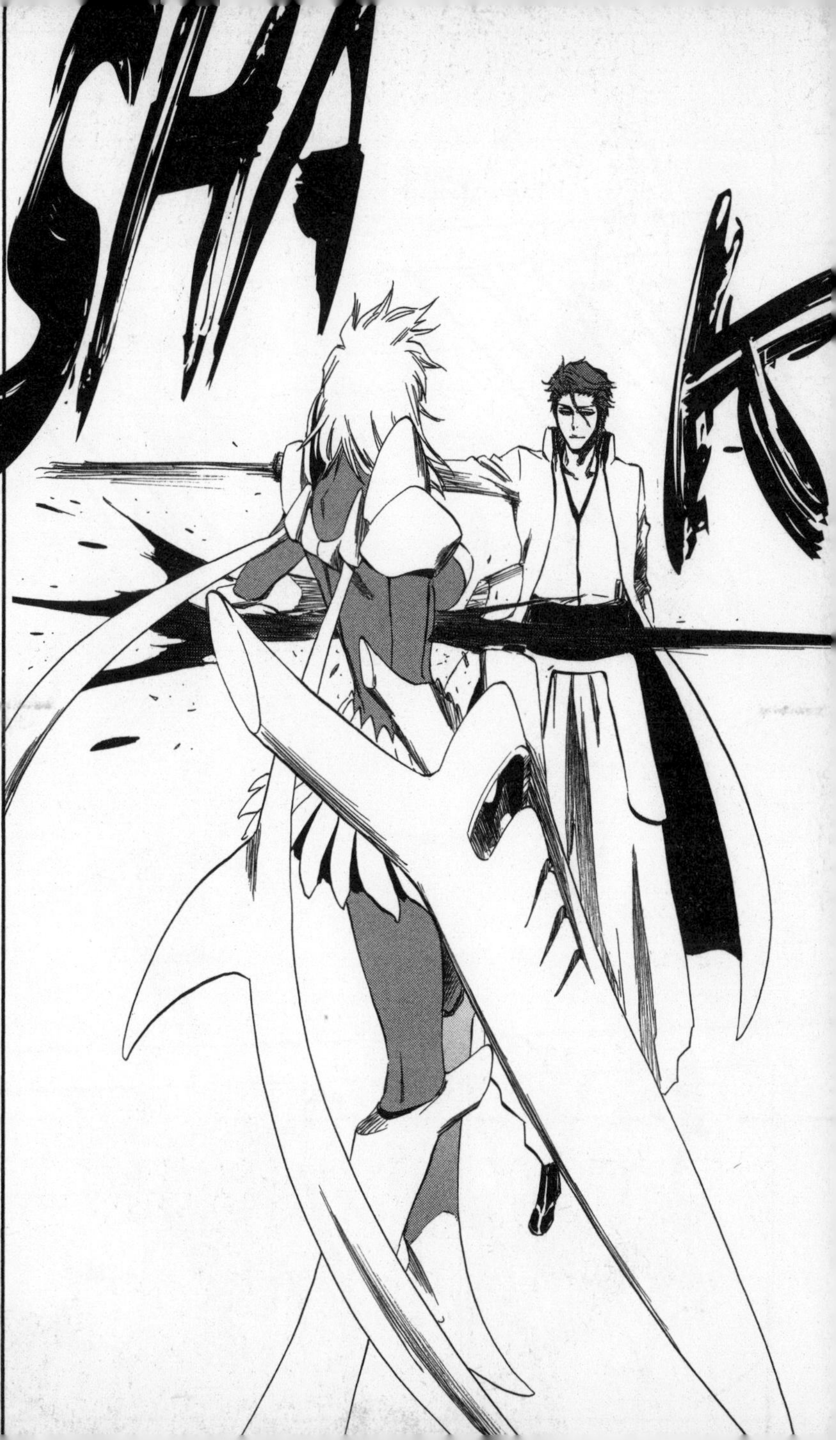
SHHAK

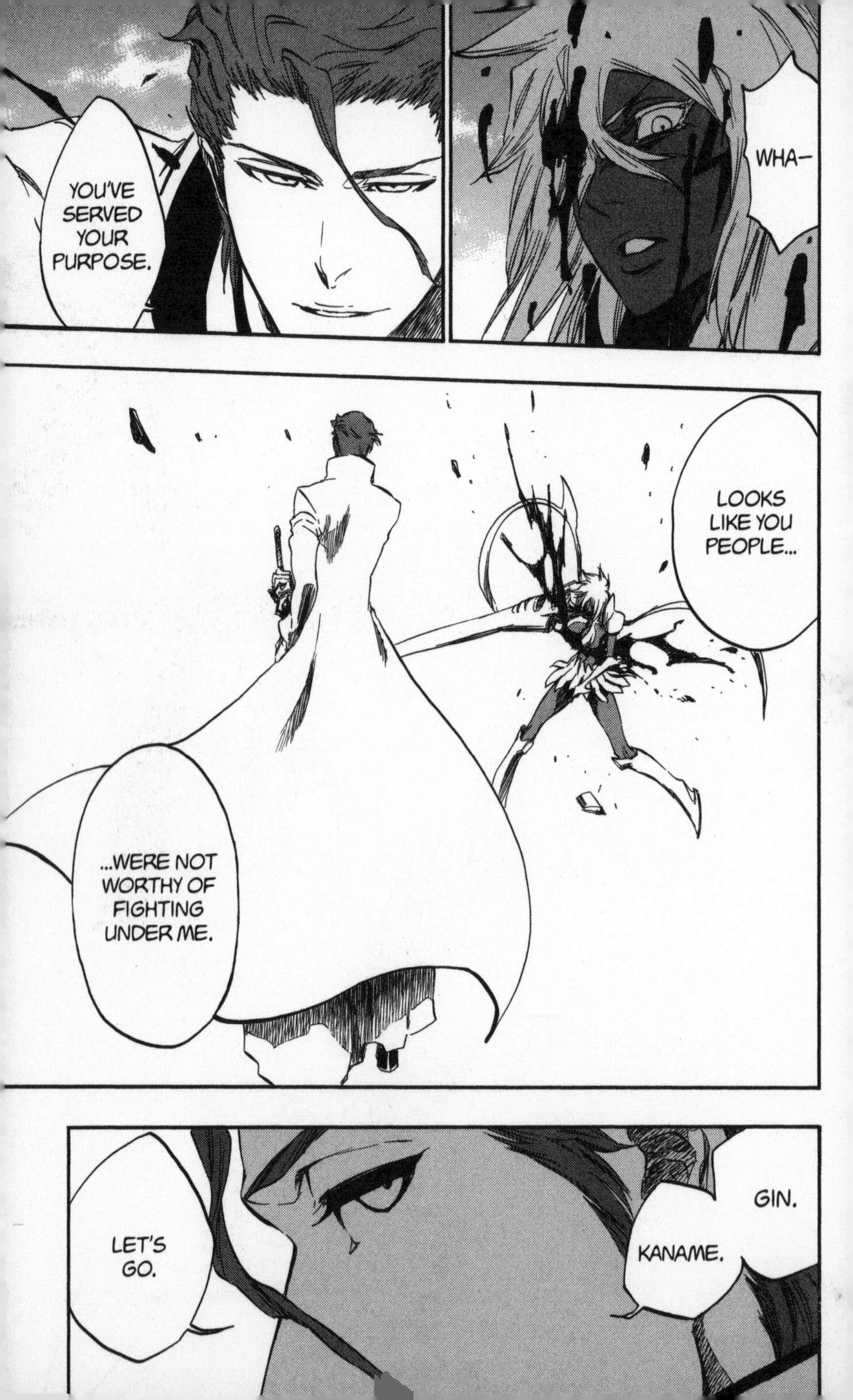
WHA-
YOU'VE SERVED YOUR PURPOSE.
LOOKS LIKE YOU PEOPLE...
...WERE NOT WORTHY OF FIGHTING UNDER ME.
GIN.
KANAME.
LET'S GO.

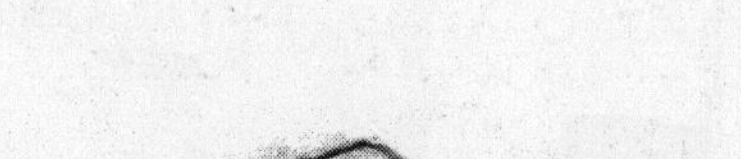

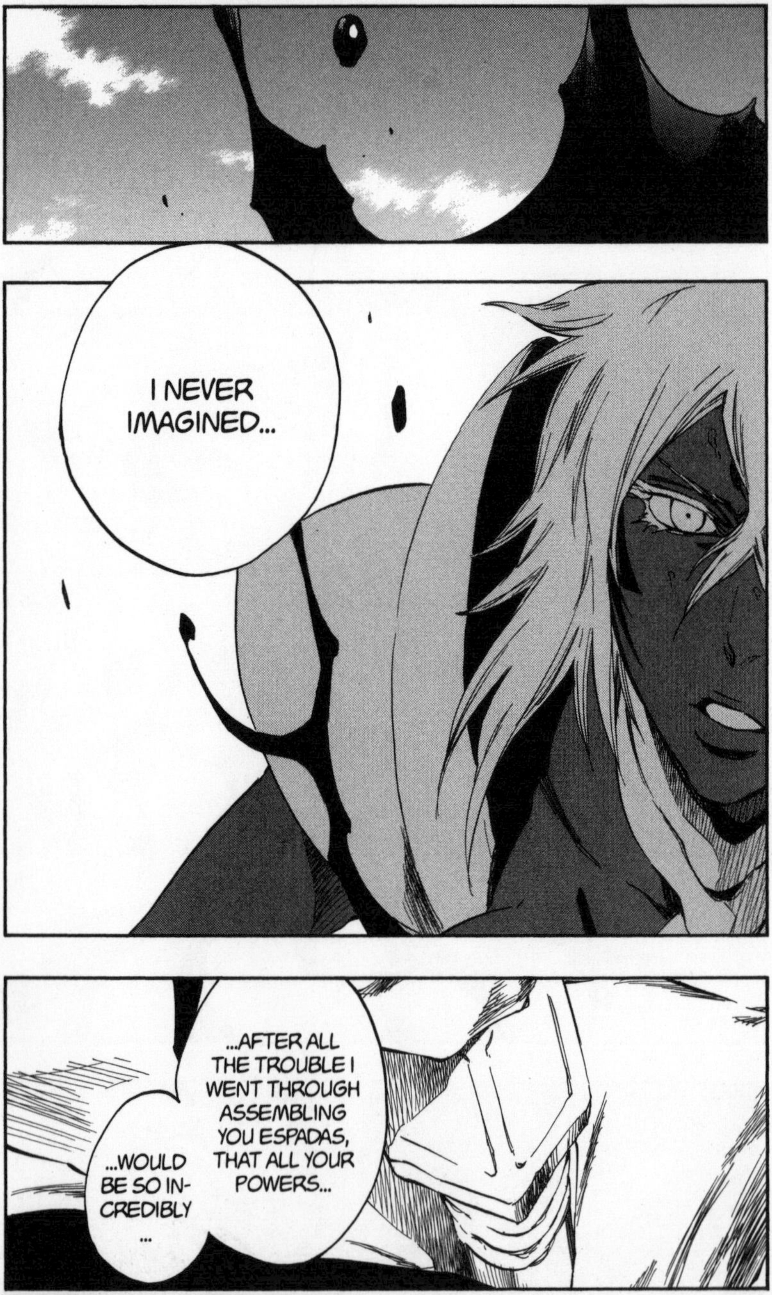
I NEVER IMAGINED...
...AFTER ALL THE TROUBLE I WENT THROUGH ASSEMBLING YOU ESPADAS, THAT ALL YOUR POWERS...
...WOULD BE SO IN-CREDIBLY ...

376. EXecution, EXtinction 2

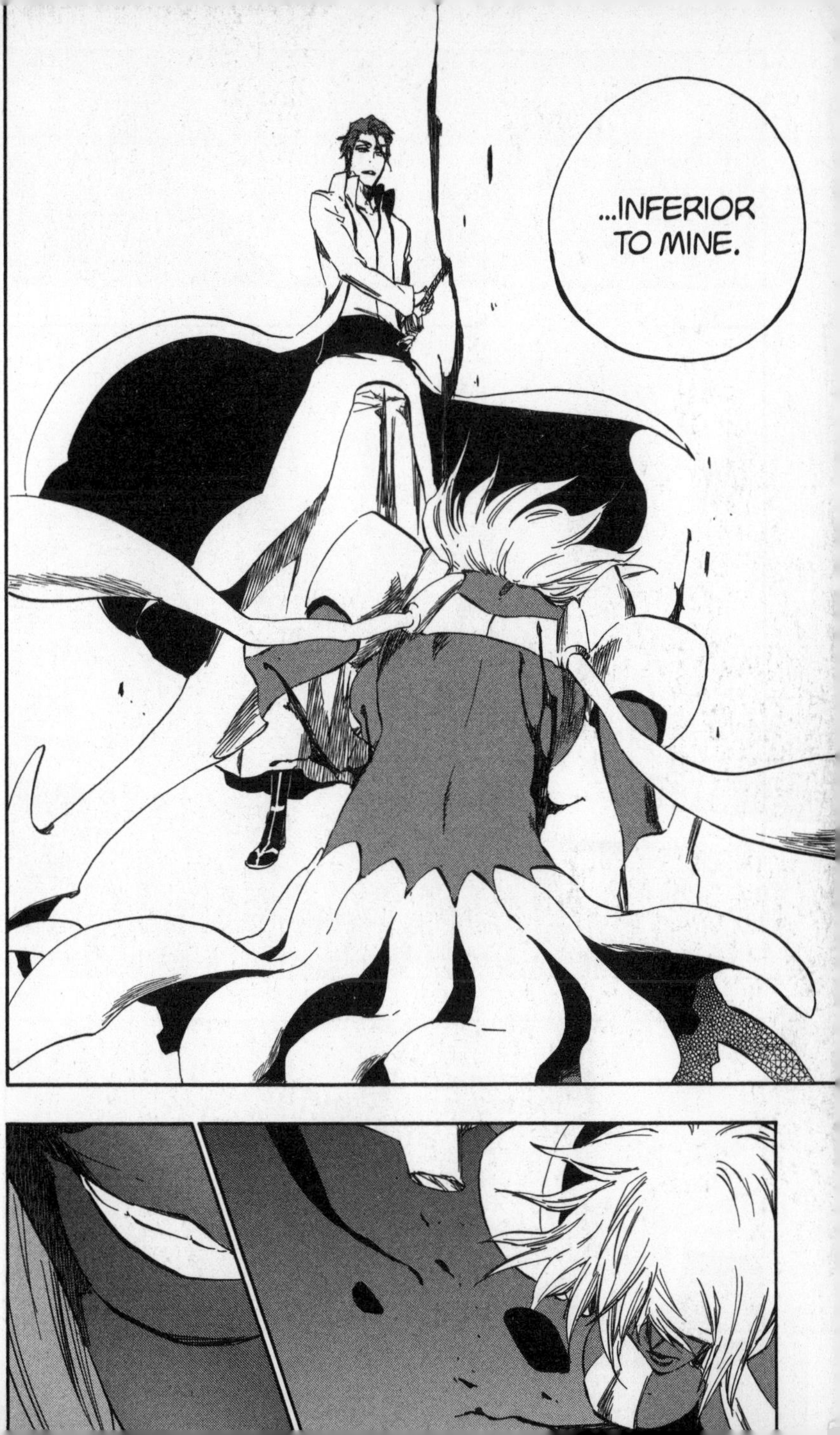
...INFERIOR TO MINE.

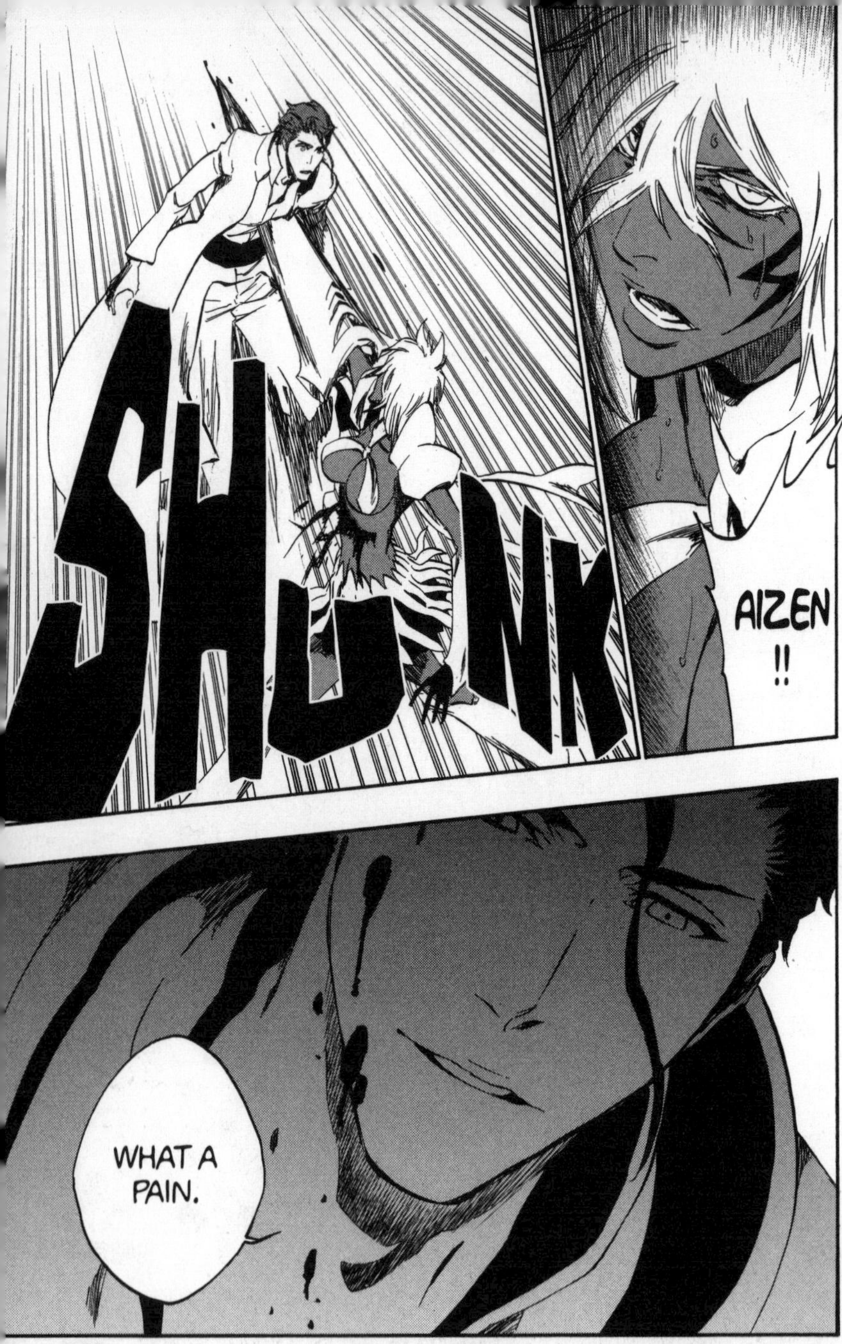
AIZEN !!
SHUNK
WHAT A PAIN.

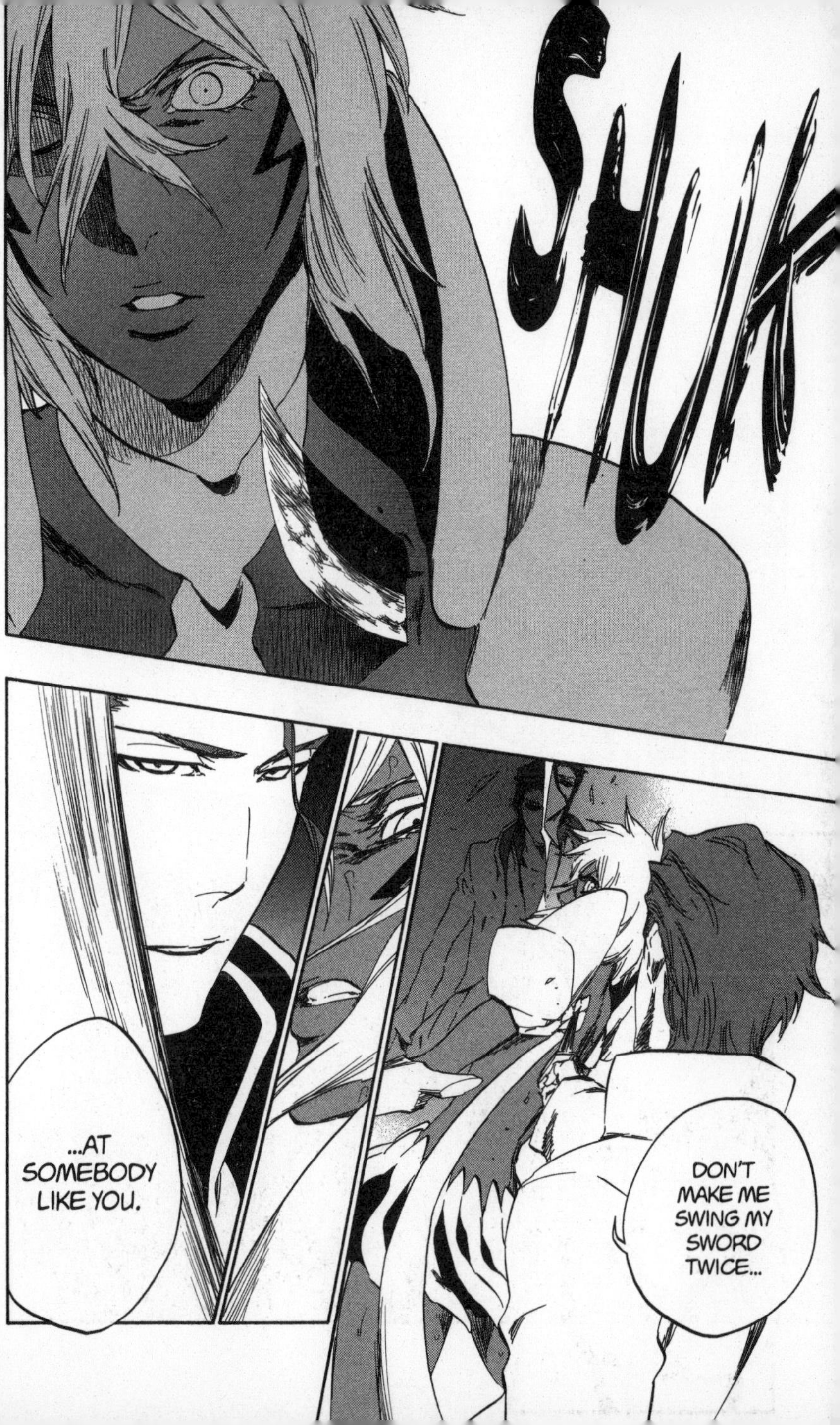
SHUK
DON'T MAKE ME SWING MY SWORD TWICE...
...AT SOMEBODY LIKE YOU.

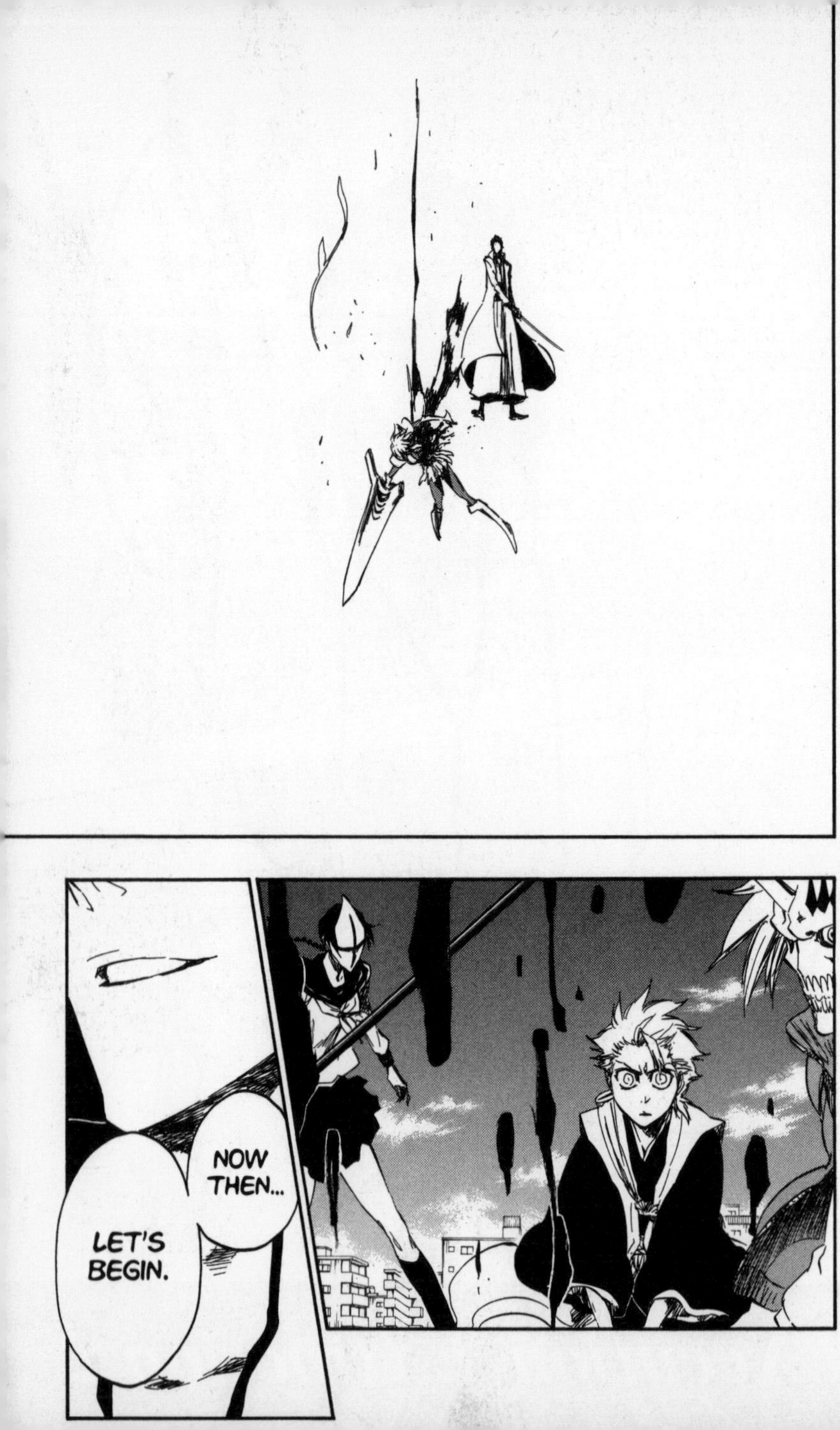
NOW THEN...
LET'S BEGIN.

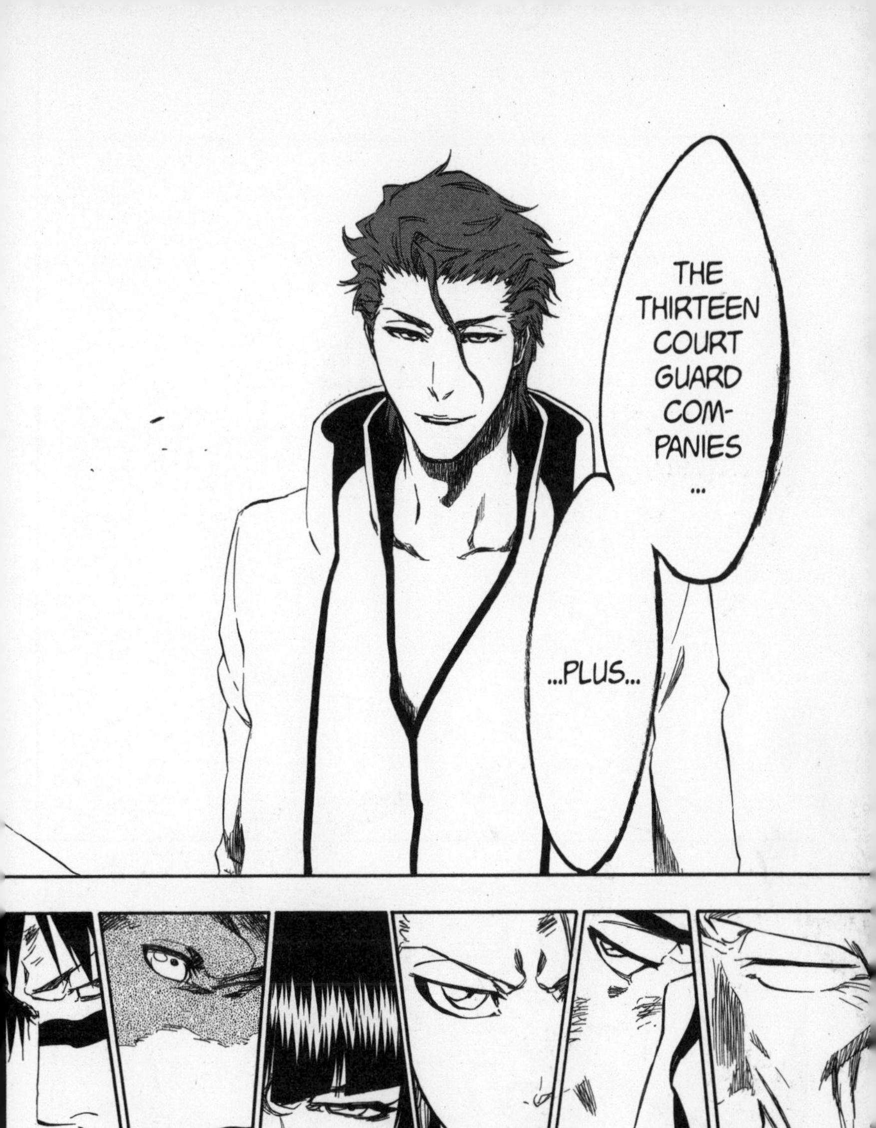
THE THIRTEEN COURT GUARD COMPANIES ...
...PLUS...

EXecution, EXtinction 2

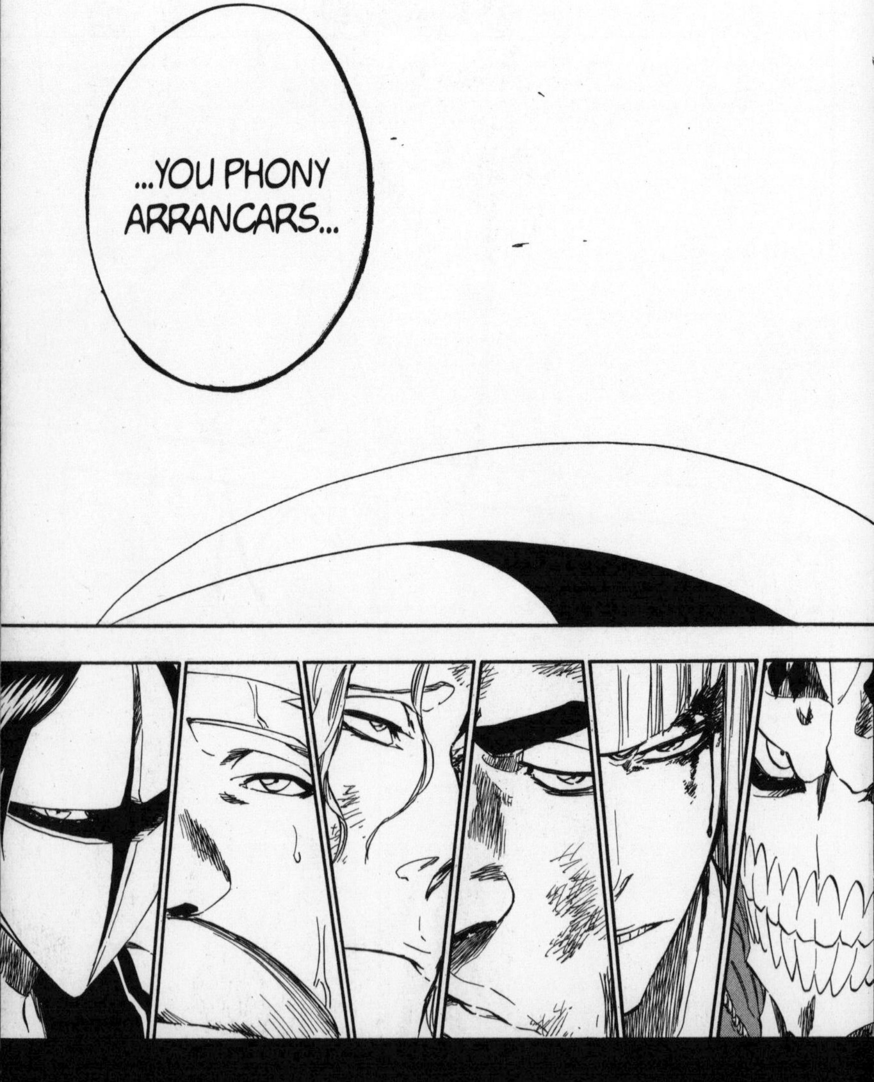
...YOU PHONY ARRANCARS...

BLEACH376.

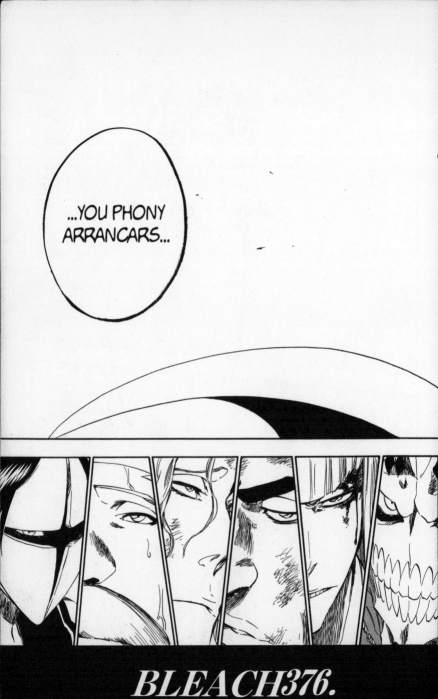

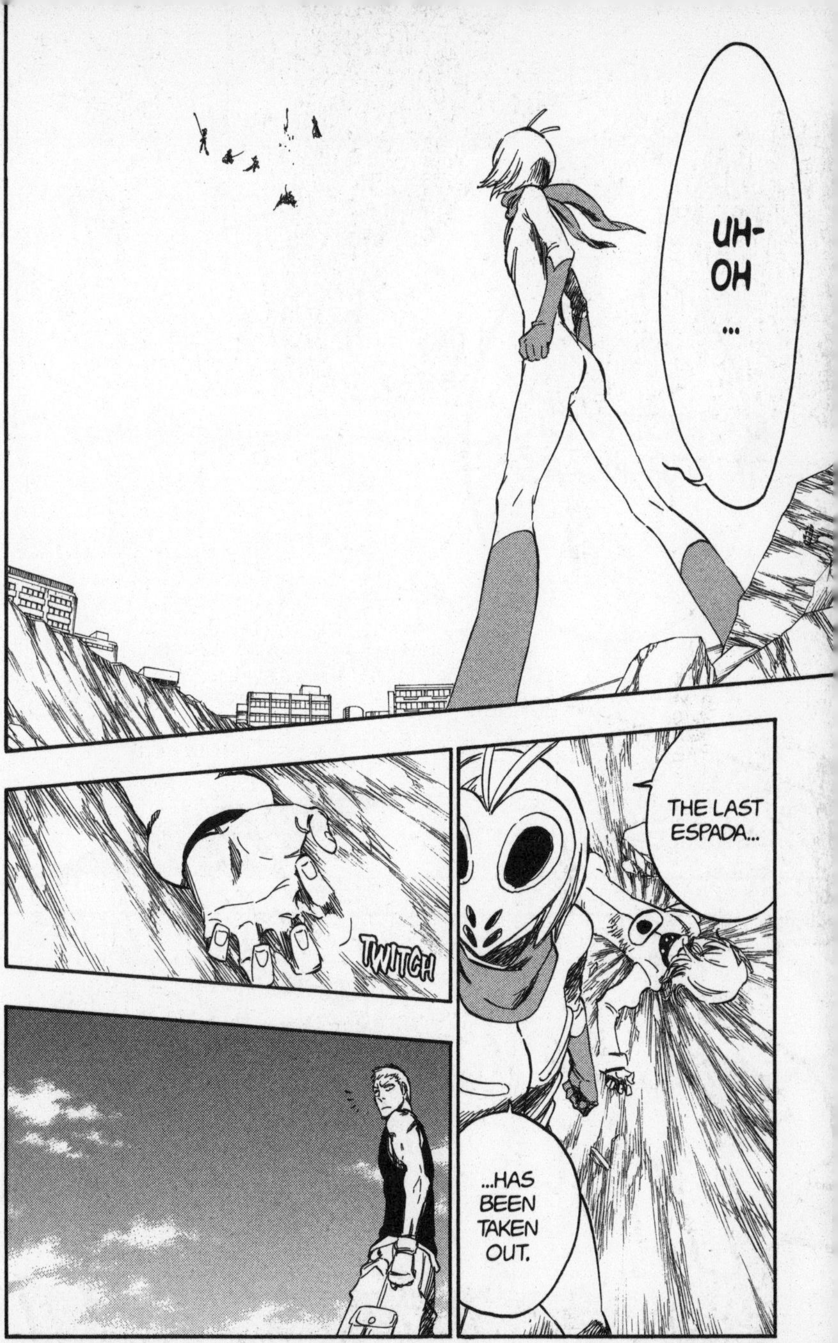
UH-OH ...
THE LAST ESPADA...
...HAS BEEN TAKEN OUT.
TWITCH

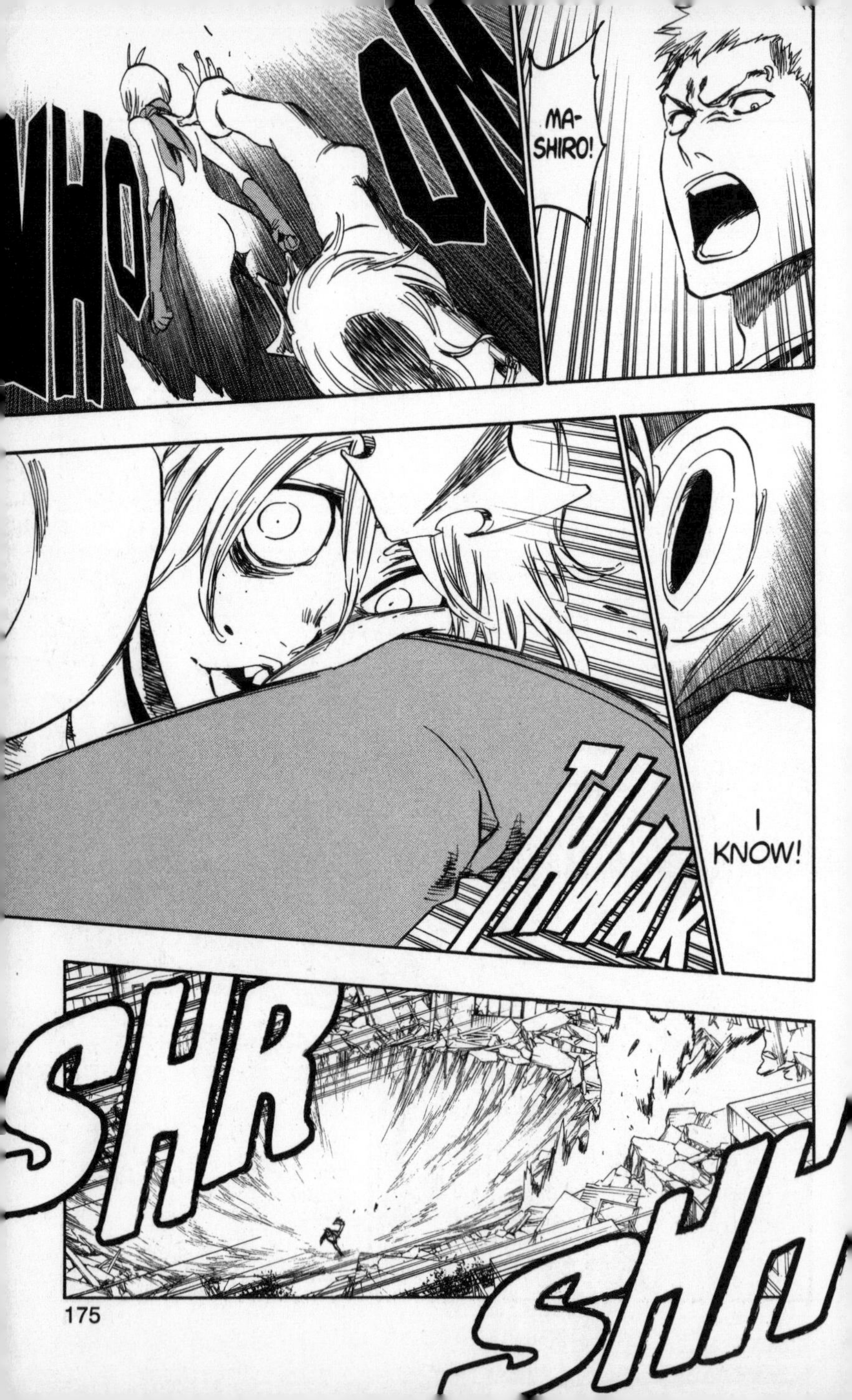
MA-SHIRO!
WHOOM
I KNOW!
THWAK
SHR
SHH

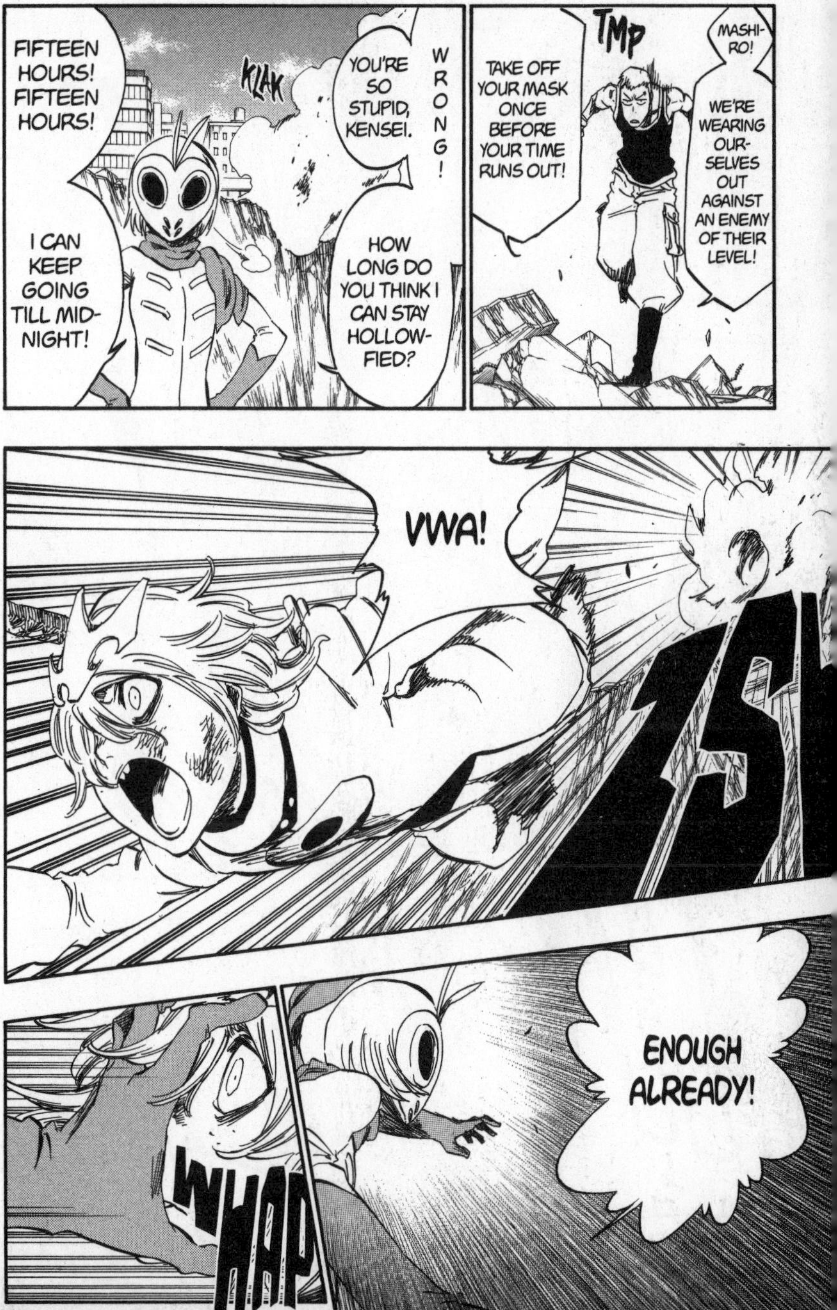
MASHI-RO!
TMP
WE'RE WEARING OUR-SELVES OUT AGAINST AN ENEMY OF THEIR LEVEL!
TAKE OFF YOUR MASK ONCE BEFORE YOUR TIME RUNS OUT!
WRONG!
YOU'RE SO STUPID, KENSEI.
HOW LONG DO YOU THINK I CAN STAY HOLLOW-FIED?
KLAK
FIFTEEN HOURS! FIFTEEN HOURS!
I CAN KEEP GOING TILL MID-NIGHT!
VWA!
ENOUGH ALREADY!
WHAP

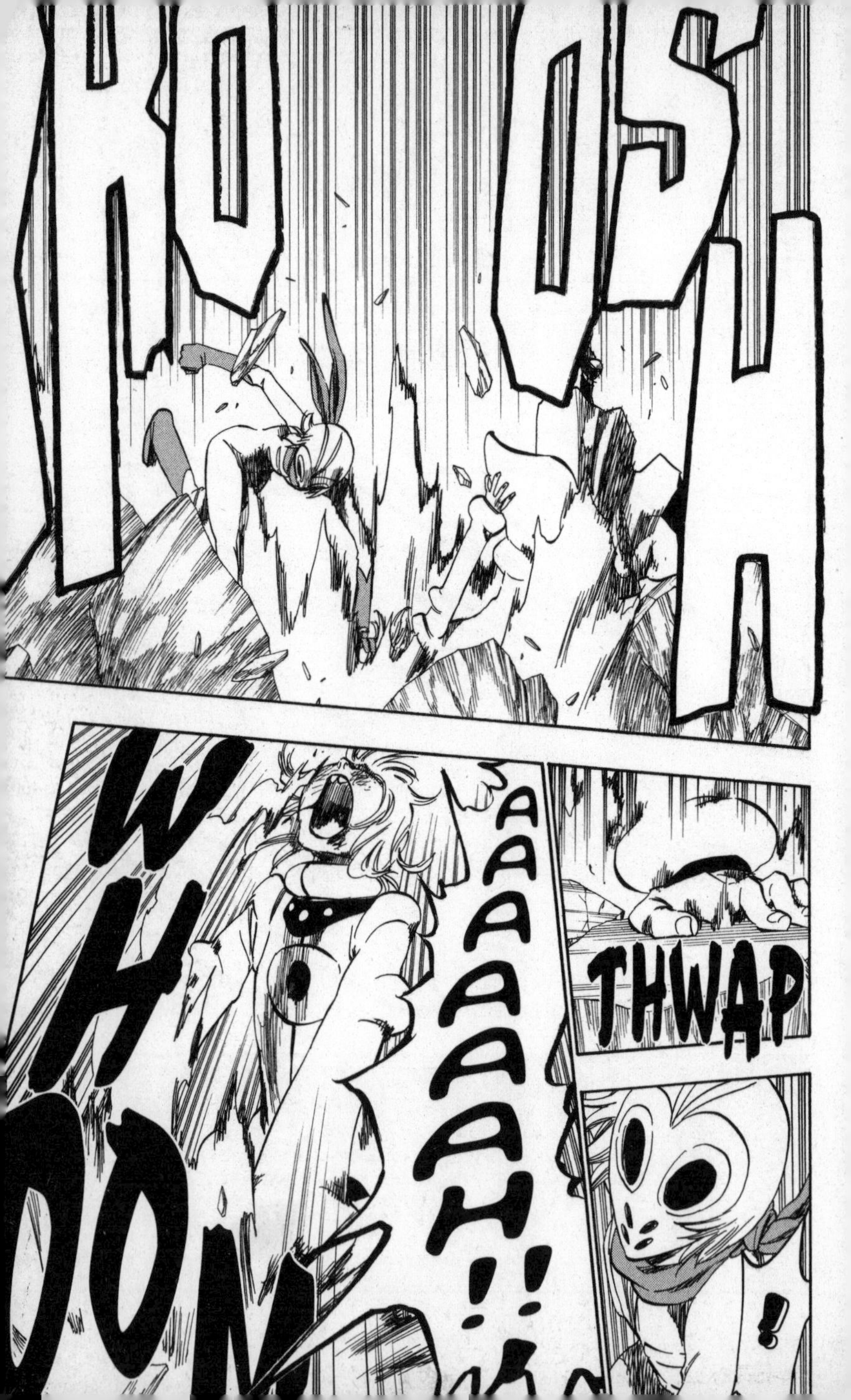
THWAP
!
WHOOM
AAAAAAAH!!

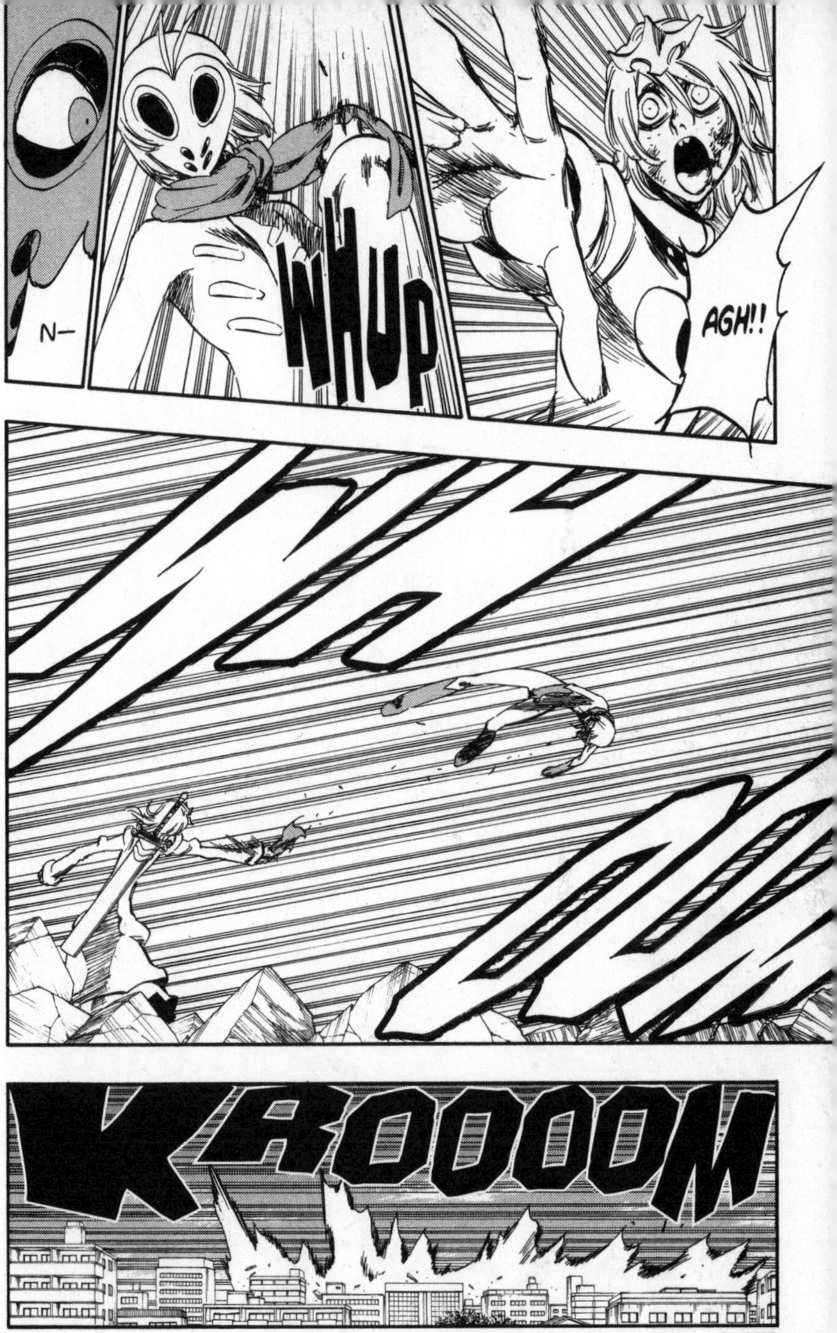
AGH!!
WHUP
N—
KROOOOM

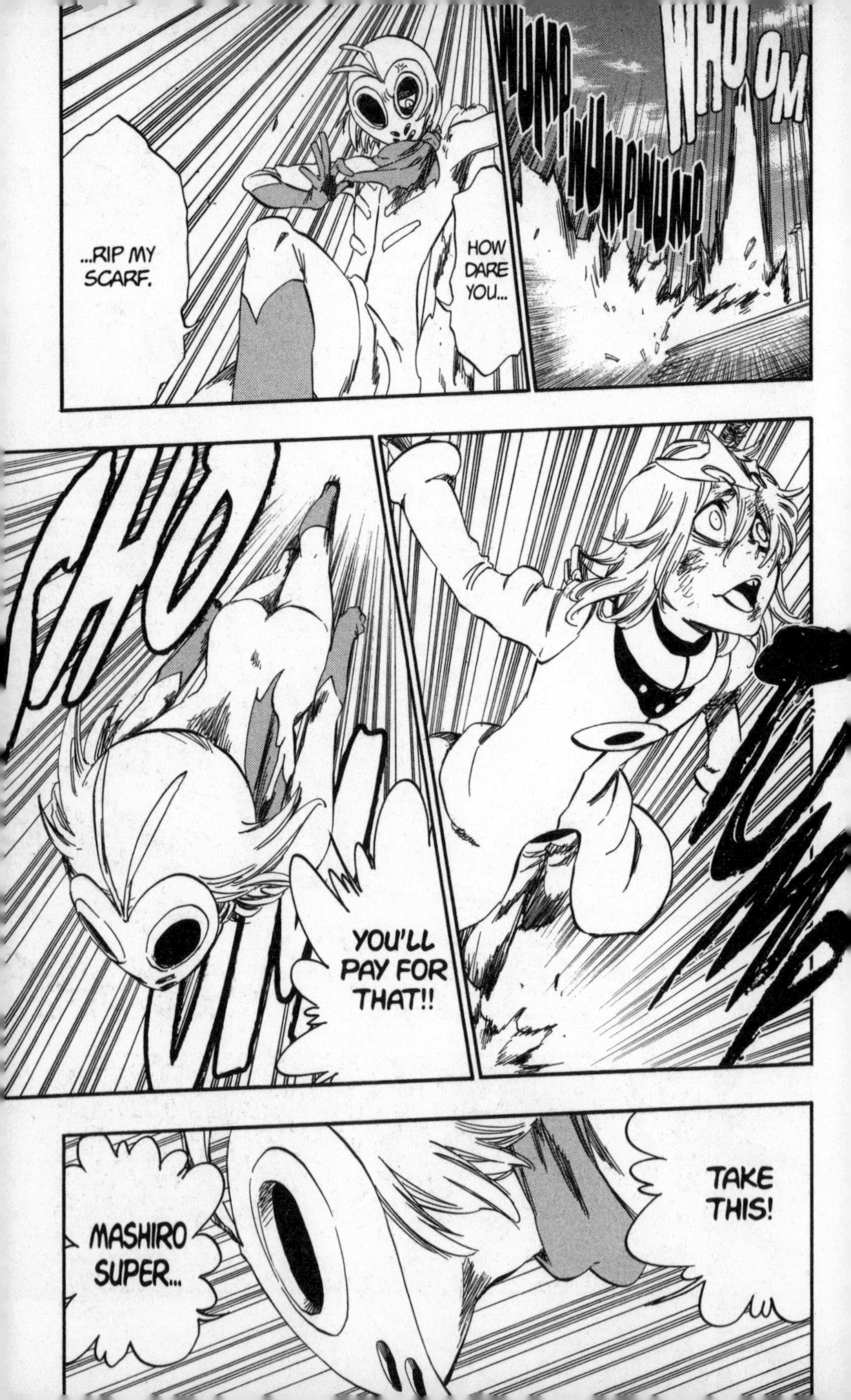
WHOOM
HOW DARE YOU...
...RIP MY SCARF.
YOU'LL PAY FOR THAT!!
TAKE THIS!
MASHIRO SUPER...

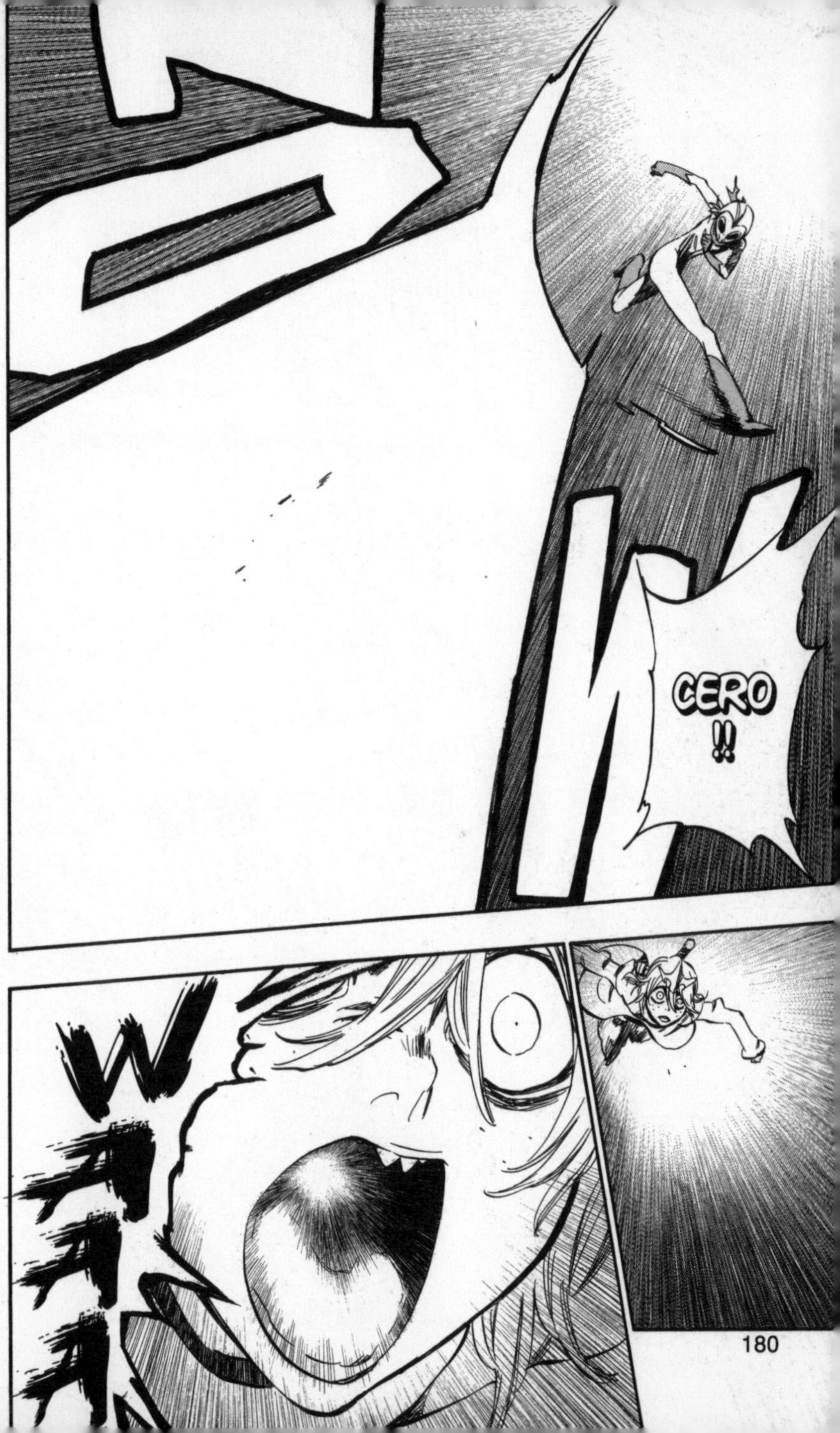
CERO !!

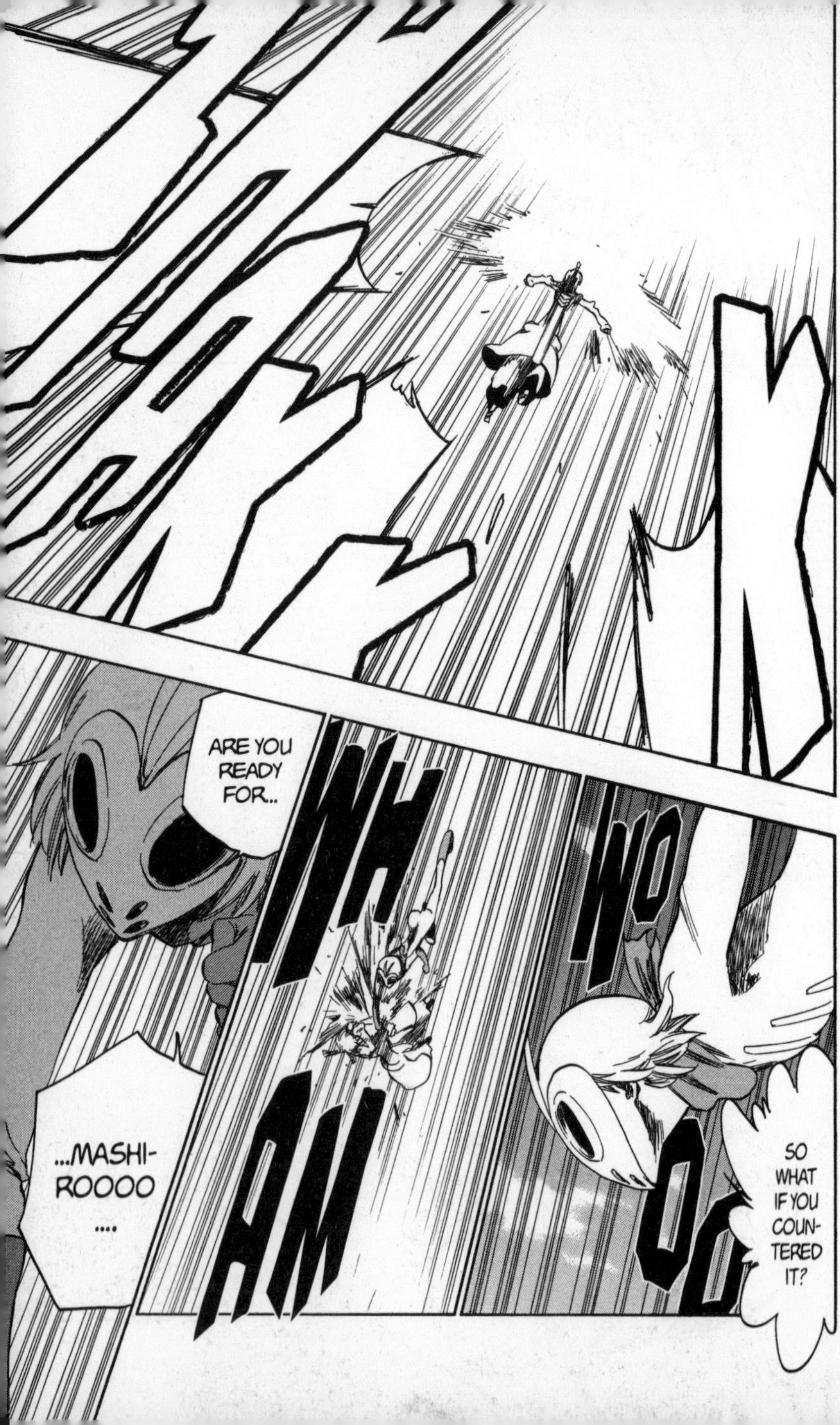
SO WHAT IF YOU COUN-TERED IT?
WHAM
ARE YOU READY FOR...
...MASHI-ROOOO ....

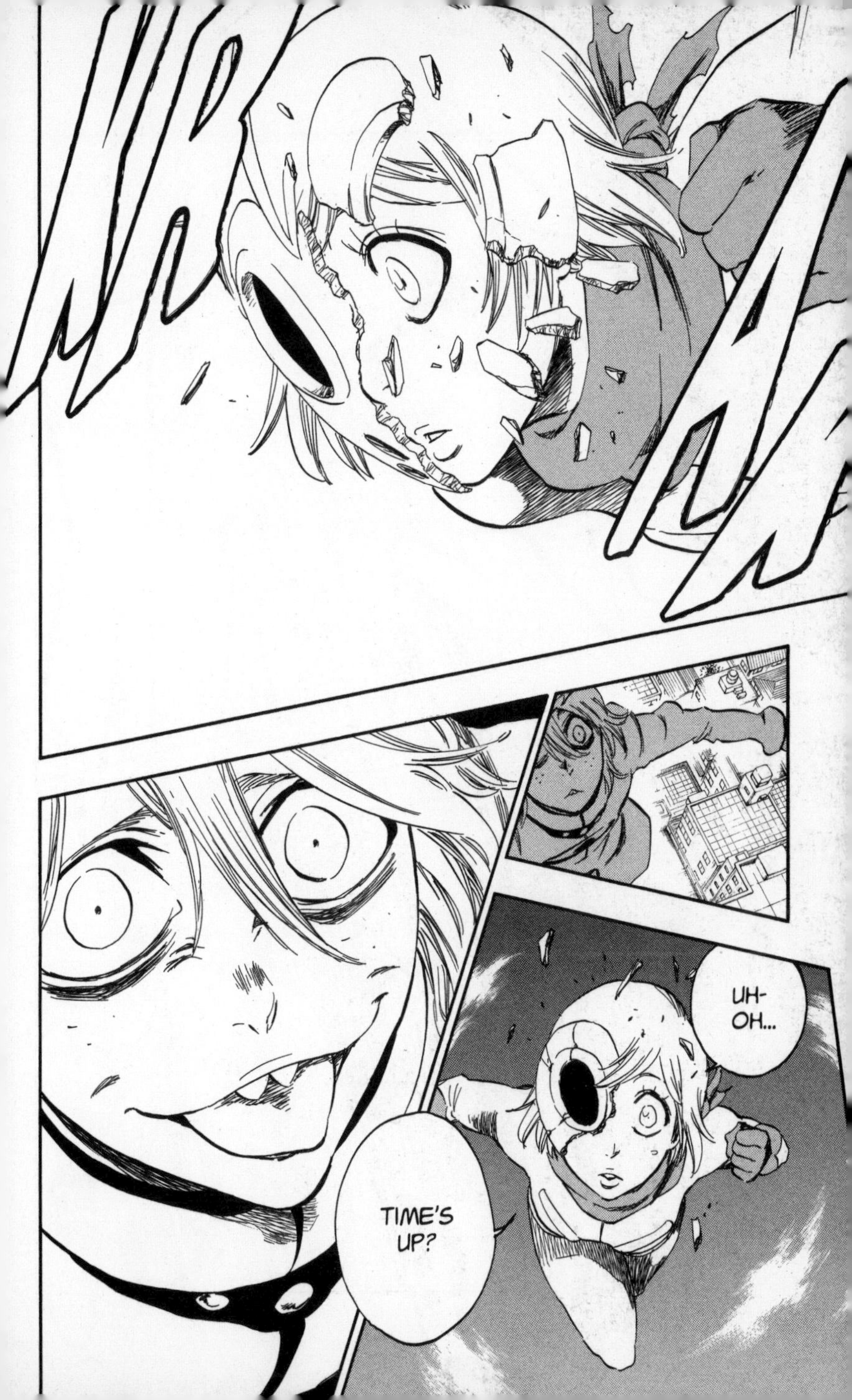
UH-OH...
TIME'S UP?

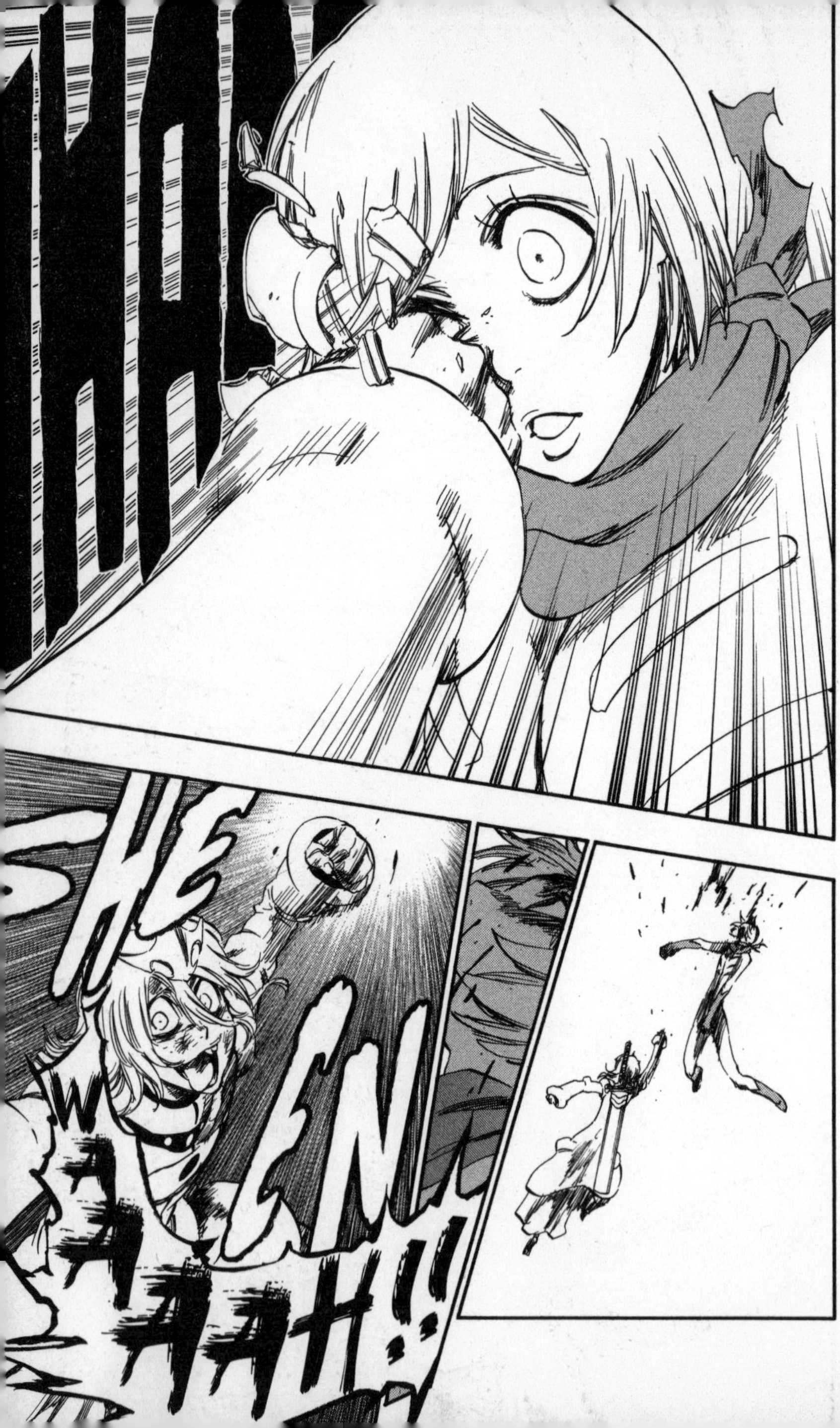

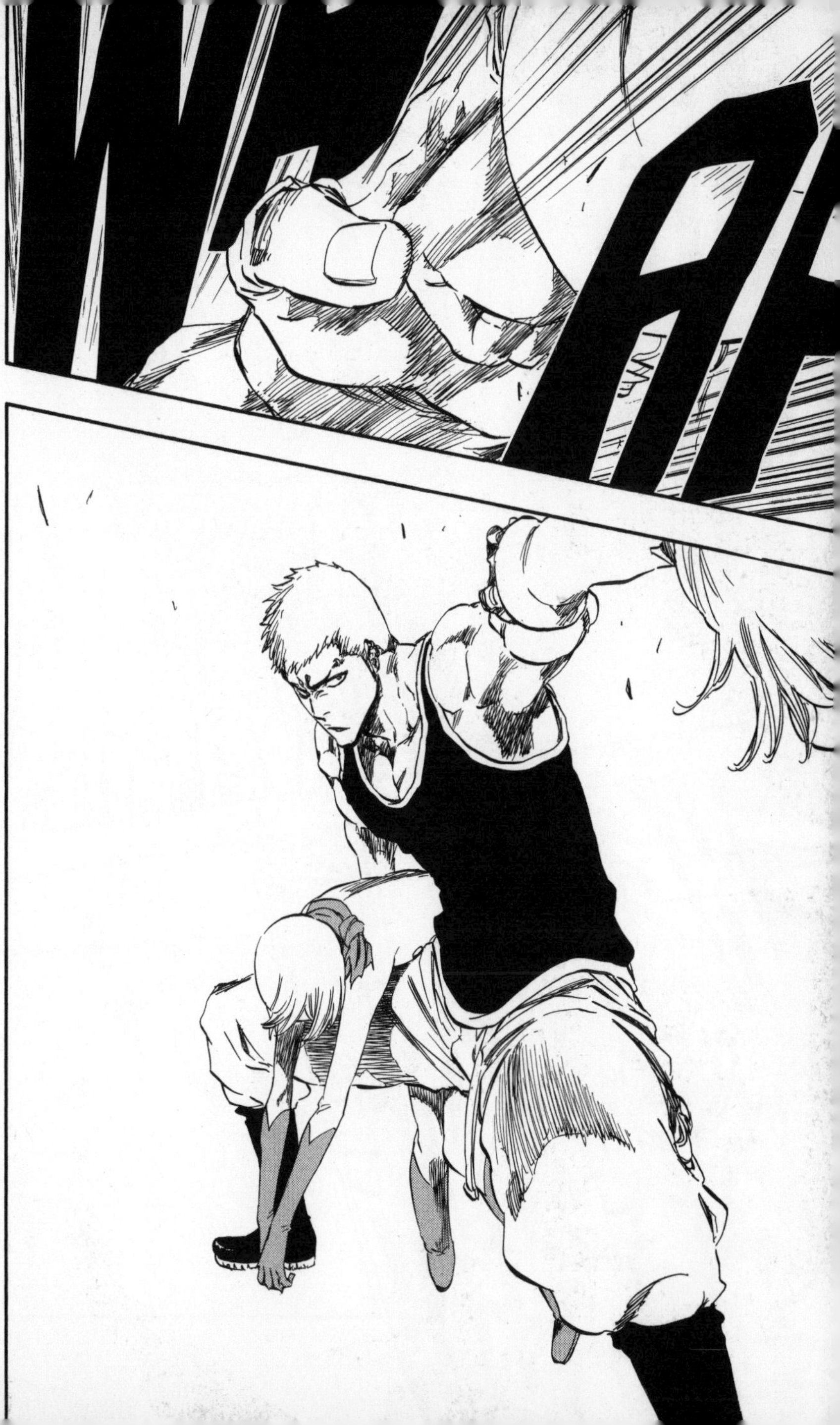

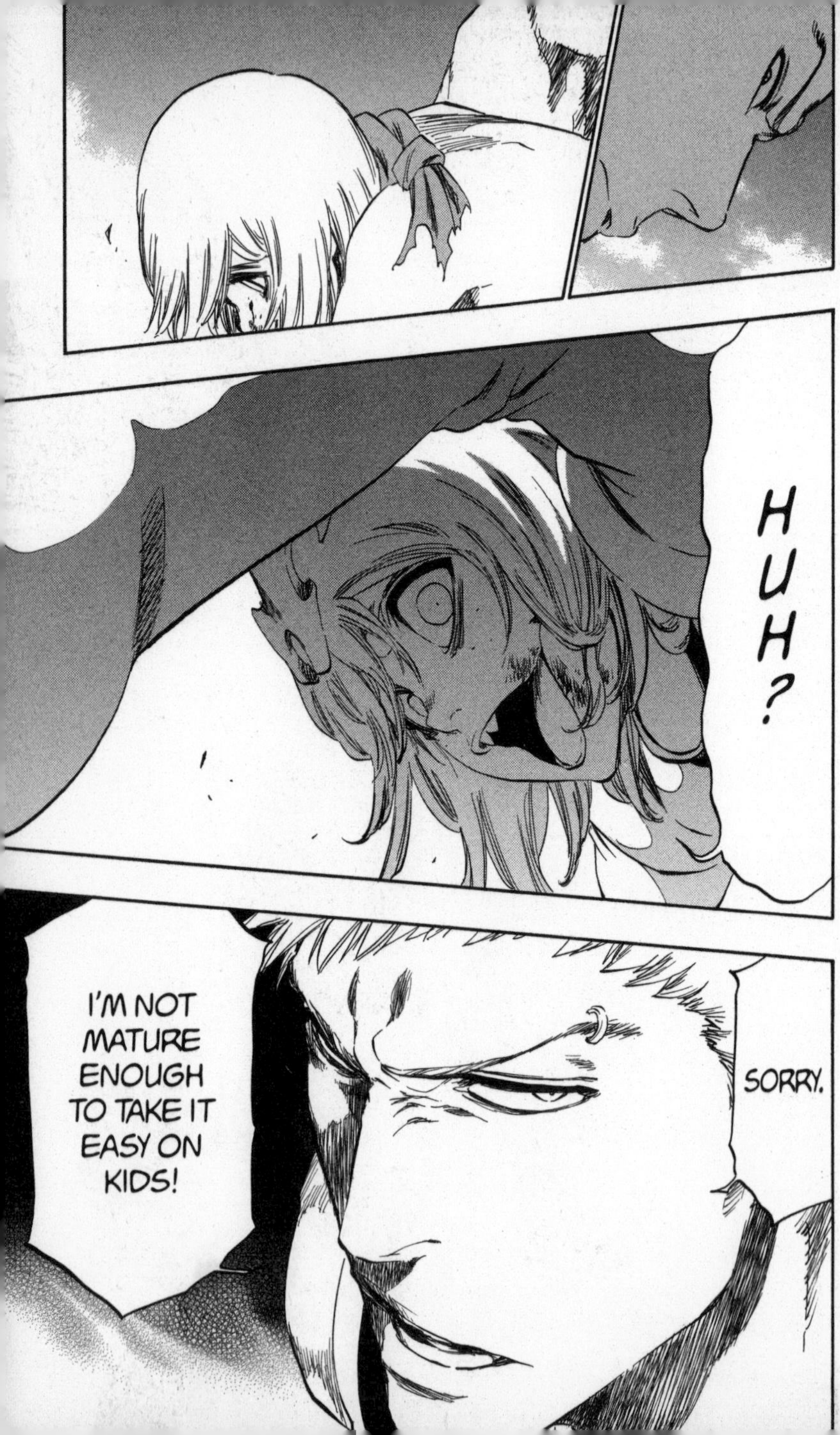
HUH?
SORRY.
I'M NOT MATURE ENOUGH TO TAKE IT EASY ON KIDS!

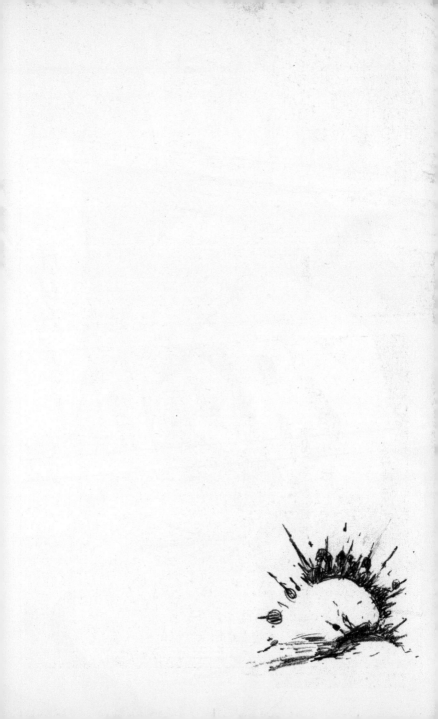

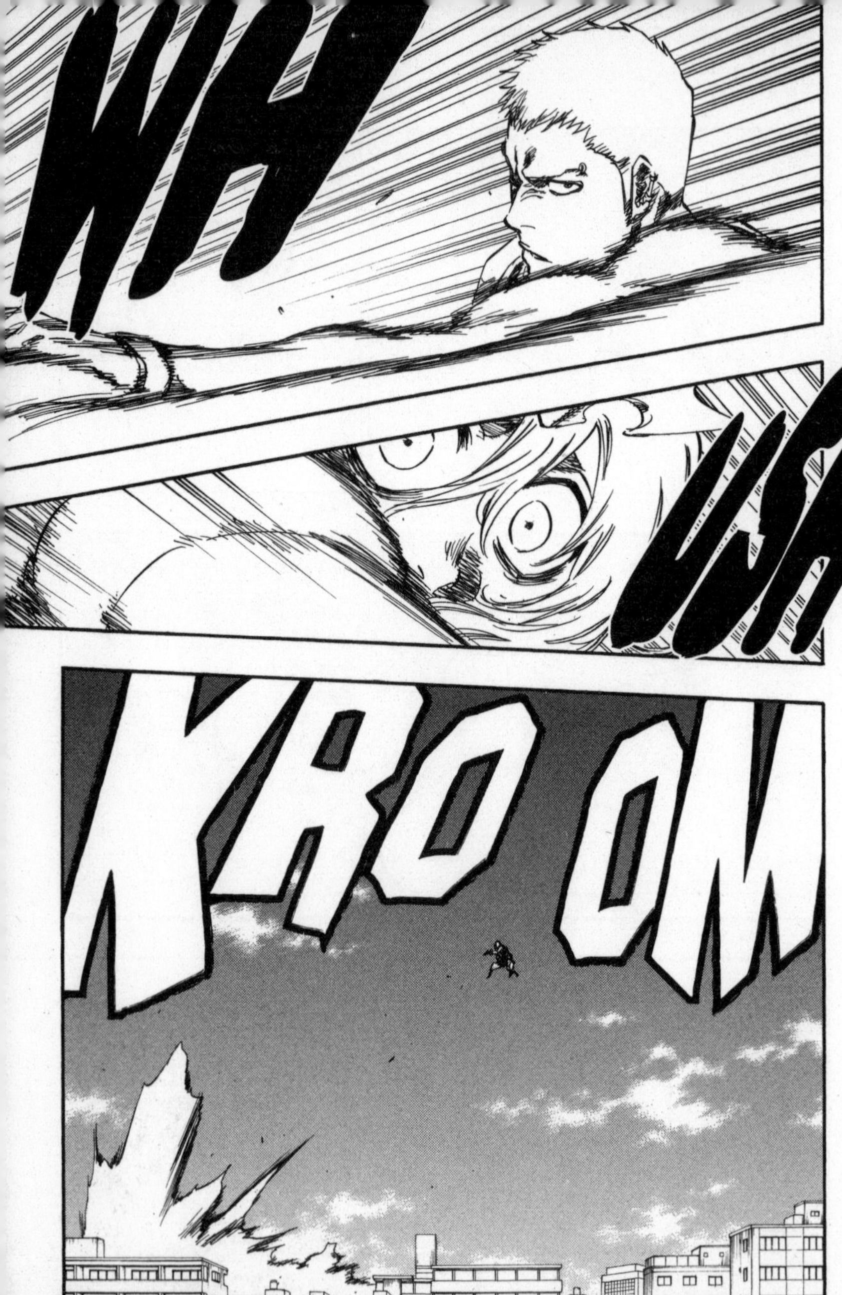
WHS
WSH
KROOM

377. Shout at the Dark

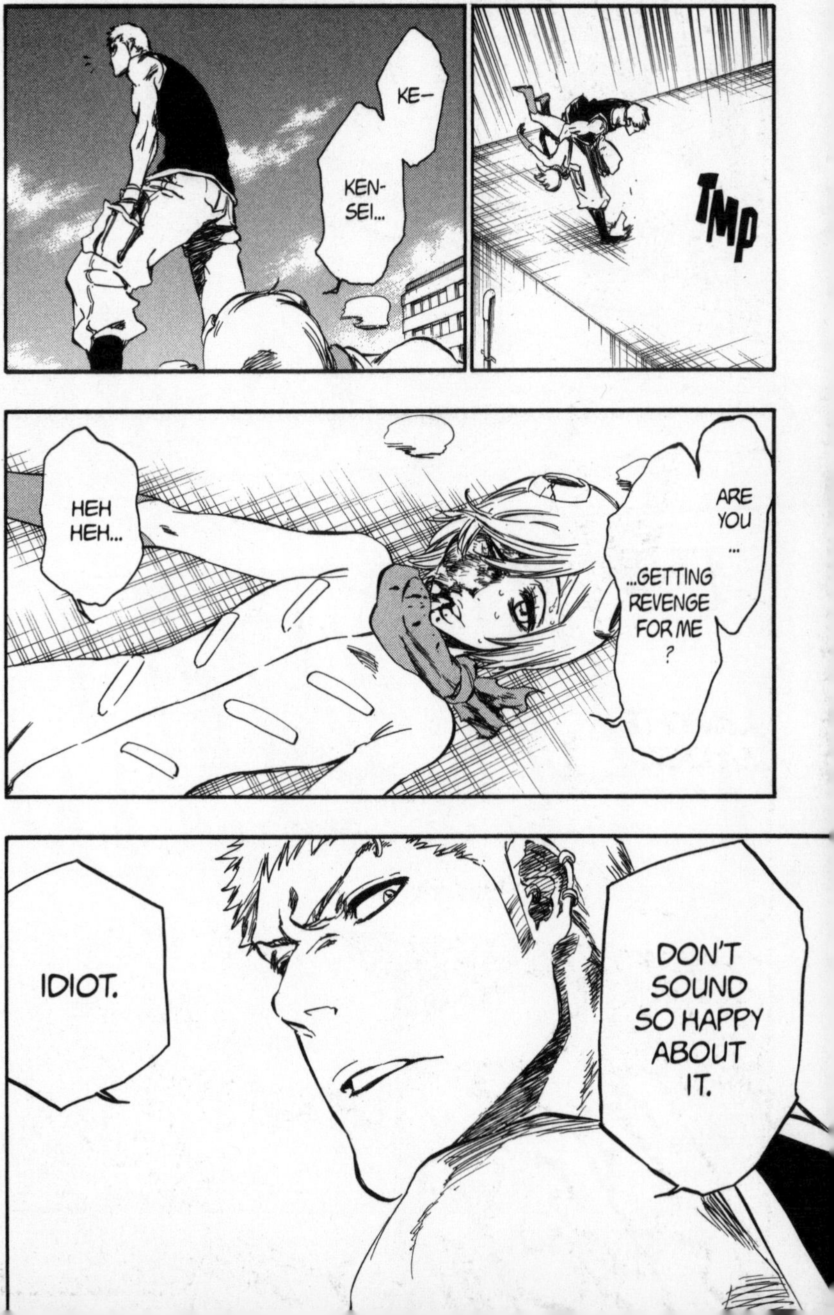
TMP
KE-
KEN-SEI...
ARE YOU ... ...GETTING REVENGE FOR ME ?
HEH HEH...
DON'T SOUND SO HAPPY ABOUT IT.
IDIOT.

READ THIS WAY

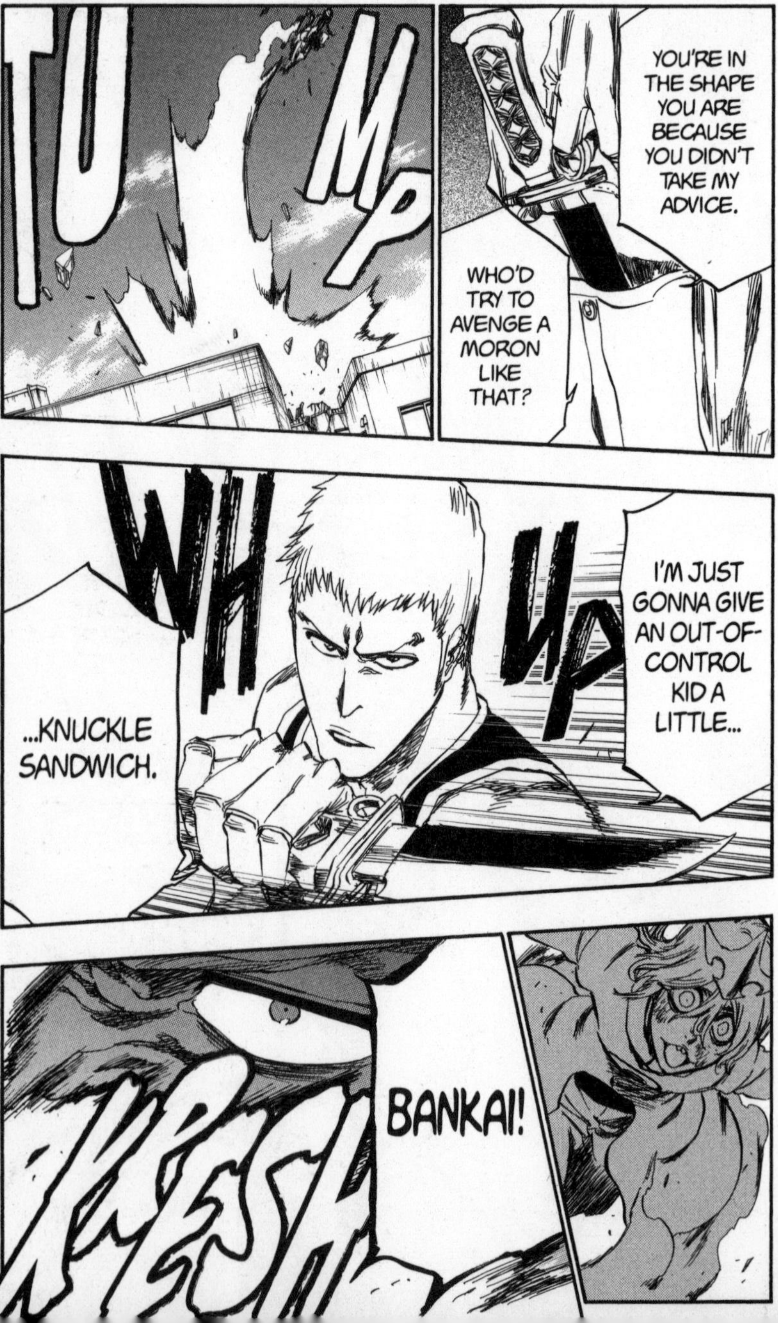
YOU'RE IN THE SHAPE YOU ARE BECAUSE YOU DIDN'T TAKE MY ADVICE.
WHO'D TRY TO AVENGE A MORON LIKE THAT?
TUMP
I'M JUST GONNA GIVE AN OUT-OF-CONTROL KID A LITTLE...
WHUP
...KNUCKLE SANDWICH.
BANKAI!

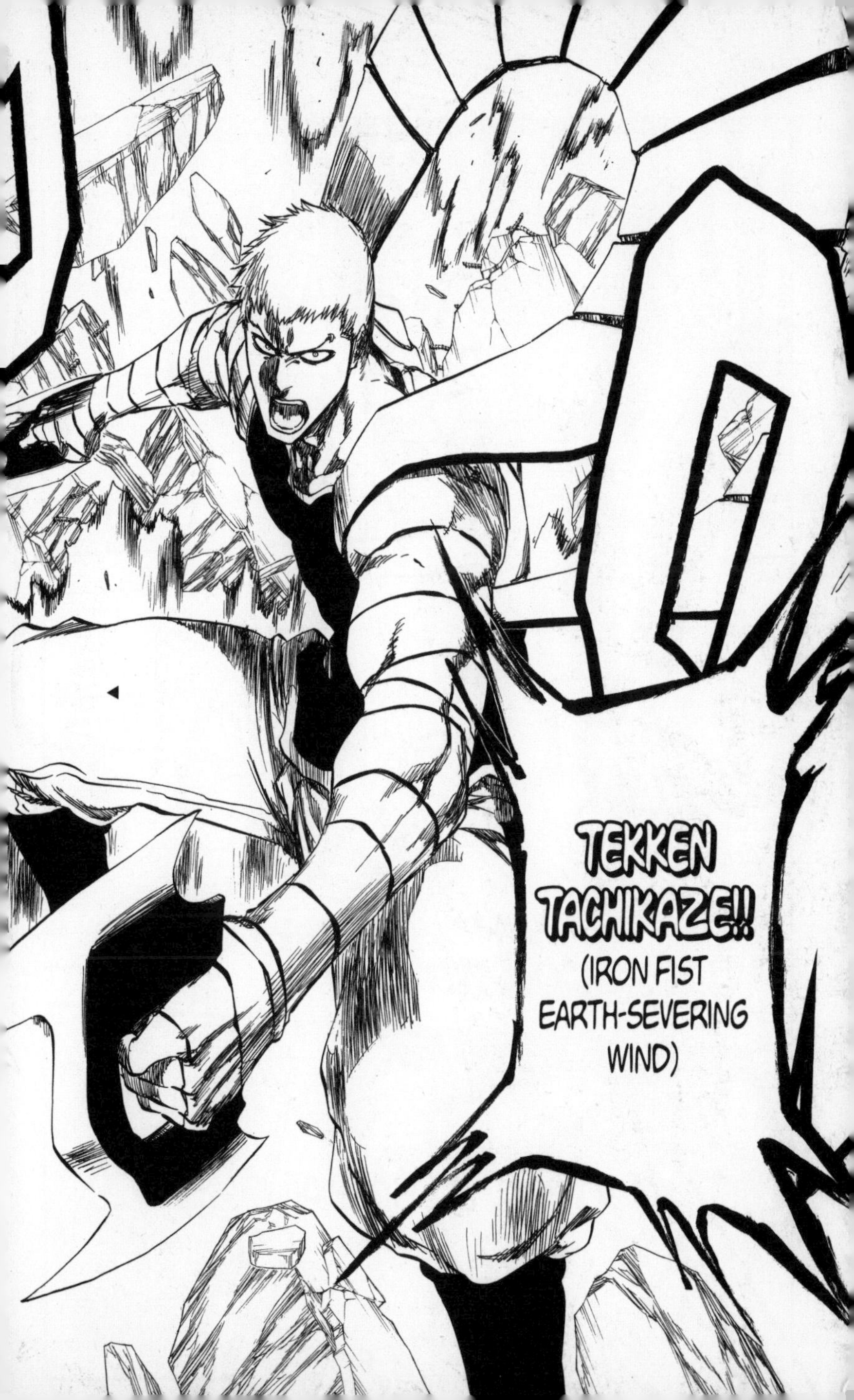
TEKKEN TACHIKAZE!!
(IRON FIST EARTH-SEVERING WIND)

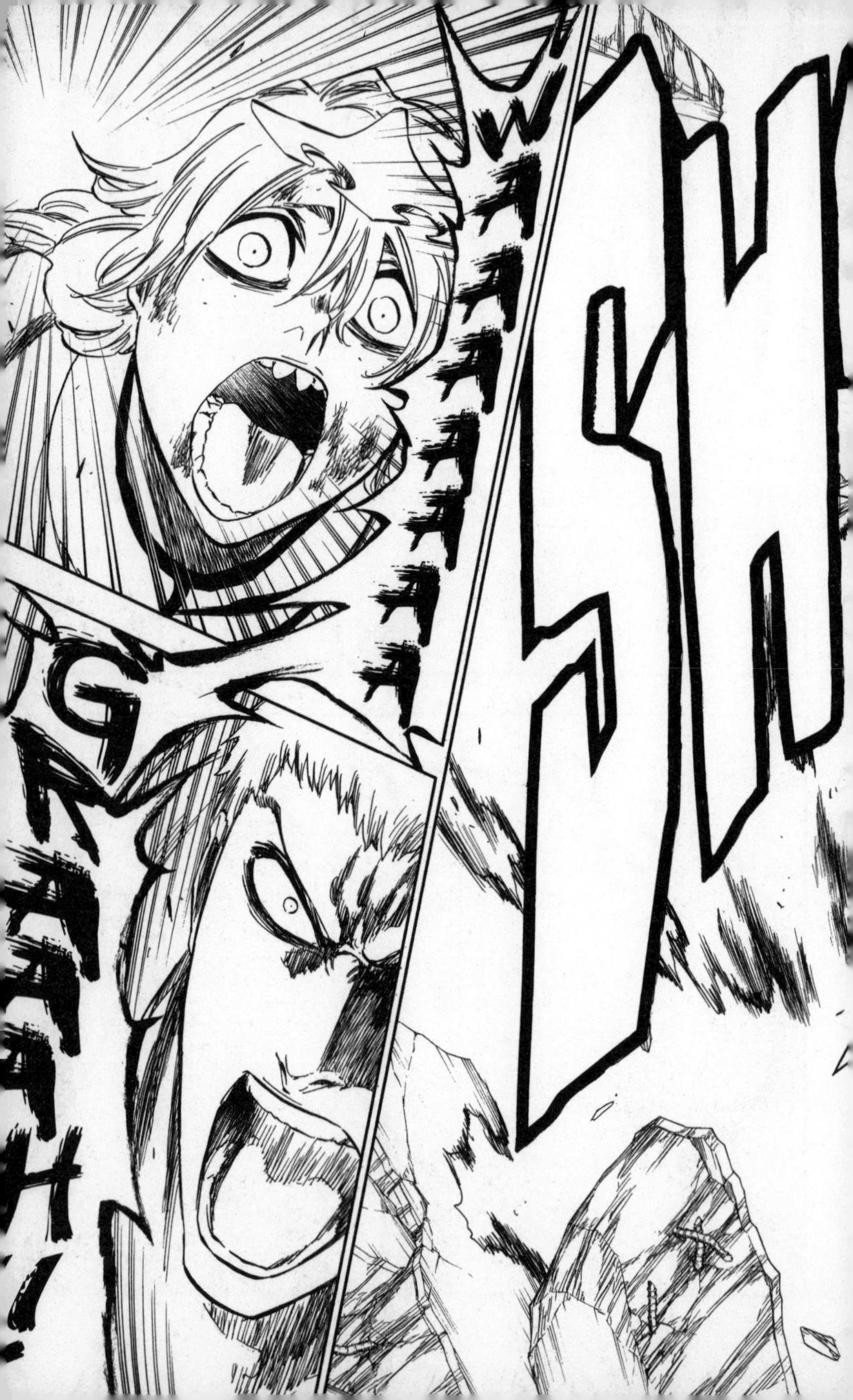
WAAAAAAA
GRAAAH!

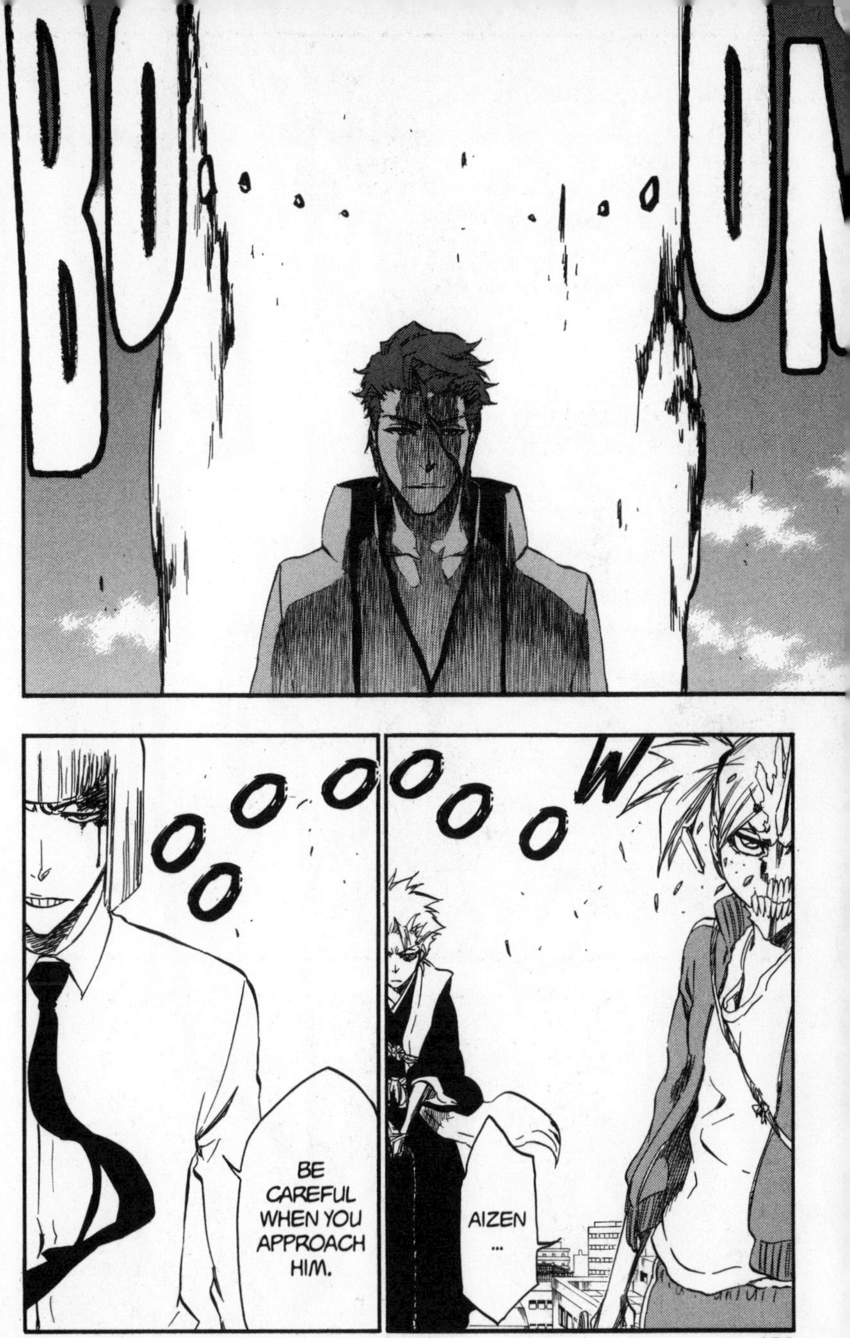
AIZEN ...
BE CAREFUL WHEN YOU APPROACH HIM.

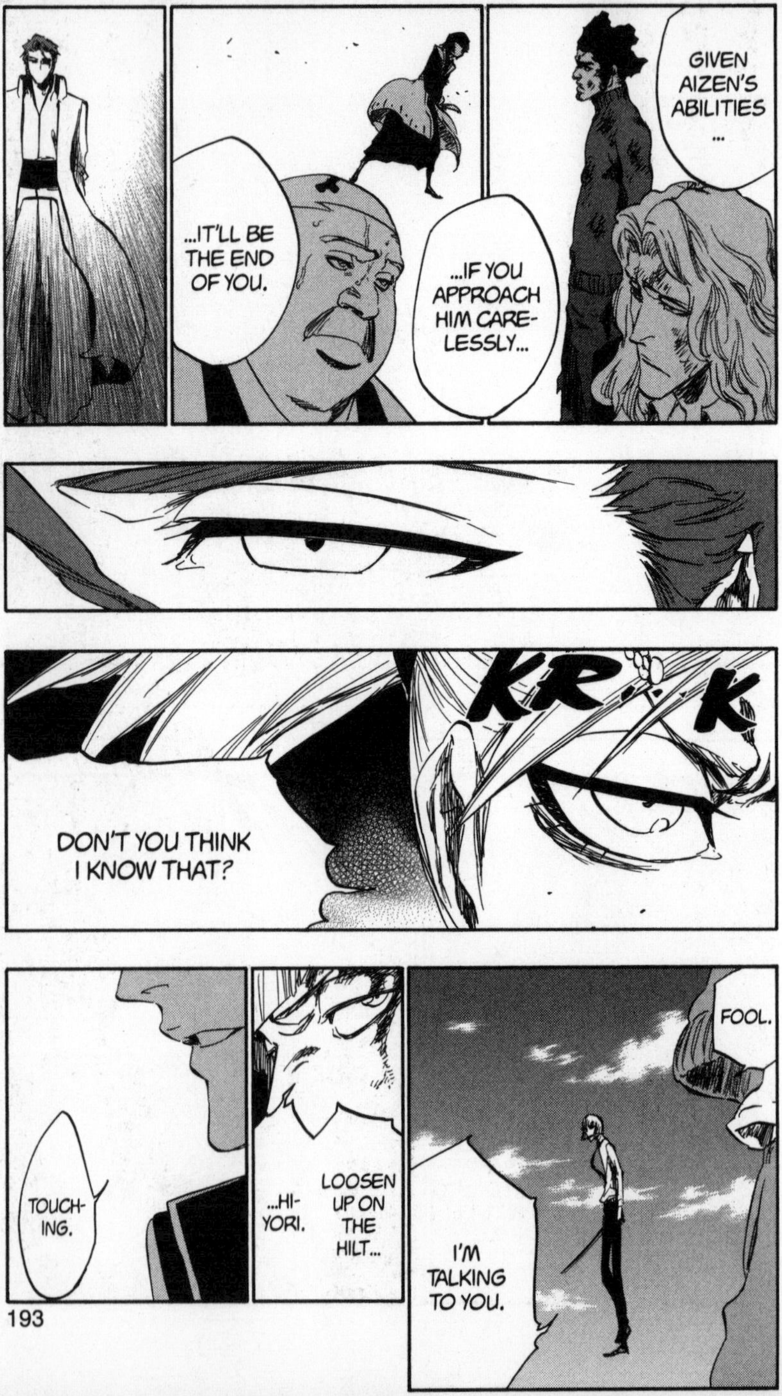
GIVEN AIZEN'S ABILITIES ...
...IF YOU APPROACH HIM CARE-LESSLY...
...IT'LL BE THE END OF YOU.
KR..K
DON'T YOU THINK I KNOW THAT?
FOOL.
I'M TALKING TO YOU.
LOOSEN UP ON THE HILT...
...HI-YORI.
TOUCH-ING.

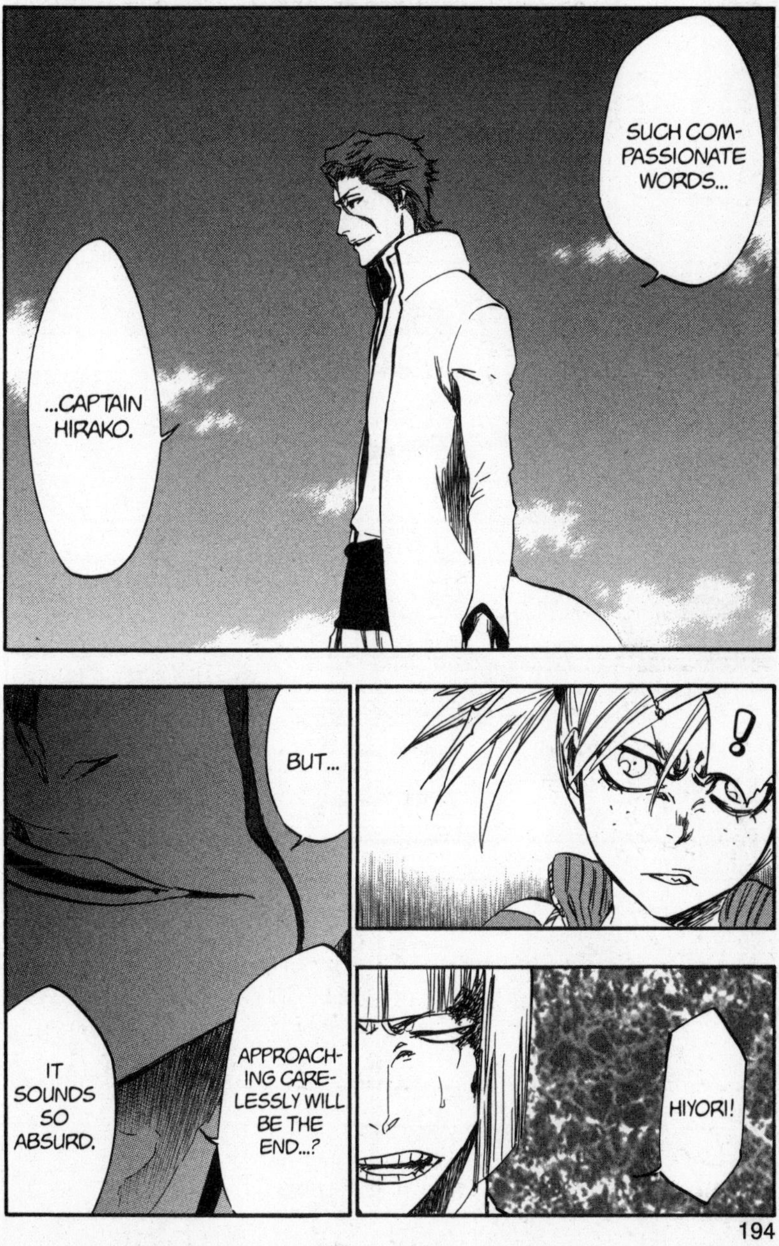
SUCH COMPASSIONATE WORDS...
...CAPTAIN HIRAKO.
!
HIYORI!
BUT...
APPROACHING CARELESSLY WILL BE THE END...?
IT SOUNDS SO ABSURD.

READ THIS WAY

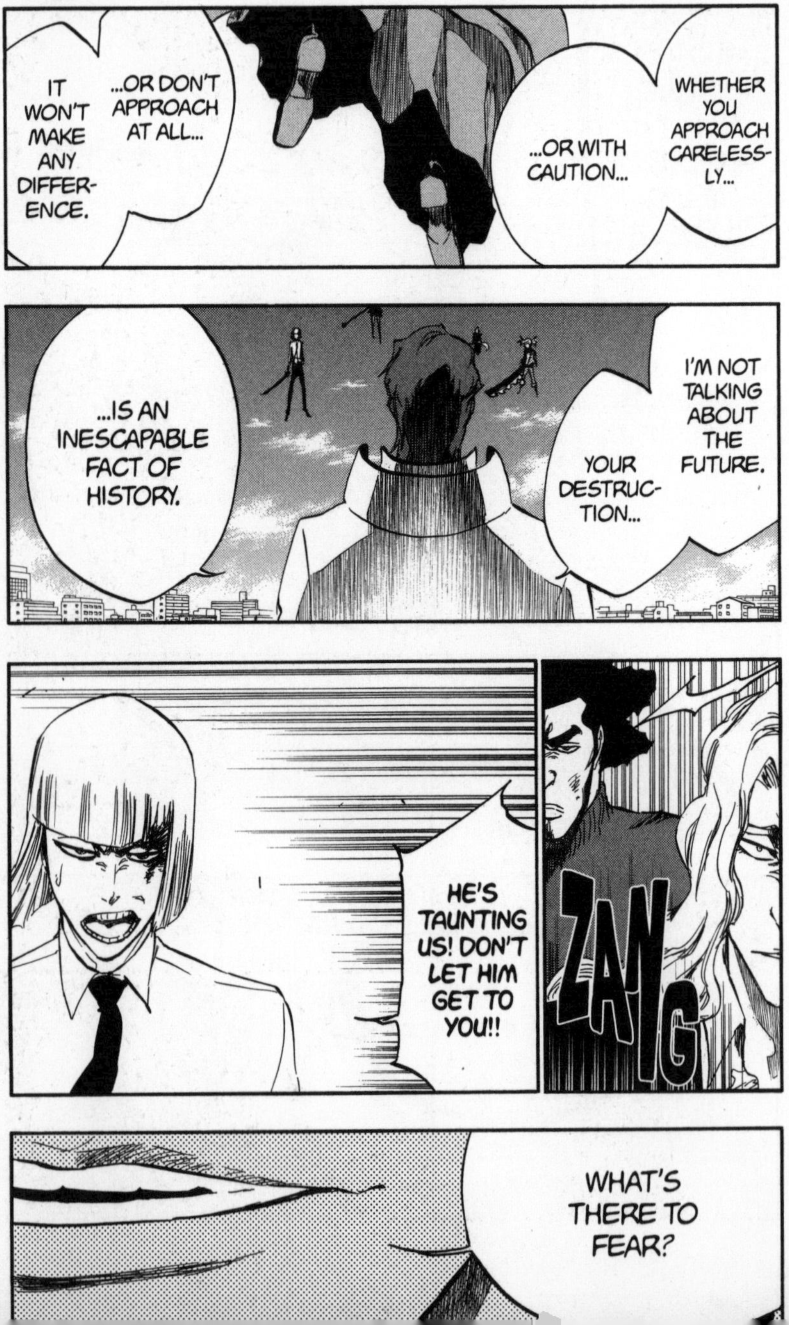
WHETHER YOU APPROACH CARELESSLY...
...OR WITH CAUTION...
...OR DON'T APPROACH AT ALL...
IT WON'T MAKE ANY DIFFERENCE.
I'M NOT TALKING ABOUT THE FUTURE.
YOUR DESTRUCTION...
...IS AN INESCAPABLE FACT OF HISTORY.
ZANG
HE'S TAUNTING US! DON'T LET HIM GET TO YOU!!
WHAT'S THERE TO FEAR?

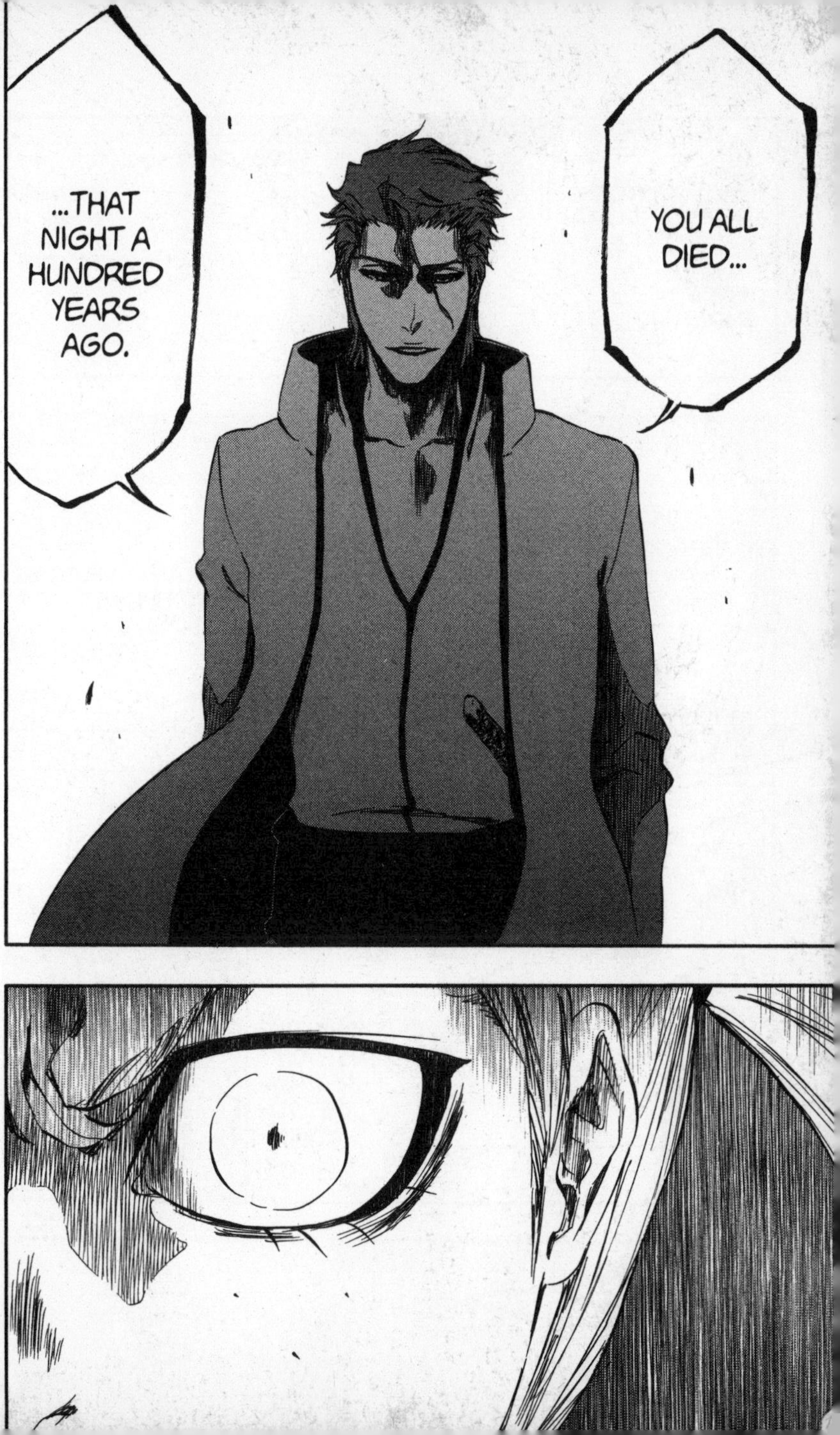
YOU ALL DIED...
...THAT NIGHT A HUNDRED YEARS AGO.

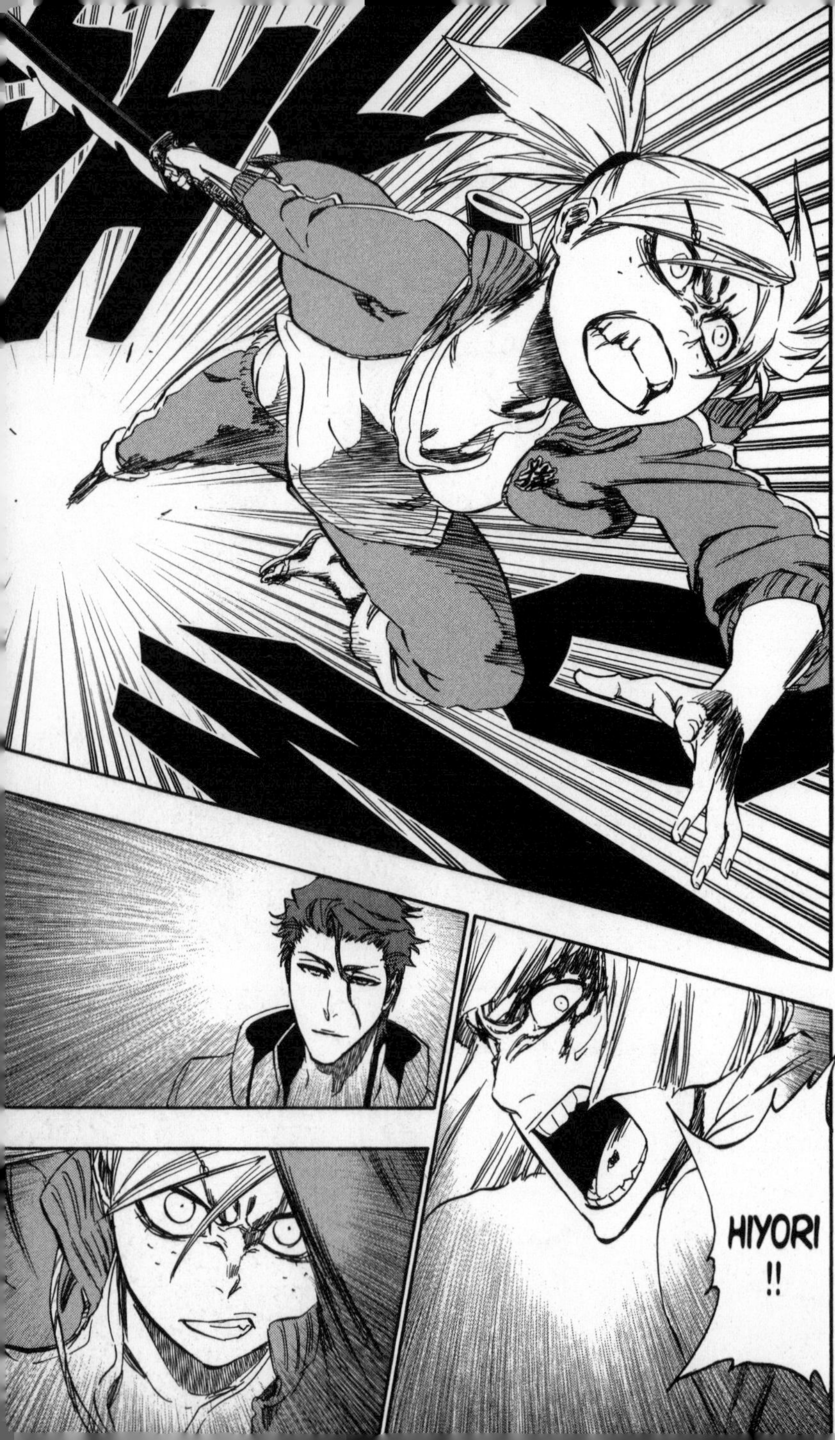
HIYORI
!!

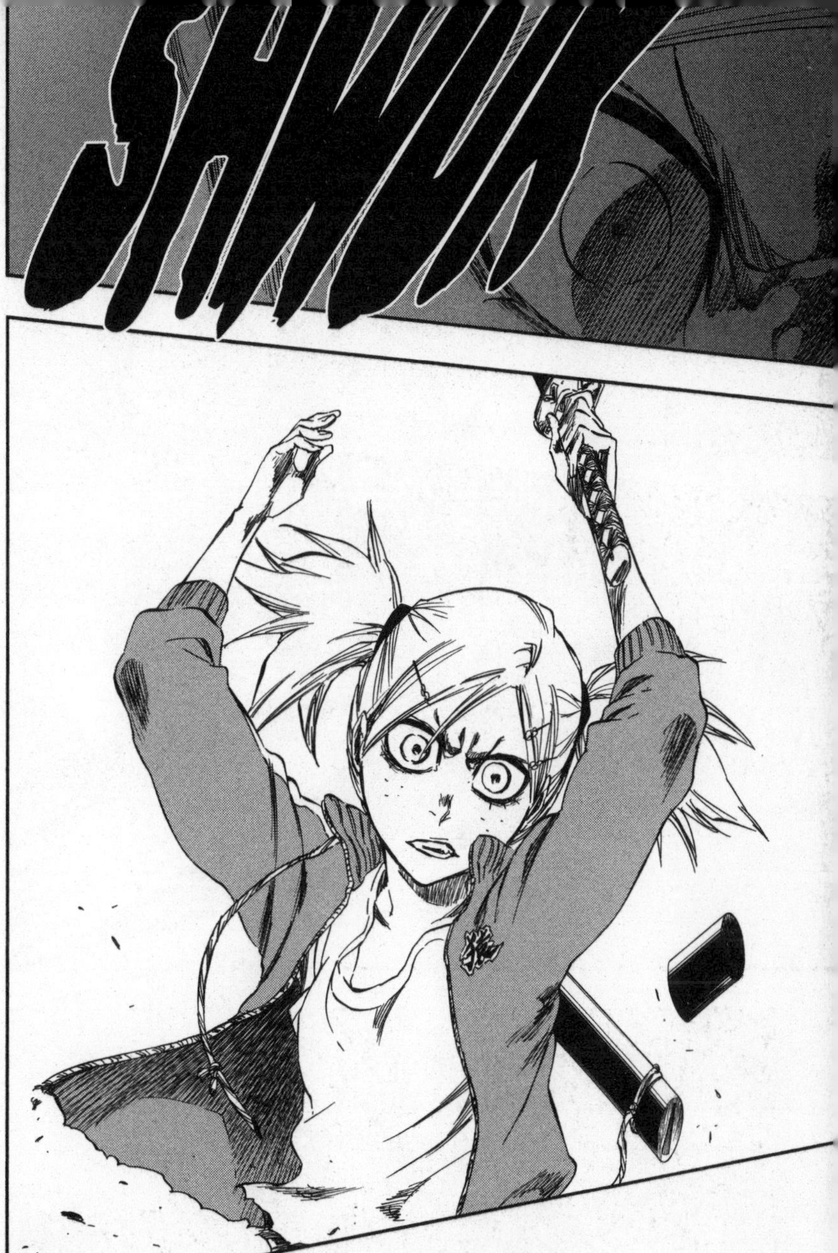

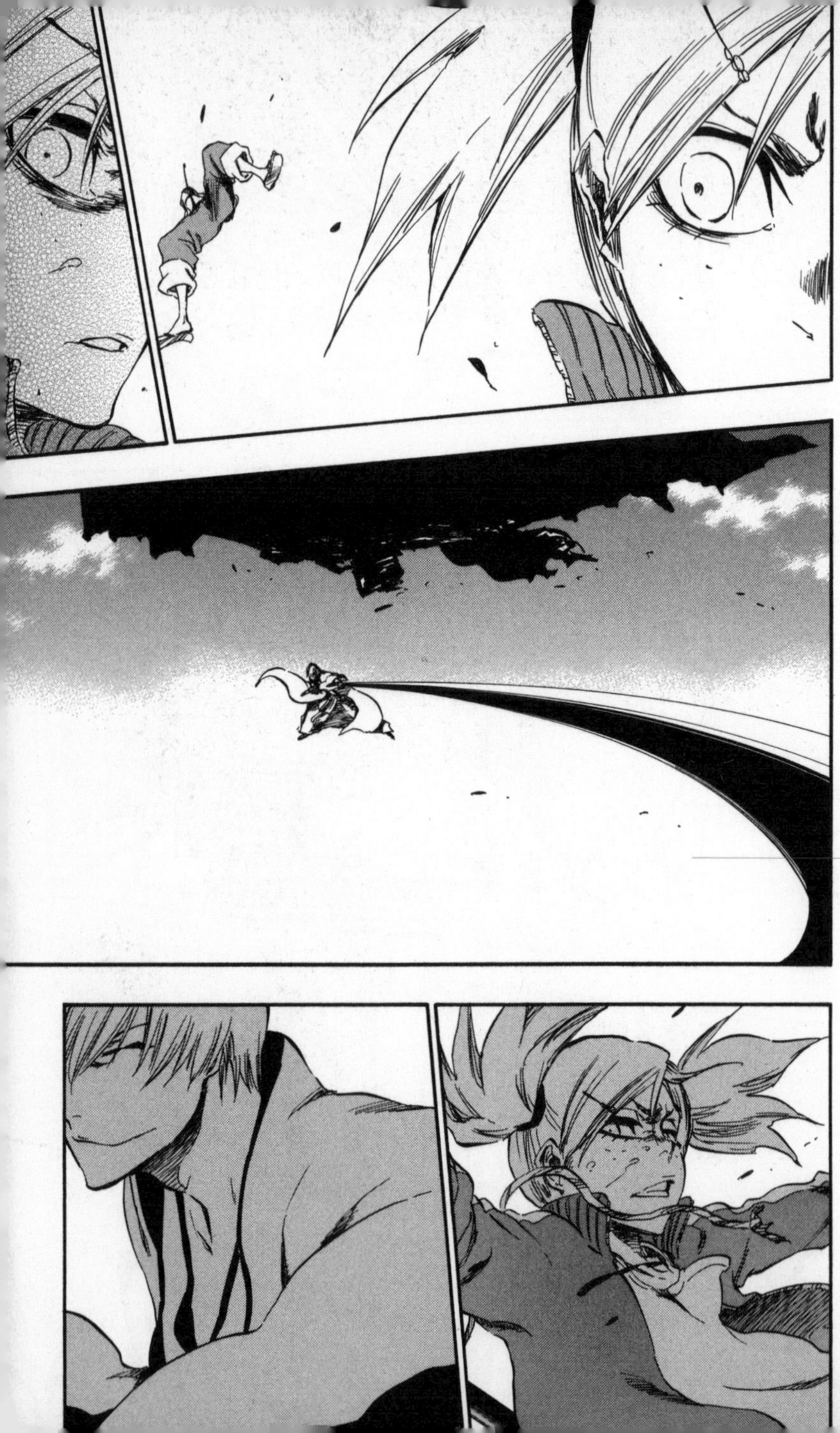

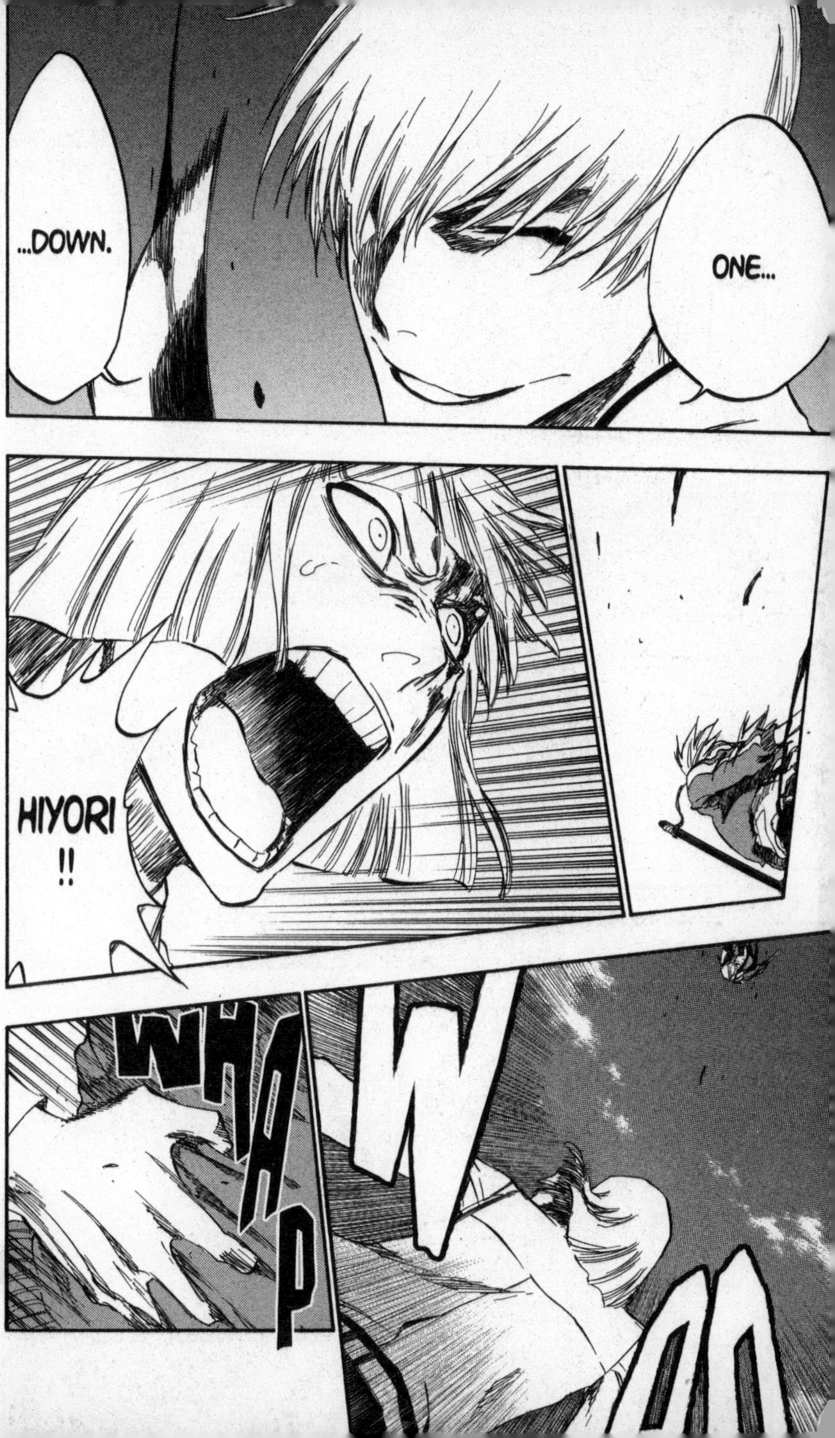
ONE...
...DOWN.
HIYORI !!
WHAP

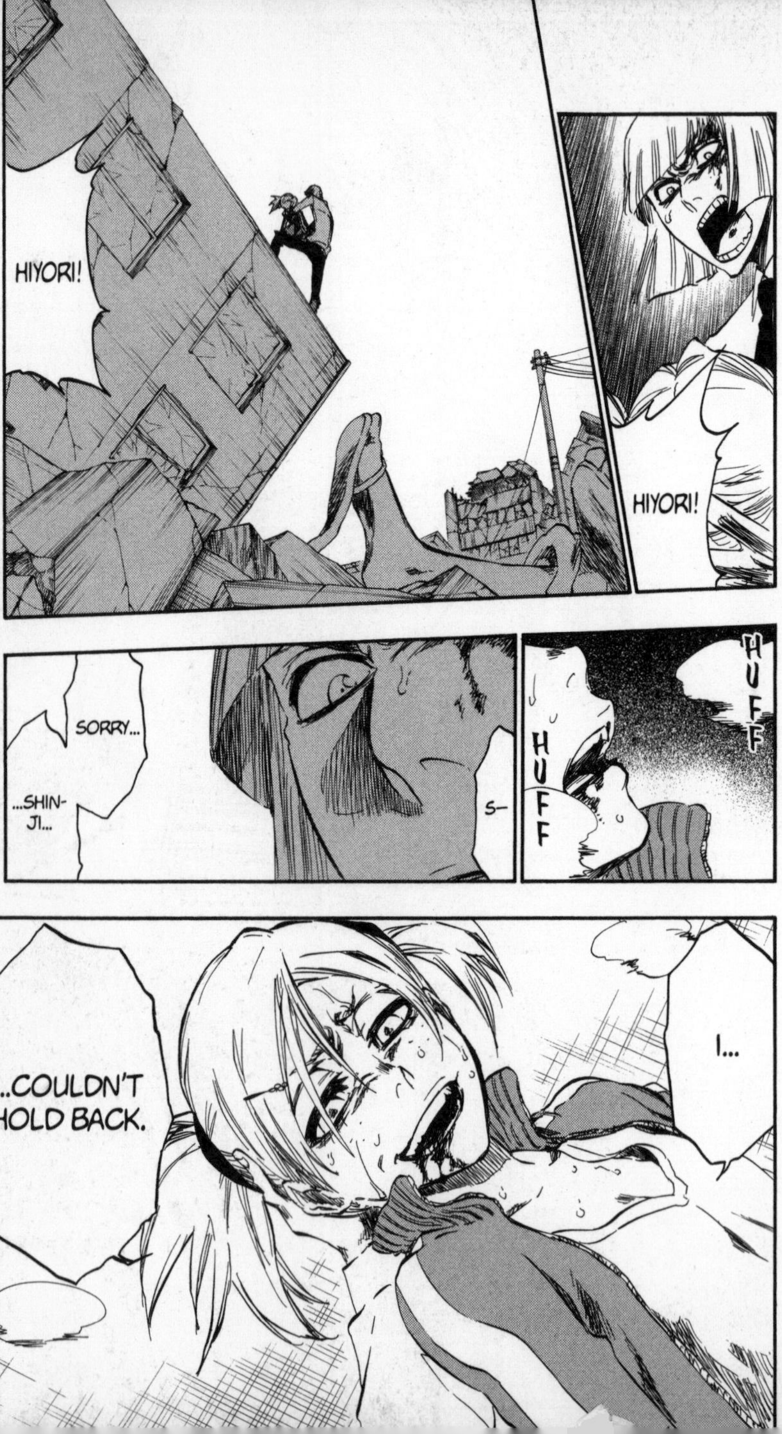
HIYORI!
HIYORI!
HUFF
HUFF
S—
SORRY...
...SHIN-JI...
I...
...COULDN'T HOLD BACK.

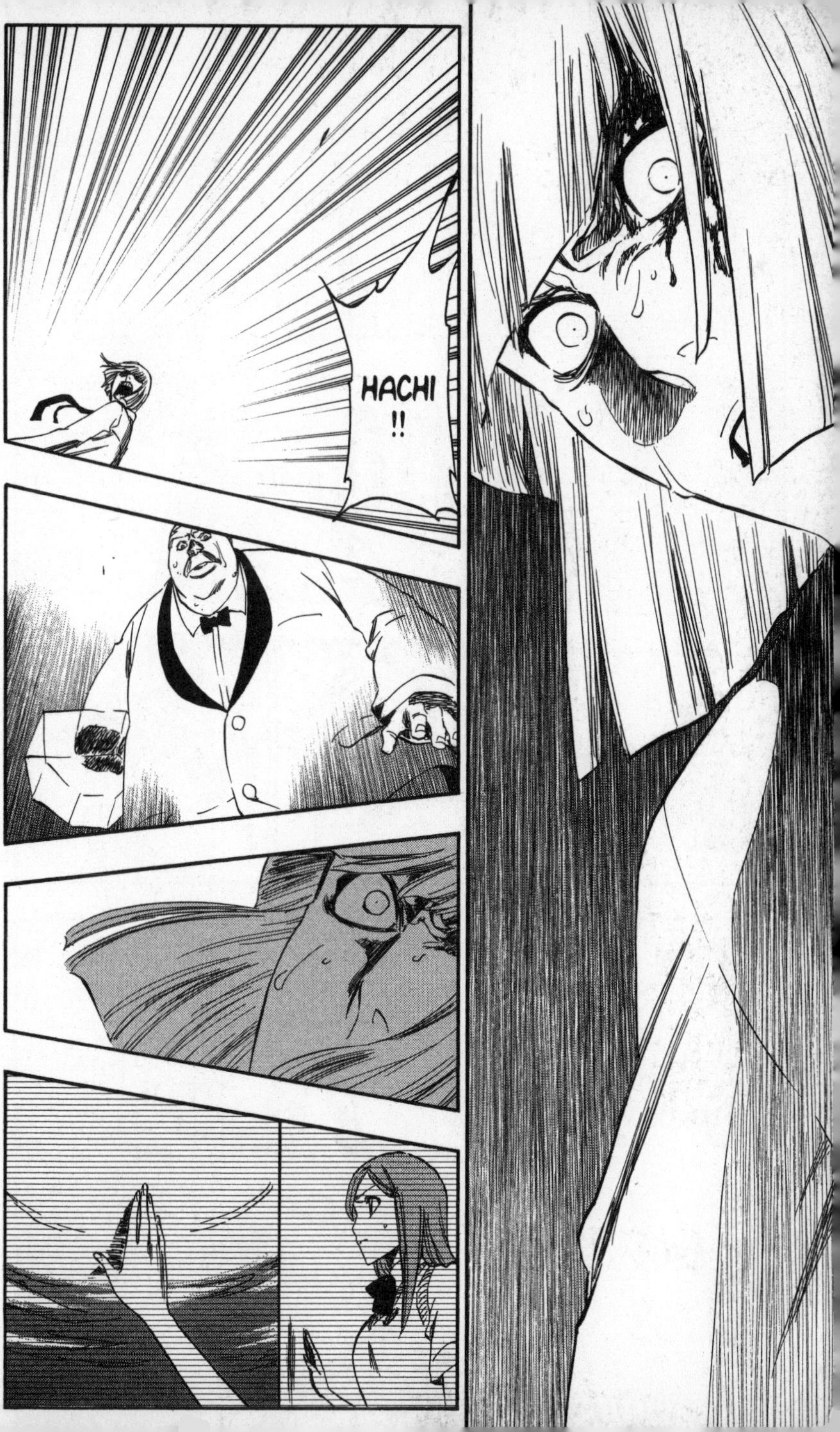
HACHI
!!

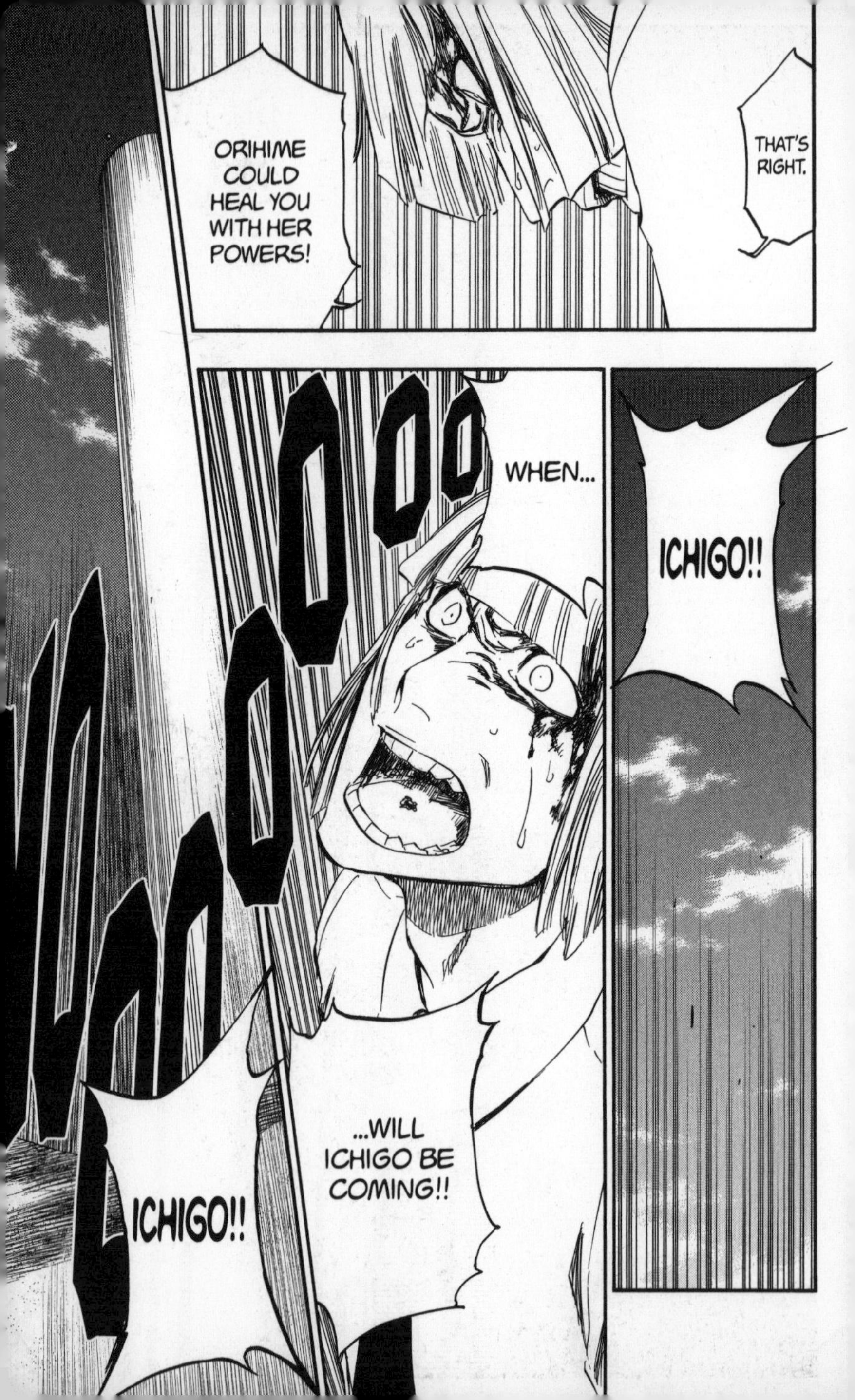

THAT'S RIGHT.
ORIHIME COULD HEAL YOU WITH HER POWERS!
ICHIGO!!
WHEN...
...WILL ICHIGO BE COMING!!
ICHIGO!!

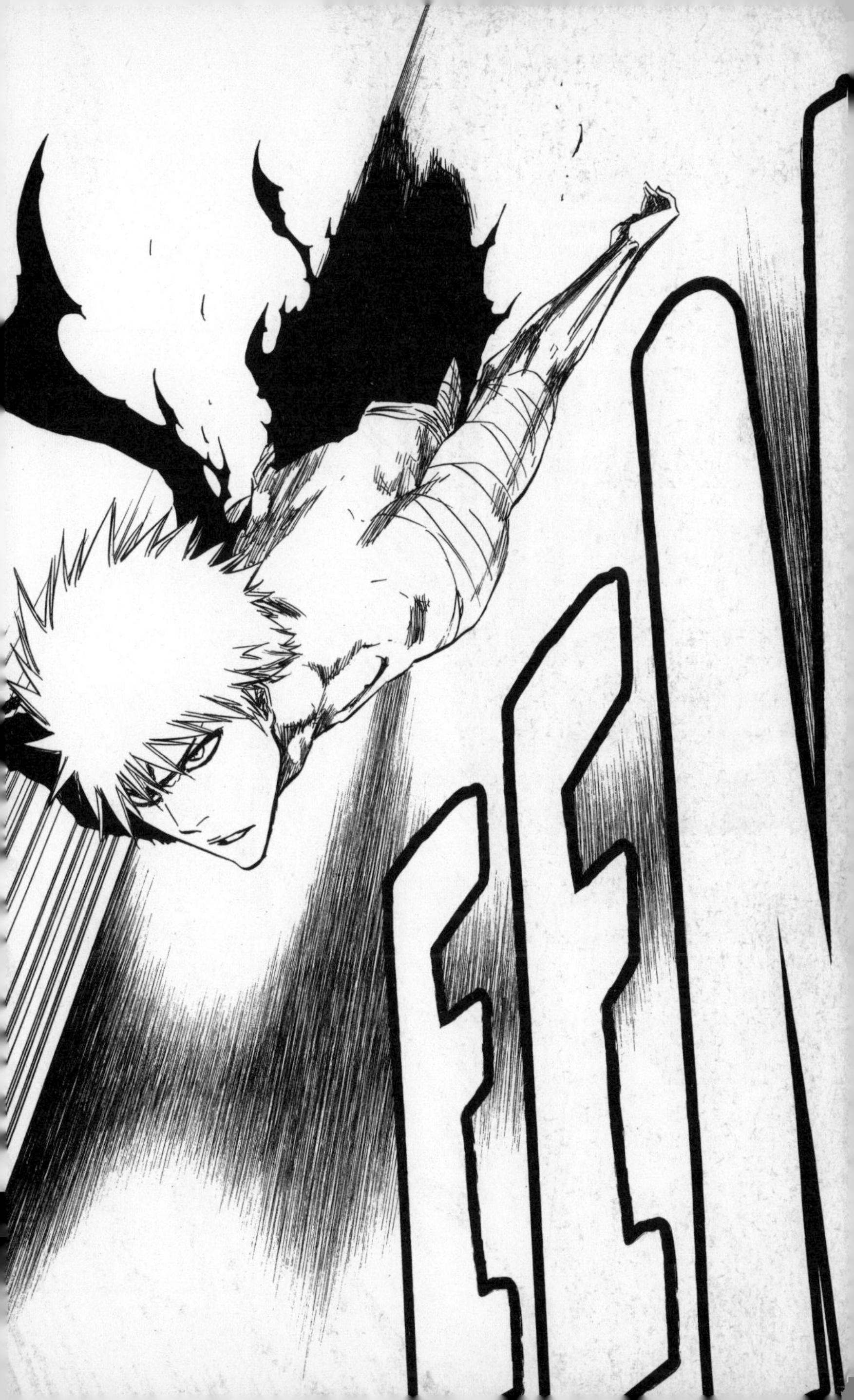

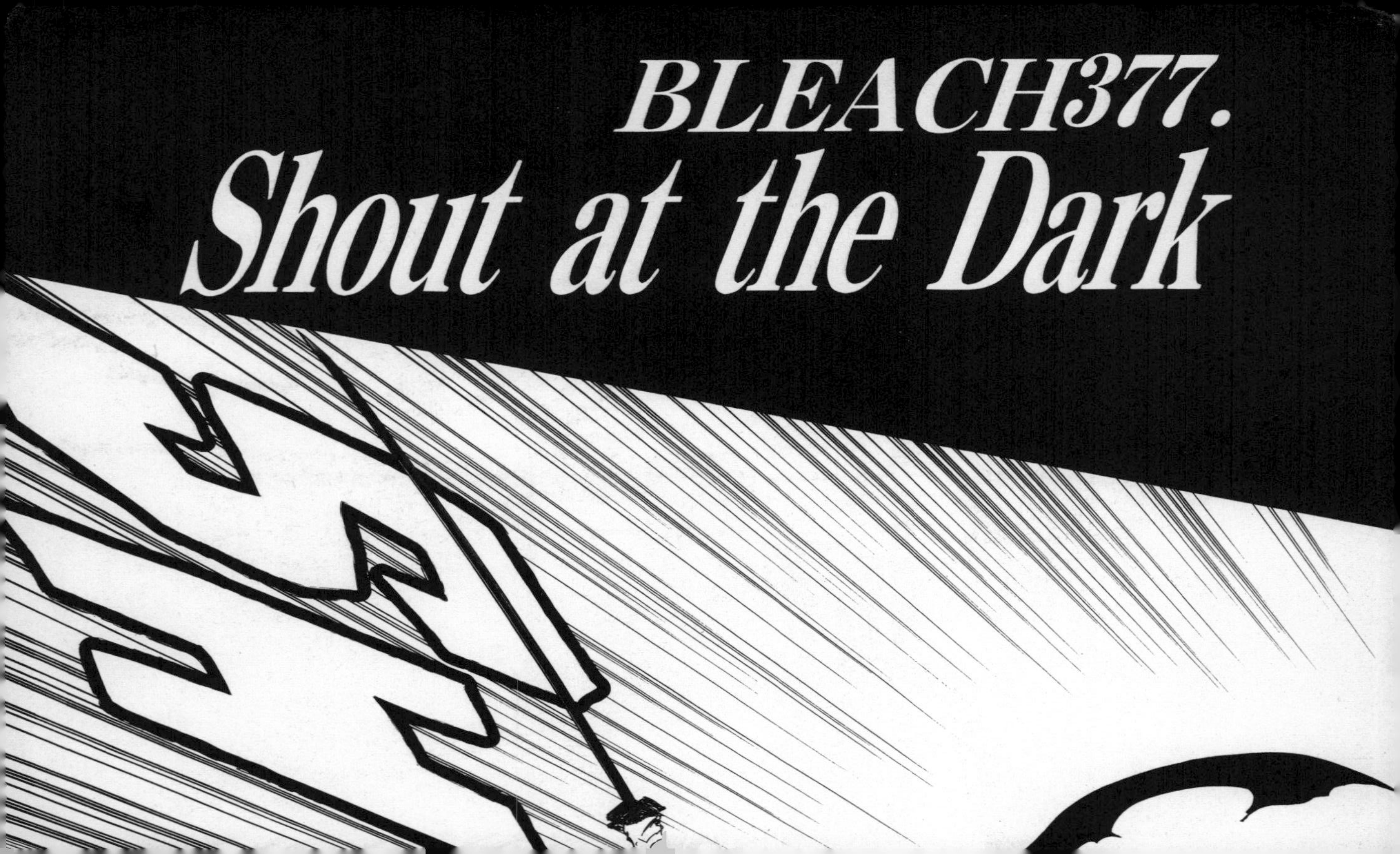
BLEACH377.
Shout at the Dark

CONTI
NUED
IN
BLEACH
44

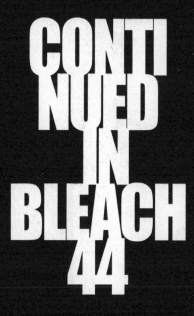

Next Volume Preview

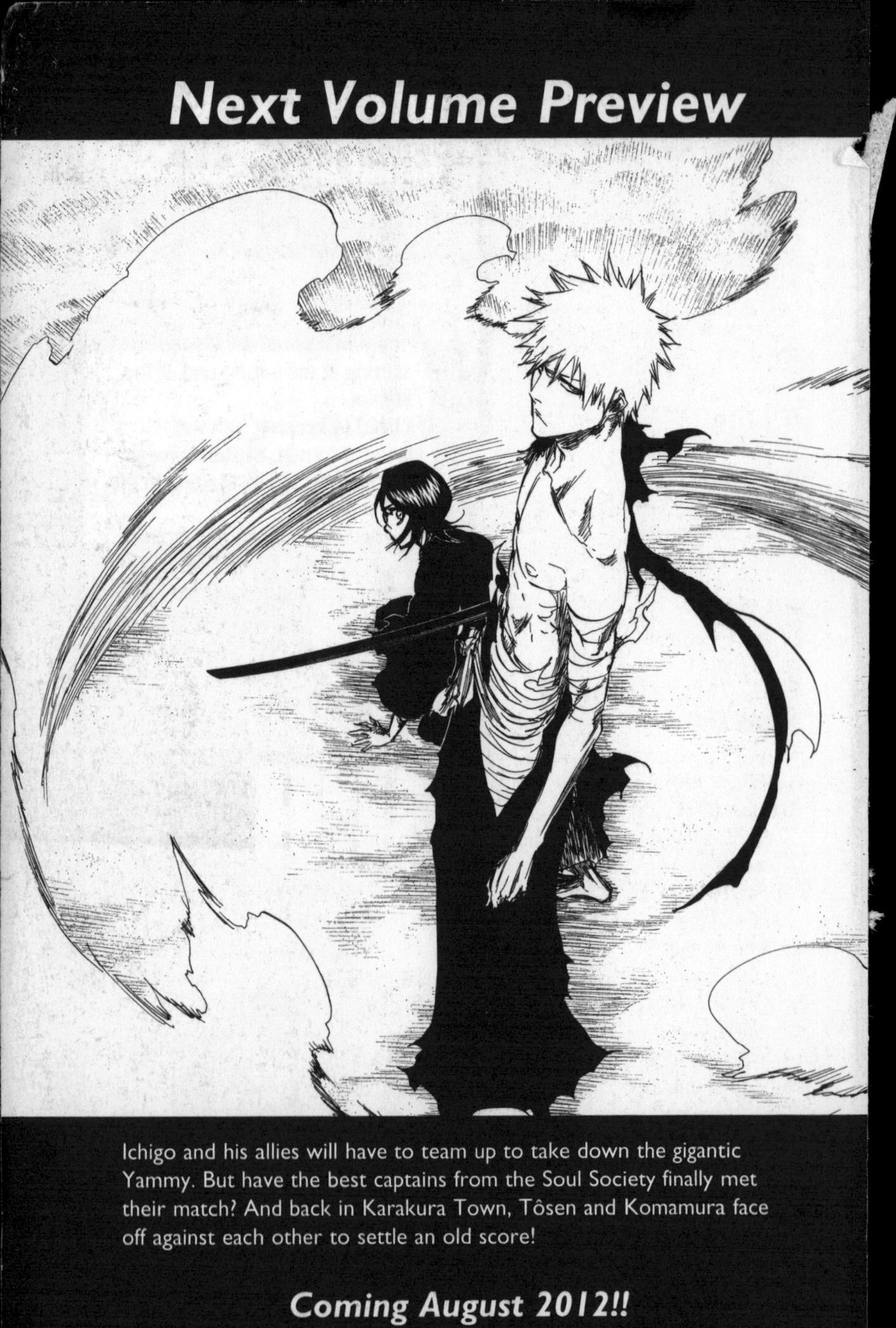

Ichigo and his allies will have to team up to take down the gigantic Yammy. But have the best captains from the Soul Society finally met their match? And back in Karakura Town, Tôsen and Komamura face off against each other to settle an old score!

Coming August 2012!!

You're Re[ading] the Wrong Direction!!

South San Francisco Public Library
3 9048 09175540 9

JUL 2012

D0573550

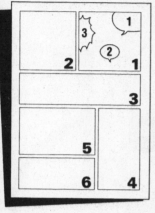

Whoops! Guess what? You're ...[starting at] the [wrong end of the comic!]

...[It's true! In keeping with the] original [Japanese format, Bleach is meant] to be r[ead from right to left, starting in the] upper-r[ight corner.]

Unlike English, which is read from left to right, Japanese is read from right to left, meaning that action, sound effects and word-balloon order are completely reversed... something which can make readers unfamiliar with Japanese feel pretty backwards themselves. For this reason, manga or Japanese comics published in the U.S. in English have sometimes been published "flopped"—that is, printed in exact reverse order, as though seen from the other side of a mirror.

By flopping pages, U.S. publishers can avoid confusing readers, but the compromise is not without its downside. For one thing, a character in a flopped manga series who once wore in the original Japanese version a T-shirt emblazoned with "M A Y" (as in "the merry month of") now wears one which reads "Y A M"! Additionally, many manga creators in Japan are themselves unhappy with the process, as some feel the mirror-imaging of their art skews their original intentions.

We are proud to bring you Tite Kubo's **Bleach** in the original unflopped format. For now, though, turn to the other side of the book and let the adventure begin...!

—Editor

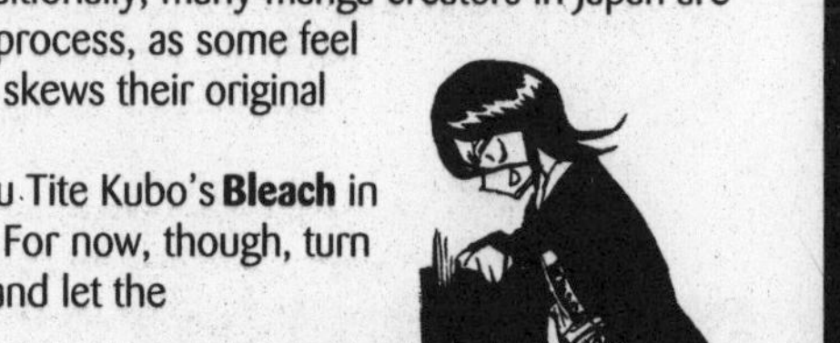